the fragile alliance

For Anita, Cathy, Julie, and Lindy,
the people who sustain me.

second edition

the fragile alliance

an orientation to the outpatient psychotherapy of the adolescent

JOHN E. MEEKS, M.D.

Director Child and Adolescent Services
The Psychiatric Institute of Washington, D.C.

ROBERT E. KRIEGER PUBLISHING COMPANY
MALABAR, FLORIDA

Original edition 1971
Reprint edition 1975, 1977
Second edition 1980

Printed and Published by
ROBERT E. KRIEGER PUBLISHING COMPANY, INC.
KRIEGER DRIVE
MALIBAR, FLORIDA 32950

Printed in the United States of America

Library of Congress Cataloging in Publication Data
Meeks, John E
  The fragile alliance.

  Includes bibliographies and index.
  1. Adolescent psychotherapy.   I. Title.
RJ503.M44   1979   616.8'914   74-32258
ISBN 0-88275-982-5

preface to the new edition:

In this edition of the Fragile Alliance two chapters on inpatient treatment have been added. This material deals in a very general and basic way with the issues of residential care. This approach is in keeping with the overall purpose of the book which is to present an orientation to the student who intends to undertake the psychiatric care of adolescent patients. Unfortunately, no single description of inpatient treatment can encompass the multitude of successful approaches which have been devised. General goals and broad concepts may be more valuable than specific recommendations in this subject area.

Another chapter has been added which considers the possibility of broadening the concept of the therapeutic alliance. It is a cautious and tentative piece of work because we are still trying to learn the limits of the psychotherapeutic method with adolescents. In the treatment of borderline and narcissistic youngsters we must share our ideas and keep an open mind. Individual successes, such as the one described with Ralph, should not blind us to the need for more generalizable technical guidelines for these difficult youngsters. The preliminary ideas offered in Chapter 6 are designed to stimulate thought and discussion.

Finally, the author wishes to thank all of those therapists who have taken the time to give encouragement and constructive criticism. It is their support which has stimulated this new edition.

preface to the second printing

I am very grateful for the friendly reception which mental health professionals have given this text on adolescent psychotherapy. I am even more pleased to learn that some professionals have found it personally useful. The basic motivation for writing *The Fragile Alliance* was a desire to render the behavior of the adolescent in psychotherapy less threatening and more comprehensible. Therapists must feel comfortable in order to assist the people who consult them. This comfort is difficult to achieve unless one understands the patient's way of asking for help. It is particularly gratifying to learn that many therapists feel somewhat more sure of themselves in their contacts with adolescents as a result of reading this book.

The major changes which have been made in this printing relate to expanded discussion of two approaches to therapy, group psychotherapy and family therapy. Neither of these modalities has been discussed exhaustively. The complexity of the topics would make such treatment impractical in a general text on adolescent psychotherapy even if the author was competent to undertake the job (which he is not). The aim of these additional chapters is introductory. I hope that they provide enough of a sense of the values and technical skills associated with family and group therapy to encourage their wider application in adolescent psychotherapy.

I should also like to take this opportunity to express my appreciation to those professionals who reviewed the original edition of *The Fragile Alliance*. Their positive comments were a source of great pleasure and their constructive criticisms were extremely valuable. Although it was impossible to alter and expand the book in all of the ways they suggested, the chapter on group psycho-therapy did arise from a reviewer's comment that the original edition did not deal with the technical problems of structuring group psychotherapy to achieve a therapeutic alliance in that form of therapy.

Society has changed in many ways since 1971 and these changes are reflected to some degree in the adolescent patient population which is currently seeking or being sent for psychotherapy. The basic issues which emerge in the interactions between the adult therapist and his adolescent patient, however, remain relatively constant. I am pleased to offer this second printing of *The Fragile Alliance* with the hope that it will help a new group of therapists to face these issues with competence and even pleasure and excitement.

contents

Part One

Part Two

Part Three

acknowledgments

Grateful acknowledgment is made to the following for permission to reprint their material:

1. Robert G. Aug, Thomas P. Bright, and International Universities Press, Inc., Excerpts from "A Study of Wed and Unwed Motherhood in Adolescents and Young Adults", The Journal of the American Academy of Child Psychiatry, Volume 9, Pages 577 — 594, 1970.

2. The American Orthopsychiatric Association, Excerpt from "Some Psychiatric Aspects of Illegitimate Pregnancy in Early Adolescence" by P. Barglow, M. Bornstein, D. B. Exum, M. K. Wright, and H. M. Visotsky, American Journal of Orthopsychiatry, volume 38, pages 672–687, 1968.

3. Doubleday and Company, Inc., New York, Excerpt from, *The Making of a Counter Culture* by Theodore Roszak, 1968.

4. Harcourt, Brace and World, Inc., New York. Excerpt from *The Uncommitted: Alienated Youth in American Society*, by Kenneth Keniston, 1965.

5. Abraham Heller, H. G. Whittington, and the American Psychiatric Association, Excerpt from, "The Colorado Story: Denver General Hospital experience with the change in the law on therapeutic abortion," The American Journal of Psychiatry, volume 125, pages 809–816, 1968.

6. International Universities Press, Inc., Excerpt from, "Psychoanalysis and the dynamic psychotherapies," by Edward Bibring, originally published in the Journal of the American Psychoanalytic Association, volume 2, pages 745–770, 1954.

Excerpt from *Selected Problems of Adolescence* (with *Special Emphasis on Group Formation*) by Helene Deutsch. 1967.

Excerpt from, "Psychotherapy of adolescents at the level of private practice" by Irene Josselyn in *Psychotherapy of the Adolescent*, B. H. Balser, editor, 1957.

Excerpt from "Drug Use in Adolescents: Psychodynamic Meaning and Pharmacogenic Effect" by H. Wieder and E. H. Kaplan in *The Psychoanalytic Study of the Child*, volume 24, pages 399–431. 1969.

7. Richard L. Jenkins and the American Psychiatric Association, Excerpt from "Classification of behavior problems of children," The American Journal of Psychiatry, volume 125, pages 1032–1039, 1969.

8. Alfred A. Knopf, Inc., New York, Excerpt from *The Rebel* by Albert Camus, 1956.

9. The University of Chicago Press, Chicago, Excerpt from *Principles of Intensive Psychotherapy* by Frieda Fromm-Reichmann, 1950.

Part

One

introduction

A rapidly growing number of adolescents are being referred for psychotherapy. This is partly because of an increase in the portion of our population which falls in this age group. In addition, social factors such as a lengthening of the adolescent period, affluence, urbanization, rapid shifts in moral standards, and the rising complexity of vocational opportunities are complicating the psychological tasks of the adolescent in America. Many of our best young people are stumbling on the threshold of adulthood burdened by problems that they cannot solve alone.

Many of these desperate young people turn to the psychotherapist for help. Some of them seek treatment on their own, at times in the face of parental misgivings. Other come reluctantly, at the insistence of their parents, school officials, courts, or other community agencies. Recently, they have come in such large numbers that they have overwhelmed the treatment facilities which are designed for their age group and are staffed by specialists in child and adolescent psychiatry. In an attempt to fill the breach, some therapists who have previously restricted their practice to adults have begun to accept adolescent referrals. Far too often, those who have accepted the challenge of the floundering adolescent have been disappointed with the results of their therapeutic efforts. Some become discouraged and decide that adolescents are untreatable, at least in their hands. Unfortunately, this group includes many psychotherapists who are highly skilled in the basic techniques of psychotherapy. We cannot afford their loss in the manpower crisis which faces us. This book is written in the hope that it will assist these therapists and those in training to feel more comfortable with the adolescent patient so that they can effectively utilize their skills with this important group of patients.

Adolescent patients can be very frustrating. Often, it seems that, despite the application of proven therapeutic techniques, the adolescent is determined to persist in his maladaptive behavior. At times, it even appears that the young patient is more intent on making the therapist miserable than in using his help. Faced with such perversity, it is not surprising that the puzzled and angry therapist wishes to return to his more satisfying adult practice.

It is possible that most of the ungratifying experiences result from a failure to understand completely the developmental dilemmas of the adolescent. These developmental dilemmas affect not only the goals and philosophy of therapy, but the very techniques which can be effectively used with the adolescent. The most polished therapeutic approach is likely to fail if developmental factors are ignored. Of course, recognizing the developmental peculiarities of this age group and making allowance for them by no means guarantee success. The problems of adolescence are tremendously complex and at times insoluble. Still, a clear grasp of the ways in which adolescence differs from adulthood and the implications of these differences in psychotherapy at least promises the opportunit to engage the adolescent in a meaningful therapeutic effort.

Our understanding of adolescence as a specific developmental stage in personality growth has increased tremendously in the last few years. Our knowledge has been enriched by theoretical, clinical, and research studies. These have come not only in the field of psychosocial development, but, with the wider availability of the writings of Jean Piaget, in the area of cognitive development also. We are approaching a capability for explaining the full implications of adolescence as an indispensable episode in the unfolding story of growth to full maturity.

Some of the research findings and theoretical constructs which bear directly on psychotherapy with adolescents will be discussed as they seem relevant in the course of the book. The concepts of Erik Erikson, which converge and focus data derived from a multiplicity of viewpoints, will often serve as an unstated organizer of the discussion.

This presentation of the psychology of adolescence will necessarily be simplified, even oversimplified. The therapist with a serious interest in treating adolescent patients should read Peter Blos's excellent book, *On Adolescence,* and *Erikson's Identity and the Life Cycle* as a minimal background. There are also several classical articles which should be part of any introductory course in adolescent functioning and adolescent therapy. These are listed at the end of this introduction for easy reference. Many other valuable contributions to our understanding of this developmental phase are included in the bibliographies following each chapter.

Since the essence of psychotherapy consists of communication within a relationship, our major emphasis will be on exploring the ways in which adolescents form and utilize human relationships and on their methods of communication. The study of communication involves not only the ways in which adolescents express themselves to others, but the styles of internal communication or thought which are peculiar to the adolescent.

Adolescents have particular problems in forming relationships. These difficulties in relating may interfere with the very launching of psychotherapy. If these shallows are successfully navigated, the therapy may still go aground on the rocky communication gaps existing between the therapist and his young patient. The adolescent not only speaks another language, but he also thinks according to different rules of syntax. It is the goal of this book to attempt an explication of these two major obstacles to the successful psychotherapy of the adolescent. In the interest of reasonable brevity, we will concentrate almost exclusively on the phase of adolescence which Blos (1963) has designated as "adolescence proper," referring only peripherally to "early" and "late" adolescence. This may clear the way for the accomplished psychotherapist or the well-trained beginner to utilize fully his psychotherapeutic knowledge and skill with adolescents.

I feel strongly that the successful therapist of adolescents will find work with these intense and fascinating young people one of his most exciting and rewarding ventures. Professional rewards include treatment responses which are often more rapid and spectacular than those attained with adults. In addition, the comprehension of adult personality functioning is enhanced. Perhaps even more stimulating is the personal reward of reawakening and rejuvenating one's zeal and competence in living through an invigorating contact with our youth.

The book is intended as a practical handbook for the clinician. Ideally, it should be read in conjunction with the theoretical readings which are suggested at the end of each chapter. The technical approaches which are suggested are by no means universally accepted. Other techniques are doubtless equally effective or superior, at least for some therapists. Those offered in this book are presented in the same spirit of open communication which characterizes the young people who inspired it. Often, I have chosen to state quite specifically the method which "should" be utilized to deal with a given problem in therapy. These assertions, which may sound dogmatic, are actually designed to illustrate one possible orientation to psychotherapy with the adolescent. I hope primarily to convey an attitude and a style of approach to patients in this age group. It seemed that this could be accomplished most compellingly through a definite and clear description of concrete therapist behaviors in the therapy setting. This is one meaning of the word "orientation" in the title of this book. The methods described represent only one orientation or viewpoint. The second meaning refers to the intended role of the book as an introductory text for the therapist who plans to work with patients in this age group.

I have tried to avoid overemphasis of any theoretical position, although my own bias for psychoanalytic explanations will be readily apparent to the most casual reader. I do not feel, however, that the treatment approaches described are dependent on any rigid theoretical school. One colleague has suggested that the development of the therapeutic alliance, as described in Chapter Four, could be understood as a successful attempt to encourage the adolescent to accept the therapist's attitudes toward emotional problems. Such behavior, he stated, could be seen as an example of modeling à la Bandura. I certainly would not quarrel with this interpretation of the approach. The purpose of the book is to help therapists of any sound theoretical conviction to apply their treatment skills with adolescent patients. As Michael Balint once commented, "Once you are in the room with a patient, theory pretty much goes out the window." That is the spirit of this book. My aim is to help the therapist to encounter the adolescent as a living, existent, and interacting human being.

Although I must accept personal responsibility for the book's shortcomings (some of which may be inherent in a single-author treatment of a topic so complex), I do wish to acknowledge the assistance of many people. Dr. Maurice Levine and Dr. Othilda Krug extended their enormous knowledge to me during my residency training in psychiatry. Their contributions formed the basis for a continuing interest in human behavior at all ages. Dr. Jack Martin read several of the chapters in their early form and offered valuable suggestions for their improvement. Drs. Robert Long, Robert Brown, and K. D. Charalampous and Miss Margaret Beckner also reviewed sections of the book and helped to clarify the pertinent issues. Special thanks are due Dr. Merlan DeBolt, whose continued assistance, encouragement, and constructive criticism at every stage in the book's conception and production made the project possible.

Finally, I am indebted to my secretary, Miss Doris Creed. Her knowledge of the English language prevented many errors and confusions. She has also served as librarian, audience, and critic in addition to her duties as clerk through many revisions. Since I cannot adequately thank her, I can only hope that she has somehow shared in my own excitement and pleasure in the effort.

The young people who inspired the book and who (suitably disguised) provide its clinical examples probably do not really want my thanks. We have settled our accounts during our therapeutic contacts. I believe that we are both satisfied with the bargain.

Articles for the "Short Course" in Adolescent Development and Adolescent Therapy

Blos, P. 1963. On Adolescence. New York: The Free Press of Glencoe, Inc.

Blos, P. 1967. The second individuation process of adolescence. Psychoanal. Stud. Child 22: 162–186.

Blos, P. 1968. Character formation in adolescence. Psychoanal. Stud. Child 23: 245–263.

Erikson, E. H. 1959. Identity and the life cycle; selected papers. Psychological Issues, Monograph 1. New York: International Universities Press, Inc.

Freud, A. 1958. Adolescence. Psychoanal. Stud. Child 13: 255–278.

Gitelson, M. 1948. Character synthesis: the psychotherapeutic problem of adolescence. Amer. J. Orthopsychiat. 18: 422–431.

Josselyn, I. M. 1954. The ego in adolescence. Amer. J. Orthopsychiat. 24: 223–237.

Josselyn, I. M. 1957. Psychotherapy of adolescents at the level of private practice. In: Psychotherapy of the adolescent. Edited by B. H. Balser. New York: International Universities Press, Inc.

Masterson, J. F. 1967. Psychiatric treatment of adolescents. In: Comprehensive textbook of psychiatry. Edited by A. Freedman and H. Kaplan. Baltimore: Williams & Wilkins Company.

CHAPTER ONE
adolescents are different

In recent years, there has been a remarkable growth of interest in adolescence as a discrete phase in the development of the human personality. The information converging from many sources has shown decisively that adolescence cannot be understood completely as merely a recapitulation of previous development. Increasing awareness of the specific role of cultural opportunities and restrictions, the characteristics of adolescent thought processes, the importance of pregenital factors and early introjects, and the synthetic role of the ego during adolescence—to mention only a partial list of recently explored areas—has served to expand our picture of the adolescent toward a three-dimensional view. Blos (1963) has greatly refined our understanding of adolescent intrapsychic process and of the specific dynamic tasks which confront the child during each subphase of adolescence. His careful description of preadolescence, early adolescence, adolescence proper, and late adolescence should be closely reviewed by the serious student. It would be impossible in this introductory chapter to explore the nature of adolescence with any degree of completeness. Instead, primary emphasis is placed on the features of adolescence which bear directly on psychotherapy, especially those features which may trouble the competent practicing psychotherapist who is relatively inexperienced in work with adolescents.

Erikson (1968) has offered us an overview of the entire adolescent process as a regression in the service of progression. It is as though the adolescent must drag himself and the adults who care for him through the mud of old conflicts, enmities, and attach-

9

ments to inoculate himself against both the seductive and frightening dangers of the past. If all goes well, he emerges into adulthood with immunity to some of the more virulent pathogens from his past and the ability to host others without apparent damage to his psychological integrity. The goal is to achieve what Erikson (1968) has called "identity" and what Blos (1967) has called the "second individuation." Both terms refer to the achievement of a workable self-awareness which accepts inner complexity and is able to relate this multifaceted sense of self-hood to others in an interpersonal and larger social context. This sense of self is still tentative and is largely a recognition of potentials, not a static and finalized state. As Erikson has pointed out, the adolescent who is involved in the quest for identity does not actually ask himself, "Who am I?", as we often loosely say. Instead, he asks, "What do I want to make of myself and what do I have to work with?" Recognition of this distinction has implications for defining the goals of psychotherapy with adolescents and setting appropriate end points for therapy which we will consider later.

Perhaps a metaphor based on the world of theatre will help to convey a sense of the adolescent experience. For the adolescent, the external world is sometimes a distant stage on which skillful players are easily producing a successful performance. The young spectator can hardly imagine that he will ever have sufficient skill to handle anything more than a walk-on part. At other times, the world is seen as a cast of faltering and untutored players, totally available to be molded to the adolescent's personal sense of drama. In short, the adolescent shifts from seeing the reality as a malleable medium in which he can implant an image of his inner struggles to viewing it as a relatively fixed situation to which he must mold himself. Generally speaking, the younger adolescent tends toward the view of himself as the undiscovered director, whereas the older adolescent gradually comes to accept a less inflated role in the grand production of life.

The theatrical metaphor was deliberately chosen to emphasize the experimental and tentative quality of the adolescent's feelings, attitudes, and relationships. One often has the impression that the adolescent is assuming a role and "playing at" life.

I do not mean to imply that the adolescent is necessarily playful or frivolous in his approach to living. The fact that he is often very serious indeed is revealed by the intense emotions which are typical of adolescence. The adolescent is playing at life with remarkable intensity. What is lacking is a readiness to make permanent commitments or form irreversible loyalties. The adolescent cannot take positions or roles which imply finality because these may prove later to be poorly suited to what he wants to make of himself or what he has to work with. Still, he can only answer these questions by involving himself with life. We cannot expect him to learn to swim without getting in the water. The adolescent's compromise solution involves trial dips which are always undertaken with the option of jumping out if the currents are too swift, if the eddies are too deep, or even if he decides he is a landlubber after all.

The average adolescent quietly conducts his experiments in living. His surface behavior remains for the most part well within the confines of acceptability. The inner struggle is hardly apparent even to the adolescent himself and is accomplished with only a few exhibitions of artistic temperament. The relative peacefulness of the ordinary adolescent experience is well described by Douvan and Adelson (1966) and Offer (1969) after large-scale studies of random normative adolescent populations.

For the most part, those adolescents who present (or are presented) for psychotherapy are a very different group. Their struggle is desperate and highly visible. For them, adolescence is quite literally a question of life or death. If they cannot find a part in the drama which fits both their sense of personal integrity and their notion of a good show, they refuse to play. The applause of an audience that they would feel they were both exploiting and being exploited by seems to them insufficient reward. They will not be roped into a command performance.

There are three general groups who might be caught in this quandary. One group is composed of those youngsters whose experiences and emotional development have been atypical to a degree which forces them to demand a role which is simply not realistically available.

An eighteen-year-old boy told his therapist that he was sure his work paralysis would disappear if only he could be entrusted with some worthwhile task. When he was asked to give an example of a worthwhile task, he told at length of his plans for restructuring the executive branch of the United States government.

Other adolescents, even more impaired by their early experience or constitution, are faced with needs and wishes which may be internally inconsistent and even explicitly psychotic. They cannot imagine any role in the real world of adulthood which would even approach a satisfactory level of gratification.

Paul, a 13-year-old, was seen for psychological evaluation during his hospitalization for a crash weight-loss program. His internist insisted on this approach after Paul's weight rose above 300 pounds despite outpatient dietary management.

Paul told the evaluating therapist that he saw no reason to lose weight, since it was his plan to establish an absolute monarchy on an uninhabited island. He anticipated that he would be totally cared for by his subjects, emphasizing the gastronomic delights which they would prepare for him. His affect was inappropriate and associations were loose. He appeared to be convinced of the reality of his delusional empire.

When he was released from the hospital, his mother attempted to carry out the dietary restrictions imposed by the internist. She relented, however, when Paul threatened her with a kitchen knife if she did not give him the food he wanted. The mother called the therapist in panic, but explained that she and Paul could not enter therapy since Paul's father "did not believe in psychiatry."

Five years later, the therapist was again contacted by Paul's mother. She wondered if the therapist would testify that Paul was emotionally ill. He was facing trial on charges of air piracy after hijacking an airplane to another country. He explained to an examining psychiatrist that he planned to mastermind a revolt in the foreign country. Paul's psychotic mission in life eventually led him to an extremely dangerous impulsive commitment in the real world.

He was found to be legally insane and committed to receive the treatment which he should have had five years sooner.

The third group of troubled adolescents consists of those who are largely whole within, but who are dismayed by the possibilities which society presents them. Many of the adolescents who come for psychotherapy can present a convincing argument for this view of their difficulty. If only society (their parents, their school, their community, their country, their world) were different, everything would be simple for them. They have studied the play and find it to be of inferior quality, lacking any suitable vehicle for their talents. Since social institutions are far from perfect, their argument has surface merit. On closer examination, however, one usually comes to feel that the particular social imperfections which trouble them most are remarkably similar to those features within themselves which they regard as unacceptable. Again, the devil without is easier to abide than the devil within, especially for the conflicted adolescent.

Unfortunately, this rejection of social institutions is not confined to youth at this point in American history. Many thoughtful adults are deeply concerned about what has been called "the quality of life" in America. Many adults are paralyzed by a sense of ineffectiveness and anonymity in the face of the staggering bulk and maddening complexity of social institutions. Our "technocracy" (Roszak, 1969) is poor in human rewards for many Americans. They feel isolated, ineffectual, distrustful, and cynical. These "alienated" adults tend toward polarization into one or another extreme philosophical system in a quietly desperate effort to restore meaning to life. Keniston (1965) has referred to "scientism" ("the ideology of devitalized reason") and "irrationalism" ("the ideology of degraded passion") as the major competing ideologies of our time. It would be a mistake to think, as some do, that American adults embrace "scientism" whereas our youth is turning to "irrationalism." Proponents of both extreme views may be found across all age groups.

This state of affairs complicates the usual "conflict of generations." It is more difficult to see the personal implications in the social complaints of today's adolescent. In actual practice, these social questions are often at the forefront in early and late stages of therapy. Initially, they are used defensively to avoid looking at the revolution within the adolescent. In the terminal phases of therapy, they are often discussed again, not necessarily with less concern, but with less anger, less utopian overtones, and usually without despair and alienation.

Naturally, the therapist of the adolescent must expect to be pulled actively into this struggle with the larger world during both stages. He will often be cast in roles far removed from his actual attitudes, capabilities, or intentions. Early in therapy, the adolescent tends to utilize the new adult in his life as a screen on which he can externalize the negative aspects of his self-image and his more distressing introjects. The therapist also may be a convenient embodiment of all the social and cultural evils which the adolescent deplores. Later, we will consider more fully both the problems that this tendency poses for the therapist in the establishment of a therapeutic alliance and some of the technical approaches which may be useful in managing this hazard.

Later in therapy, the therapist frequently finds himself unrealistically elevated and venerated to the point of idealization. Although this reaction of the adolescent is not nearly so distressful to the therapist, it can also interfere with the adolescent's emotional growth if it is not properly utilized and eventually dissolved. The counter transference problems which occur when one is faced with adulation are especially marked when this attitude follows upon a previous disdain for the therapist.

Many therapists find it difficult to respond therapeutically to this peculiar style of adolescent relating. The observing ego, with which the therapist has allied himself in working with adults, seems rudimentary or absent in many adolescents. The seasoned psychotherapist expects his patients to distort his intentions and his personality, as long as the patient is able to localize the origins of the distortions within himself and to reflect on their possible meanings. In early therapy with adolescents, one commonly encounters an intensity of feeling and a lack of introspection which produce a degree of uncooperativeness and explosiveness usually seen only in very disturbed individuals in adult psychotherapeutic work.

To understand why the adolescent relates as he does, we will need to consider some of the developmental problems which the adolescent faces and the impact of these problems on the ways in which he deals with other people. The discussion of approaches by which these patterns can be turned to the adolescent's developmental advantage is deferred to the chapters on technique.

THE ADOLESCENTS STYLE OF RELATING

When adolescence begins, a youngster is subjected to a multipronged attack on his sense of self-esteem. The invading forces include the impact of unpredictable and uneven sudden changes in body configuration and size, an unacceptable upsurge of forbidden impulses, and the adolescent's own need to devalue his parents, thereby losing a valued part of himself. The subjective response to this onslaught is a vague, anxious sense of inner loss and injury. The adolescent, as a result, is eager for new human relationships but is equally driven to use these relationships primarily to bind his psychic wounds. Although he desperately needs human identification patterns to restore a sense of direction, he is unable for several reasons to involve himself in any relationship which requires him to take a consistent interest in the other person. His attachment to other people—other adolescents as well as adults— is primarily narcissistic.

This does not mean that the adolescent will necessarily exploit the people to whom he relates, although he may. It merely means that the tie to others is strongly colored and mainly determined by the adolescent's inner needs. The actual characteristics of the other person are not totally ignored, but they are important primarily as orientation points around which the adolescent weaves complex fantasies and suppositions which are emotionally important to him. Other equally obvious characteristics are simply ignored if they do not fit the adolescent's view.

An inhibited 14-year-old boy in therapy for six months expressed amazement on learning that his therapist was married.

"You seem more like the 'swinger' type," he exclaimed.

The therapist had worn a clearly visible wedding band throughout his contact with the adolescent. The same therapist had been accused of being hopelessly old-fashioned and an obvious square by other adolescents with different needs.

The adolescent's hunger to merge with an individual who seems to have a workable identity structure must live in uneasy coexistence with the fear that merger may actually occur. The adolescent's opposition to therapy, his therapist, and the therapist's ideas are often reactions to a fear that the fragile identity he is nurturing may simply be overwhelmed by the strength of the therapist's personality. Perhaps, this is the core of the dread of dependency which the adolescent frequently demonstrates. Certainly, one is often impressed that youngsters who are most fearful of the dependent role in the psychotherapeutic relationship have parents who frequently intrude into the adolescent's psychological privacy in an attempt to dictate his style of life.

The observable adolescent style of relating to others is the outer manifestation of inward distress. The adolescent often shows an intense but still fleeting and superficial attachment to other people. There is a searching quality, frequently described as fickle, as the adolescent reacts to real or fantasied qualities in new objects which promise an external solution to his inner turmoil. It is also characteristic that he hopes for total solutions and therefore is regularly disillusioned by those to whom he attaches himself. Of course, with the progression of adolescence, the attachments take on an increasingly adult form, although an ebb and flow of mature and immature attitudes toward the loved or admired person will continue until young adulthood. The impact of these characteristic adolescent styles of relating on the problem of establishing a therapeutic alliance will be immediately apparent to the reader. Not only will the styles of relating affect the early phases of therapy, but they must also be considered in attempting to understand "transference" phenomena in this age group. These problems are considered more fully in Chapters Three and Four.

THE THOUGHT OF THE ADOLESCENT

For many years, the peculiar thought processes of the adolescent have been noted by both the clinician and the creative artist.

Prior to the monumental contribution of Jean Piaget, however, the unusual nature of these cognitive processes has been explained on the basis of the emotional changes characteristic of the developmental phase. Piaget has pointed out that we must also consider the way in which the intellectual functioning of the adolescent influences his behavior and emotions.

According to Piaget (Piaget, 1967; Flavell, 1963), the capacity for *formal operations* appears in early adolescence. This style of thought allows the youngster for the first time logically to manipulate thought itself. In the preceding phase of *concrete operations*, the child developed a capacity for logical manipulation of isolated problems and an understanding of the interrelationships of material objects. The advent of formal operations allows the construction of general theories of the interrelationship between various facts, problems, and ideas. As the adolescent develops the capacity to think about thought itself, he is able to manipulate mere possibilities. Piaget states further that the emergence of a new stage in conceptual development is invariably marked by an increase in the egocentric use of the new cognitive ability and by a preoccupation with testing and utilizing the recently acquired skill. The adolescent is therefore fascinated with his shining toy of truly abstract thought, and he plays with it endlessly.

The adolescent applies this ability for abstract thinking to his world and overemphasizes its strengths and capacities as a tool for reshaping the reality around him. Clinically, this tendency appears as a belief in the omnipotence of thought and a grandiose overestimation of the adolescent's capacity to alter his world by merely thinking about it. There is often a sense of impatience with adults, who seem to be dawdling and needlessly complicating problems which could easily be solved by a logical approach. In many youngsters, this development is accompanied by a quickness and acuity of logical thinking which is truly outstanding. In this regard, it is of interest to note that many mathematicians and theoretical scientists, who deal almost entirely in symbolic logic, make their most important theoretical contributions during late adolescence and early adulthood.

This development in the cognitive area reinforces the emotional predisposition to narcissism during adolescence. The omnipotent, messianic preoccupations in the thought of the adolescent may be determined not only by his narcissistic withdrawal from the real world and internal objects, but also by the parallel developments in the unfolding of the cognitive apparatus. It seems that the adolescent needs and deserves the opportunity to play with his thoughts and to develop elaborate if unrealistic and fanciful plans to revolutionize social, political, and scientific practice just as the infant needs to shake his rattle and the latency child to build his collections as they master and consolidate earlier cognitive development.

A related area in which the adolescent makes use of his newly developed skill in manipulating thought is in the discussion of ideologies. The adolescent is struggling toward a sense of commitment to some life view and therefore spends a great deal of time thinking about and talking about life styles and the meaning of existence. This interest in ideology is readily observed in the articulate, studious, middle-class adolescent with his endless dialogue about life goals and values. However, as Shainberg (1966, 1970) has shown, the preoccupation of certain constricted and limited adolescent boys with their automobiles is also an implicit representation of their mechanized sense of self.

The therapist who wishes to treat adolescents must be prepared to listen to extended discussions which he would dismiss as intellectual defensiveness and resistance in adult patients. In fact, he should not only listen, but at appropriate times join the ideological discussion. Some guidelines for dealing with intellectualizing in adolescents are offered later.

THE ADOLESCENT AND SOCIETY

The adolescent's view of adult, organized society contains inherent elements of ambivalence. If the adolescent intends to find a place for himself in society, he naturally will have a strong curiosity about the nature and structure of this organization he plans to join. However, as described above, the adolescent is above all things a deductive thinker. His curiosity about society does not necessarily lead to an active study of its institutions, methods of operation, and reward systems. In addition, he is sadly deficient in knowledge of the behavior of human beings. Since he is utopian in outlook, he can develop only a limited interest in a historical perspective. He is more likely to devote himself to extensive fantasy, speculation, and theorization based on the most superficial and cursory examination of the data.

The adolescent who "drops out" and cannot accept the possibility of amalgamation into the adult world may be more interested in a depth study of society, but the value of his efforts may be decreased by the strong bias which accompanies his work. He is interested only in verifying his opinion, already self-validated, that society is corrupt, unchangeable, and inimical to basic human needs.

Even the adolescent who is more favorably inclined toward the adult world will have some mixed feelings about accepting an apprentice or student's role despite the value of this intermediate step on the path to adulthood. The adult world is, after all, his parents' world. The adolescent is still engaged in the struggle to escape dependent ties to his parents. He is reluctant to place himself in a comparable position with other adults. It is very difficult, especially for the younger adolescent, to accept his limitations comfortably, even those that are simply human. Internal conflicts, as well as shortcomings, tend to be externalized and dealt with as though they were environmental enemy forces. The adolescent cannot be entirely at peace with his world because he is not at peace within.

The capacity to tolerate inner strife is developed only gradually. Often, the adolescent cannot afford to learn the truth about society when that information would interfere with some of his self-protective fictions. This is often most clearly apparent in his dealings with the aspect of adult society closest to him, namely, his parents.

This state of affairs is complicated by adult society's views of the adolescent, which is often as irrational and unconsciously determined as are the adolescent's attitudes. Pearson (1958) has described the unconscious competitive, fearful, erotic, and envious attitudes which parents often harbor unconsciously toward their adolescent children. Brody (1968) has viewed adolescents as a minority group, noting that they are often responded to, as a group, with stereotyped attitudes and expectations that could only be described as prejudiced. He also suggests that this state of affairs plays an important role in the formation of an "adolescent contra-culture" with compensatory claims of superiority to the dominant adult society. The author has tried to describe the effect of these kinds of adult attitudes on the management of adolescent behavior elsewhere (Meeks, 1967).

Adolescents struggle along an unstable interface between their peer culture and adulthood. In even the smoothest adolescence, there is some mutual shaping and accommodation between the adolescent and his parents. The game is one of negotiation and compromise, no matter how much some adults may wish that a stricter approach would simplify life. Our society eventually guides the adolescent into an acceptable adult role in most instances, but, after all the arguments, threats, cajolery, coercion, and capitula-tions, we find that the process of molding our youth also has al-tered our notion of adulthood. Maturity and youth constantly shape one another.

Viewed objectively, the battle of the generations would seem to end in victory for both sides in the yield of a wider and more flexible set of adaptive skills. Subjectively, however, both sides often feel defeated. Too often, the young person feels that he has compromised his ideals whereas the adult suffers a nostalgic long-ing for a simpler and somehow nobler past, now lost forever.

THE ADOLESCENT AS UNCLE TOM

Several recent studies have suggested that the much-discussed adolescent rebellion is more myth than fact, especially in adoles-cent girls (Douvan and Adelson, 1966; Offer and Offer, 1968; Offer, 1969; Grinker, 1962; Offer et al., 1970). Some of these au-thors have expressed concern that American adolescents are ac-tually tame organization men who never battle through a real adolescent rebellion and therefore never achieve full autonomy (see also Friedenberg, 1959, 1963; Goodman, 1960). These authors feel that the apparent conflict between the generations represents an unimportant skirmish whose main function is to obscure the fact that the important battles are not fought.

This view probably represents a failure to understand the nature of the adolescent revolution. The revolt that absorbs the adolescent is primarily internal and is directed more against memories of old attachments to the parents than toward current adult domination and control.

Erikson (1968) has argued well that autonomy and a clear sense of identity are always found in some workable and personally meaningful alliance with dominant cultural themes and available role patterns. Although one may yearn personally for the more individualistic, self-directed, and ethically oriented American character of past generations, such an identity may be poorly adapted to current American culture. A workable personality for twentieth-century America may need to emphasize easy amiability and compromise rather than strict adherence to principle in all matters. Current social conditions may favor a generalized, although possibly superficial, friendliness rather than a pattern of mannered formality counterpointed with passionate involvement with a few intimates. The social conditions of urbanization, easy geographic mobility, corporate business structure, and massive population growth which have fostered these styles of relating are factors to which the adolescent must adapt, not conditions that he has created.

Adolescents, despite their affinity for ideological discussion, are not effective agents of real social change. They are more frequently noisy and highly visible riders on a bandwagon they cannot afford to miss. It seems unfair to expect the adolescent, struggling with internal turmoil and possessing only a superficial understanding of the cultural landscape, to do the adult world's dirty work of social criticism and reconstruction. It is enough that he stand ready to follow intelligent and passionate leadership, carrying the banners of the cause and shouting its slogans. Adolescents, as a group, are well-informed and thoughtful consumers of new or at least historically relevant ideologies. They are in no position to assume the responsibility of devising and manufacturing them. It has been suggested that the hope for a solution of our social problems lies with our youth. This may be true, if sensible and knowledgeable adults will provide reasonable blueprints for reconstruction. Our youth will labor untiringly if they are provided a job description that makes sense to them and then are left to their own techniques of implementation. Even an author as favorably impressed by the current youth culture as Roszak (1969) says of the young person's desire for new ideologies, "The appetite is healthily and daringly omnivorous, but it urgently requires mature minds to feed it."

The adolescent who comes to psychotherapy needs assistance in gaining enough freedom from his internal strictures so that he can voluntarily commit himself to the life style of his own choice. His therapist·has no right to select the leaders the adolescent will follow, only the responsibility for assuring a reasonably free election.

ADOLESCENT ADAPTATION

Although the adaptive techniques and ego defenses utilized by adolescents are not unique to this age, some characteristic patterns of emphasis can be observed. These general preferences give adolescent patients a particular style and flavor which distinguish them from adult patients to some degree. An awareness of coping behaviors which are typical for the age group is an essential background that allows the therapist to recognize deviations which may have diagnostic importance.

The friendless adolescent and the adolescent who prefers adult companionship are good examples of patterns which should alert the therapist to probable areas of emotional conflict. The turn toward peers is an almost universal adaptive technique for the adolescent. This hunger to have friends is related to at least four pressures on the adolescent.

1) His internal need for narcissistic support. Friends of the same age group can provide support not only by offering the sense of acceptability inherent in belonging to a group, but also by sharing guilt and thus reducing the shattering impact on self-esteem of a superego outraged by the increase in libidinal and aggressive drives at puberty.

2) The strongly felt need to loosen both dependent and unconscious erotic ties to the parents in preparation for eventual independence and mature love. The companionship of peers offers

some substitution for the loss of support entailed in this process of leavetaking.

3) The absence of a comfortable, or even bearable, sense of individual identity. Faced with the anxiety of this internal struggle to define a bearable sense of self, the adolescent often prefers the safety of belonging to a "we" to the terror of becoming an "I" (Deutsch, 1967).

4) To a large extent, group formation is forced on the adolescent by social realities. The process of secondary education and the college experience in a specialized and technological society requires us to place large numbers of adolescents together apart from their families. This spatial contiguity, coupled with the "minority group" status of the adolescent, strongly encourages the formation of intense ties between young people.

Adolescents use their peers to back their demands for greater freedom and to validate their grievances toward their parents and the remainder of the adult world. In unity, there is some strengthening of their vulnerable position. As the rebellious students say, "They can't bust us all!"

The use of the group to avoid awareness of anxiety is especially evident in the preoccupation of adolescent groups with "fun" and "action." The complaint "there is nothing to do" is not so much the jaded grumbling of a pleasure-mad sophisticate as the anxious lament of a trembling soul desperate to stay one jump ahead of a pursuing host of internal demons.

THE POWER OF WORDS

At times, the adolescent pauses in his flight to turn and face up to the enemy within. He rarely makes this stand alone. His choice of weapons against the demons requires the company of at least one other person who will be asked to serve as a listener. A listener is essential to the plan of action, since the adolescent seems intent on subduing his inner problems with words. He plans to talk them to death, and the adult listener sometimes wonders who will succumb first, the demons or the listener.

This adolescent chatter often has an incessant, driven quality because it is used in the service of intellectual defense. The content of the verbalizations may be frankly introspective at times. These monologues may contain rather accurate insights into some of the adolescent's conflicts which he is able to face by maintaining some distance from their associated affects. Still, as Blos (1963) has pointed out, the defense of intellectualizing does permit greater tolerance of instincts and is therefore largely a positive emergency measure during adolescence.

More often, the voluble ruminations are not so clearly related to the adolescent's personal feelings, but take the form of philosophic discussion. A very personal concern can usually be discovered underlying the philosophic issue when these weighty pronouncements are carefully attended.

A very unhappy 13-year-old spent her first few therapy hours bitterly accusing the adult world, including her therapist, of hypocrisy. No adult, she proclaimed, was what he pretended to be. This led to long and bitter tirades against religion and against her parents for forcing her to attend a church whose articles of faith she could not in conscience accept.

Shortly thereafter, when a therapeutic relationship was established, she wished to discuss her dangerous sexual provocation of older boys whom she told that she was 16. She noted in a letter to the therapist, "I've been yelling about all those hypocrites. I guess I'm the biggest one of all."

At a deeper level, she seemed to be referring to the incongruity between her rigid infantile superego and the emerging sexual feelings which seemed foreign to her. She had some awareness that her precocious leap into heterosexual behavior was "hypocritical" in the sense that it was defensive and by no means an expression of an actual readiness for heterosexual encounter. In her conflicts over denied dependency on her mother and her overwhelming guilt, she tried to maintain equilibrium by a spurious sexual aggressiveness.

If the adolescent can be garrulous at times, he can also be unbelievably taciturn. Total retreat into a glum and irritable silence is more disturbing to most adults than intellectual prattling. The intuitive feeling, often voiced by parents, that withdrawal is more serious than open conflict is correct. Usually, these silences cover a sense of being overwhelmed. During such times, the adolescent frequently adopts ascetic attitudes which cause him to experience almost unbearable feelings of guilt and shame. No progress in integrating the new instinctual striving is made in this atmosphere of self-suppression. At best, the adolescent can use these self-imposed exiles to lower the amount of external stimulation and to lick his wounds. At worst, he can paint himself into a misanthropic corner that he has too much pride to leave, even when he would like to do so.

MISDIRECTION

Magicians discovered long ago that it was not necessary for the hand to be faster than the eye if the observer could be led to look in the wrong place. To accomplish this, the magician uses large and obvious movements to divert attention from more subtle movements which are essential to the trick. Blackstone used to open his act by producing a live goat on stage. The great fuss he raised with his cape diverted attention from the fact that behind the cape he was carrying the goat under his arm! The technique is known as misdirection.

Adolescents seem to use these diversionary tactics frequently, especially in hiding attitudes and affects which they do not care to face or to have others notice. The method is especially effective when the affect to be hidden is a quieter, more gentle feeling. It is not always easy to detect the sadness and dependent longings a young person is experiencing when one's anxious and irritated attention is commanded by his belligerent and angry rantings.

The defensive technique that I am calling misdirection, then, could be defined as the exaggerated expression of one felt affect in order to hide from the self and others the presence of a concurrent, less acceptable affect.

The utilization of this defensive operation explains why the adolescent often seems to go to extremes in the expression of a single feeling, especially of anger. Misdirection gives the adolescent a one-dimensional affective tone when it is employed. He appears at these times to be a real "Johnny-One-Note" on the emotional scale. The stereotyped and unchanging nature of the affective expression can be a clue that other shadowy feelings may be lurking behind the fireworks in the foreground.

This defensive pattern is somewhat related to the "reversal of affect" described by Anna Freud (1937). Reversal of affect refers to the adolescent's attempt to avoid the struggle and anxiety aroused by his positive attachment to his parents by reversing these feelings into a bitter hatred. A less virulent technique of disparagement of the parent has been described as a typical adolescent defense against an actively seductive parent of the opposite sex (Sachs, 1966).

Of course, a similar pattern has a wider defensive value in simplifying and resolving identity conflicts. Erikson (1968) has discussed this as a demand for "totality" when a richer sense of "wholeness" cannot be achieved. The adolescent who grasps at totality amputates not just single affects, but larger portions of his personality in order to achieve a constricted, but comfortable, sense of identity. He sacrifices richness and complexity to obtain a shallow sense of certainty (see also Shainberg, 1970).

APOLLO VERSUS DIONYSUS

Special mention should be made of the adolescent's varied attempts to adapt to his superego conflicts. These behaviors are a frequent source of confusion to the adult observer. Very often, when it comes to the adolescent and his conscience, things are simply not as they seem to be.

Pattie was a 15-year-old girl whose rebellious behavior and apparent sexual promiscuity became so outrageous that her distraught family in desperation placed her in a psychiatric hospital. On the ward, she paraded her precocious pulchritude in a seductive display which made Sadie Thompson look like an inhibited old-maid school teacher. Since the adolescent boys on the ward were all racing about, tongues awag, approaching something which might have been called heterosexual panic, Pattie was seen in emergency daily therapy sessions.

In the first two sessions, she contented herself with systematically dismembering her parents with a cool, detached sophistication. By the third session, however, she was ready to give her therapist the full treatment. She somehow eluded the censoring eye of the nurses and arrived for therapy (barely) clad in a brief miniskirt, topped by a low-cut, skin-molded peasant blouse. She spun around in the office, modeling her outfit. Then, hands on hips, she leaned seductively forward and innocently asked her therapist,

"Now do you see anything wrong with these clothes?"

Her therapist retained his composure and looked at her steadily for a long moment.

"I think you secretly feel like a dirty slut," he said. "And I think that must be a lousy way to live. Why don't we talk about why you're doing this to yourself?"

Pattie broke into tears.

"You stupid ass," she shouted and fled the office.

Her flamboyant exhibitionism lessened over the next few days. During the weekend, she remarked to a ward nurse,

"Dr. X (her therapist) is not such a bad shrink. At least you can't fool him."

As her therapy proceeded, it became clear that Pattie's extravagant delinquency was simultaneously an effort to disclaim and escape a rigid superego and an unconsciously calculated effort to force others to control her behavior.

The variety of similar patterns is virtually endless. Many adolescents who appear to exhibit poor ego structure and deficiencies in impulse control are actually thrashing helplessly in the grip of an infantile superego which will not permit the comfortable and orderly expression of impulses. These adolescents can permit gratification only by linking pleasure with self-destructive and self-punitive extremes. They feel that it is okay to sin a little or even a lot if you promise to die tomorrow.

Not all of them are so flamboyantly "going down in flames" as was Pattie. The self-destructive behavior may be quieter and more subtle. The adolescent may merely fail his school work, "rebelliously" refuse to accept honors, or demonstrate a sullen refusal to enjoy anything. The built-in self-punishment evens the tally and therefore allows some expression of pleasure-seeking behavior. The combination often appears to the puzzled, angry (and sometimes envious) adult as a self-indulgent and willful flaunting of social expectations. The typical adult response makes it easy for the adolescent to externalize his superego conflict. The limiting adult is invested with the viciousness, rigidity, and anhedonia which actually reside in the adolescent's own superego.

GHOSTS, GOBLINS, AND THINGS THAT GO BUMP IN THE NIGHT

Many adolescents show an intense interest in the supernatural. Some of their morbid preoccupations and beliefs would be quite pathological if expressed by an adult. Usually, these interests do not seem unpleasant or frightening to the adolescent. In fact, they are usually presented in a playful manner and may be the basis of entertainments such as visiting "haunted houses" in groups. Astrology and other occult sciences also hold great fascination for many adolescents.

Frankie, an intelligent, nonpsychotic 16-year-old girl, bounced cheerfully into a therapy session. Bubbling with enthusiasm, she announced, "Now I know how to make myself invisible!"

Frankie had frequently discussed a fantasy wish to be invisible which seemed to have multiple dynamic origins. She now explained, "You get a human head and three black beads. You put one bead in each eye and one in the mouth. Then you draw this design on the head and bury it. You water it with the finest brandy for three days and then...."

"Wait, wait," said the therapist. "I'm still back at the beginning. Where do you get the human head?"

"Oh," said Frankie airily. "That's no problem. You just go out and get one."

Even risking the pun, the gleam in her eye could only be described as devilish.

It is striking that much of the interest in the supernatural seems related to the question of death and immortality. One gains the impression that not only is the fear of death very real to the adolescent but death often seems imminent. However, in typical adolescent fashion, this fear is usually handled in a counterphobic manner.

There seem to be two primary sources of this inclination toward the occult within the adolescent. The first we have already encountered as the adolescent's belief in the omnipotence of thought. Reality ties are loosened and magical thinking is easily accepted. It is a logical short step from a personal alteration of reality to a world peopled by witches, ghosts, and seers.

The second factor is the adolescent's effort to relinquish his parents and many aspects of his childhood self. In a psychological sense, death and mourning are an immediate part of the adolescent experience. Since the adolescent's greatest fear is fear itself, he sometimes happily embraces his demons and, gulping back his fears, takes them out for a romp.

This adolescent propensity is reinforced currently by a generalized awakened interest in the irrational and mystical. Since this social movement is closely linked with the increasing use of psychedelic drugs, it is more fully discussed in Chapter Fifteen, "The Adolescent on the Drug Scene."

SUMMARY: IMPLICATIONS FOR PSYCHOTHERAPY

These developmental characteristics of adolescence pose many problems in psychotherapy. Because of the adolescent's style of relating and his preference for peers, it is often difficult to establish a therapeutic relationship. This is true not only because of the adolescent's distrust of the therapist, but because of the countertransference attitudes which this negative approach arouses. In the next chapter, we consider the personality characteristics which may help the therapist to establish a therapeutic alliance with adolescent patients. Later, we will be concerned with the techniques of establishing the therapeutic alliance and with the problems which are encountered by the therapist and patient even after therapy is well under way and through the time of termination.

CITED AND RECOMMENDED READINGS

Blos, P. 1963. On adolescence. New York: The Free Press of Glencoe, Inc.

Blos, P. 1967. The second individuation process of adolescence. Psychoanal. Stud. Child 22: 162–186.

Brody, E. B. 1968. Minority group adolescents in the United States. Baltimore: Williams & Wilkins Company.

Deutsch, H. 1967. Selected problems of adolescence (with special emphasis on group formation). New York: International Universities Press, Inc.

Douvan, E., and J. Adelson. 1966. The adolescent experience. New York: John Wiley & Sons, Inc.

Erikson, E. H. 1968. Identity: youth and crisis. New York: W. W. Norton & Company, Inc.

Flavell, J. H. 1963. The developmental psychology of Jean Piaget. New York: D. Van Nostrand.

Freud, A. 1937. The ego and the mechanisms of defense. London: Hogart Press, Ltd. (New York: International Universities Press, Inc., 1946).

Freud, A. 1958. Adolescence. Psychoanal. Stud. Child 13: 255–278.

Friedenberg, E. Z. 1959. The vanishing adolescent. Boston: Beacon Press, Inc. (New York: Dell Publishing Company, 1962).

Friedenberg, E. Z. 1963. Coming of age in America. New York: Random House.

Gardner, G. E. 1959. Psychiatric problems of adolescence. In: American handbook of psychiatry, Vol. I. Edited by S. Areti. New York: Basic Books, Inc.

Goodman, P. 1960. Growing up absurd. New York: Random House.

Grinker, R. R. 1962. Mentally healthy young males (homoclites). Arch. Gen. Psychiat. 6: 405–453.

Keniston, K. 1965. The uncommitted: alienated youth in America. New York: Harcourt, Brace & World, Inc.

Meeks, J. E. 1967. Some observations on adolescent group leaders in two contrasting socioeconomic classes. Int. J. Soc. Psychiat. 3: 278–296.

Offer, D. 1969. The psychological world of the teenager. New York: Basic Books, Inc.

Offer, D., D. Marcus, and J. L. Offer. 1970. A longitudinal study of normal adolescent boys. Amer. J. Psychiat. 126: 917–924.

Offer, D., and J. L. Offer. 1968. Profiles of normal adolescent girls. Arch. Gen. Psychiat. 19: 513–522.

Pearson, G. H. T. 1958. Adolescence and the conflict of generations. New York: W. W. Norton & Company, Inc.

Piaget, J. 1967. Six psychological studies. New York: Random House.

Roszak, T. 1969. The making of a counter culture. New York: Doubleday & Company, Inc.

Sachs, L. J. 1966. Disdain as defense against parental seduction. J. Amer. Acad. Child Psychiat. 5: 211–225.

Shainberg, D. 1966. Personality restriction in adolescents. Psychiat. Quart. 40: 258–270.

Shainberg, D. 1970. "It really blew my mind": a study of adolescent cognition. Adolescence 5: 17–36.

CHAPTER TWO
therapist qualifications: an essay

NEVER TRUST ANYONE OVER THIRTY

There is a widespread belief that young adults relate comfortably with adolescents and are accepted as leaders with greater ease than older individuals. Lewis (1969a) has suggested that young individuals "may represent good identification models whose cultural values have not ossified, and who share an interest in the legitimate age-appropriate interests of youth." There may be considerable truth to this, in that the very young adult is closer to the cultural changes that produce much of the generation gap. Often, however, this affinity is markedly strained when points of disagreement appear between the adolescent and his slightly older mentor. The young adult's closeness to his own adolescent struggles can tempt him to relive them vicariously through the adolescent or to fight against that temptation with rigid moralistic attitudes of rejection and condemnation. Often, the young adult lacks the security of personal identity which would permit him to view the adolescent's impassioned trials and missteps from a perspective of tolerant understanding.

This is not to say that youth automatically prevents one from doing good psychotherapy with adolescents. The point is that being older does not automatically disqualify one. The adolescent *can* and *will* trust someone over 30!

The personality characteristics of the therapist are important, however, regardless of his age. The attitudes that he holds toward himself, toward society, toward the nature of human motivation, and toward young people are the factors which will dictate his effectiveness with adolescent patients.

GENERAL CHARACTERISTICS

There are some general characteristics which are probably necessary equipment for all psychotherapists. The first of these relates to the basic way that one views his fellow men and their behaviors. Some people are mystified and dismayed by aberrant behavior. They do not look below the surface of apparently strange and incomprehensible actions to their origins in strivings which are universally human. Needless to say, a nonjudgmental view which considers all behavior as potentially comprehensible within a human framework is essential in psychotherapy. Those who deal with the panorama of human adjustments by conveniently dividing the world into good and bad people will be unable to guide any patient through the moral dilemmas of psychotherapy and will be especially ineffective in work with adolescents. This does not mean that the therapist takes no stance in regard to the adolescent's behavior. Obviously, some actions are self-destructive and symptomatic. Timid avoidance of direct confrontation on these issues is as destructive as prudish condemnation. The important point is that even the most repulsive and self-defeating behaviors are comprehensible. The patient needs to know that we believe deeply that there are good reasons for everything he does, even when what he does is not good for others or for himself. The therapist's main activity is to help the patient discover his real goals and reasons. I hope that this book is pervaded with examples of this attitude as it affects the therapeutic response in many different clinical situations. It is basic to psychotherapy of the adolescent.

The therapist can be more successful in helping the adolescent patient understand his inner motivations if the therapist is not an intrusive person. It may seem paradoxical to speak of respect for the patient's privacy while discussing the goal of inner revelation. In fact, this apparent contradiction is not real. Most of us react with some measure of caution to a listener who seems too eager to know all about us. Too active curiosity may kill the cat of spontaneous self-revelation. The adolescent is especially sensitive to psychological intrusion. Early in therapy, he may react to the most casual question as though it were a third degree. He needs to understand that we want him to get to know himself. Our need to know about him is justified only by our status as a hired guide. What he does, thinks, or wishes is our business only because it is necessary to our work. Since we can only do as much of this work as he wishes, we should encourage him to reveal only those matters that he is ready to expose for purposes of exploration. In fact, it may be important occasionally to caution the adolescent about excessive candor early in therapy (St. John, 1968).

The adolescent therapist's recognition that human drives, appetites, and wishes are universal does not blind him to the variability in the expression of these urges. As Noshpitz (1969) has said, "The wishes are pretty much the same from person to person, but the disguises—ah, there we have the full panoply of human personality to contend with."

We have discussed in the previous chapter some of the disguises which are especially prevalent during adolescence. We must also recognize that the expression of drives varies within a social context. Prevailing mores influence which disguises are deemed acceptable or even praiseworthy and which are regarded as evil, perverse, or pathological (Lewis, 1969b; Hughes, 1969).

ULTIMATE VALUES

In my opinion, however, the therapist must not drift into a bleak and apathetic relativism based on cynical reductionalism. Dynamically oriented psychiatrists have occasionally slipped into this kind of arrogant contempt for human achievement. I rather suspect that there is a bit of narcissism involved in the insistence that religious insights, artistic creations, and innovative constructs in the business and scientific worlds are "just" the expression of inhibited libidinal or aggressive drives. The psychological pundit then becomes the only person who is actually dealing with basic truth. He rides high until someone points out that *his* activity consists of "just" sublimated voyeurism and his speculations of "just" mental masturbation.

This simple-minded reductionalism not only ignores the historical fact that man has always searched for transcendental meaning in life, but ignores the importance of ego synthesis and the boundless potential of human mutuality. Adolescents especially need help in recognizing that man does not live for gratification alone, but also moves toward a sense of coherence and meaning within a value context which includes some explicit or implicit stance toward the needs and values of other people. Dynamic psychology has shed a great deal of light on the nature of the drives which energize man's quest for the "good life." All well-trained therapists may be justifiably proud of their knowledge in this regard. On the other hand, we must humbly recognize that our knowledge of the "fuel sources" does not fully enlighten us regarding the details of overall structure of human personality and, further, that it tells us virtually nothing of the best directions for the human spirit to pursue. We know a lot about psychic gasoline, little about detailed structures of the vehicle, less about road maps, and almost nothing about proper destinations.

One essential derivative of the views of the human condition expressed above is optimism. The therapist works best with a basically hopeful viewpoint, tempered by a realistic recognition of the difficulties involved in psychological maturation and the relatively limited help which one person can offer another in the process of moving toward maturity. All human beings need hope, and psychiatric patients are often critically low in their supply. They look to their therapist for replenishment. The therapist can meet this need without perjuring himself or being unrealistic if he has an optimism based on a realistic faith in the human desire for emotional growth and the healing potential of psychotherapy (Harrison and Carek, 1966).

A sense of trust in the basic goodness and worth of all people, regardless of how repulsive their superficial defensive armoring may be, is indispensable to the establishment of a therapeutic atmosphere. Maurice Levine (1942) has described this inner goodness as the "third layer," which may be obscured by a first layer of hostile or avoidance defenses against interpersonal contact and a second layer of anxiety, narcissism, and irrational infantile needs. At the level of the third layer, however, all men long for a warm and fair interaction with their fellow men.

CHARACTERISTICS SPECIAL TO THE ADOLESCENT THERAPIST

This "basic trust" in others must extend to those caught in the developmental squeeze of adolescence if one intends to work effectively with adolescents. Persons who respond to adolescents with stereotyped negative expectations will have little success in treating them. There are people who cannot overcome a tendency to find adolescents irritating or boring for a variety of personal reasons. Other therapists will find that they can respond positively to some adolescents but not to others. It is best that both groups accept their own limitations and refer the disliked adolescents who happen to come their way to others for psychotherapy.

Of course, it is not necessary to approve totally of every adolescent whom one treats. Fromm-Reichmann (1950) even goes as far as to say, "If a person comes to see the psychiatrist, this implies a need for changes in his personality; and if a psychiatrist accepts a person for treatment, this means that he recognizes that person's need for change and that he hopes to be instrumental in the patient's ultimate attainment of these necessary changes. This being so, the question of whether or not the patient in his present mental condition and with his present personality trends is to the psychiatrist's liking is beside the point." Possibly, this viewpoint expects too much of the therapist and ignores the realities of his vulnerabilities. It may be worthwhile for therapists to aspire toward such an ideal goal, but this aspiration should not blind them to their real limitations. Almost all therapists will occasionally encounter a patient whose first and second layers of personality will produce so much anxiety in the therapist that he will be unable to work effectively with the patient. If the therapist cannot overcome this feeling through introspection or consultation with a colleague, he would be unfair to make the patient a victim of his limitations.

Another personality characteristic important to any therapist is a fine sense of tact. The old adage that you can say anything to a patient if you say it the right way is especially applicable to the adolescent patient. With his exquisite narcissistic vulnerability, the adolescent demands a delicate touch. This is easy to overlook, since the adolescent himself, in his single-minded lunge toward an authentic adulthood, rarely shows great tact in his dealings with the therapist.

Skill in tactful confrontation is essential in the early stages of therapy and comes to have a growing importance in the intensely emotional interchanges which characterize later stages of treatment. The ability to be direct and yet courteous in a tumultuous interaction implies a high level of personal comfort in dealing with feelings stirred by the adolescent. A squeamish avoidance of confrontation and interaction cannot substitute for honest communication which still respects the adolescent's feelings. Tact does not imply an absence of firmness or a failure to face issues.

The adolescent therapist must be comfortable enough with himself to leave aside any pomposity or excessive professional dignity. The adolescent will quickly recognize these as evidences of personal insecurity. As such, they will frighten the adolescent, since his own self-esteem is extremely shaky and in need of support from a strong and secure adult. This security is best conveyed by a simple, honest presentation of oneself as an ordinary person who has some useful skills learned in the ordinary way, namely, by study and training over a period of time. The adolescent therapist does not deny his rational status as an expert, but avoids claiming any special consideration or adulation as a human being. He should not try to impress his patients with his importance, brilliance, or skill.

THE ADOLESCENT THERAPIST AND MORALITY, NEW AND OLD

Since the adolescent is most often threatening in the spheres of morals, ideology, and identity, the individual with marked conflicts in these areas may find it difficult to be comfortable with the adolescent. This is perhaps especially true of the therapist with latent, unexplored problems of this kind, the therapist who long ago settled for "totality" rather than "wholeness" for himself (Erikson, 1968).

The adolescent questions and attacks primarily those values which Veblen called "institutional process values." These are the values which receive their authority from tradition or other forces superordinate to individual men. These include those de riving from religion, status, and the vague coercive strength of the "establishment." They may be contrasted with "instrumental process values" which are more pragmatic and oriented toward problem-solving on a personal human plane. Wheelis (1958) has discussed the role of both processes in cultural change and in the inertia against change.

Obviously, with their basis in tradition and their proscriptive content, the institutional process values are critically scrutinized by the adolescent both as external representatives of his superego strictures and because of their importance in the development of ideological structures.

The therapist who is unaware of his own inflexible assumptions in this area may find the adolescent's challenge of traditional values quite troubling on a very personal level. His sense of outrage may block any effort to treat the adolescent's productions objectively and therapeutically. On the other hand, the therapist who is still actively seeking his own identity and still in rebellion against cultural values is probably no better prepared to deal with the adolescent. He may inflame the adolescent's natural tendency toward iconoclasm and overlook the more important civil war within his patient which can only be resolved successfully through compromise and accommodation to psychological reality. The uncertain therapist may go even further in abdicating his responsibility and look to the adolescent patient to provide him with a workable ideology in a changing cultural scene. This unfortunate reversal can only result in chaos, not just in the therapeutic situation, but in the adolescent's life. Problems of this kind are especially likely to arise when therapists have strong utopian wishes which are untempered by a historical perspective on the complexities of social living and some of the inherent paradoxes in human makeup.

These issues are especially troubling in our current historical climate. We are deeply involved in a social experiment which is extremely perilous. There is a growing distrust and repudiation of any authority outside of the individual. There is a movement to destroy all institutional process values. Many people fear that a society without structuralized institutional controls will de-

teriorate into bestial anarchy and chaos. Their concern is well
founded in the bloody history of mankind. There seems to be
little evidence that individual man is naturally inclined to reside
comfortably in a utopian age of Aquarius.

The therapist must try to prevent his anxieties (or his enthusiasm) about this social revolution from obscuring the adolescent's
main purpose in attacking social institutions. Despite historical
currents, the individual adolescent's primary goal is to alter his
own rigid conscience. It is the therapist's responsibility to assist
him in this task with all the honesty and objectivity he can muster.
In my experience, when this job is properly managed, the adolescent's politics become quite responsible, although they do not
always agree with mine.

ON ACTING ONE'S AGE

The adolescent therapist needs to be content with his own life
and his own age level. This includes a comfortable awareness of
the areas of living in which he is disappointed with himself. Arrival at maturity always includes facing up to some ambitions that
have not been realized and mourning some fantasies which have
never been gratified in reality.

The adolescent patient of the same sex easily becomes a potential vehicle for the accomplishment of frustrated self-expectations. Where the therapist has floundered, his adolescent alterego,
benefited by the therapist's sage advice and counsel, may succeed.
Once the adolescent's idealized image of the therapist is abused
in this manner, it becomes very difficult to reestablish a therapeutic relationship which the patient can trust as totally committed to his best interest. Instead of being helped to become his
own person, he has been issued as a new edition of the therapist.

Equally destructive to the adolescent patient is the therapist
who feels defensive regarding his own deficiencies. Adults of this
kind frequently react to adolescents as a threat and are fearful
that the younger person will surpass them. Their response to this
anxiety may be a subtle or overt suppression of the adolescent.

The challenging, competitive, depreciating, provocative adolescent can elicit this anxious suppression in adults who are generally

fairly self-assured. Many adolescents are masters at ferreting out the hidden emotional vulnerabilities and tender spots we all harbor. Some of them can work on these relentlessly in an attempt to assuage some personal sense of inadequacy or to justify the avoidance of emotional involvement with the therapist. The only dependable defense that the therapist can mount against such an attack is personal comfort with his own peculiar configuration of strengths and shortcomings. Sometimes, it is necessary to tell some of the more clever, shrewd, and manipulative adolescents honestly that we realize they can probably outsmart us if they wish, adding that we can only hope that they will decide to use their talents to help themselves rather than to prove their superiority. Some of them can eventually understand that beating the therapist is a hollow victory which brings no worthwhile trophy or prize.

Still, the therapist's self-esteem frequently takes quite a beating. He cannot depend on adolescent patients for any narcissistic supplies, since the adolescent has little to spare early in treatment, whereas, later, adulation cannot be accepted without harming the patient. The therapist must look for his emotional gratification outside of his therapeutic work. His own life must be sufficiently gratifying so that he does not need to have his emotional needs met by his patients. There are other rewards in treating adolescents which we describe in the chapter on termination, but the therapist must not look to them for sustenance. He must be sustained by other people outside of his work.

This need for sustaining human relationships in one's personal life is especially felt during the runs of "bad hours" which therapists often encounter. To my knowledge, no one has ever adequately explained the phenomenon, but most therapists have noted "good weeks" and "bad weeks" with their patients. At times, it seems as though every patient is getting worse and holding the therapist totally responsible for this plight and hating him for it. Even the strongest therapist's shoulders begin to bend under the weight of session after session of depression, discouragement, and anger. His free time is interrupted by frantic parental and patient telephone calls which report runaways, suicide threats, and a variety of demands for instant miracles. At this point, the most dedicated therapist wonders why he did not choose some sane and safe profession, say lion taming. He buys a book on the circus world and begins to read.

Surprisingly, if he maintains some degree of therapeutic objectivity and struggles with the problems, the tide turns. Suddenly, it seems that all his patients are improving and growing. He feels like a veritable genius and even his adolescents cautiously admit that he seems to know what he is doing. He throws away the circus book and wonders whether he should write the definitive work on psychotherapy. At the height of his elation, everything crashes again, and he pulls his circus book out of the wastebasket and tries to find his place.

Of course, this is an exaggeration, but it carries a grain of truth. The swings do disturb therapists, especially those who are experiencing them for the first time and do not yet appreciate their cyclic nature. I have the impression that they are more noticeable with adolescents because of their volatility and tendency to go to extremes. Sometimes, the reasons are apparent. Experienced psychotherapists dread the end of vacations not just because they hate to give up their pleasant regression, but because they expect that their patients will be angry over their absence when they return. Because of the prevalent anger, they expect some difficult hours. Other rough periods may be related to periods of time when the therapist is relatively less effective because of personal problems, fatigue, or minor illness. Still, there are those runs of "bad sessions" which appear inexplicable. These are probably due simply to the chance concurrence of periods of resistance and negative transference in several patients. Of course, such periods are actually evidence that therapy is effective and the patients are involved. A therapy which "runs smooth" is a therapy in which nothing of importance is happening. Still, we are inclined to accept consensual validation. If 10 patients in a row tell us that we are not helping them, that we are personally obnoxious, incompetent, and a little stupid, too, it is not easy to retain balance, objectivity, and self-respect. The same thing could be said in reverse about the "good periods" when everyone seems to agree that we are unusually gifted, charming, helpful, and lovable. Through both kinds of excesses, the therapist must try to maintain a sense of professional competence and balanced optimism. 'Tis easier said than done.

THE LOVE GENERATION

The temptation to utilize the adolescent to gratify frustrated libidinal needs is perhaps even more dangerous than the possibility of using them for narcissistic self-enhancement. Although it is probably extremely rare for a therapist actually to act out sexual feelings toward an adolescent, the frequent occurrence of disruptive erotic countertransference and vicarious participation in adolescent sexual behavior is easily detected. It appears, sometimes with disarming honesty, sometimes masquerading as humor or unwarranted prudishness, in the material which younger therapists bring to supervision. It also makes itself known in the fantasies, dreams, and therapeutic blunders of the more seasoned practitioner.

Of course, it is not surprising that the adolescent is capable of stirring forgotten yearnings, especially in America. Not only is the healthy and vigorous adolescent undeniably attractive as a sexual object, our culture, contrary to all reason, assigns him a comfort in instinctual expression far beyond that enjoyed by the mature American. When this mythical image is coupled with the adult's nostalgic mourning for missed opportunities during his own adolescence, the mixture is potentially explosive. In these situations, the adolescent is not a passive victim. Because of his intense need for affection, the adolescent often can be quite seductive toward his therapist. The psychotherapist who would really prefer to *be* an adolescent, rather than treat an adolescent, is likely to encounter serious problems in the erotic area.

What is needed, of course, is not total freedom from such stirrings, but a comfortable awareness that they are present, and, more importantly, that they are illusory. If the therapist does not have a clear grasp of these realities, he can be easily led astray by the adolescent patient. Because of his internal difficulties with his own superego, the adolescent must become a master of corruption. Since he practices daily on his own inflexible superego, he is likely to endeavor with equal fervor and subtlety to corrupt the superego of the therapist. In his skilled presentation, sadistic behavior can be disguised as healthy rebellion and movement toward autonomy; a narcissistic exploitation of another individual may be presented as growing sexual freedom and a healthy interest in heterosexuality. If the therapist has difficulty calling a spade a spade in his own life, he may wake up at various points in therapy to find that the adolescent has taken him on quite a stroll down the primrose path.

THE THERAPIST AND RESPONSIBILITY

All of this touches indirectly on another necessary qualification for treating adolescents. This is the capacity to define one's area of responsibility and then to assume it without excuses or complaints. Adolescent patients frequently raise very confusing issues around the nature of the therapist's responsibility. Because of their dependency conflicts, the adolescents often say verbally that they are totally responsible for their own lives and the therapist need not concern himself. At the same time, they may communicate nonverbally partial or total irresponsibility which invites the therapist to prevent disaster.

Obviously, since his goal is to maximize independence and autonomy, the therapist wishes to take as little direct responsibility for the adolescent as is consistent with common sense. Some therapists even say that their only responsibility is to make the adolescent aware of his real motivations and to discuss the likely consequences of any decisions in reality, leaving the final responsibility for his behavior always to the adolescent. This is a tempting posture, but I do not believe that it is consonant with psychologically reality or with a realistic view of ethical professional behavior. It breaks down when faced with pathological self-destructive aims and in dealing with excessive aggression toward others. The therapist must recognize that at times the adolescent cannot take responsibility for himself because his "self" is overwhelmed by guilt, rage, or other turbulent emotions. The therapist must serve as an emergency ancillary ego at these times. If he does not accept this responsibility, tragic results such as suicide or homicide may prevent the adolescent from ever having a chance at autonomy and self-direction.

The important guiding principle is that the therapist takes responsibility for the adolescent's behavior only when it is essential for the youngster's welfare and the continuation of therapy. He relinquishes this responsibility at the earliest safe moment. He also encourages the adolescent to explore his reasons for soliciting the rescue operation in the first place. The therapist's behavior is regulated by the adolescent's cues and direct and indirect requests. Individuals who have a personal need to control or dominate others or to have others dependent on them are poorly suited to function as adolescent psychotherapists. They will tend to assume responsibility for the adolescent's life because they need to do so, not because the adolescent is asking for temporary assistance to prevent the overthrow of his rational decision-making capacity.

We must also consider the question of what the therapist is responsible to provide within the therapy contract. Obviously, the therapist does not offer to provide an active cure to a passive and helpless patient. Clearly, the therapist must teach the patient to share the responsibility for the process and the outcome of psychotherapy. The therapist, however, does have the responsibility for knowing what psychotherapy is all about and how the patient should function in order to derive maximum benefit from the undertaking. He has the further responsibility to convey this information to the patient in a way he can understand. The mechanics of this process are detailed in Chapter Four, "The Therapeutic Alliance with the Adolescent."

The therapist has a continuing responsibility to recognize those times when the adolescent is unable to function well as a patient. At these times, it is the therapist's job to notify the adolescent of this state of affairs and to help the adolescent to understand the forces that sidetracked the treatment process. The adolescent must do the important work of therapy. The therapist's primary responsibility is to provide on-the-job training and some tactful quality control. The therapist can never "give" insight. If the therapist knows his job and stays in his proper role, he may help the adolescent to find his own insight by saving him the effort of looking in the wrong places. This does not imply passivity. In the role of expert guide, the therapist must often be quite active in asserting his leadership. On the other hand, he must be as unobtrusive as possible when the adolescent is on the right track.

THERAPY FOR THE THERAPIST

It is probably apparent to the reader that the kind of flexible and objective self-awareness described above can usually be achieved only through the hard-won insights of an intensive personal experience in psychotherapy or psychoanalysis. For most individuals, this is probably true, although one cannot overlook the occasional person who seems to reach a balanced knowledge of himself without the aid of formal therapy. Furthermore, many individuals seem to have a kind of personal integration which some adolescents can utilize as an anchoring and orienting focus even though the adult shows little of the flexibility extolled above. These people, who are often referred to as "strong personalities," can offer a great deal to the troubled adolescent if their strength is real so that they have no need to recruit converts to their idiosyncratic view of life. The therapeutic experience such a person can offer the adolescent may be limited in its scope and goals, but it may be sure and valuable within its limitations.

SUMMARY: WHAT PRICE INSIGHT?

In closing these remarks on the optimal personality makeup of the aspiring therapist of the adolescent, we should mention one final "true believer." This is the psychotherapist, usually (but not always) unanalyzed himself, who has perverted an oversimplified psychoanalytic understanding into an institutionalized process value system. Such a therapist holds with a religious fervor to the belief that "real" therapy consists solely of making unconscious conflicts conscious. The inadvisability and occasional danger of such an approach with most adolescents have been pointed out by several authorities in the field. The adolescent is struggling, with already overburdened equipment, to effect a synthesis of conflicting tendencies within his personality. He cannot be assisted by an approach which further accentuates the schisms within him and ignores his desperate need for his defenses.

The effective therapist for the adolescent patient is above all things a pragmatist. His personal value systems, even if committed to such a lofty and irreproachable value as absolute intrapsychic awareness, cannot be allowed to take precedence over the central task of aiding the adolescent to achieve *any* organization of his warring personality fragments that is reasonably safe for the patient, fairly benign and constructive toward his environment, and yet productive of a personal sense of vigorous direction in living. A sense of the pluralism of human behavior and value patterning, an acceptance of the fascinating variety of viable and useful human identities, is useful to any therapist but is of critical importance to those who treat adolescents.

It should go without saying that such a view breeds both respect for one's younger fellow men and a healthy sense of humor in watching oneself and the adolescent patient as both struggle with their roles in the human comedy.

CITED AND RECOMMENDED READINGS

Erikson, E. H. 1968. Identity: Youth and Crisis. New York: W. W. Norton & Company, Inc.

Fromm-Reichmann, F. 1950. Principles of intensive psychotherapy. Chicago: University of Chicago Press.

Harrison, S. I., and D. J. Carek. 1966. A guide to psychotherapy. Boston: Little, Brown & Co.

Hughes, H. S. 1969. Emotional disturbance and American social change. Amer. J. Psychiat. 126: 21–28.

Levine, M. 1942. Psychotherapy in Medical Practice. New York: The Macmillan Company.

Lewis, J. M. 1969a. Changing moral concepts. South. Med. J. 62: 290–294.

Lewis, J. M. 1969b. The development of an inpatient adolescent service. Presented at South. Psychiat. Assoc. Meeting, Oct., 1969. *In press:* Adolescence.

Noshpitz, J. 1969. Drugs and adolescents. Presented at a seminar on childhood and adolescence by the Department of Postgraduate

Education, University of Texas Southwestern Medical School at Dallas, April 25–26, 1969.

St. John, R. 1968. Developing a therapeutic working alliance with the adolescent girl. J. Amer. Acad. Child Psychiat. 7: 68–78.

Wheelis, A. 1958. The quest for identity. New York: W. W. Norton & Company, Inc.

CHAPTER THREE

the diagnostic evaluation of the adolescent patient

THE PERTINENT QUESTIONS

Even the ideal therapist cannot treat all adolescent emotional problems on an outpatient basis. A careful program of evaluation should precede the decision to attempt this therapeutic approach. The purpose of the evaluation is to answer six questions about the adolescent as accurately as possible.

1) What is the best level of psychological development which the adolescent has achieved?

This question is complex and difficult to answer for any psychiatric patient. In adolescents, who frequently deal with developmental stress by either regression or an equally confusing premature leap forward, the problem may be bewildering. The distinction between regression and fixation, so important to prognostication, is often very uncertain during the fluidity of the adolescent phase.

Only meticulous attention to a complete developmental history and the capacity to decipher the latent content of the adolescent's behavior and verbalizations can yield the data for even a tentative conclusion on this point.

2) What kind of object relationships has the adolescent established, especially with his parents?

Correct assessment of this side of the adolescent's development is obscured by the phase-specific peculiarities of relating which were described earlier. It is particularly hard to derive a realistic view of the adolescent's previous style of relating to the parents in the face of reversal of affect, disparagement, and other defenses calculated to help the adolescent divest himself of these tries to the parent.

Again, the history plays a crucial role in arriving at the answer to this question. The adolescent's less guarded description of his relationships with peers may also be of assistance. Particular attention should be given to the covert expectations, hopes, and fears which the adolescent holds in regard to his friends. These frequently reveal a great deal about the strengths and conflicts present in the previous relationships with parents.

3) Why is the patient ill now?

In many youngsters brought for therapy during adolescence, the answer is simply that they are ill now because they have always been ill. This is true of youngsters with very severe behavior disorders which result from a basic failure in the socialization process. The parents may be antisocial themselves, overtly or covertly, or simply so rejecting of the child that they have never provided the affection and direction necessary to even rudimentary emotional development and identification with society's rules and goals. These youngsters are brought to psychotherapy in adolescence, not necessarily for the first time, primarily because their increased strength, cleverness, and motility have widened and deepened the impact of their antisocial behavior on their environment.

Other individuals, struggling with adolescence reasonably well, become ill in response to external traumatic events. Although their symptomatology is colored by their developmental phase, the focus of therapy should be on the mastery of the precipitating event.

Still, most adolescent patients are victimized by specific developmental stresses. Their illness is precipitated by the onset of adolescence and the tasks inherent in that period. This is not to say that their conflicts are purely adolescent. Very often, perhaps usually, adolescence merely activates and highlights points of relative weakness in the personality structure. These unsolved growth problems may not have been troublesome in earlier stages, but careful review of the developmental history usually reveals their presence underground prior to their eruption into open view during the volcanic upheaval of adolescence.

For most adolescents, this reactivation of latent conflicts has positive value which outweighs its negative implications. During the "trial run" at adulthood which adolescence permits, the young person has another opportunity to discover, demonstrate, and correct personality flaws without the severe and possibly irreversible consequences which might attend their emergence after commitment to adult goals and responsibilities.

4) Is the adolescent conflicted?

This question could be restated in two other ways. Is the adolescent's behavior and adjustment ego-alien? Is the adolescent motivated to change?

The problem in answering these questions is the adolescent's reluctance to admit directly to a sense of conflict. He is much more likely to try to bluff it out and make the best of a bad thing, although there are some exceptions to this rule, especially in older adolescents. His indications that he is unhappy with himself and would welcome assistance are likely to be subtle and carefully hedged. Many experienced therapists think that even the adolescent who asks for psychotherapy is more likely asking for help *against* his parents than for help *for* himself.

Many therapists, especially those who are relatively inexperienced, place too great an emphasis on verbalized motivation. All patients who approach therapy honestly are ambivalent about it. Conscious motivation is a straw in the whirlwind of primitive emotions unleashed by exploratory psychotherapy. Most patients weather these storms only because their attachment to the therapist strongly reinforces their rational wishes to improve. Often, it is possible to assess the true nature of the adolescent's motivation only after a trusting involvement with the therapist has developed. Actually, before this stage has arrived, the adolescent himself does not know whether he is "motivated" or not.

5) Does the adolescent have the capacity to view himself with reasonable objectivity and the willingness to describe his view to the therapist?

This is, of course, a central question, since in outpatient therapy the therapist will have to rely heavily on the adolescent to report honestly both his behavior and his feelings as a basis for the therapeutic work. One cannot expect too much, however, especially in younger patients. Some defensiveness, distortion, and self-protection are anticipated and do not contraindicate outpatient work. All adolescents can be expected to "play games." One only expects that they will gradually develop a capacity to discuss the rules of the game and the prizes they are trying to win.

6) Will the adolescent's family permit and help the adolescent to change?

These six questions are clearly interrelated to one another. One might even say that they are largely different ways of looking at the same basic question: how sound is the basic personality structure in this particular youngster?

The adolescent who has previously functioned in large measure at age-appropriate levels and has achieved fairly gratifying and stable object relationships probably has the capacity, if given proper assistance and if his family can allow it, to utilize the therapist as an ally in productive self-scrutiny. This remains true even if the presenting behavior is chaotic and bizarre. Trying to decide the true nature of the premorbid adjustment in the face of the distortions of the adolescent and his parents is truly a perplexing enigma. A tremendously important therapeutic step will have been accomplished if this problem can be resolved with substantial accuracy.

The remainder of this chapter is devoted to a description of the mechanics of the evaluation procedure followed by a fuller discussion of the diagnostic questions mentioned above and, finally, by the application of the answers to therapeutic planning.

THE EVALUATION PROCESS

There are no set rules stipulating the form which the evaluation of the adolescent patient and his family should take. Procedures must be dictated by the circumstances of the individual case and by the particular preferences and skills of the examiner. Any approach which permits a contact with the adolescent and his family comfortable and extensive enough to allow the collection of sufficient data to answer the diagnostic questions posed above is acceptable. However, experience can offer some guidelines which will apply to most adolescents.

It is often preferable to set up the initial contact directly with the adolescent, especially the older adolescent. Many adolescents are very concerned that the therapist will form an alliance with their parents. Other adolescents may not resent the coalition between parents and therapist, but may be encouraged to take a passive role, hoping that the adults will straighten things out for them. Scheduling the initial interview with the adolescent clarifies the therapist's intention to appeal to that part of the adolescent which is striving for autonomy, self-direction, and responsibility. It also offers the therapist an opportunity to observe how the adolescent responds to this invitation to maturity.

When the adolescent patient is opposed to the consultation, he also gives us the opportunity to observe how effective his parents can be in dealing with him. Many parents will ask how they should present and explain the necessity for the evaluation. This permits the therapist to demonstrate his willingness to help the parents, as well as his expectation that the parents take a significant portion of the responsibility for helping their youngster.

The parents should be advised to be honest with the adolescent not only about the nature of the interview, but also about the parents' reasons for requesting it. The therapist may freely offer advice about appropriate wording, since this is basically an attempt to educate the parents to a psychological view of their youngster's problem.

The father of a 15-year-old boy who was tyrannizing his family and involving himself in minor delinquencies called to discuss therapy for his son. When the therapist suggested an interview with the boy, his father said, "I don't think he'll come. He is already mad at us, especially my wife. He'll think we're trying to say that he's crazy."

"Do you think that he is?" the therapist asked.

"No, but he is acting very strangely. Sometimes he sits and stares at nothing for hours."

"I wonder if he's afraid that he may be going crazy," the

therapist said. "Maybe you should discuss your concern with him, tell him that you are worried about him, and think he is probably worried about himself."

After further discussion of the appropriate approach to the boy, the father finally asked, "What if he still doesn't want to come, even after all that?"

"From what you tell me, that's very likely the way it will be," the therapist said. "What do you feel you should do as his father if it turns out that way?"

There was a long pause. Then the father emitted a long sigh which seemed a mixture of resignation and resolution.

"He'll be there," the father said.

The therapist simply cannot be a party to any parental plan to skirt the issue by pretending the youngster is coming for a physical checkup, to discuss school planning, or to take some tests for an ill-defined purpose. Such dishonesty would defeat the whole effort to establish an atmosphere of honesty, trust, and open communication. In situations where there is a high level of family conflict, however, it is appropriate for the parent to present the evaluation as a family undertaking. The adolescent may be told, "We have arranged for a series of interviews with Dr. X since we all seem to be having trouble living successfully as a family." Since this is quite true, there can be no disadvantage in emphasizing it to the adolescent. Suggesting this approach also has the advantage of making this point quite clear to the parents.

Some parents will not be able to accomplish the task of bringing their adolescent to his initial interview in a reasonably acceptable frame of mind unless the therapist departs from this usual pattern and provides them with some direct assistance. In these instances, the therapist should honestly admit to the parents that his contact with them may pose some problems later with their youngster. The parental interviews should focus tactfully on the parents' already demonstrated problem in discharging their appropriate function in family leadership. If their problem cannot be resolved in a few contacts with the therapist, this supplies an early negative answer regarding the parents' capacity to assist the therapy. The therapist must then consider whether therapy for the adolescent would be more appropriately conducted on an inpatient basis or whether an extensive period of therapy for the parents should precede any effort to work directly with the youngster. It is impossible to treat the adolescent if he is in omnipotent control of his environment or if his parents are determined to destroy him if he remains in their company.

Many therapists do not follow the procedure outlined above. They feel that they can evaluate the adolescent more effectively if they follow a more traditional child psychiatry approach and obtain a full developmental history from the parents prior to the interview with the adolescent.

Both approaches probably have their advantages and pitfalls. It is probably wise to choose the approach which feels most comfortable and then to utilize it consistently. The therapist gradually becomes acquainted with the particular "side effects" of his favored style and develops skill in managing them. As stated earlier, the end result is more important than any rule of procedure.

At some time during the evaluation, however, the therapist has the right and the responsibility to insist on seeing the parents, no matter who is seen first. The occasional adolescent who objects to this reasonable request is actually revealing an aspect of his problem which needs to be carefully explored and acceded to only under the most unusual circumstances. The therapist who agrees to this arrangement usually finds that he is the next object of his patient's secretive control and that his therapeutic usefulness is nil.

When the adolescent is interviewed, the therapist must decide how many sessions are needed to gain the necessary information for treatment planning. This may vary from one or two interviews with an articulate adolescent who is "ripe" for therapy to four or five or even more if the adolescent is silent, or otherwise highly defensive.

Many therapists find that one or more family sessions are useful in the course of a diagnostic evaluation. These may even include other siblings or relatives, such as grandparents, who live in the home. These family sessions not only may reveal patterns of family interaction which might be missed in individual interviews, but may assist the family in defining their problems and understanding what must be accomplished later during therapy.

PARTICULAR PROBLEMS IN THE DIAGNOSTIC INTERVIEW WITH THE ADOLESCENT

Negativism

The initial task in the diagnostic interview with the adolescent patient is to define the purpose of the interview and to help the adolescent to recognize and deal with his reactions to the procedure. Unless some measure of cooperation can be obtained, the diagnostic process cannot proceed. The most common problem with the adolescent patient is an open reluctance or refusal to participate in the interview. Even in dealing with this initial negativism, however, the therapist can gain important diagnostic information. Although the manifest emphasis is on conscious feelings about the present situation, the adolescent will display his usual defensive techniques and reveal some of his conflicts when confronted with the request that he talk openly about himself. The therapist should make note of these responses, but should comment on them only as they relate to the evaluation procedure. This is especially true in the younger adolescent, who may be more frightened by the implications of a psychiatric evaluation than patients of any other age group. These children are old enough to realize some of the implications of psychiatric referral, but are not old enough to have the objectivity of the adult or older youngster. The strong upsurge of instinctual impulses with which they are struggling, as well as their tendency to confuse fantasy with action, makes the discussion of their inner feelings very threatening. In addition, many of them attribute their problems to their guilty secrets—especially masturbation—and often live in terror of being revealed. In short, they are already secretly convinced that they are crazy—a confirmation they certainly do not need!

Early Negotiations

In all adolescents, the decision to consult a psychiatrist, even when self-initiated, gives rise to intense feelings. If the examiner does not attend carefully to these reactions and help the patient to deal with them, he will have great difficulty in obtaining the information he requires. The reactions which one anticipates are closely bound to the age of the patient. The early adolescent is likely to respond to the stress by denying that he has problems of any kind. The 14- to 16-year-old patient is likely to admit that there are problems, but then to blame them on his parents. The older adolescent is better able to appreciate that at least some of his difficulties are related to his own attitudes and feelings.

Adolescents of all ages, however, are skilled negotiators. Those who are resistant to the exploration of their problems begin testing the therapist even during the diagnostic process. They are interested to know whether the therapist will take an authoritarian, parental role with them. The testing may take the form of direct invitation. After having revealed something of himself in spontaneous conversation, the adolescent may suddenly ask, "Wouldn't you like to ask me some questions?" The unwary examiner may accept the invitation and confirm the adolescent's ambivalent hope and fear that he is faced with still another adult who wishes to arrange his life. A better response might be to comment, "I think you are doing very well in telling me about yourself. Please go on." With the younger adolescent, one might go even further in encouraging responsibility by commenting, "I sometimes ask a lot of questions with younger children, but with guys your age I have found this usually isn't necessary."

The patient may also try directly or indirectly to force the therapist to promise that he will reward the youngster for discussing certain topics or for simply participating in the diagnostic evaluation. This may be presented negatively, "I don't see how talking about all this is going to help me." At other times, the appeal may be more openly dependent. "Mother says if I tell you all about my problems, you can straighten me out."

Can You Help Me?

Of course, the therapist cannot permit himself to be pulled into such an unprofitable contract. The focus must be returned to the obvious fact that diagnostic understanding must precede any reasonable decision about what can be done to help matters. The youngster can be told that he and the therapist can discuss this question when the diagnostic work is completed. Some openly rebellious adolescents would challenge this comment by declaring that they already understand themselves and know that they do not need psychotherapy or help of any kind. The therapist must either ignore or challenge this opinion, since obviously it would dictate an untimely end to the diagnostic process. The manner in which the therapist chooses to respond to this ultimatum will depend on his tentative understanding of the particular adolescent. If anxiety appears to be the predominant obstacle to discussion, the approach would be sympathetic and supportive. The therapist might agree that the youngster has demonstrated ability to solve many of his own problems. The therapist can explain that he has no wish to interfere with that process, but can also comment that perhaps there are some problems which the youngster has not entirely solved as yet and which may be difficult to discuss. It may be wise at that point to add, "At any rate, I'd like to get to know you a bit better." The therapist can then ask a neutral question regarding the youngster's school, hobbies, or plans for the future. This may permit a more natural flow of talk with more subtle introduction of important topics. The youngster may comment, for example, that he is interested in motorcycles, but that his parents will not buy him one. The therapist can then open the discussion of the parent-child relationship in a natural manner by asking, "They're not too interested in motors, eh?"

Youngsters who appear more angry and rebellious may require a more direct approach. The therapist may need to state openly that he feels the patient is simply stating his opposition to the consultation when he says that he does not need any help. Since most rebellious youngsters have not originated the idea of psychiatric referral, this fact may be recalled to them. The therapist can then inquire directly about their feelings and wonder whether the attitude toward the diagnostic evaluation is mainly derived from anger. This may allow a discussion of the youngster's feelings about doing things that his parents recommend or demand of him, including his feelings about the evaluation. If he is able to reveal his rebellious attitude toward his parents, he may go on to a more extended discussion of his feelings about rules and authority figures.

Other youngsters are merely being provocative and teasing when they say that they do not need help. They do not expect an answer to their dare, but are testing to see whether the therapist is an anxious and defensive adult who must rise to every bait thrown his way. They are best managed by ignoring the gauntlet and pressing forward with the real business at hand. Others deserve a light, "Frankly, I hope you're right. My schedule is pretty full right now. However, someone thought you needed help and it's my job now to form my opinion. I can't just accept yours. Let's go ahead and see whether you and I agree or disagree."

You Better Not Help Me!

Not infrequently, however, one encounters an adolescent who has successfully erected a defensive facade which depends upon an apparent omnipotent control of the environment. Often, these youngsters are quite successful in manipulating their families. Since they do manage to externalize their illness, they feel quite strongly that they "have it made" and feel absolutely no wish to have their arrangement interfered with. As a rule, such youngsters would not be candidates for outpatient psychotherapy and would have to be either placed in a controlled environment which they could not manipulate or managed quite differently by their parents before they would be amenable to psychotherapy.

On Keeping Your Cool

Commonly, the early interviews with an adolescent resemble a verbal fencing match more than a typical psychiatric interview. It is impossible to anticipate the myriad forms which the adolescent's testing behavior may assume during the diagnostic evaluation. The therapist must rely on his basic commitment to an open-minded, objective evaluation to guide his interaction with the adolescent. Since it is difficult, if not impossible, to work a confidence game on a person who is disinterested in larceny, the therapist can usually avoid being drawn into fruitless arguments with the adolescent. Like Sergeant Friday, the therapist should "just want the facts."

Since therapists are human, however, they probably will lose some of their rounds with adolescents. The therapist who wishes to work with adolescents must be able to shrug these off and return to the work at hand. A relaxed humorous comment to the effect that the adolescent won that round can sometimes actually improve the relationship between the patient and the therapist. Adolescents often have great difficulty in laughing at themselves and are therefore very critical of adults who are too stiff and self-important. Perhaps the adolescent, with his own narcissistic problems, intuitively recognizes that he cannot work with an adult who is similarly afflicted. At any rate, a sense of humor and a casual attitude are valuable attributes in interviewing adolescents. They are rivaled in importance only by the trait of honesty.

Tell It like It Is

Adolescent patients frequently test this characteristic also. The adolescent who is engaging in behavior which is either extremely antisocial or very bizarre often asks the therapist's opinion about the seriousness of the problem. It is important that this question not be dismissed lightly. The therapist can reply that he can see that these are things that would worry anyone and must be a source of great concern to the adolescent. When this concern appears to be lacking, the therapist may well comment on this and wonder why the child is so disinterested in his own welfare. This may include an objective recounting of the personal risk involved in the behavior in question, including its effect on the youngster's opinion of himself.

An intelligent 18-year-old dropped out of college, although his work was at an acceptable level. He readily accepted psychiatric referral, since his parents were extremely distraught and he saw the evaluation as an opportunity to prove to them that his decision was entirely rational.

He was extremely cooperative during the initial interview, but demonstrated a breezy nonchalance about his decision to leave school. He spoke at length about how "up tight" his parents were, laughing at their distress over his withdrawal from school. His own philosophy of life emphasized the pleasures of the moment, and he was good-naturedly critical of the competitive attitude at the college he had been attending.

Toward the end of the first interview, the therapist commented that the patient described his situation as though he were recounting a story about a friend. He was told that the incongruity between the importance of his decision to leave school and the absence of any strong feelings in the matter puzzled the therapist.

The young man became grave, but did not reply. On the following day, he called for an appointment, stating that the therapist's words had caused him to do some thinking. He had slept poorly and wanted to discuss some of his thoughts and feelings.

In the next interview, he began to explore his long-standing competitive relationship with his father, although it was much later in therapy before he began to appreciate the origins and extent of his inability to succeed and his true motives for leaving college.

Youngsters who have given up on themselves more completely, such as the seriously delinquent adolescent who has wholeheartedly adopted a negative identity, cannot so readily utilize the invitation to treat themselves more kindly. Still, the invitation must be clearly conveyed and continually repeated. Even the delinquent who actually does harm others pays a great personal price in the bargain. He must be asked why he always seems to express his aggression by drowning others in his own blood.

ONCE THE INTERVIEW GETS GOING

If these gross resistances to the diagnostic process can be managed, the interview with the adolescent can be conducted more or less in the same way as the diagnostic interview with an adult. The reader who would like to review the basic principles of psychiatric interviewing might profitably read Ian Stevenson's (1959) excellent presentation in *The American Handbook of Psychiatry*.

Although it would be beyond the scope of this book to deal exhaustively with the techniques of psychiatric interviewing, some points of special interest in the initial interview of the adolescent should be mentioned.

The Adolescent and Silence

Silence is an important technique in psychotherapy, but most psychiatrists feel that it should be avoided in initial interviews. There is always the danger that the patient, who as yet has no relationship with the therapist, will interpret silence as disinterest and unresponsiveness. It is even less advisable to permit the adolescent to stew alone in mute discomfort. Silence is likely to accentuate the adolescent's anxiety, his fearful fantasies regarding the therapist, and his difficulty in perceiving the sympathetic and helpful attitude of the therapist. Any discussion, no matter how apparently or actually trivial or unrelated to the purpose of the evaluation, is preferable to an anxious silence. If necessary, the therapist should carry the conversation, periodically inviting the youngster's participation, and gradually assuming a more passive role as the child begins to talk more. As we have noted earlier, careful attention should be given to the youngster's feelings regarding the evaluation itself. Silence often results from anxiety or anger directly related to the evaluation.

The Adolescent and Confidentiality

Confidentiality is a point of great concern to many, perhaps most, adolescents. At times, the fear that the therapist will report their conversation to the parents becomes virtually a paranoid preoccupation. Often, this worry is not verbalized openly, but can be detected through its influence on the course of the interview. The adolescent may suddenly appear anxious after revealing something about himself and even retract the statement. The alert therapist will usually be able to guess when the question of confidentiality is troubling his patient. The problem should be openly discussed, not because this will always settle the issue, but to demonstrate an openness and honesty that may gradually convince the adolescent that he can trust the therapist.

Again, in the question of confidentiality, the therapist is confronted with the need for negotiation and discussion with the adolescent. If one promises complete confidentiality, this may pose serious problems. If the adolescent later confides plans for serious antisocial behavior, preparations for a suicide attempt, or other dangerous actions which require intervention, the therapist will have to break his promise in order to enlist the aid of parents or others. The admission by the adolescent patient that he is using illegal drugs without his parents' knowledge poses a delicate dilemma in this area, which today's adolescent therapist faces with painful regularity. Therapists generally do not promise to withhold knowledge of criminal activity from a minor's parents. In the case of the drugs, the activities not only are felonious, but are potentially quite dangerous to the adolescent. Still, many therapists who would be quite concerned and anxious in the knowledge that a female adolescent patient was engaging in active sexual behavior accept drug usage without blinking an eye! The problem of psychoactive drug usage is complex and is considered in detail later, but it is clear that it is another subject in which the adolescent should not be assured of blanket confidentiality.

What then can the therapist promise? First of all, and probably most reassuring to the adolescent, the promise can be given that the therapist will not convey any information to the parents without informing the adolescent of his intention to do so in advance. The adolescent's greatest fear is of a secret coalition between his parents and his therapist.

Second, the therapist should state clearly that the adolescent's feelings are confidential. Only the adolescent's actions will ever be considered for possible discussion with his parents, and then only if in the *therapist's* judgment the particular actions represent a danger to the therapeutic process, other people, or the adolescent himself.

ENTER THE PARENTS

Although some therapists suggest that the adolescent should be asked whether he is willing to permit the therapist to talk with his parents, this probably only confuses the youngster and creates an atmosphere of unreality. Parental involvement in their affairs is a fact of life for most adolescents, unless they have already left home. To play along with the adolescent's fantasy that he can solve his conflicts with his parents by wishing them out of existence can only block any rational therapy. The adolescent's parents have a right to know, in general terms, what their youngster's problem is, how serious it seems to be, the reasons behind the therapeutic recommendations, and what they can do to assist their youngster. These assertions remain true even when the adolescent's complaints against his parents are well grounded in objective evidence of parental inadequacy. To ask the adolescent's permission to talk with his parents implies that troubling family interactions can be safely ignored. This would not seem to be a very productive premise with which to begin therapy.

It does seem appropriate to offer the adolescent the option of attending the postdiagnostic conference with the parents. Youngsters of this age do have a right to be fully informed of plans which involve them. Conducting the treatment-planning session as a family interview may also be helpful in promoting an atmosphere of objective exploration toward family problems which have previously been the occasion for disruptive anger and mutual recrimination. This is also a good time to spell out the ground rules of psychotherapy (if this is the recommendation), including the rules regarding confidentiality mentioned above. This subject is explored more fully in Chapter Six, "The Parents of the Adolescent Patient." Many adolescents, even when offered the opportunity of attending the postdiagnostic conference with their parents, will prefer to have an individual interview at the end of the diagnostic period to discuss the findings and recommendations.

OTHER DIAGNOSTIC PROCEDURES

At times, one needs information about the adolescent which requires referring him for psychological testing, physical examination, or other procedures. These recommendations tend to be resisted by adolescent patients. If the interview situation, which at least resembles typical social interaction, is frightening, the prospect of being tested with instruments that the patient does not understand poses an even greater threat. Adolescents are aware that psychological tests are designed to extract information which the patient may not have intended to reveal. Because of his many secrets, the adolescent certainly does not want his mind read.

It is important to explain honestly to the adolescent why the additional studies are necessary and what information they may reveal. When the adolescent is not given this information and allowed to discuss it fully, he often reacts to the diagnostic studies as though they were devious attempts to "get the goods on him." An electroencephalogram (EEG) may be interpreted as an underhanded effort to find out if he has damaged his brain by masturbating or by taking drugs or, in more disturbed youngsters, as a way of finding out his dirty thoughts.

In the postdiagnostic conference, it is important to report fully the findings of the special procedures and to correlate them with the youngster's life experiences. If, for example, an EEG has been ordered to rule out psychomotor epilepsy in a youngster with episodic rage reactions, the negative findings should be correlated with the absence of postictal phenomena, amnesia, and other clinical data which have already been discussed with the patient.

It should be noted briefly that projective tests may give a very misleading picture of the adolescent unless they are administered and interpreted by a psychologist with extensive experience with adolescents. Youngsters in this age group frequently appear much more ill than they actually are if their test productions are judged by adult norms.

DIAGNOSTIC INTERVIEWS WITH PARENTS

Several goals must be kept in mind simultaneously during the diagnostic sessions with the parents of an adolescent patient. The parents' feelings about their child's problems may range from a deep concern, verging on panic, through rage and wishes to reject the child, to subtle enjoyment of the youngster's behavior. Most often, the parents are puzzled and frightened, especially if the adolescent appeared to be adjusting adequately during earlier childhood. Their intense feelings result in a loss of perspective, which causes difficulty in gaining information about past family relationships and events in the youngster's earlier life. The parents must be offered the opportunity to ventilate these feelings, not only to clear the way for consideration of historical data, but because of the importance of such feelings to an understanding of the adolescent's current life situation.

Usually, it is possible to learn a great deal about the parents' conscious and unconscious attitudes toward the adolescent by carefully noting which aspects of the current situation they choose to emphasize in their discussion with the therapist. However, some caution should be exercised in drawing conclusions from observations made during the emotional turmoil which often characterizes initial diagnostic contacts. Defensive reactions both to the family crisis and the prospect of revealing their family problems to an outsider may produce confusing distortions.

The mother of a 14-year-old delinquent girl was referred for therapy by her daughter's therapist. The referring psychiatrist, who had performed the diagnostic evaluation on the family, apologized for the referral, stating, "I don't think there is much you can do. This mother would really just like to pretend that this girl is not her daughter. She's the coldest fish I ever saw."

Actually, the mother wept throughout most of her first therapy hour. She expressed her conviction that her daughter's problems were completely her fault and recognized that she was still struggling with antisocial impulses, especially in the sexual area, herself. When asked why she had not told the referring physician of these concerns, she could only say that she was in a state of shock after the daughter's delinquencies came to light.

"I guess I thought someone was going to come and arrest me," she said.

DEVELOPMENTAL HISTORY

The importance of detailed information about psychological development in children has been challenged in recent years. A number of studies have demonstrated that the accuracy of parental recall is rather poor. It is still worthwhile to spend some time in asking about the adolescent's earlier development even if one cannot accept the parents' statements as literal truth. One can often detect evidence of gross difficulties in psychosocial progression, such as serious maternal depression during infancy, separations from one or both parents, family deaths, and periods of poor adjustment such as difficulty in toilet training. It is also possible to draw some tentative conclusions about the extent of parental investment in the child and the quality of the parent-child relationship in the past. Parental statements in this area must be explored and taken as tentative, since the current family conflict may influence memory selectively and impart a retrospective overemphasis or denial of negative aspects in the parent-child relationships. Often, persistent attention to the history is rewarded with valuable data, such as the parental recollection that their belligerently independent adolescent has shown considerable evidence of excessive dependency on one or both parents in the past.

Even if the information gathered in a developmental history only approximates the actual occurrences, the process of inquiring about longitudinal development helps the parents to refocus their efforts toward understanding their youngster's problems. The very act of exploring the past suggests to the parents that their youngster's problems are comprehensible and possibly soluble. The investigation of the family history may also bring to light any feelings of guilt which the parents harbor about their role in the adolescent's difficulties. When these are openly discussed, the therapist can compliment the parents for their frankness, suggest that emotional problems are rarely so simply understood, and state his intention to discuss frankly with them all factors which may have had importance in creating the family difficulties.

Some therapists prefer to have the parents interviewed by a colleague. This has some disadvantages in that the parents are better able to support the therapy fully if they have had a valuable personal experience with the therapist. For this reason, it seems wise for the adolescent's therapist to spend some time with the parents, even if he is unwilling or unable to conduct the parental diagnostic interviews. The trust which can result will be invaluable during difficult periods in the adolescent's therapy. Even if there are few difficult periods, adolescents who undergo successful psychotherapy will move toward independence from the parents. Many parents find this transition emotionally painful, even if they intellectually recognize that it is necessary. A positive relationship to the therapist may permit the parents to tolerate essential growth without consciously or unconsciously sabotaging the therapy.

DIAGNOSIS IN ADOLESCENCE

There is a danger in assigning a clinical diagnosis to the adolescent. Erikson (1968) has pointed out that the adolescent is very susceptible to the expectations of his society. The adolescent's present and future role is partially defined by the reaction of his culture to him. It is clear that some clinical psychiatric diagnoses, such as schizophrenia and psychopathy, carry powerful implications for future functioning, and are in effect statements that the adolescent's problems are chronic and his prognosis poor. The effect is to decree an identity as a sick individual for the adolescent. Since the troubled adolescent is especially unsure of what and who he is, he may be very sensitive to such definitions of his identity. For this reason, it is important to exercise caution in assigning clinical diagnoses during the fluidity of the adolescent period. Even if the patient and his family are not directly appraised of the diagnosis, it will certainly affect the therapist's attitude toward his patient and will indirectly be perceived by the youngster.

This cautionary statement does not alter the fact, however, that there are adolescents who *are* doomed to a lifetime of psychiatric disability (Masterson, 1967). In fact, some investigators feel that the early onset of schizophrenic symptoms, coupled with a history of childhood problems of poor academic performance, poor peer relationships, and evidence of "minimal brain dysfunction," strongly suggests a poor prognosis for the schizophrenic (Offord and Cross, 1969). It is unfair to assign the adolescent prematurely to the life pattern of chronic psychiatric illness, but it is equally unfortunate to hold out false hope and to apply expensive and unwarranted treatment approaches to families and youngsters who are already burdened with the crushing problems of coping with process schizophrenia.

The diagnostic classification system offered by the Group for the Advancement of Psychiatry (GAP) (1966) suggests that the diagnostician attempt to differentiate between "acute confusional state of adolescence" and "schizophrenic disorder, adult type." A third category of "other psychoses of adolescence" is included to permit the classification of those symptom pictures which cannot be easily fitted into one of these two categories. This classification system also recommends avoiding terms such as borderline psychosis, prepsychotic states, latent psychoses, or pseudoneurotic psychoses, utilizing instead the appropriate personality disorder category with a notation of severity and a description of the disturbances in ego function drawn from a specially prepared symptom list.

The GAP report has also dropped the diagnostic terms "psychopath" and "sociopath." Instead, they utilize the general category of "tension discharge disorders" with two subcategories, "impulse-ridden personality" and "neurotic personality disorder." Generally, the latter group is more amenable to outpatient psychotherapy. The diagnosis suggests an inner state of conflict which is expressed through symbolic unacceptable behavior. Potential personality strengths exist which may be mobilized by appropriate psychotherapeutic help. Impulse-ridden personalities suffer from more serious deficiencies in personality structure. Treatment must include extensive retraining, external controls on behavior, and gradual correction of early deficiencies in ego development.

The entire GAP report should be carefully reviewed, not only because of its usefulness as a nosological system, but because of its thoughtful discussion of the complex theoretical issues underlying the classification of emotional illnesses in children.

In general, it would seem preferable for the clinician to make every effort to arrive at the best possible clinical diagnostic category in every adolescent whom he evaluates. This clinical diagnosis may then be viewed as highly tentative, since it is recognized to represent a cross-sectional statement regarding personality structure during a period of life in which longitudinal changes may be quite rapid and very extensive. Masterson's (1967) research indicates that diagnostic categories do have predictive value, however, despite the problems of correct assessment.

THE DIAGNOSTIC SUMMATION

Despite the need to establish a tentative clinical diagnosis, prognostication and treatment planning depend more on an over-all assessment of the strengths and weaknesses of the adolescent's personality functioning than on any diagnostic term. The diagnostic data should be reviewed with an eye to the six questions posed earlier.

1) What level of psychosocial development has the adolescent achieved?

Although the adolescent may be obviously preoccupied with pregenital concerns and behavior at the time of referral, other diagnostic data may lead you to suspect that this represents a regression. A documented history of performance at a better level is one observation which would encourage a better prognosis. In addition, the patient may present dreams, fantasies, or a style of relating during the diagnostic interviews which will belie the primitive psychological picture suggested by the presenting symptoms.

A 16-year-old boy was seen for evaluation because of stealing, destruction of property, and periods of staring vacantly into space. His parents stated that he was uncontrollable and they were concerned that he might become homicidal.

In his interview, he varied between angry silences, anal obscenities, and tight-lipped avowal to "get" his parents for arranging the consultation. Whenever the therapist asked a question or made a comment, the boy would lean forward menacingly and snarl, "What?"

The therapist repeated himself a few times, and then realized what was happening. He commented amiably to the boy, "I get the feeling that you're trying to scare me out of saying anything. You must be pretty worried about what I might say."

"I don't give a shit what you think of me," the boy snapped.

"How about what *you* think of you?" the therapist asked.

For a moment, the boy lowered his guard and grinned. "Well, now *that* might be worth talking about some," he said.

Actually, he was not able to talk about his crippled self-esteem and floundered through the remainder of the interview, angry and suspicious. However, his brief comment did reveal that he was potentially capable of engaging in a human relationship at something other than an anal control level.

It is particularly difficult to assess correctly the best psychosocial level achieved by the adolescent because of the tendency for regressions during this phase of development to be "ego regressions" rather than "libidinal regressions." Anna Freud (1965) has noted that in ego regression primitive impulses are accepted and acted upon, rather than giving rise to internal conflict. The adolescent's ego is relatively weak and is therefore easily drawn into the regressive process. The absence of resistance to the infantile impulses and the lack of conflict can cause the adolescent's immaturity to resemble fixation more than regression. This can lead the therapist to conclude incorrectly that the adolescent is fixated at pregenital levels.

2) What kind of object relationships did the adolescent have with his parents prior to the onslaught of adolescence?

Although historical data will be of central importance in answering this question, much can be learned from observing what the adolescent emphasizes in rejecting his relationship to his parents. Generally speaking, those adolescents who have been most dependent on their parents are the most adamant in their demands for independence. Very often, their shrill and uncompromising insistence on total freedom and denial of any attachment to their parents are accompanied by behavior which is unconsciously calculated to pull their parents into their affairs. The louder the adolescent screams that his parents treat him like a baby, the more likely it is that he is struggling with intense dependency yearnings toward them.

A similar situation exists in some adolescents who are extremely angry with their parents for not being omnipotent. These children have, for a variety of reasons, invested their parents with a fantasied capacity to protect them from all harm and to ensure their success in all endeavors. When this illusion collapses with the onset of adolescence, the youngster feels cheated. Often, the parents are denounced as phonies, hypocrits, or idiots. The tone of disappointment is conveyed by a joke which a teenage girl told her psychotherapist.

A teenage boy approached his father with questions about the Viet Nam war, campus riots, and the sexual revolution. He wanted his father to give him clear-cut judgments and answers, but instead the father, after each question, equivocated, noting that the situation was very complex and that there was no simple answer. He ended his comments each time by saying, "You're just going to have to make up your own mind on that, son."

After this happened four times, the son finally said, "Dad, would you rather I wouldn't bother you with all these questions?"

"Gosh, no!" said the father. "You have to ask questions. How else are you going to learn?"

In the joke, it is the father who fails to recognize that there are some things that he cannot teach, but in fact the disillusioned adolescent himself is begging, "Say it ain't so, Pop!"

We have already mentioned the adolescent who utilizes disdain to protect against incestuous feelings. One may also suspect oedipal conflicts when the adolescent reports and demonstrates a pattern of constant bickering with and withdrawal from the parent of the opposite sex, especially when this is accompanied by accusations of sexual repression and unattractive personal qualities. This follows a general rule of thumb with the adolescent. When he stresses and emphasizes one particular vector of affect, you may get a glimpse of significant problems if you sight backward along the arrow in a reverse direction. Often, the adolescent unknowingly betrays his real feelings when he "doth protest too much."

3) Why is the patient ill now?

Generally speaking, adolescent illnesses which are precipitated by clear-cut external events, such as the death of a family member, or which result primarily from the stress of the developmental crisis of adolescence respond well to outpatient psychotherapy. This is true even when the regressive features of illness are quite marked. On the other hand, even deviations which appear relatively minor on the surface may be very difficult to resolve if they reflect long-standing personality patterns. Generally, a chronic situation of this kind suggests a strong family involvement in the behavior pattern. Typically in these instances, the impetus for consultation comes from outside the family group. In these cases, the final three questions will usually be answered in the negative. The adolescent is not conflicted, the family has no real wish to permit or aid in change, and the adolescent will be unable to observe his own feelings objectively as a result of his comfortable immersion in a neurotic family pattern. Some alternate treatment approaches for these youngsters and their families will be discussed later.

It should be noted that adolescents and their families are no more skilled than other psychiatric patients at recognizing the events which precipitate emotional illnesses. Often, the examiner must take the responsibility for noting temporal connections between life occurrences and the onset of symptoms of illness. The examiner can then search for the dynamic connections between the meaning of the particular event, the developmental history of the adolescent, the adolescent's verbal and nonverbal behavior during the diagnostic study, and the course of the illness. Only in this way can the true significance of the traumatic event be fully understood.

4) Is the adolescent in conflict?

As stated above, except for some older adolescents, one rarely encounters an adolescent patient who views his symptoms as totally ego-alien, completely originating within himself, and subject to solution by self-understanding. Like the adult patient with a weak ego structure, the adolescent is largely alloplastic, self-justifying, and resistant to any therapy which would require him to face up to himself.

The examiner must content himself with minor clues that the adolescent is dissatisfied with himself. These brief self-disparaging comments, veiled hints of guilt, and half-admitted anxieties are viewed as the surface evidence of the presence of workable discontents below ground which can be tapped later, when the adolescent is comfortable enough to permit exploration.

The examiner should also ask the parents if the adolescent has expressed discontent with himself or with his symptoms. Naturally, their answers must be studied in the full light of their motivations. Angry, rejecting parents may see the most anxious youngster as blissfully unregenerate. On the other hand, indulgent, overinvolved parents may misread deep self-concern in the faint scribblings of manipulative mock remorse.

Only when there is some real evidence of inner conflict, even if faint, should the adolescent be considered for individual outpatient treatment. If the conflicts are only between the adolescent and the outside world, the adolescent will not be motivated to form a therapeutic alliance. These youngsters will require other treatment approaches, at least initially, to produce any hope of success. Often, this question cannot be answered definitely without a trial period of treatment. Many adolescents with neurotic personality disorders appear to be impulse-ridden personalities until the pattern underlying their "senseless" acting out can be appreciated.

5) Does the adolescent have the potential capacity to observe his own feelings and behavior and to report them with some degree of objectivity?

Many aspects of the diagnostic information must be considered in seeking the answer to this question. The presence of at least low average intellectual ability is probably a necessary basis for a therapeutic approach which relies on a verbal readjustment of attitudes and experiences. Youngsters with unchangeable reality problems, including serious impairments in organic brain functioning, may be unable to face themselves honestly without benefit of a specially constructed living situation which could be adjusted to their special needs. Outpatient psychotherapy, with its emphasis on personal responsibility, may place undue demands on the coping mechanisms of these youngsters.

We have already described briefly the adolescent who has

adapted neurotically but successfully to a neurotic family situation. If the parents can offer such a youngster sufficient gratification within the family pathological configuration, there may be little impetus for growth and honest evaluation of the skewed contract which the adolescent has accepted. One can often suspect such a state of affairs when the adolescent accepts the absence of satisfactory peer relationships without complaint and without any apparent drive to achieve them.

Other youngsters may reveal chronic impairment of the capacity to put feelings into words or to share their feelings with others. Rather than showing the disguised and distorted feelings which one expects in adolescent patients, these youngsters either seem totally cut off from knowledge of their inner experience or else have never developed the trust in another person which would encourage them to make the effort of trying to explain themselves to someone. The examiner should accept this view of an adolescent patient with great reluctance and only in the face of overwhelming evidence. Many adolescents have temporary problems in recognizing and describing their emotions which would not interfere with the eventual utilization of outpatient psychotherapy. With only a diagnostic evaluation to guide him, the examiner can erroneously assume that these defects are chronic and irremedial, especially if he is angered or frightened by the adolescent's initial inability to cooperate.

Frankly psychotic adolescents are obviously unable to assess their feelings and behavior realistically. These youngsters usually require inpatient treatment until their reality testing becomes more reliable. Many of those with transient psychotic symptoms may then be candidates for outpatient psychotherapy.

A final group of youngsters who cannot objectively observe their own behavior are those who are intoxicated with their control of the environment and are virtually convinced of their own omnipotence. Usually, their conflicts can be studied only when they are prevented from discharging their every anxiety in action. As a rule, this can be accomplished only with the control and leverage offered by an inpatient setting.

6) Will his family help the adolescent to grow or at least permit him to do so?

In adolescent patients, this is usually not a serious problem. Most of the youngsters come to therapy after at least having begun to fight for autonomy. The therapist usually will find that, although the parents may be distressed by this turn of events, the family has recognized that the previous homeostatic balance must be altered.

In the older adolescent, this alteration can often be effected without the parents' active assistance. In fact, in the course of successful psychotherapy, the adolescent can learn to recognize and to accept a reasonable degree of parental ambivalence toward his effort to wrench himself away from the family.

In the younger adolescent, however, the parents may need to involve themselves in the therapy. Most parents are sufficiently troubled by the overt family strife to be somewhat more cooperative than many parents of latency-age children are.

Occasionally, one does encounter parents who are desperately committed to maintaining a pathological tie to their child, even in the face of the adolescent's efforts to force a separation. These parents typically seek the therapist's aid in forcing the youngster to remain under their infantilizing control. In such a situation, it is probably not therapeutic to offer psychotherapy for the adolescent until the parents can be brought to a healthier point of view.

A 17-year-old female high school senior was brought for psychiatric evaluation because of her refusal to accept her father's selection of the college she was to attend.

The girl's objections to the college seemed fairly reasonable, since all of her friends were planning to attend a coeducational school in the area, whereas her father insisted that she attend an exclusive girls' college located some distance from her home. The girl was an extremely good student and correctly pointed out that the girls' school was noted more for its social prestige than its academic excellence. It was also obvious that she was attempting to assert her right to make this important decision in her life for herself.

The father, an extremely successful businessman, was an autocrat of the old school who had little interest in friends or intellectual achievement. He was self-made and put great store on his daughter's associating with "the right people."

He asserted that his daughter's choice of school was very suspect and might be based on a wish to "run wild."

When the therapist asked about his evidence for this assertion and otherwise demonstrated a wish to explore the disagreement rather than accepting his view without question, he became quite angry. He stated that he certainly knew what was best for his own girl and had only hoped that "a doctor" could help bring his daughter to her senses. When the therapist asked whether the girl should have any decision-making power in regard to her college education, the father replied sarcastically, "Certainly! To the exact same degree that she intends to pay for it!"

Fortunately, very few parents view their adolescent children as chattel property as this father did. Most of them are anxious or diffident and require support to function with the kind of supportive firmness which their children need. The techniques and problems of involving parents in the therapy of the adolescent are discussed more fully in Chapter Six.

THE POSTDIAGNOSTIC FAMILY CONFERENCE

When the diagnostic information appears reasonably complete, it is necessary to arrange for one or more conferences with the parents and the adolescent to discuss the findings and recommendations. As previously stated, many therapists like to invite the adolescent to sit in with the parents during this conference, whereas a few prefer to have separate meetings with the parents and with the adolescent.

As we have described elsewhere (Meeks and Martin, 1969), this conference is difficult to manage due to the intensity of feelings present both in the family members and in the examiner. However, the necessity for such a conference and its crucial role in setting the stage for the entire therapeutic undertaking cannot be ignored. A tremendous hurdle to successful treatment will have been passed if the family can leave this conference with some sense of direction and with the feeling that the therapist respects their individual feelings.

Unfortunately, this goal is easier to state than it is to achieve.

The interested reader is referred to McDonald's (1965) excellent paper on the diagnostic process for a clear description of the problems and techniques of conducting this interview.

No matter how skillful the therapist becomes in conducting the postdiagnostic conference, he will not be able to use the skill without a clear diagnostic conception. The family dynamics, clinical diagnosis of the child, and the genetic and dynamic understanding of the adolescent must be carefully thought out prior to the postdiagnostic interview. Without this preparatory work, the therapist cannot hope for the kind of conciseness and clarity which will be necessary for effective communication with the family.

RECOMMENDATIONS OTHER THAN OUTPATIENT PSYCHOTHERAPY

Full consideration of the diagnostic data will often suggest that individual psychotherapy for the adolescent is not the treatment of choice. It is difficult to specify these situations with exactitude, but some general suggestions can be offered. These may be organized around the specific recommendations which might be made.

Hospitalization

The decision to hospitalize the adolescent is not to be taken lightly. The face that the adolescent frequently views psychiatric hospitalization as a verification of his worst fears about himself is only one of several reasons that inpatient treatment is fraught with danger. The inevitable presence of restrictive structuring in even the most liberal group situation, the loss of contact with normal peer experiences and opportunities, and the invitation to regression and an accentuation of dependency conflicts all militate against a positive result in hospital treatment of the adolescent.

Easson (1969) has stated that only the adolescent who can neither handle his inner drives nor utilize meaningful relationships with other people to help himself needs inpatient psychotherapy. He points out that even the severely narcissistic youngster with good ego strength can manage himself and continue his psychological growth. Youngsters with very weak egos who can form warm relationships with family members and peers can be guided into a successful adjustment through such external support.

There are adolescents, however, who can be treated properly only within a psychiatric hospital. The program for the hospital treatment of the adolescent has to be especially constructed to meet the needs of this age group. Many structures have been devised and utilized with success, ranging from programs which mingle adolescents with adult patients to those with separate adolescent units. Some attempt to separate the functions of the child's psychotherapist and his administrative psychiatrist, whereas other programs insist that these functions be combined in the same individual. Still, most programs develop common features which include a recognition of the adolescent's need for vigorous activity, both physical and mental, some plan to develop group cohesion and a "protherapy" orientation among the adolescents, and a system of limitations and privileges designed to control the adolescent's propensity to live out his problems rather than discuss them (Holmes, 1964; Lewis, 1969; Lewis et al., 1970).

Generally speaking, individual programs tend to be designed either for brief hospital care or for prolonged intensive treatment. There are many problems in attempting to combine both these approaches in a single unit.

BRIEF HOSPITALIZATION. The brief care units are valuable for the adolescent who is caught in an acute crisis situation. This may include those who might be diagnosed as showing an "acute confusional state," as well as some adolescents who are reacting to transient stress with suicidal or homicidal impulses. Some adolescents who have "gone wild" as a way of dealing with superego conflicts also may benefit from brief containment. Some youngsters with an acute toxic psychosis also require brief hospitalization for detoxification and evaluation.

For these youngsters, hospitalization is aimed at dealing with the emergency situation, utilizing drug therapy, containment, and support to avert disaster. Usually, the evaluating therapist will wish to manage the youngster's hospital care, hoping to establish a therapeutic relationship during the hospital stay. Outpatient therapy can then be utilized to deal with the chronic personality problems which predispose the youngster to emotional breakdown.

A 16-year-old boy, home from prep school during the Christmas holidays, developed marked suicidal ideation as the time for returning to school approached. A suicidal attempt led to an emergency diagnostic study. Evaluation revealed marked confusion and a strong tendency toward impulsivity. The preoccupation with suicide as a solution to a chronic sense of failure suggested that hospital care was the only reasonable plan.

During a three-week hospitalization, the boy formed an intense tie to the therapist and revealed a good capacity for self-observation and verbalization of feeling. Arrangements were made for the boy to return to school locally and attend outpatient psychotherapy sessions three times a week. Soon, it was possible to reduce the sessions to twice weekly and to explore the youngster's long-standing neurotic conflicts. The therapy continued for two years with no further need for inpatient care.

EXTENDED HOSPITAL TREATMENT. Those adolescents who require long-term hospital treatment comprise a different group. This recommendation should be reserved for those with marked defects in early ego development. They require a prolonged corrective living experience. For these youngsters, there is no disadvantage in the structured nature of the hospital setting. Structure is essential to fill their need to learn adaptive techniques, control of their impulses, and skills in interpersonal relations. The potential of the inpatient setting to induce regression is not a hindrance to their care, but can rather be turned to the advantage of the adolescent. The enormous dedication and skill which are necessary to cope successfully with the regressive transference manifestations which appear in the adolescent in residential therapy are well described by Rinsley (1965, 1967).

When this type of therapy is to be recommended, it is often wise to extend the diagnostic period, especially that portion spent with the parents. This precaution allows the development of the closest possible relationship with the parents, which may be utilized to aid them in dealing with their resistance to separation from the patient. In many adolescents who require hospital care, this will be a very difficult job, since the parents have often crippled the adolescent in order to bolster their own defensive structure. The parents will often resist hospitalization in order to protect their personal equilibrium. In the resistance to the separation, grossly irrational fantasies tend to be projected onto the therapist who recommends hospitalization, the institution, and the staff of the hospital. Often, these can be dealt with if the therapist has had sufficient contact with the parents to establish open communication and a sense of trust. At times, a period of unsuccessful out-patient treatment is necessary, both to demonstrate that hospitalization is essential and to gain enough therapeutic ground to permit the parents to accept the recommendation. In the youngsters who truly need this intensive treatment approach, problems are chronic and proper preparation is more important than speed of disposition.

The techniques of actually providing inpatient treatment are discussed in Part Three of the book.

Family Therapy and Group Psychotherapy

The indications for recommending group psychotherapy or family therapy as primary treatment approaches are covered in the chapters dealing with these modalities (Group Psychotherapy, Chapter 8; Family Therapy, Chapter 9).

Wait and See

In many mild adolescent disturbances, the therapist may attempt to help the parents and the adolescent to define their problems more productively during the diagnostic contact and during the postdiagnostic family conference. This does not differ materially from the crisis-intervention technique described above. If some success is achieved in clarifying the issues, the therapist may wish to recommend that the family attempt to work on the problems for a period of time without outside help. If this recommendation is made, it is important to discuss specifically with the family what will be done during the "wait" and what behaviors and attitudes they should hope to "see." Although time is often helpful in the resolution of adolescent crises, many pathological solutions may be avoided by the constructive use of counsel during the wait.

Waiting for further developments may also be wise in cases which will probably eventually need treatment but where the adolescent or his family shows marked current ambivalence about entering the treatment process. Often continuing or accelerating problems will intensify the discomfort the family feels and help to focus the need for a commitment to therapy.

SUMMARY: FROM UNDERSTANDING TOWARD THERAPY

Some of the issues surrounding the diagnostic evaluation of adolescent patients resist rigid codification. Although certain approaches seem to be regularly useful, flexibility is the keynote in the attempt to obtain useful and reliable diagnostic information.

Our next task is to consider the ways in which dynamic understanding can be translated into effective therapy with the adolescent patient. This task can be undertaken only when a therapeutic alliance is established. The next chapter attempts a description and working definition of the therapeutic alliance, as well as a discussion of how one can effect such a tie with the distrustful, narcissistic, and "fickle" adolescent.

CITED AND RECOMMENDED READINGS

Easson, W. M. 1969. The severely disturbed adolescent. New York: International Universities Press, Inc.

Erikson, E. H. 1968. Identity: youth and crisis. New York: W. W. Norton & Company, Inc.

Freud, A. 1965. Normality and pathology in childhood. New York: International Universities Press, Inc.

Group for the Advancement of Psychiatry. 1966. Psychopathological disorders in childhood: theoretical considerations and a proposed classification. Vol. VI, Report No. 62. Publications office: 419 Park Ave. South, New York, N. Y. 10016.

Holmes, D. J. 1964. The adolescent in psychotherapy. Boston: Little, Brown & Co.

Lewis, J. M. 1969. The development of an inpatient adolescent service. Presented at South. Psychiat. Assoc. Meeting, Oct., 1969. *In press: Adolescence.*

Lewis, J. W., J. T. Gossett, J. W. King, and D. I. Carson. 1970. Development of a protreatment group process among hospitalized adolescents. Timberlawn Foundation Report No. 40.

Masterson, J. F., Jr. 1967. The psychiatric dilemma of adolescence. Boston: Little, Brown & Co.

McDonald, M. 1965. The psychiatric evaluation of children. J. Amer. Acad. Child Psychiat. 4: 569–612.

Meeks, J. E., and J. Martin. 1969. Teaching the techniques of the postdiagnostic family conference. J. Amer. Acad. Child Psychiat. 8: 306–320.

Offord, D. R., and L. Cross. 1969. Behavioral antecedents of adult schizophrenia. Arch. Gen. Psychiat. 21: 267–283.

Rinsley, D. B. 1965. Intensive psychiatric hospital treatment of adolescents: an object-relations view. Psychiat. Quart. 39: 405–429.

Rinsley, D. B. 1967. Intensive residential treatment of the adolescent. Psychiat. Quart. 41: 134–143.

Stevenson, I. 1959. The psychiatric interview. *In:* American handbook of psychiatry, Vol. I. Edited by S. Areti. New York: Basic Books, Inc.

CHAPTER FOUR
the therapeutic alliance with the adolescent

THE CONCEPT OF THE THERAPEUTIC ALLIANCE

For many years, psychoanalysts have described the need to develop and utilize a conscious, cooperative portion of the patient's personality as an observing ally during the storms of transference feelings which appear during analysis. In Freud's 1912 paper, "The Dynamics of Transference," he pointed out that, paradoxically, transference is both the force which binds the patient to therapy and encourages cooperation, as well as the major resistance to analysis. Balint (1952) has called the binding force the "adult, affectionate and aim inhibited form" of the transference. Bibring presented a paper on the "therapeutic alliance" at the Psychoanalytic Congress in 1936. Fenichel wrote of the "rational transference" in 1941. In his book on analytic technique, Greenson (1967) emphasized the importance of this relationship with the therapist, which he preferred to call the "working alliance."

All of these concepts refer to the necessity for a pact between the analyst and an observing portion of the patient's ego aimed at an honest and uncritical examination of the patient's inner experience.

Recently, it has been recognized that a similar alliance must be found in order to conduct dynamic psychotherapy properly. The psychotherapist allies himself with the healthier, more reality-oriented aspect of the patient's ego for the purpose of observing the maladaptive, neurotically defended, and conflicted portions of the personality. There is general agreement that this alliance is created through the orderly interpretation of affective and defensive behavior toward the therapist. In fact, Friedman (1969) has suggested in an excellent review article that this aspect of the therapeutic bond is a result of progress in therapy rather than an initiator of therapeutic change. Certainly, the result of maintaining a therapeutic alliance with the adolescent patient is a strengthening of the observing ego—"the capacity for self-scrutiny without self-judgment and without action" (Long, 1968).

WILL THE REAL OBSERVING EGO PLEASE STAND UP?

In adolescents, the observing ego is something of a paradox. At times, the adolescent seems completely emerged in self-observation. Ruminative preoccupation with inner feelings, interminable musings over real or imagined inadequacies, and detached experimentation with new feeling states and altered states of consciousness all appear to signal the emergence of a capacity to stand aside and observe one's own psychological structure and functioning. This capacity is demonstrably unstable, however, and the adolescent also expends great effort in denying his impulses, affects, and needs. Often, this tendency to disavow his inner life is reinforced by an explosive tendency to act, rather than to think or feel.

A primary reason for this unstable state of affairs is the adolescent's conflict with his superego. The emerging capacity for self-observation can flower only as the harsh and unrelenting superego of early adolescence is gradually modified toward a more flexible and humane code of conduct.

STRENGTHENING THE EGO IDEAL

Blos (1963) has described and Long (1968) has amplified the adolescent's use of a special friendship to accelerate the development of the ego ideal. The special attachment is made to a friend of the same sex, usually somewhat older. "The essential thing is that the older (or bigger) person displays some essential traits that are lacking or that the young adolescent feels are lacking in himself" (Long, 1968). These traits are then idealized to provide the missing perfection of the self so that narcissistic balance is partially restored. This relationship is later internalized as a stabilizing but also liberalizing introject. The friend's values are gradually abstracted and detached from their origin and come to exist completely in their own right in the adolescent's mind. To quote

Long again, "Because the boy can now better accept his instinctual drives and control and direct them, he can now look upon himself as more of a man and can be to a significant degree more objective about himself, and eventually also more objective in looking at his parents. That is, the establishment of the ego ideal acts as a supporting plank for the development of an observing ego."

In the processs of developing a therapeutic alliance with the adolescent patient, the therapist may find that he has become the youngster's "special friend" in the sense described above (see Adatto, 1966). Even when this does not happen, the therapist's permission to discover and relate to an older friend of this kind may be one of the most important gains in therapy. When the capacity for noncritical self-observation appears, many adolescent patients seem virtually to "cure themselves" with relative rapidity.

It should be emphasized that the primary function of the therapeutic alliance with the adolescent is to assist the youngster in understanding the link between his feelings and his behavior *in the present*. The adolescent's anxiety about the future and his fear of regression contraindicate extensive focusing on the genetic determinants of his behavior. In psychoanalysis of adults, and to a limited extent even in dynamic psychotherapy with adults, the therapeutic alliance is utilized to promote and regulate a controlled regression. This approach cannot be utilized extensively with the adolescent. Early developmental defects and severe fixations cannot be worked through during early adolescence because the necessary degree of regression would threaten the progressive and synthetic thrust of the developmental period. Brief regressive episodes appear spontaneously and account for the fluctuating transference of adolescent patients. However, only the older adolescent can tolerate the careful study of these ego states. The therapist must usually focus his efforts on helping the adolescent to recover from regressions. As a rule, adolescents respond to a correct and appropriate interpretation by a progressive developmental leap forward rather than by further regression and exploration of genetics. If the therapist tries to interfere with this tendency by encouraging the development of a regressive transference, many adolescents will bolt from therapy. The conscious, rational alliance must be emphasized, not the irrational, infantile bonds to the therapist.

Since the alliance is of central importance yet is often difficult to achieve with the adolescent, the techniques and problems associated with this phase of therapy are discussed in some detail.

FOSTERING THE THERAPEUTIC ALLIANCE

The basic technique of establishing the therapeutic alliance is the timely interpretation of affect and defense as stated above. This process can be restated as helping the adolescent to recognize that his behavior is motivated by inner feeling states. Early in the therapeutic situation, these feeling states are commonly impatience, frustration, feelings of helplessness, and a sense of narcissistic impairment over the need to consult a psychotherapist. Some of the typical early defenses against these painful affects include rebelliousness; passive compliance; timidity; disdainful, condescending attitudes toward the therapist; and cool, aloof intellectualizing. Recognizing these defenses and the feeling states which they disguise is the first order of business in psychotherapy. This may be overlooked when the adolescent's primary defense is passive compliance. These adolescents appear to be "good" patients, eager to get right to work on their problems. The therapist should not be deceived into confusing this frightened obsequiousness with a true therapeutic alliance.

More often, the adolescent therapist must proceed to the clarification of the connection between feeling and action by means of a difficult way station, namely, through interrupting the adolescent's propensity to act in order to avoid feeling. When the therapist challenges this pattern, he is quickly cast in the role of a critical parent, a superego figure. It is a difficult but crucial undertaking to convince the adolescent that "Why did you do that?" is a neutral question, rather than a statement of moral disapproval.

SAYING NO THE EGO WAY

Adolescent acting up and acting out must be limited by the therapist. The only rational basis for the authority to direct behavior proceeds from the therapist's knowledge of the conditions required for effective therapy. In short, the adolescent is told that his behavior is none of the therapist's business except that some actions interfere with the therapeutic process and these must be controlled or therapy will not proceed properly. Often, it is also possible to demonstrate that acting out disrupts the youngster's psychological harmony or threatens to harm him. The therapist tries to convey his wish that the adolescent win the developmental war while keeping it clear that it is the youngster's battle and that the therapist cannot fight it for him. This position is more convincing to the adolescent when it becomes apparent that the therapist has the same benevolent, inquiring attitude toward all symptomatic behavior, whether it is "wrong" or not.

Sarah, a 15-year-old girl in psychotherapy because of promiscuity and poor academic performance, was openly sceptical of the therapist's assertion that his disapproval of her promiscuous behavior was not based on moral indignation. She jeered at the assertion that there were reasons behind her behavior that she did not understand and which could not be explained by her statement that she was "hypersexed." She continued to believe that the therapist was "another square" with "hang-ups about sex" who was trying in typical bluenose fashion to interfere with her fun.

After some positive transference had developed, the girl began to study secretly. Eventually, she brought an excellent report card to a psychotherapy session as a seductive gift to the therapist and as proof of her value. She was at first offended, and then amazed that the therapist did not praise her "good" behavior. Instead, the therapist noted that she did not seem to be enjoying the grades and that this suggested she had worked hard because she felt for some reason that it was expected of her. She talked for a few moments about her motives for improving her academic performance, then said, "You know, I've been telling you what a sex expert I am. Actually, the only reason I was willing to come see you in the first place is that I have never enjoyed sex. Not once. I love the idea of sex, but in practice it's lousy for me. Yet I practice and practice and practice. I know that sounds crazy."

The therapist agreed that this must be a puzzling state of affairs and suggested that he and the patient try to understand it together.

The adolescent is exquisitely sensitive to any manipulative control which threatens his tenuous sense of autonomy. Unless the therapist maintains his neutral, sympathetic but inquiring attitude toward *all* the adolescent's behavior, he cannot convince the adolescent that his goal is to foster understanding, not to dominate the patient through psychological warfare.

"DON'T KNOCK YOURSELF"

The therapist should be quick to point out tendencies toward judgmental and self-critical attitudes in the adolescent. The adolescent should be encouraged to look for the sources of his behavior, attitudes, and affective states, rather than call himself names. The goal of therapy is to increase self-understanding and inner psychological strength and flexibility, not to suppress annoying behavior. Often, the demonstration of therapeutic neutrality and of the motivational origins of behavior can be made effectively through the office interaction with the patient.

A 16-year-old boy started his first three therapy sessions by slouching in his chair and lighting a cigarette. The therapist's inquiry about the meaning of the behavior made him angry.

"You mean I can't even smoke in this crummy office?"

"I didn't say there was a rule against it. I just have noticed that you never talk about smoking, yet you light up the moment you hit that chair."

"So what?"

"So we're here to understand why you do the things you do."

"Because I want to, okay?"

"Well, if you want to go through a session standing on your head and playing a harmonica, I guess that's okay, but I'd probably ask you why you wanted to."

The boy grinned, and then asked carefully, "Are you going to tell my parents I smoke here?"

"We can talk about that in a minute, but I wonder why

you're doing something here that you know your parents dis-
approve of."

The boy hung his head. "Yeah. I know I shouldn't smoke.
It would kill my parents if they knew. I don't know why I'm
always bad."

"I don't think it's going to help to criticize yourself. Let's
try to understand what's really going on here."

"Well, I kinda wanted to see what you'd say about the
smoking."

The smoking represented an attempt to corrupt the therapist by implicating him as an accessory in a forbidden behavior. Without a persistent effort to expose the reasons behind the smoking, the therapist would have been either
maneuvered into a compromised position or forced into an
arbitrary prohibition. In either case, no therapeutic alliance
could develop. Later, when the therapist was calmly able to
confront the boy with his tendency to manipulate people, the
boy said, "Yeah, I like to have my way with them, I guess."

The therapist did not pick up on the sexual implications
in the wording, but commented, "I'm sure there are reasons
why you can't trust people enough to be honest with them.
That's one of the things we might try to understand."

Eventually, the boy was able to talk easily about what he
called his "crook tendencies," both in terms of their disadvantages to him and the situations in which they appeared. The
capacity to observe himself in action and in feelings was finally achieved.

TOWARD TRUE FREEDOM

The youngster discussed above was finally able to realize that
"just wanting" to perform certain actions was actually the end result of many forces within himself. This recognition is extremely
important in the treatment of the adolescent. The startling realiza-
tion that his freedom of choice is being sabotaged by unknown inner forces greatly strengthens the adolescent's motivation for
therapy. The young person's wish for freedom and autonomy will
then be a support to the therapeutic effort to change rebellion into

true freedom and self-direction rather than merely to substitute slavish submission to instinctual drives for earlier submission to the parents.

Several psychological forces within the adolescent interfere with his acceptance of this liberating insight. The typical narcissistic, omnipotent defensive conformation of adolescence, reinforced by the preoccupation with formal operations and the omnipotence of thought, is severely threatened by the idea of unconscious motivation. The adolescent feels a desperate need to see himself as absolute master of his fate. The idea that he is not infinitely malleable but must adapt himself to his own instinctual drives, his own conscience, and external social demands is offensive and frightening. The flip side of total control is total helplessness. When the bubble of his omnipotence is punctured, the adolescent tends to feel completely vulnerable and pitifully weak. The therapist must be extremely supportive and sometimes quite forceful to convince the adolescent that ignoring a fire in the basement or merely trying to "think it away" is an excellent way to get oneself burned. The therapeutic support consists of helping the adolescent to see that his real abilities to devise methods of putting out the fire or confining it to safe areas are much greater than he thought. In short, the therapist supports the adolescent's ego skills to discourage his reliance on magic omnipotence.*

In dealing with the same technical problem, Holmes (1964) has suggested the interesting technique of having the rebellious adolescent role-play cooperative and friendly behavior for a short period of time. He feels that this device often mobilizes affects which have been absorbed in the egosyntonic symptomatic behavior.

'TIS AN ILL WIND—

It is important not to drift into a pattern of only observing and studying pathological and maladaptive behaviors within the therapeutic alliance. A fair and objective evaluation of the adolescent will always reveal areas of strength and competence, often unrecog-

---

* I have described some of the techniques for dealing with a similar problem in latency age children who cheat at games. Many of the technical approaches hold with adolescents also (Meeks, 1970).

nized by the patient. These must be included in any total observation of psychological functioning. This is also true of the adaptive value of ego defenses. For example, a distrust of appearances may result in interpersonal touchiness in the adolescent, but it also characterizes the personality of many successful social and scientific innovators. If the adolescent is to learn to trust the objectivity and honesty of the therapist, he must have the opportunity to see the therapist patiently look at all sides of every question. This strengthens the patient's faith in the therapist's position of friendly neutrality. It is a demonstration of the therapist's wish to avoid intruding and his determination to provide the adolescent with as much information as possible so that the youngster is better prepared to reach his own decisions.

ADOLESCENT ATTITUDES TOWARD A THERAPEUTIC ALLIANCE

The wishes and fears with which adolescents face the beginning of therapy have very little congruence with the goals of the therapist. Consciously, the adolescent is fearful of becoming embroiled in another dependency relationship, whereas unconsciously he hopes and fears to find in the therapist the gratification of various irrational and childish wishes. Because of these emotional currents, the adolescent typically utilizes various techniques to avoid the establishment of a therapeutic alliance. He may project negative attributes onto the therapist or externalize his difficulties and invite the therapist to criticize or reject him. Other adolescents attempt to convert the therapeutic situation into a friendly parent-child relationship in which they will be advised and assisted. Others are overwhelmed by massive superego pressure and can only condemn themselves and beg for mercy.

UNHOLY ALLIANCES

The distortions of the therapeutic relationship just described can usually be managed by the patient application of the principles previously enumerated. However, Keith (1968) has described another group of resistances which he appropriately designates as "unholy alliances." These must be recognized and avoided in order to achieve a usable therapeutic alliance. Keith classifies these structurally as unholy alliances 1) with the id, 2) with pathological ego defenses, and 3) with the superego.

Id Alliances and the Swinging Therapist

All of the unholy alliances are dangers with the adolescent patient. Id alliances are especially seductive, since the therapist is often eager to appear more understanding, tolerant, and "hip" than the other adults whom the adolescent criticizes. The therapist who finds himself discussing specifics of sexual behavior, techniques of outwitting parents, or the absurdity of official authority early in therapy may well suspect that he has been drawn into an unholy alliance with the id or with id derivatives. The result of such an alliance is the weakening of the adolescent's controls and an upsurge in impulsive acting-out behavior. The lack of a true alliance may be demonstrated through overt hostility which the adolescent soon directs toward the therapist, probably with the unconscious goal of inviting external control. It is of crucial importance to avoid this alliance with the adolescent because of his tenuous controls and his resultant fear of his strong feelings and impulses. Because of these fears of loss of control, many adolescents will react to an id alliance with intense anxiety which leads to defensiveness, silence, and attempts to avoid the entire therapy process. The therapist is viewed as an actual threat, a tempter who is encouraging them to lose control of themselves and give rein to the worst aspects of their nature.

This pitfall can be avoided by remembering that it is unwise to interpret or discuss aggressive or sexual material until the distinction between thought and action is clearly established and the adolescent understands that the therapist's encouragement of free expression includes only thoughts and feelings. Only a comfortable recognition that the therapist is opposed to impulsive and unwise action can create a proper atmosphere for the open expression of strong feelings and lead to a true therapeutic alliance. To fantasy that one is omnipotent is a dangerous luxury. It is a game of pretense that the therapist must not play even temporarily. Stated differently, the adolescent can never be seduced into a therapeutic alliance, and the therapist who attempts to deal with his uncomfortable patient in this way is likely to end up with an unworkable and unholy alliance with the id.

A 15-year-old girl was referred for psychotherapy after her parents learned that she and her boyfriend were having sexual intercourse regularly. In early sessions, she admitted that she was promiscuous and eagerly volunteered specific information on her sexual fantasies and adventures in seduction. The therapist ignored her racy stories and merely commented repeatedly on the absence of affect in her friendships as well as her cool and distant way of relating to him. Her titillation gradually ceased and she began to describe her feelings of contempt for all her sexual partners and eventually her wish to outsmart the therapist and show him up as "another dumb, horny male."

Over a period of time, it was possible to create a friendly and honest therapeutic alliance which allowed a moderately successful exploration of the girl's serious character problems which had prevented her from forming close emotional ties. Therapeutic results were first apparent when she began to develop satisfying friendships with girls for the first time since early childhood.

Alliances with Pathological Ego Defenses

The primary pathological ego defense which may be utilized in an unholy alliance by the adolescent is intellectualization. The intelligent, psychologically minded adolescent, often well-read in popular psychology (or even Freud, Erikson, Fromm, etc.) can discuss fascinating insights for hours on end while remaining totally untouched by therapy. The defense may even be actively used to act out competitive and demeaning attitudes toward the therapist under the guise of enthusiastic cooperation. If the therapist, relieved that he does not have to struggle with one of those belligerent, uncooperative adolescents, joins in an alliance with this defense, a therapeutic alliance will not appear. Instead, therapy will deteriorate into sterile, philosophical discussions gradually producing feelings of boredom and despair in both therapist and patient.

There is a place in the therapy of the adolescent for ideological discussion and even for the defense of intellectualization. However, it is important first to establish a therapeutic alliance strong enough to allow the experiencing and reporting of affect. This can only be accomplished by refraining from extensive discussion of conceptual content early in therapy when affective contact has not been established with the adolescent. The intellectualizing patient should be asked to define all jargon such as "hostility," "ambivalent," "erotic," "incestuous," "really meaningful," "I-Thou relationship," and the like. He is asked what he means by those words and asked to tie them to concrete experiences and his feelings during his involvement in those real-life interactions. The therapist, of course, avoids any technical terms, using instead emotionally laden, everyday words such as "mad," "angry," "burned up," "sexual," and even slang sexual phrases if these do not seem unduly seductive with the specific patient. Generalities are discouraged and specifics are sought. The goal, of course, is to bring real emotion into the session. When affect does appear, either in the description of events outside the psychotherapy session or in direct relationship to the therapist, this is encouraged by a demonstration of interest and acceptance.

An 18-year-old college freshman was seen for psychiatric evaluation when he became psychotic following the ingestion of LSD. Even after the brief overt psychosis cleared, he remained rather grandiose, preoccupied with cosmic issues of good and evil. Psychotherapy with limited goals appeared feasible despite the fragility of the personality structure.

Initially, the general philosophic structure and preoccupation were accepted, although not encouraged. The therapist occasionally interjected the observation that personal feelings were important and seemed absent from the patient's thinking. The patient's objection that he intended to rise above his feelings was received with friendly scepticism. The extremely intelligent young man was reminded of historical examples in which philosophical systems were distorted by the personality quirks of their innovators. At the same time, the patient's infrequent references to "human weaknesses" in himself were applauded as evidence of his desire to know himself and thereby avoid the blind errors of other ideologists. Gradually, a capacity for self-observation was developed, although the therapist had to continually disavow the patient's attempt to cast him in role of maharisha.

The conviction that people did not rise above their feelings was constantly reiterated and was demonstrated to the patient in his own behavior whenever possible. The therapist himself continually insisted that *his* only area of competence was in understanding emotions and that this skill was the result of special training, rather than any supernatural power or mysterious talent. Gradually, the patient was able to admit that much of his aloof, mystical superiority covered anxiety and feelings of inferiority and that philosophical detachment was often his way of dealing with feelings of frustration and helplessness.

Greater caution was necessary in approaching the intense anger which he covered with a fervent pacifism and masochistic turnings of the other cheek. Only after repeatedly showing him evidence of his capacity to have strong feelings without acting on them was it possible to comment directly on his anger. The intensity of his fear of losing control of his aggressive impulses was illustrated by his delusional projection of a "conspiracy of evil" which he felt was trying to make him "homicidally insane" during his initial psychotic episode.

One of the points which I have tried to make in this case illustration is the need to accept the positive aspects of adolescent intellectualization. Since adolescents place such importance on logical thought and ideological speculation, it would be a gross technical error to dismiss their intellectual efforts in therapy as useless and unacceptable resistances. Instead, one accepts intellectualization but does not support it. The therapist continues to point out that feelings are *also* important. A patient and persistent effort is made to bring affect into the therapy hours without making a direct critical attack on the defense of intellectualization. The therapist does not ally himself with the pathological ego defense, but neither does he try to force the adolescent to abandon it before he is ready. In behavioral terms, the therapist positively reinforces affective expressions and attempts to extinguish intellectualization by failure to reinforce that behavior.

To a lesser extent, adolescents may attempt to draw the therapist into alliances with other pathological ego defenses, especially denial and reaction formation. In these instances, the therapist maintains his neutrality and encourages greater objectivity without directly assaulting essential defenses. In the emergency states which appear during adolescence, many pathological defenses will be utilized by adolescent patients. The wise therapist approaches them with respect and caution, but it is rarely necessary for the therapist to give his stamp of approval to distortions of inner or outer reality.

The Unholy Alliance with the Superego

It is almost impossible to avoid completely an unholy alliance with the superego in adolescent psychotherapy. It is natural for the adolescent to maneuver to externalize his conscience. This developmental characteristic will be brought into the adolescent's relationship with his therapist, since it is universally present in the adolescent's interactions with all significant adults. This propensity is commonly expressed by the strategy of acting up provocatively to seduce important adults into meting out sadistic punishment. This pattern is described in detail in the section of Chapter One which discusses the adolescent's interaction with his environment. The therapist, as an important environmental figure, must be constantly alert to the danger of being drawn into this kind of relationship with the adolescent patient. The unavoidable technical requirement to limit defensive acting out automatically places the therapist in a precarious position from which he can all too easily slide into a superego alliance.

A 13-year-old boy's easygoing amiability was successfully interpreted as a resistance against his inner feelings. The boy's father was an angry, harsh, competitive man who frequently struck the youngster whenever he challenged any of the father's rules or statements. The youngster was able to discuss some of his anger in a session during which he was able to recognize that his excessive deference and compliance toward the therapist was a defensive continuation of a pattern that he utilized with his father to cover his inner feelings of rage.

However, in the next session he was silent and sullen. Near the end of the session, he suddenly stated that he was "going" and headed for the door.

The therapist, rather surprised, tried to keep him in the room, and a mild shoving contest developed. The therapist recognized his error and was not surprised to encounter a very negative youngster in the next session. He discussed the boy's need to "pick a fight" and indicated his interest in understanding how the boy felt about remaining in the office. The youngster was congratulated on the greater honesty he was demonstrating in his relationship with the therapist and was assured that his anger could be discussed.

Of course, the adolescent *does* need to externalize superego issues in order to find ways to modify his harsh conscience while using the external agent as a temporary protection against the unwise expression of impulse. The adolescent therapist can expect to be used in this way and can be helpful by tolerating some distortion of his intentions. An almost daily example occurs around the question of continuing therapy during difficult periods. Some version of the following conversation is a periodic commonplace during the therapy of many adolescents.

Adolescent (in anger): I never did need to come here. I sure as hell don't need you, and I'm not coming back in here for any more of these silly talks.

Therapist: That's not too surprising. We both know you have a tendency to run away from things when they make you too nervous, but you're strong enough to stay and talk about your feelings.

Adolescent: Why should I sit through this? Do I have to come back?

Therapist: You know that you need therapy. That's not the question. What are you really up to with all this quitting talk?

Adolescent: Okay, Okay, I'll be here next week. I should have known you wouldn't let me quit.

Therapist: Why do *I* have to stop you from doing something that wouldn't be good for *you?*

Adolescent: Aw, forget it. I'm not going to quit your precious therapy.

Therapist: Sorry, I can't forget it. Just not quitting won't cut it. We need to look at how you're trying to set me up.

Adolescent: God! Even my parents aren't this hard to get along with.

Therapist: Maybe they're mainly interested in how you behave—*what* you do. I'm interested in *why* you do things and how you feel. Sometimes it's easier to do what you think I want than to look at your feelings. The only reason that it's any of my business whether you quit or not is that it would interfere with your therapy.

Adolescent: Very funny! But you *did* say that I need to stay in therapy. You *are* telling me what to do!

Therapist (laughs): Yeah. Simon Legree rides again.

Adolescent: Aha! You admit it!

On it goes as the adolescent forces the therapist into a superego role. Still, the therapist must resist the temptation to criticize the adolescent for his provocation, to threaten him, or otherwise behave in a punitive way. This does not mean that the therapist avoids superego issues. Later, we consider the methods of dealing with material in this area in a way that encourages emotional growth.

The immediate point is that only the observing ego is a dependable ally in therapy with the adolescent. Even when a superego alliance produces a diminution of acting-out behavior, there is little true gain in maturation. The surface improvement tends to be ephemeral in most cases. In other instances, it is maintained through an ascetic constriction of personality which chokes off spontaneity and the capacity for pleasure—a terrible price to pay for superficial socialization. There has been no gain in independence and autonomous control in either case.

RECOGNIZING THE ALLIANCE

If the therapist is able to avoid unholy alliances and to respond with appropriate empathy, tact, and precision to the adolescent's defensive operations, evidence of a therapeutic alliance begins to appear. It is important to recognize and acknowledge this important new skill in the adolescent without implying a paternalistic endorsement of "good" behavior. Perhaps, the most meaningful acceptance of the alliance is a comment which merely recognizes its value in the therapeutic process. Its value is purely "instrumental." It is a tool which permits more effective therapeutic work.

In order to credit the adolescent with his discovery, however, it is necessary to recognize its appearance. The alliance may show itself in various forms, depending on the style and personality of the adolescent patient. One recognizes its presence primarily through a subtle change in the tone of the sessions. The atmosphere is somehow no longer totally adversative. The therapist recognizes intuitively that he can relax somewhat, since his patient has at least become interested in observing and understanding the frightened, wary, guarded, and devious styles of relating which have characterized him in earlier sessions. In short, the therapist no longer feels that he is working totally alone in opposing the patient's resistances.

CHECKPOINTS FOR THE ALLIANCE

This general "feel" for the situation can be checked against some behavioral specifics which usually attest to the development of an alliance.

1) The patient occasionally says, "I'm not sure I know why I did that," or "I think I understand why I got *so* upset," or "Can *you* understand what I really was upset about?" In other words, the patient demonstrates a tendency to reflect on his affective experience, or at least a willingness to allow the therapist to suggest an underlying motivation for an intense feeling state. This is particularly meaningful if the affective experience in question directly involves the therapist. "I think the reason your comment made me so angry is—."

2) A switch from threatening actions to discussing thoughts and exploring their origins. Instead of "I'm not coming back here," a change to "When you say things like that, I get so angry at you I feel like quitting."

3) Paradoxically, the development of the therapeutic alliance may also be indicated by a more tolerant attitude toward episodes of loss of impulse control. These episodes are discussed with moderation and objectivity, rather than withheld, bragged on, or criticized with an air of self-loathing. However, the attitude is not merely intellectualization, since the accompanying affects are not isolated but are discussed. The adolescent can say, "I lost a battle, but overall I feel I'm winning the war."

4) A recognition and discussion of affects appearing during the session. The patient is able to comment, "I don't know why, but this discussion makes me very nervous."

5) A recognition and acceptance of ambivalence as an internal reality. No longer "My parents treat me like a baby," but rather "Sometimes I want to grow up, but at other times it scares me to death."

6) A reflective, curious response to appropriate confrontations and interpretations rather than a defensive, critical reaction.

All of these attitudes may appear as isolated occurrences without signaling the arrival of a therapeutic alliance. They represent merely some specific behaviors which may serve as checkpoints for verification of the general air of cooperation described above. Without the overall sense that the therapist has been accepted as a working partner, these behaviors mean nothing.

MAINTAINING THE ALLIANCE

The therapeutic alliance is a delicate structure which is constantly threatened by the anxiety which results from its operations. The successful functioning of the alliance leads repeatedly to upsurges of aggression and erotic feelings which are threatening to the working coalition, especially since these feelings frequently become directed toward the therapist. The adolescent, with his constant search for real objects, has great difficulty in understanding the meaning and nature of transference. We discuss the overall management of transference in adolescent psychotherapy in the next chapter. It is mentioned in this context merely to note that it is a major force acting against the maintenance of the therapeutic alliance.

The fluctuations which characterize ego functioning during adolescence are themselves a threat to the steady maintenance of a therapeutic alliance. During periods of marked regression, the rational therapeutic alliance may be scuttled along with other reality-oriented ego functions. The adolescent therapist must be flexible and adapt himself to the startling changes in level of functioning and defensive patterning which the adolescent shows from one session to the next. The adolescent patient himself often does not view these "moods" as changeable reflections of aspects of the self. He tends to see each new ego state as the way he "really" feels and the way life "really" is. The therapist must try to utilize the therapeutic alliance to assist his patient in accepting his complexity and variability. Westman (1970) has suggested that when the adolescent seems to ask "Who am I?", the therapist can often be most helpful by replying, "Many people. It depends on circumstances inside you and conditions around you." The therapist assists the adolescent to maintain a sense of "wholeness" and personal continuity despite rapid and puzzling changes in mood and attitude.

EXTERNAL THREATS TO THE ALLIANCE

In addition to internal dangers, the alliance may also be threatened by external events. Parents may unknowingly or consciously sabotage the alliance for a variety of motives. Possessive parents may be threatened by the affectionate tie between the therapist and the child. Controlling, hostile parents may view the therapist as an agent of their control and convey this image to their youngster. Other parents may actually be threatened by the improvement they observe in the adolescent if these changes interfere with family patterns which are important to neurotic stability. Some ideas regarding the management of these problems are presented in Chapter 6, dealing with the parents of the adolescent patient.

Other external occurrences may produce such intense affects that the adolescent is forced to erect rigid defenses which cannot be explored for a period of time. These occurrences may be the illness or death of an important person in the adolescent's world or an overwhelming defeat or disappointment in the adolescent's personal struggle for competence and acceptance. During these periods, the adolescent needs to withdraw and mourn. The therapist must recognize the legitimacy of this need and accept a role of passivity and empathic sharing until the adolescent is prepared to work again. More active intervention during such a period may permanently impair the therapeutic relationship.

These instances do permit the therapist to observe the adolescent's style of dealing with loss. He can determine whether the adolescent acts to avoid grief and mourning by total introjection of the object rather than by a gradual identification with the desirable characteristics of the loved one and rejection of those characteristics that do not fit his personality needs and his aspirations (Laufer, 1966; Root, 1957; Rochlin, 1965). When the mourning process goes awry or is avoided by the adolescent, the therapist may act to encourage the appropriate expression of grief and the constructive adaptation to loss. However, when the adolescent's grief and mourning are appropriate, the therapist should remain unobtrusive and grant the necessary time for the work to be completed.

WHAT TO DO UNTIL THE ALLIANCE COMES— AND WHEN IT DOES NOT

The therapeutic alliance may simply never materialize. This can result from the failure to respond accurately or effectively to early defenses or affects in a particular patient. In these instances of therapeutic error, an open discussion of the problem may permit a new start. If this is not possible, transferring the patient to a different therapist may be considered. Before carrying out transfer, however, it is worthwhile for the therapist to examine his decision closely to be sure his plan does not merely represent a rejection of the adolescent based on countertransference. Even when this proves to be the case, a transfer may still be in order. However, the therapist and the adolescent will benefit if the real reason for the transfer is recognized and discussed.

The problems are somewhat different when the patient was simply never a candidate for outpatient psychotherapy. No matter how carefully the diagnostic process is conducted, some errors will occur. When this is recognized, one must present the problem and the new recommendations to the patient and his family without undue embarrassment or apology. This situation is discussed further in the chapter on termination.

WHY DOES THE ADOLESCENT STRIVE FOR THE ALLIANCE?

After surveying all these problems, one might wonder why the therapeutic alliance ever survives the vicissitudes that it meets. These negative forces we have just enumerated are countered by two positive effects which tend to balance them. The first of these is the sense of freedom and release which usually results from increased self-awareness. The adolescent is motivated to persevere because of the sense of mastery which accompanies therapeutic gains. This rational advantage is bolstered by the adolescent's pleasure in the identification with the working therapist. The frequency with which adolescent patients develop the ambition to be a psychotherapist reveals both the identification and, at least very often, the defensive fear of passively losing identity unless they turn passive into active and "go the therapist one better." In my opinion, this defense should not be challenged. Instead, the adolescent should be permitted to regard himself as a junior partner and eventual peer so long as he does not use his psychological insight destructively toward himself or others. After all, when the therapeutic alliance is functioning properly the adolescent is literally functioning as his own therapist much of the time. Even when the adolescent uses his new found skill destructively, the perversity of such a practice can be interpreted without attacking the identification.

Sarah, the 15-year-old girl with the symptom of promiscuity described earlier, had many preoedipal problems with her mother illustrated by multiple oral-autoerotic behaviors in early childhood.

In the middle course of therapy, she had developed considerable expertise in observing and interpreting her behavior and feelings. During this time, she related an interchange with her mother. The mother saw the patient's kittens, already quite large, nursing the mother cat. She reacted with anger and disgust that such large kittens "would not leave their mother alone." Sarah interpreted her mother's disapproval of libidinal pleasure and associated to her mother's negative statements about sexuality. She then told of accusing her mother of being chronically unhappy because of neurotic self-denial (a correct interpretation, by the way). She told the mother she really should see a psychiatrist. The mother became quite angry and criticized Sarah for needing psychiatric help, since that revealed her lack of "true Christianity."

Sarah was initially indignant at her mother's reaction "when I was only trying to help her." The therapist noted he had been unable to detect much sympathy or understanding in Sarah's comments. Could it be that Sarah was angry and critical of her mother, simply using her insight as a more effective weapon of attack?

Sarah was able to accept the interpretation and turn to an exploration of the origins of her overreaction to her mother's attitudes toward the cat. She eventually recognized her identification with the aggressively demanding kittens and her guilt because her mother acceded to her wishes but then induced guilt through an air of sadness and martyrdom.

Later in therapy, she came to a sympathetic and affectionate understanding of her mother. She was able to support and encourage the mother to find community activities in which the mother's dependency needs could be met comfortably and without shame or disgust.

EVIDENCES OF A FAILING ALLIANCE

The recognition that the therapeutic alliance has collapsed usually comes from the same intuitive grasp of the total therapy situation which was mentioned as the best evidence of the presence of the alliance. One senses a new tendency toward opposition, not so much toward the therapist but toward the work of therapy. Again, the therapist senses that he is struggling alone in his efforts to utilize the therapeutic session to aid the process of self-understanding. The adolescent is no longer manning one of the oars, and the therapist must paddle upstream without assistance.

Again, there are isolated events which help to confirm the over-all impression.

CHECKPOINTS FOR FAILURE OF THE ALLIANCE

1) An absence of any evidence of self-observation and explora-tion. The adolescent is again immersed in experience and shows little interest either in understanding his role in creating his per-sonal emotional experiences or in dealing effectively with these experiences.

2) Subtle or gross actions directed toward the therapist which are dismissed as unimportant even when they are noted. Examples would include coming late, missing sessions, interrupting the therapist, frequently misunderstanding the therapist's words, and other manifestations of hostility, but also bringing gifts, praising the therapist, and other seductive behaviors.

3) The reappearance of defensive attitudes which were previ-ously interpreted, understood, and discarded. Again, this is ac-companied by a bland disregard of the implications of the be-havior.

4) A return of manipulative behavior and attitudes toward the therapist. Stated differently, there is a return to neurotic inter-personal interaction with the therapist expressed in action rather than verbalized for exploration.

REESTABLISHING THE ALLIANCE

If the therapist identifies a disruption of the therapeutic alli-ance, he can then work to repair it. The therapist should recog-nize that no other work will be useful until the alliance has been reestablished. No matter how much inherent interest the content of the sessions may hold, the therapist should utilize only that por-tion of the material which may help to rebuild the therapeutic alliance. In the absence of a working alliance, the therapist's inter-vention will be ineffective or even antitherapeutic.

How, then, can the therapist reestablish the alliance? The first step is the identification of the cause of the disruption. As men-tioned above, the most common sources of disruption are the anxiety and uncomfortable affects released through the activity of the therapeutic alliance itself. One very honest 13-year-old, confronted with her resistance, stated the problem succinctly: "The trouble with looking at yourself is that it doesn't feel good."

Of course, this is the very stuff of which therapy is made. The therapist should accept the inevitable fact that properly conducted psychotherapy produces pain and all people try to avoid pain. The adolescent patient has every right to complain about this and to expect his therapist to sympathize. Mankind has always chaffed under the painful demands of reality. Surely, we can be sympathetic and supportive when the adolescent frets at these nettles. Of course, the therapist's sympathy is directed at helping the adolescent to bear this realistic fact of life, not toward shielding him from it.

When confronted with a break in the therapeutic alliance, the therapist needs tactfully to acknowledge with his patient the change in their relationship. Often, the therapist will have to explain to the adolescent that this change is not viewed as "goofing off," obstinancy, or rebelliousness. The distinction between resisting the therapist and resisting the therapeutic process often needs extensive clarification if the adolescent is to learn how to observe this interaction objectively and without feeling criticized by the therapist. It is essential to help the adolescent to understand that his interactions with the therapist will be treated in the same objective, curious, nonjudgmental way with which the therapist responds to his other affective experiences.

Tammy, an attractive and petite 17-year-old blonde, requested psychotherapy one night in the midst of a family row over her poor school performance. She told her therapist that her real reason for wishing to be in therapy was a feeling that life was passing her by and that she was unable to form close friendships that were meaningful to her. Over the first few psychotherapy sessions, Tammy formed a warm relationship with the therapist and utilized her capacities for introspection with some success in understanding her relationship to her hard-working, intense, and somewhat driven mother. She was able to recognize that her poor academic record reflected both a repudiation of her mother's anxious way of life and a fear of competing with the mother.

Throughout this time, she periodically complained that she did not seem to be popular. Although she first blamed this unpopularity on her moral standards, which she felt were higher than those of most of the girls at her school, she gradually recognized that she was somehow "turning off" the boys who showed an initial interest in her. As this became a focus in therapy, the therapist commented on the fact that Tammy did not seem to take her femininity seriously and seemed in many respects to treat relationships between boys and girls as though they were a game that did not involve any intense feelings. Tammy's response at the time was to distort the comment somewhat and to state defensively that she had engaged in some necking and that she was not afraid of sexuality.

However, in the next interview Tammy was visibly anxious and found it difficult to talk. She fidgeted in her chair and regularly pulled at her skirt. She tended to avoid the therapist's direct gaze and frequently blushed whenever she would try to speak. After a few minutes of this, she was able to become somewhat comfortable, but seemed to be talking at a very superficial level and showing none of her characteristic curiosity about her own feelings, thoughts, and behaviors.

When the therapist commented that it seemed Tammy had lost a good deal of interest in exploring her feelings, Tammy felt that she was being criticized. After the therapist clarified that this was not the case and suggested that feelings about therapy and the therapist could be openly discussed, Tammy was able to say that she was feeling somewhat annoyed with the therapist when she left the previous session and was aware that she was quite upset. She stated further that she could not remember the topic of discussion from the previous session and volunteered that this was unusual for her, since as a rule it was quite easy to remember her sessions. The therapist supported her honesty in this and encouraged her to continue talking about any reactions that she might have had toward the therapist.

Initially, she spoke with some timidity, but gradually this diminished as Tammy began to complain that the therapist was "finding problems" that she did not know she had. Because of this, she could not be sure whether therapy was helping her or making her worse. She noted that generally she enjoyed a good mood most of the time but that she had been rather depressed for the entire past week. At this point, the therapist reminded her that he had commented that she sometimes treated life as a game and refused to take it seriously and suggested that perhaps she found this necessary because of some tendency toward depression, which she was attempting to avoid. The therapist supported her honesty in facing up to some of these sad feelings and wondered with her which course of action held the greatest promise in the long run.

"Well, if you can stand a blubbering idiot, I guess I can weep my way through it. I suppose I've known this all along myself," Tammy replied.

It seems that Tammy's discomfort was related to sexual feelings toward the therapist which were activated by his direct recognition of Tammy's femininity. However, in the absence of a therapeutic alliance strong enough to deal with this kind of material, the appropriate response was in the direction of dealing with the uncomfortable affects stirred by the therapy process in the interest of reestablishing a therapeutic alliance. The techniques of management of sexual transference in adolescents are discussed in the next chapter.

If the disruption of the alliance arises from some unfortunate event in the adolescent's life, a period of unobtrusive and undemanding support will need to precede any attempt to reestablish a therapeutic alliance. As mentioned above, the therapist must allow the adolescent to take the initiative in indicating an interest in continuing the exploratory work of the treatment unless the grief reaction itself is seriously distorted. More likely than not, the adolescent will indicate his readiness to go back to work by complaining, "We don't seem to be getting much done in here lately!" The complaining adolescent may be quite surprised to see his therapist, somewhat worried during the mourning period, suddenly smile and say, "Man, I can't tell you how relieved I am to hear you say that! Let's get with it."

Parental sabotage of the alliance must be recognized and differentiated from stresses arising from the therapy itself. Often, parental interference is signaled by comments which disavow previous areas of conflict with the parents. The adolescent, on the contrary, reports "therapeutic sessions" with the parents and may imply that they can help him more than the therapist. Especially if such periods coincide with or follow anxious phone calls from the parents, the suspicion of parental sabotage is justified. These problems are discussed more fully in a later chapter, but it is well to recognize that the problem cannot be handled unilaterally with the adolescent patient once it has reached this level. The parents themselves must be helped either through a collaborative therapist or directly by family conferences.

THE ALLIANCE IN PERSPECTIVE

The therapeutic alliance is not only essential to any psychotherapy; it coincides with an important developmental task of the adolescent period—the emergence of the observing ego. Therefore, the development and maintenance of a therapeutic alliance with the adolescent patient assume a double importance. We have explored some of the particular problems and pitfalls in establishing a therapeutic alliance during this phase of psychosexual development. We have also tried to point out that the maintenance of the alliance is inextricably linked to various other aspects of therapy, especially the transference tendencies of the adolescent and the problems of the adolescent's parents. The capacity to establish a therapeutic alliance is an essential skill for the therapist of the adolescent. Outpatient therapists are referred increasing numbers of adolescents who do not fit easily into our previous expectations regarding the form of the therapeutic alliance. The next chapter explores some of the problems and possibilities associated with efforts to form a workable alliance with these youngsters.

CITED AND RECOMMENDED READINGS

Adatto, C. P. 1966. On the metamorphosis from adolescence into adulthood. J. Amer. Psychoanal. Assoc. 14: 485–509.

Balint, M. 1952. Primary love and psycho-analytic technique. London: Hogarth Press, Ltd. (New York: Liveright Publishing Corporation)

Freud, S. 1912. The dynamics of transference. Standard Edition, Vol. 12, pp. 121–144.

Friedman, L. 1969. The therapeutic alliance. Int. J. Psychoanal. 50(2): 139–153.

Greenson, R. 1967. The technique and practice of psychoanalysis, Vol. I. New York: International Universities Press, Inc.

Holmes, D. 1964. The adolescent in psychotherapy. Boston: Little, Brown & Co.

Keith, C. R. 1968. The therapeutic alliance in child psychotherapy. J. Amer. Acad. Child Psychiat. 7: 31–43.

Laufer, M. 1966. Object loss and mourning during adolescence. Psychoanal. Stud. Child 21: 269–293.

Long, R. 1968. The osberving ego and adolescent development. Rev. Inst. Nac. Neurol. (Mexico) 2: 8–21.

Meeks, J. 1970. Children who cheat at games. J. Amer. Acad. Child Psychiat. 9: 157–171.

Rochlin, G. 1965. Griefs and discontents: the forces of change. Boston: Little, Brown & Co.

Root, N. N. 1957. A neurosis in adolescence. Psychoanal. Stud. Child 12: 320–334.

Westman, J. 1970. Personal communication.

CHAPTER FIVE
atypical alliances in the psychotherapy of adolescents

INTRODUCTION

Although the model of the therapeutic alliance described in the previous chapter is one that the therapist should always strive for, it cannot always be achieved. In some ways it must be regarded as an ideal since as Adatto (1966) has pointed out, many adolescents in psychotherapy will utilize the therapist as a real object in their psychological development. Some youngsters, particularly psychotic and borderline youngsters, youngsters with severe narcissistic pathology and youngsters with severe character problems exxaggerate the adolescent tendency to force the therapist to play a role in their lives which is quite different from the image of a neutral, objective guide.

It seems evident that many of these adolescents cannot tolerate the degree of distancing and neutrality implied in the traditional therapeutic alliance. Their sense of self is so fragmented and distorted that they cannot develop the degree of relatedness to a real person in a specific role which would allow an even-handed and non-judgmental discussion of their psychological functioning. However, from a pragmatic clinical viewpoint, it seems that many of these youngsters benefit materially from a psychotherapeutic interaction in spite of the absence of a therapeutic alliance dominated by observing ego functions.

Progress in the absence of an ideal alliance is a psychotherapeutic process which is still poorly understood and relatively unexplored. Many therapists are very uncomfortable when they are pressed into a role in the adolescent's life which seems at variance with their own professional identity as a psychotherapist.

This chapter is presented as a very tentative exploration of some of these atypical therapeutic relationships which still have the potential for a productive result.

The author is aware that some of the relationships described may approximate the "unholy alliances" described in the previous chapter as situations to recognize and avoid in psychotherapy. Although this idea may appear paradoxical, the case illustrations may clarify the techniques and attitudes involved.

REVISITING THE OMNIPOTENT TRANSFERENCE

As noted in the chapter on ongoing psychotherapy, some basically neurotic adolescents develop omnipotent transferences toward their therapist which require exploration, interpretation and disillusion. There are patients, however, who cannot tolerate this approach to their omnipotent projections, at least early in the therapeutic relationship. This tends to be the case in youngsters with borderline or severely narcissistic personality structures.

The work of Kohut (1971) and others has added a great deal to our understanding of the nature of narcissistic psychopathology and its expression within the therapeutic relationship. These narcissistic adolescents have significant fixations in this realm of emotional development which go far beyond the "normal" narcissism and omnipotence of the adolescent developmental phase. Because of their personality structure they have an intense need to aggrandize the therapist and idealize him and at other phases in treatment to solicit from the therapist endless admiration of themselves. For these youngsters this style of relating is not a defense but a demonstration· of serious deficiencies in their previous experience with parenting figures. They require a gradual living through of this way of relating to another human being in order to repair damaged or non-existent intrapsychic personality structures. If the therapist is able to accept these unrealistic feelings neutrally in the same way that he regards other distortions of his true nature and function, the patient is often able to gradually relinquish the unrealistic view as he gradually realizes that competence can replace omnipotence in his own security system.

Kohut (1971) has described a process of normal development characterized by a gradual disillusionment with the narcissisticly invested idealized parental image. This disillusionment occurs without any direct verbal disavowel of omnipotent powers on the part of the adult. The unavoidable frustration of unrealistic hopes regarding the adult lead to gradual relinquishing of unrealistic wishes. In the psychotherapeutic relationship, relinquishing this illusion is, of necessity, telescoped in time and tends to be enormously painful and regularly accompanied by alternating periods of depression and rage directed toward the therapist.

Davy, a sixteen-year-old caucasian male was admitted to a psychiatric hospital because of a suicide attempt. In the hospital setting he appeared markedly inhibited, frightened of his age-mates, and often near psychotic in his fearfulness of the environment and in his capacity to drift into long periods of reverie during which he seemed totally disinterested in his surroundings. The developmental history revealed that Davy had always been extraordinarily dependent on his mother who regarded him as an extremely sensitive, intelligent, and "very special human being". He had never had good peer relationships and had tended to be the scapegoat in his classes throughout his school experience.

In his individual sessions Davy spoke very little to his therapist regarding personal matters. He was quite willing to discuss his hobbies which included sports (though he did not participate personally), literature, and music. In all of these areas Davy was extraordinarily well informed and showed a quick and incisive logic which was quite impressive for his age. When pressed to discuss his personal difficulties including the suicide attempt, he would become evasive. If the pressure was continued, Davy would simply clam up.

However, in family therapy Davy began to express his concern about being overly dependent on his parents and began to ventilate feelings of frustration and anger when his mother's behavior seemed to him to be infantalizing. He also began to rebel against his scapegoated position in the peer group to the extent of becoming involved in physical fights on two occasions when he felt he was being "pushed around". As his general functioning improved it was decided that Davy could be discharged from the hospital and followed in outpatient treatment. This decision was maintained in spite of the fact that Davy quickly reverted to his social isolation on his return home. Although he continued to verbally decry his inability to relate to people outside his family, he could not bring himself to make any active efforts to change that state of affairs.

In his individual treatment, Davy began to speak more freely about himself and his ideas. At the same time he seemed overly interested in the virtual "honor" of being a patient of his therapist. He was preoccupied with the therapist's national reputation, complimented the therapist on the brilliance and subtlety of his simplest statements and sang the therapist's praise to his family and anyone else who would listen. During this period he confided a variety of grandiose wishes and fantasies about himself and also recounted some embarrassing and frightening daydreams and wishes. He was particularly concerned regarding some homicidal fantasies and admitted that his suicide attempt was partially an effort to "rid the world of a potential murderer."

As the months went by, the unqualified admiration of the therapist continued but a new theme of identification with this power and Davy's self adulation became more and more clear. For example, Davy would develop complex, imaginative metapsychological theory systems and present them in detail to the therapist. The manner of presentation suggested that Davy was attempting to earn the admiration of the therapist through emulation of the therapist's area of interest. Although there were some undercurrents of competitiveness, these seemed much less important than the desire to be praised by a "hero" figure.

Gradually, however, Davy began to look for clay feet. He devised situations, such as refusing to attend school, which created crises in which the therapist was powerless. He also showed a wry humor directed at the exalted image of the therapist which he had created. Usually Davy reacted with open anger and disappointment when the therapist had to cancel appointments. During this period, however, Davy suddenly accepted an absence with cheerful indifference. When asked why he wasn't upset this time, Davy replied, "I've come to accept that it's just part of having a semi-famous psychiatrist."

Davy was quite depressed during this period. The disappointment of recognizing the therapist's human limitations and lack of magical power was clearly painful. Davy varied between grief and rage toward the therapist. Only gradually was he able to begin to struggle realistically with his own life. After two and a half years of therapy Davy grudgingly admitted, "I guess I'm a lot less crazy than I was two years ago and I suppose you had something to do with that." For the therapist this was quite a comedown from his previous grandeur in Davy's eyes but for Davy it was a significant improvement in his ability to recognize the genuine value of another human being.

Kernberg (1968) has described in detail the primitive defenses which the borderline youngster uses. He comments particularly on the defense of splitting which is often employed in varying combinations with the unrealistic idealization just described. It is important that the therapist listen attentively to the negative feelings of rage and frustration expressed toward others during the period when the therapist himself is idolized. It can be safely assumed that this hostility and depreciation will eventually be expressed in the transference also. Other youngsters may begin therapy by presenting the negative side of their tendency to split. These youngsters may continue to idealize their parents or other adults and utilize the therapist as the target of their negative projections. This is particularly likely because of projective identification, commonly utilized by these youngsters, which leads to the fear that the therapist harbors those impulses and actions which are in fact struggling for expression in the youngster's own mind. It is difficult to engage these young people in treatment but once they become involved the therapist may later become the idealized object for them.

Ralph was referred for psychotherapy as a 16 year old near the middle of his sophomore year in high school. The referral was initiated by Ralph's mother over Ralph's protest and with only lukewarm support from the father. The mother requested to speak with the psychiatrist before Ralph was seen and was given an appointment.

She explained that she had been quite concerned about Ralph for two or three years. She stated that Ralph had never been an outstanding student but had accomplished an acceptable performance in elementary school. She also noted that in the earlier grades Ralph was friendly, socially accepted, cheerful, and "resilient." When Ralph was in the 6th grade the family moved and Ralph had to enter a different school. The mother felt that this experience was very hard on the boy although he did make some new friends and appeared to be adjusting to his new situation. The 7th grade also did not present problems, but in the 8th grade Ralph began to have significant problems with the other youngsters. He stated that he was not liked and began to be more reticent at home. Ralph began to have difficulty getting to school on time in the mornings. His grades also began to deteriorate.

Near the end of the 8th grade the parents consulted a psychologist who stated that he felt too much pressure was being placed on Ralph. The mother stated that much of this pressure came from her husband, an extremely successful and aggressive businessman who owned his own company. The mother stated that Ralph's father was affectionate and relaxed with their 13 year old daughter but focused his attention on Ralph entirely around school performance, work at home, and other achievement goals.

Both parents were quite intelligent and basically

cooperative. After the school conference they made an effort to follow the advice they had been given. The father stopped complaining to Ralph regarding his poor performance although he continued to voice anger and disappointment to Ralph's mother regarding the boy.

Near the end of the 8th grade year Ralph's best friend Danny moved out of the area. At that point Ralph seemed to completely give up all social contacts. He did make an effort to keep in touch with Danny by mail but seemed to always compare himself unfavorably with his lost friend. He was particularly upset when Danny wrote with the news that he had a serious girl friend. At that time Ralph told his mother, "Danny's made it and I haven't."

Ralph's steady slide continued through the 9th grade. Toward the end of that year the parents took him to a psychiatrist who evaluated Ralph and told the parents that he had very poor self esteem and was moderately depressed. Ralph went to the psychiatrist reluctantly. He had attended only two sessions when school ended and Ralph got a job. He quit therapy telling his parents that he would return to treatment in the fall. However, in the fall he refused to see the psychiatrist again, stating "I've got it all together." The parents insisted that he go back for at least one session. Ralph went late to his appointment and told the psychiatrist, "Don't let my mother make any more appointments." At the beginning of the 10th grade Ralph indicated that he wished to enroll in distributive education which allowed him to attend school a half day and work. His grades continued to be poor although he seemed to be performing acceptably in his job as a gas station attendant. The mother felt that he had gotten rather heavily into pot. She stated that a few weeks before Ralph had told her that he was quitting marijuana.

The mother felt Ralph was worried about his masculinity. A friend of his once told her that Ralph gave up too easily in regards to making friendships with girls. The friend indicated that Ralph had called one girl for a date but when he received a negative reply he withdrew and refused to call any more girls. Ralph said at the time that he would never have a girlfriend.

The mother stated that she felt Ralph was extremely depressed. He had recently said to her, "You think life is great and wonderful. I hate it." When mother wept in response to hearing this despairing comment Ralph became angry with her and shouted, "Stop that, that's what made me such an old lady". On another occasion he told the mother that when he was 21 he would get a gun and finish all of this. The mother felt that Ralph looked depressed almost all of the time. She was very worried about Ralph and seemed particularly concerned about her relationship with the boy. She and Ralph had had excellent communication up until about two years ago. He had told her during the time when they were closer, "You're proud of me, but I'll never make father proud of me." The mother agreed that she and the father had argued a good deal during Ralph's early life. She admitted that she might be somewhat indulgent and overprotective but felt that father was unreasonably demanding of precocious independence from Ralph. Father was especially strict regarding table manners and total obedience to rules when Ralph was a young child.

During this interview the therapist asked to speak to Ralph's father. She seemed somewhat hesitant stating that she felt Ralph's father "had given up on Ralph." The therapist sensed that mother was trying to "sell" Ralph to him. She seemed concerned the father would discourage the therapist from making a treatment effort with her son. When the therapist insisted, however, she agreed and Ralph's father did accept an appointment.

The father was a very handsome man, noticeably younger in appearance than his wife though they were in fact approximately the same age. He was cooperative and stated "Ralph's having a lot of problems with his own feelings about himself". When asked to expand on that he replied "The ones I fasten on depend on my mood. I'm moody and I reflect a lot." He stated that in his opinion the family had "normal family frictions" and probably "doesn't communicate too well".

The father focused a gread deal on Ralph's performance difficulties, admitting that Ralph's poor school achievement bothered him. He was even more bothered by the fact that Ralph was difficult to get up in the mornings and customarily went late to all scheduled activities. Father admitted he was extremely annoyed by the fact that Ralph did not seem to care whether he was on time or not. Interestingly the father states that he felt Ralph had "given up on himself". He noted that Ralph's one ambition was to be a guitarist in a rock group but that in fact Ralph had demonstrated no musical talent. The father stated that the only thing he and Ralph did with mutual pleasure was ice skating.

Both parents indicated that Ralph had told them that a traumatic event occured during his 8th grade year that he could not discuss with them. This secret Ralph stated was the cause of his depression and continuing problems.

An interview with Ralph was scheduled in spite of the fact that both parents had some concern that he would not keep the appointment. They asked if there was any point in "forcing" Ralph to come to the interview. The therapist told them that Ralph should come to the appointment if they had to drag him there. In fact, Ralph came reluctantly but voluntarily. He was overweight, unattractive, clearly depressed, and just as clearly sulky and petulant. His long hair was lank and appeared dirty and his dress was somewhat sloppy and disheveled. He spoke reluctantly and there was considerable conscious witholding, but in addition there was genuine psychomotor retardation. Though there was no apparent thought disorder it did seem that Ralph occasionally became confused and had some difficulty in maintaining his train of thought. He stated rather early in the interview in a somewhat challenging way that he was not going to talk about his real problem. The therapist elected to pursue a friendly cross examination since Ralph's manner somehow suggested that that was what he expected and needed. This interrogation gradually revealed the following points.

1. Someone has let him down in a very serious and painful way but Ralph cannot talk about this.
2. Ralph has a secret too embarassing and painful to disclose.
3. "Half the time" Ralph feels hopeless and thinks that his problems are insoluable.
4. The effort to solve his problems is too much trouble anyway.
5. He cannot trust the therapist because the therapist might use information against him or simply not understand him or both.

Ralph says that both parents irritate him especially his mother. She irritates him first of all by being too nice and explaining too much and secondly by singing nursery rhymes and "acting like a kid sometimes." Ralph thinks that at times he blames his parents for his problem. His blaming does not take any definite form, "just the way they are. They raised me." Ralph states that he has never told his mother that he is angry at her because she is very senstitive and "it would hurt her." When asked how he would know she was hurt he states that she would cry. Ralph is unable to say anything specific about how his father irritates him but with some prodding says, "bugging me like waking me up or sometimes treating me like a little kid."

Ralph quickly seemed uncomfortable about these complaints toward his parents and added, "It's probably all just my fault, I don't know." He stated that he did not have any friends but that he would like to have some if they were "the right kind." When asked what sort of youngster would be the right kind he stated, "Someone who doesn't hurt me. Someone I can trust, and someone who is popular."

The therapist formed a diagnostic impression of an extremely narcissistic boy with a severe depressive neurosis. The presence of multiple neurotic traits of compulsive rumination, phobic tendencies and a suspiciousness which verged on the paranoic suggested poor ego structure and the possibility of a borderline personality organization. Both the parents and Ralph were told that Ralph's problems were extremely serious. Ralph stated that he still did not wish to have therapy and he was told firmly that he only had two choices, either to come in for individual sessions or to be part of family therapy. He was told that he did not have a right to refuse therapy in view of the pain and concern which his unhappiness was creating in his family. The effect of this comment seemed to be more supportive and face-saving than upsetting to Ralph. He was able to accept individual treatment on this basis.

The first few months of treatment with Ralph were characterized primarily by long silences and an extreme dirth of material. However, he seemed to be relaxing somewhat and occasionally would enter into brief discussions with the therapist. The therapist maintained an extremely active, cheerful, and chatty manner although Ralph's sullen silence and unresponsiveness sometimes caused the one-sided happy chatter to sound a bit like the babblings of a good-natured idiot. After about four months of treatment Ralph announced that he would like to describe the traumatic events which happened to him in junior high but that he was not sure he could. This, of course, represented a significant break-through since previously he had stated that he was absolutely unwilling to discuss this matter. The therapist took this as permission to prod, pry, cajole, and actively pursue this material. Three or four sessions later Ralph was able to describe the events which happened to him in the 8th grade. Basically they consisted of a competitive run-in with a youngster who became his enemy. This youngster had considerable skill at teasing and was able to get groups of youngsters to laugh at Ralph on a few occasions on the school grounds. The ultimate upset occured when this enemy drew a caricature of Ralph on the wall of the schoolhouse with spray paint, particularly emphasizing Ralph's somewhat oversized nose. All of the other kids laughed and thought the picture was funny. Ralph was humiliated.

Over the next few sessions Ralph continued to discuss the

impact of these events on his attitudes and thinking. It became clear that he had developed an almost paranoid attitutde toward other youngsters which at times approached "ideas of reference." For example, if Ralph would see two youngsters laughing together he would wonder if perhaps they were talking about him and laughing at him. He also came to feel that school work was not important. He dreaded attending school each morning and could hardly force himself to go, thus accounting for this chronic tardiness. He became more and more seclusive and did not wish to talk with his family since he felt sure that they would not understand his problem. He was concerned that his father would criticize him for not dealing more effectively with the situation while his mother would be overly sympathetic and excessively supportive. Specifically he felt that his mother would tell him that he was a handsome and likeable youngster when he felt convinced that he was in fact, ugly, obnoxious and unlikeable.

Several months were spent dealing with Ralph's reaction to these events in early adolescence. The therapist focused particularly on the absence of any memory of overt anger, desire to retaliate, or obvious competitiveness in Ralph's response to his peer problems. Initially Ralph flatly denied having any such feelings but gradually began to recover some memories of anger and competitiveness. These bothered him a great deal and he confessed them with tremendous guilt. At the time of entry into treatment Ralph was an avowed pacifist who stated that he had strong moral opposition to violence in any form. Violence for Ralph included many behaviors normally regarded as appropriately aggressive and competitive. For example, he felt that one should never criticize another person even for constructive reasons since that might inflict pain on the other individual.

At this point in treatment the material shifted slightly and Ralph began to talk about his difficulty with girls and his intense desire to have a girlfriend. As he described the relationship he wished for, it became clear that his fantasied goal was a symbiotic union with an adored girlfriend against the rest of the world. It was crucial to Ralph that his girlfriend be absolutely beautiful not only in his own eyes but in the consensual evaluation of the entire world. He recognized that this was unrealistic but maintained that it was crucial to him. Ralph would initially be reticent and reluctant to describe fantasies of this kind, but once they were voiced he would adopt a stubborn defense of his right to have his emotional wishes met. His attitude was, "I don't care if its crazy, that's what I want anyway." In connection with the discussion of his sexual development and his attitudes towards himself as a male, Ralph gingerly approached another secret. He was never able to confess it on his own, but when the therapist suggested that he had many guilt feelings about masturbation, Ralph wept and admitted that that was the subject he had been alluding to. Again he adopted the attitude that the only solution to this problem was for the therapist to assist him in giving up this totally unacceptable habit. When the therapist finally told him that he thought that was unlikely until the time that Ralph had a sexual relationship with a girl, Ralph was annoyed and declared that the therapist had thereby "undone all the good we've done here."

Ralph continued to argue that the habit of masturbation could be overcome if only the therapist could help him. Ralph insisted on explanations as to why the therapist would not join him in this effort. He was extremely reluctant to accept the reality of the sexual drive and felt that he should rise above it in much the same way that he insisted he should be able to overcome any feelings of anger or competitiveness.

These complaints were merely specific instances of Ralph's general dismissal of the value of therapy. Although he now attended regularly and without protest, he maintained a sullen grumbling attitude toward the treatment effort, frequently noting that it had not helped him. The therapist's attitude toward all of these complaints was to accept them without comment in spite of the fact that the family was reporting to the therapist that Ralph's behavior had improved considerably and in spite of the fact that Ralph admitted reluctantly that his report card had improved dramatically during the last reporting period. He assured the therapist that that was the result of having easy courses and in any event was of no importance to him.

At this point in therapy Ralph presented another obsession which he stated was virtually exhausting him. In describing the development of this obsession Ralph inadvertantly revealed that his social contacts had increased considerably. However, in these interpersonal situations Ralph would predictably become anxious at times and would feel he had to get away and be alone so that he could "think about the world". What Ralph meant by "thinking about the world" was devising hiw own mind solutions to all human problems. He felt that if he could solve racial predjudice, poverty, war and general human suffering so that everyone in the whole world could be happy, then he himself could be content and happy also. If he failed in these mental gymnastics, happiness would be impossible for him. He was quite convinced at times that if he would persevere with enough effort and time he could succeed at this grandiose undertaking. At other times he recognized the obsession as "a ridiculous mind game" that was serving a defensive function in containing his interpersonal anxiety and his fear of the novel situations that were beginning to occur in his life.

Shortly after this Ralph found another solution to his dilemma. He announced to the therapist that he was quite sure that the therapist was somehow contacting the youngsters and teachers in his school to "Put in a good word for him". He admitted that this seemed impractical and when pushed he would admit that possibly it was only a feeling or thought that he had, but none-the-less he felt "pretty sure" most of the time that the therapist was in fact actively interceding to cause people to treat him better. The "delusion" was particularly interesting in that it was accompanied with a great increase in Ralph's social activity and his comfort with it. He began to date and his parents reported that he now had several friends who frequently called him and came by to visit. Ralph's attitude toward this benevolent interference in his life was somewhat mixed. He admitted that he was pleased that the therapist wanted things to go well for him but stated that he felt somewhat badly that he could not do it himself. At no time, however, did he ask the therapist to stop interfering nor did he seem angry or resentful about the fantasied intrusion into his personal life.

This phenomenon persisted for approximately four months and then was abruptly dismissed as "a silly idea." During these four months Ralph solidified his social situation and his academic performance converted to a virtual straight A report without much apparent effort or studiousness on Ralph's part.

Around this time Ralph stated that he felt he only needed to come in weekly. This decrease in frequency of sessions was accepted by the therapist. Ralph used his weekly appointments primarily to report ups and downs in his fortunes in the dating game. He would periodically repeat his worries that he was ugly and that no girl would ever like him. These self-derogatory ruminations slowly became less and less frequent. Ralph gradually developed a capacity to formulate a psychological understanding of why certain relationships did not work out well. He became much more aggressive in pursuing girls that he liked. Although their physical attractiveness remained extremely important to him, he no longer pursued only the girl he regarded as the most beautiful in the class. He now preferred girls who were very attractive but also of interest to him as human beings. After a few months of weekly meetings Ralph stated that he thought he could handle his life on his own. This decision came soon after Ralph established a "steady" relationship with a girl. Ralph talked a good deal about this relationship which sounded basically healthy although the couple did spend a great deal of time alone. There did seem to be considerable mutual dependency in the bond. Still, Ralph and his girlfriend did socialize in group situations and both of them retained friendships with other youngsters.

In his final therapy session Ralph was obviously quite moved and with some difficulty expressed very sincere gratitude to the therapist for his help. It was clearly difficult for Ralph to do this since he had never been able to express any appreciation, open affection, or simple acknowledgement when his parents did nice things for him.

It had been three years since Ralph terminated his two years of psychotherapy. The therapist has received periodic follow-ups from the mother indicating that Ralph's improvement has continued. He is performing outstandingly in college and is engaged to be married following graduation next year. There is no evidence of psychotic thinking or of unusual interpersonal relationships.

It is also of interest to note that one year following termination of psychotherapy the father in this "perfect" family abruptly announced that he was leaving his wife for a much younger woman. At that time the mother came to the therapist for a period of supportive psychotherapy to assist her in dealing with this shocking event. She has been functioning extremely well since that time.

THE THERAPIST AS A CORRECTIVE SUPEREGO FIGURE

Another atypical treatment relationship which frequently proves constructive without actually measuring up to a genuine therapeutic alliance occurs with some youngsters who present with superego pathology. Johnson in her writings regarding the treatment of youngsters with superego lacunae has provided important guidelines in this area. She feels that a major aspect of the treatment relation with these youngsters is concerned with the search for an incorruptible adult model. In treating youngsters with superego defects the therapist must remain comfortably alert to the inevitability of efforts to corrupt his conscience. One can be sure that the patient will, with varying degrees of subtlety, try to get the therapist to join him in breaking rules or at least in condoning the youngster's asocial or antisocial behavior.

One therapist described a situation with a patient who was being interviewed in the course of a stroll. The adolescent was drinking a soda and as the therapist and patient passed a fence with a large sign which said "NO TRESPASSING" the patient casually tossed his empty bottle over the fence. The therapist was briefly in a quandry since any action on her part seemed to be corrupt. If she said nothing the patient could assume that she countenanced the littering. If she allowed the patient to climb the fence in order to retrieve the can that would involve defying the clearly posted sign. Fortunately, she had the presence of mind enough to stop and reflect out loud on the dilemma. She said that though it was hardly the end of the world, she preferred to follow rules even in this somewhat trivial matter. She considered the possibilities open to her and the patient's interpretation of them. She carefully avoided suggesting that the patient had deliberately put her in this moral bind. Her demeanor made it clear that she did not intend to move on or continue the discussion until a solution within the rules could be fashioned. After a few minutes of this the patient said sarcastically but with an undertone of respect, "Oh, if you're such a goody two shoes I'll get you out of this one." He picked up a fallen limb, raked the bottle to the fence, retrieved it and dropped it into a waste receptacle. The therapist complimented him on his ingenuity and thanked him for solving her dilemma.

Other youngsters may utilize the therapist more directly to strengthen their reality testing and superego controls as Aichorn has described. A handsome and muscular 15 year old boy with a history of multiple juvenile offenses regularly insisted to his therapist that he "didn't give a damn" what the therapist thought of his behavior. In spite of this avowal he gradually began to describe his planned antisocial behavior in advance during his therapy sessions. For example, he would tell the therapist that he badly needed some material object that he did not have the money to buy. He would then talk about the possibility of stealing the object or of dealing in drugs in order to obtain funds. The patient would then state that he knew the therapist disapproved of such activities but would then challenge the therapist as to how the problem could be solved without getting into trouble. At these times the therapist would offer various alternatives such as doing extra work around the home to obtain funds or saving up his allowance. Inevitably the patient would scoff at the advice but invariably he would follow it. The patient would then return to the next session to complain that the solution was dumb and that he preferred to do things as he had done them in his antisocial past. In spite of this constant harping and apparent hostility the patient continued to grow and develop, not only avoiding legal problems but showing steady improvement in school work, family relationships, and socialization.

Another 15 year old boy with strong delinquent tendencies and a history of almost homicidal rage outbursts and physical fights showed sudden and persistent improvement in his functioning shortly after he was hospitalized on an adolescent psychiatric unit. During group psychotherapy another patient asked the boy why he had stopped fighting with everyone and the patient explained, "My doctor is a champion boxer. I'm not about to tangle with that guy". The patient had learned that the therapist was a boxer from a hospital employee who had known the therapist in high school. In fact the therapist was 10 pounds lighter than the patient and had not boxed in 20 years. In situations of this kind the patient creates the therapist in some image which allows emergency control of his frightening impulses. It is important to recognize that although these images may be somewhat primitive and at variance with the self image of benevolent nurturing preferred by the therapist, they may be temporarily important to the patient. For a brief period the patient may need to provide himself with the fantasy of someone strong enough and aggressive enough to counter the tempestuous violence within himself. The image of this helpful authority can be gradually modified as the therapist demonstrates in his direct management of the patient a kinder, warmer but still reliable style of impulse control.

As noted in the introduction, we are on relatively uncharted ground when we accept or at least do not directly disavow such unrealistic images of ourselves. For one thing, we are much more vulnerable to countertransference errors because we are less guided by our tradition and training. Treatment relationships of this kind approach patterns described in psychodrama and go well beyond Alexander's notion of the corrective emotional experience. Since the therapist at least passively takes a role in the externalized drama created by the adolescent patient, there is considerable danger that the adolescent may be used for self gratification. For example, if the patient places one in the position of a powerful superego figure the therapist may unconsciously enjoy exercising this power and authority over another person's life. This gratification may prevent the therapist from helping the adolescent take control of his own destiny.

It is apparent that these special relationships must be regarded as temporary stages in treatment. Aichorn (1935) stated that the therapist who assisted the delinquent youngster by permitting and encouraging narcissistic transferences could not continue the treatment at the point where the patient became more neurotic and thus available for a more intensive and dynamic treatment experience. However, Aichorn actively pursued a transference of this kind and may have thereby limited his availability as an object of other transference tendencies. In some cases it does appear that the patient can come to understand his need for a distorted image of the therapist, work through this need and proceed to a more traditional alliance with the same individual.

The therapist must take complete responsibility for sorting out the emotional currents in these atypical treatment alliances. In the traditional therapeutic alliance, this responsibility can be shared to a greater extent with the patient. Supervision with peers or with more experienced psychotherapists is an important aid in maintaining objectivity and in preventing countertransference errors. Self scrutiny is also very important.

In reviewing these somewhat unusual psychotherapeutic encounters one can utilize the same questions which shed light on transference patterns with any patient.

"How does the patient seem to wish to view me?"
"What does he want from me?"
"What is this role that he is placing me in doing for his psychological functioning?"

The answers to these questions require a careful understanding of the patient's developmental history, his current level of psychological functioning, and his overall life situation. When the questions can be answered with some degree of accuracy the therapist can consider further questions.

"To what extent is it ethical and comfortable for me to serve this function for the adolescent patient?"

Giovachini (1974) has described one type of patient who is extremely difficult to tolerate because his transference pattern challenges the basic identity of the therapist as a helping person. Other unrealistic transference needs may be disturbing because of particular unresolved conflicts in the life of the therapist or because of current life problems which may be present in the therapist's personal realm. For example, if the therapist is involved in a legal action or other situation which requires genuine aggression, it may be too uncomfortable to be viewed as a fierce and combative figure by an adolescent patient.

One final question must be asked about the therapeutic relationship.

"Can this style of relating conceivably lead eventually to healthier psychological functioning for the adolescent patient?"

It does seem possible in some cases to assist a troubled adolescent without ever achieving a genuine therapeutic alliance. As implied earlier, perhaps the mechanism of growth is related to the adolescent's use of the therapist as a "real object." In these cases the patient creates in the person of the therapist a particular adult image which can be internalized to complete aspects of development which had not been previously realized. As in the case of Ralph, these notions regarding the therapist may be quietly discarded when the patient no longer requires them. In other situations, as was the case with Davy, the unrealistic expectations of the therapist are relinquished only with great reluctance and pain.

SUMMARY

Some preliminary ideas regarding treatment relationships which vary from the traditional therapeutic alliance and yet seem useful have been described in a tentative way. The positive potential of such treatment patterns as well as the dangers inherent in departing from a strict adherence to a therapeutic model have been described. In the following chapter we will turn to a consideration of the continuing process of psychotherapy.

BIBLIOGRAPHY

Adatto, C.P. 1966. On the metamorphosis from adolescence into adulthood. J. Amer. Psychoanal. Assoc. 14: 485-509.
Kohut, H. 1971. The analysis of the self. New York: International Universities Press.
Kernberg, O. 1968. The treatment of patients with borderline personality organization. Int. J. Psychoanal., 49: 600-614.
Johnson, A.M. 1965. Sanctions for super-ego lacunae of adolescents. In: Searchlights on delinquency. Edited by K.R. Eissler. New York: International Universities Press.
Aichorn, A. 1935. Wayward Youth. New York. Viking.
Aichorn, A. *op cit.*
Aichorn, A. *op cit.*
Giovachini, P.L. 1974. The difficult adolescent patient: counter-transference problems. Adolescent Psychiatry, 3: 271-282.

CHAPTER SIX

the problems of ongoing psychotherapy with the adolescent

GOALS OF PSYCHOTHERAPY WITH THE ADOLESCENT

Most, if not all, psychoanalysts would agree that the adolescent patient is not a candidate for a thoroughgoing and complete psychoanalysis (Adatto, 1966; Corday, 1967; Josselyn, 1957). It would be even more foolish to attempt total resolution of the adolescent's conflicts through psychotherapy. The goal, instead, should be to assist the adolescent to achieve an ego synthesis which would permit him a moderate degree of gratification within the limits of social reality (Gitelson, 1942, 1948). This synthesis may include many areas of unresolved conflict managed, bound, and partially neutralized by productive, growth-oriented compromise character formations. After all, the proper concern of adolescence is the construction of a viable and sustaining identity. The further refinement of personality is the task of young adulthood.

TECHNIQUES OF PSYCHOTHERAPY WITH ADOLESCENTS

Bibring (1954) has divided basic therapeutic techniques into the categories of suggestion, abreaction, manipulation, clarification, and interpretation. He has noted that psychoanalysis emphasizes clarification and interpretation, utilizing the other activities only to further the interpretive work. He includes within the meaning of the term *manipulation* all those actual emotional interactions between the patient and his therapist which Alexander might have called "corrective emotional experiences." Bibring says, "Manipulation . . . can be defined as the employment of various emotional systems existing in the patient for the purpose of achieving therapeutic change either in the technical sense of promoting the treatment, or in the curative sense, for manipulative measures too can be employed in a technical as well as a curative way."

Although the term *manipulation* seems a poor one in terms of its other connotations, if it can be taken in the neutral sense which Bibring intends, it can be used to describe the most important technical device utilized in the psychotherapy of the adolescent. If interpretation is the basic key in psychoanalysis, then the adolescent's relationship to the therapist, with the opportunities that this permits for new emotional learning experiences and the more effective utilization of "emotional systems existing in the patient," is the comparable key in adolescent psychotherapy (Gitelson, 1948). It is within this interaction that the adolescent can gradually recognize his emotional needs and learn which of them must be modified and which can be gratified safely in interaction with other human beings.

It is difficult to define precisely the differences between interventions which are appropriate to these goals as opposed to those which would be appropriate in psychoanalysis. Buxbaum (1954) has suggested that psychotherapy should focus on interpreting defenses rather than impulses. Although this is a useful distinction, it gives little practical guidance regarding the proper management of manifestations of impulse when they appear as transference phenomena in the course of psychotherapy. Bibring (1954) suggests that the basic difference between psychoanalysis and other dynamic therapies lies in the degree to which other therapeutic interventions take precedence over interpretation. Certainly, the interpretation of unconscious conflicts plays a relatively minor role in the psychotherapy of the adolescent.

When we attempt to state what *is* important in adolescent psychotherapy, we are reminded, as Freud stated long ago, that therapy resembles a chess game and, aside from the opening and closing moves, must be learned largely from experience and the study of the experience of others. This chapter does not try to substitute for this experience, but does try to define the goals of the game and to demonstrate some common strategic problems and their management.

UTILIZING THE THERAPEUTIC ALLIANCE

The Therapist as a Trusted Adult Friend

The very existence of a comfortable therapeutic alliance has substantial inherent and immediate value to the adolescent. It permits the adolescent to be dependent without the dangers involved in his dependent ties to his parents. The adolescent needs a trusted adult outside his family group, but may have few opportunities to find such a relationship in a society characterized by isolation of the nuclear family, overcrowded and impersonal classrooms, and neighborhoods without social cohesion. It is a necessary and valuable function of therapy to provide this kind of relationship.

The therapeutic alliance allows a moderate degree of psychological support, guidance, and reassurance to the adolescent. Most adolescents seek and will utilize advice and opinions from their therapist, especially if the therapist shows no special interest in controlling them or in demonstrating his adult superiority. In many adolescents, marked psychological growth follows merely from the opportunity to speak freely with an adult who quietly demonstrates his interest and respect.

Closely related to the supportive function is the educational role of the therapist. Often, the adolescent longs for an adult who can offer factual answers to troubling questions. Adolescents still worry that they may be sexually abnormal despite the increase in sexual sophistication in our time. The questions are more refined, and often more disguised, since few modern teenagers consciously fear that masturbation will drive them to insanity or cause hair to grow on the palms of their hands. Fear of homosexual impulses, concern about the size and appearance of genitals, worries over sexual attractiveness, concerns about body size or shape, unrealistic self-expectations in the dating game, fears of being hypersexed or hyposexed, and the like are commonly brought to the therapist. Although these questions can rarely be settled by education alone, since they often are partially rooted in unconscious conflicts, the adolescent deserves truthful answers. This at least helps the adolescent to distinguish those concerns which are realistic from those which are related to his personal problems.

A 16-year-old boy finally was able to drop his bravado and

confess his feeling that girls did not like him. He felt that he was ugly, even grotesque. He said that this bitter conviction was a major cause of his multiple delinquencies. The therapist asked how he knew that girls did not like him. As the boy discussed his interaction with girls, it became clear that he treated them in a haughty and superior manner to avoid being rejected.

The therapist encouraged him to try being friendlier to a few girls in his class and to report his results. He returned discouraged. He had tried friendliness, but nothing happened. The boy was further encouraged to ask one of the girls for a date. The therapist explained that the boy looked like a regular guy to him. He should take a chance, even though there was always the possibility that his offer would be rejected. The boy was told that girls expected to be pursued and that he could not expect them to show interest in him if he did not woo them. The therapist even helped plan an evening which a girl would enjoy and appreciate. Along with the practical advice, the youngster was openly encouraged and supported. The invitation was accepted, and the evening proved at least a partial success. The boy began dating fairly actively. His emotional reactions to dating experiences opened the door to exploration of the boy's sexual conflicts. Among other things, it soon became clear that the virtual delusion that he was ugly was related both to his "ugly" (that is, sexual) thoughts about girls and his perception of his mother's view of men and her early reaction to the sight of his penis.

Without the practical help and advice on dating procedures, which barely stopped short of dialing the telephone for him, the work of therapy could not have continued.

Dating is only one social reality which the adolescent may not understand. Some have a poor concept of how families, schools, communities, and governments function. The disillusionment which often follows the loss of childish belief in the perfection of hallowed institutions may lead to a bitter cynicism. After some of this disappointment is worked through, extensive reeducation regarding many aspects of the social and political facts of life may aid the process of maturation. Although the therapist should not present himself as a fount of wisdom on all subjects, he can raise questions and cite experiences which broaden the adolescent's view of his world. Since honesty is the cornerstone of the therapeutic relationship, this implies a willingness to admit that institutions are considerably less than perfect. As a rule, these discussions are much more valuable after the adolescent's superego can permit him to admit that he is not perfect either. He can then use knowledge of society's faults and problems as a guide to productive adaptation rather than a defensive self-justification.

The Therapist as Guide in the Search for Self-Understanding

These pedagogic and supportive roles, however, are secondary to the primary therapeutic goal of increasing the adolescent's insight into his own emotions and their effect on his attitudes and behavior. The therapist tries to teach the interested adolescent everything possible about his physical functioning and the world in which he lives, but this information is less valuable than those things which the adolescent learns about his own wishes, attitudes, and style of relating to other people. Information of this kind, however, cannot be taught at the level of intellectual discourse. It emerges almost as a byproduct of the experiential interaction between the adolescent and the therapist. The adolescent gradually reveals his emotional makeup in the interplay with his therapist. It is through the exploration of this living, vital experience with another individual in the here and now that the adolescent may be helped to know himself.

TALKING WITH THE ADOLESCENT—ON BEING NATURAL

In order to have a relationship of suitable intensity with the adolescent, the therapist must learn to conduct psychotherapy in a reasonably relaxed, conversational style. Most adolescents cannot tolerate a silent, totally passive, "blank screen" technique or a stiff and stilted style of therapy, especially not early in the treatment process. For a variety of reasons, including their tender narcissism, their distrust of adults, and their expectation of moral criticism, they usually react to silence and formality with intense anxiety and increased defensiveness. The difficult technical dilemma is to be reasonably talkative and responsive without being directive or intrusive. Once the adolescent gets unwound and comfortable, the therapist's silence is viewed as a positive willingness to listen. This recommendation to "chat" with the adolescent does not imply an awkward attempt to speak "hip talk" or to act like an adolescent. The adolescent is usually "turned off" by an adult who does not conduct himself like a grownup. What is appreciated is an openly friendly, quietly cheerful manner designed to make the adolescent as comfortable in the office as his inner feelings will allow him to be.

LET US FIGHT IT OUT

Arguing with adult psychotherapy patients is generally discouraged and even recognized as an indication of countertransference. Adolescents, on the other hand, expect to argue. They spend a great deal of their time arguing with parents and friends. In these arguments, they are often learning and changing, although they rarely admit it at the time. Frequently, an adolescent patient ends one session fiercely defending some viewpoint against his therapist and opens the next session by emphatically stating the very opinion he was battling only a few days before. The adolescent usually does not bother to credit the therapist for those ideas and insights which he appropriates. Naturally, the wise therapist leaves well enough alone and does not demand a credit byline. Although the adolescent himself may push an argument to the bitter end, he expects his therapist to be able to admit when he is wrong. The adolescent therapist cannot afford the appearance of arrogant certainty and pompous self-assurance. If he uses his knowledge too forcibly, the therapist may find that he has won an argument but lost a patient. In fact, whenever possible, the therapist should admit areas of ignorance, especially when the adolescent is knowledgeable on the subject. Since adolescents are always being taught by adults, they appreciate the opportunity to demonstrate their knowledge. Usually, it is easy to find areas in which the adolescent knows more than the therapist if the therapist is comfortable enough to accept this reversal of roles. Often, these occasions develop around the discussion of dynamics and motivations. When the adolescent realizes that his opinions and ideas are respected and considered on their merit even when they conflict with a statement made by the therapist, the therapeutic relationship is strengthened. Since many adolescents find it almost impossible to admit it when they are wrong, they admire the adult who can do so without a loss in self-esteem. Since they often feel that they "know it all" while actually fearing that they know nothing, they can relax with an adult who easily admits areas of ignorance and imperfection while demonstrating a comfortable self-respect.

THE ROLE OF CONFRONTATION AND INTERPRETATION IN PSYCHOTHERAPY OF THE ADOLESCENT

Confrontations and clarifications involve showing the patient *what* he is doing either without knowing it or without recognizing its importance or its connection with other behaviors and attitudes. In interpretation, we address ourselves to *why* the patient performs certain actions or expresses certain thoughts. Interpretations are often further distinguished as interpretations of defense or resistance and interpretations of content or impulse. These distinctions have some value in organizing a discussion of interventions, but within the reality of the psychotherapy process, they often merge and overlap. In our example of the youngster who smoked in his therapy session, the confrontation (*what* the youngster was doing) led quickly to a consideration of the *why* of his behavior. This is the proper sequence of effective interventions, since they must concern observable behaviors or attitudes which are important to the patient in the here and now. This is especially important in adolescent psychotherapy, since the adolescent typically encodes his most important messages in behavior rather than words (Easson, 1969). Effective confrontations which decipher these loaded behaviors often lead to anxiety and the emergence of powerful affects. Often, the impulses behind these affective storms are extremely apparent to anyone who has some understanding of unconscious motivations. The adolescent may reveal rather directly impulses and fantasies which are seen in adults only in states of extreme regression whether these are pathological or deliberately induced through careful psychoanalytic work. These impulses should not be interpreted. Nothing can be gained by pointing out the adolescent's homosexual, incestuous, or homicidal wishes even when these seem virtually conscious.

This kind of awareness is not useful to the adolescent and can only further compromise an already overburdened ego. The therapist instead extends himself to support the adolescent's ego, encouraging healthy defenses and emphasizing the adolescent's control over unacceptable impulses. One of the most important jobs for the adolescent therapist is to recognize those times when the adolescent is fearful of losing control. The therapist then offers help by recognizing the anxiety and by trying to assist the adolescent to find ways in which he can deal with the emerging impulses.

A large, aggressive, 16-year-old borderline youngster was regularly confronted with the fact that much of his behavior suggested a need to intimidate and compete with his therapist. This led to extensive discussion of his father's worship of his athletic prowess which was accompanied by excessive physical affection which verged on homosexual seduction.

In one session, the boy became extremely excited, anxious, and agitated as he compared himself with the therapist. He shouted that he was more intelligent, stronger, and "more of a man" than the therapist. The therapist agreed that he was a fine young man, but also noted that he seemed worried that he would misuse his capacities or only use them to show up other people. The therapist expressed his confidence that the boy would make constructive use of his abilities. The youngster calmed down somewhat and recognized that he had been saying, in effect, that he had a "superpenis." He laughingly asked, "I guess I made it sound like it was long enough to polevault with, eh?"

In the next session, he reported a wild session of joking fantasy with a male friend in which they carried the idea of penile size to more and more ridiculous extremes. They had collapsed in hysterical laughter over the recognition that the man with a "super SUPER penis" would not be able to wear normal clothing or even drive a car for fear of an erection. The homosexual nature of the fantasy was implied as the patient and his friend joked about the insoluble problems which the girlfriend of such a man would face.

The therapist accepted the joke and joined in the laughter. Later, he added that the youngster seemed also to be making an important and serious point about manhood, namely, that there was much more to being a man than physical attributes or even intellect. Although positive potentials were important, their constructive utilization was of even greater consequence. This episode seemed to be a turning point, and gradually the youngster was able to apply some of his competitive energy in more productive pursuits.

In short, confrontations are commonly used in the psychotherapy of the adolescent. On the other hand, interpretations of unconscious content are rarely indicated. When such impulses must be mentioned, as in our example above, the emphasis is properly on the fear of their expression. Such interpretations of fear of loss of control are accompanied by acceptance and support of any defense which is adaptive (or even just harmless) that the adolescent can muster to regain his sense of self-mastery. It should be noted that defenses suggested by the therapist are rarely useful to the adolescent. In fact, suggesting specific activities to handle an anxiety and replace acting out behavior usually interferes with the therapeutic alliance. The adolescent reacts as he does to well-meaning adults who counsel, "Instead of running all over town with those weirdo longhaired friends of yours, why don't you stay home and read a good book?" Only the adolescent can really feel his itch, and only he can figure out where to scratch himself.

Although I feel that this basic approach holds generally with adolescent patients, I am indebted to Dr. Merlan DeBolt for reminding me of one important exception to the rule. This occurs with adolescents who are painfully aware of wishes, ideas, or fantasies which they regard as insane and terrifying. These youngsters need open discussion of their fears of homosexuality, incest, or murder to accomplish what DeBolt has suggested might be called a "corrective associational experience" or a "corrective ideational experience." This allows them to learn that these ideas need not lead to action or to psychosis, but may be treated as uncomfortable but harmless thoughts. Confusions of this kind frequently develop in youngsters with limited intellectual ability or borderline ego function.

Mark was an attractive, husky boy of 16 who had a tested full scale IQ of 87. His academic performance was extremely poor in the highly competitive school setting that his ambitious parents forced on him. In addition, he showed an intense and unreasoning contempt for his mother despite all her efforts to show affection and concern for him. This antipathy was pushing Mark toward delinquency.

Gradually, the therapist began to recognize that Mark was terrified of being alone with his mother. Over a period of several months, a therapeutic alliance developed and the therapist felt that he must approach the matter directly with Mark.

"Mark," the therapist said one day, "I get the feeling that your mother scares you."

"Naw," Mark said. "But she *is* trying to ruin me."

"I'm not sure I understand what you mean by that."

"Well, it ain't something I can tell you, but she's trying to ruin me."

The therapist considered his choices. From a number of things Mark had said, he felt sure that the boy's fears of his mother were generated primarily by incestuous wishes. He also knew that Mark's thinking was extremely concrete and that he would probably misinterpret his mother's hysterical mannerisms. He decided to take the bull by the horns.

"Mark," he said, "have you ever had the feeling that your mother wanted you to fuck her?"

Mark hardly hesitated. He seemed relieved that things were out in the open.

"Yeah. She *does* want me to. It's not just something I think. She doesn't sleep with my dad. I don't think she ever has. She wants *me* to screw her."

The therapist knew that since Mark was adopted, it would be impossible to prove to him that his parents, in spite of separate bedrooms, did have intercourse. Instead, he elected to focus on Mark's direct perceptions of family reality.

"When did you first get the idea that she wanted you to have sex with her?"

"When she used to take nude sunbaths outside my window. I'd watch her and get a hard on."

The therapist explained that any teenage boy would react with excitement to the sight of a nude woman, whether it was his mother or not. He assured Mark that his feelings were perfectly normal under the circumstances.

The next several sessions were devoted to convincing Mark that if he acted on his idea that his mother was seducing him it would lead to much trouble for him. The therapist patiently explained that some women, including Mark's mother, had a strong need to be admired and loved. They did not know how to meet these needs except by sexually teasing men, even including their own sons. However, they were not really aware of what they were doing and would be horrified and frightened if the men responded to their sexual provocation. Mark was told flatly, "Boys do not screw their mothers, no matter how things may appear."

Following this period of therapy, Mark began to make a few friends outside of the home and even attracted a girlfriend. He continued to be somewhat cautious and distant around his mother, but did not constantly criticize her as in the past. He came to refer to his incestuous wishes as "those dumb thoughts I used to have."

GENERAL MANAGEMENT OF TRANSFERENCE
WITH ADOLESCENTS

Younger adolescents feel intensely and use projection with abandon. They often are totally unaware that their picture of another person is constructed within their own mind. Their "transference" feelings usually seem totally real to them. This holds not only in therapy, but in their relationships with other adults and peers. We have discussed the narcissistic needs which give rise to this style of relating in the chapter on the dynamics of adolescence. Because of this characteristic, the primary problem in managing transference in adolescent therapy is simply to convince the adolescent that the projection originates within his mind, not in external reality. This undertaking is, like much of life, easier to describe than to accomplish.

First of all, there is the adolescent's compelling need to be right in his opinion of others. He is struggling to construct a world which makes sense to him and within which he can live. Marked distortions are desperately defended, since to relinquish them would expose him to a confusing external world and to confusion within himself. He would be left without confidence in himself as one who can see life, including other people, clearly. Part of his desperate defensive structure designed to control his sexual and aggressive drives is founded in this obsessive concern with "being right" and being in control.

For most adolescent patients, considerable educational work must precede any clarification of transference distortions. The aim of this educative effort is to lead the adolescent to put his trust in a groping, gradual objectivity, rather than in an impulsive, intuitive, and subjective global grasp of interpersonal relationships. Later, when his intuitions are less defensive in origin, he can learn to trust them again and to utilize these "hunches" in conjunction with a reasoned, "secondary process" approach to life.

Many techniques may be valuable in accomplishing this goal. Often, it is wise to begin with work on those distortions produced by other people. The adolescent may describe a friend who has changed his attitude radically toward the patient or another person. The patient may be shown how both attitudes were based more on the friend's inner needs than on the characteristics of the object. It can be further pointed out that this is a common tendency in human relationships. The technique of universalization may be extensively utilized in this area. The therapist may wish to offer a benign personal anecdote if one comes to mind.

This educative groundwork will need to be repeated until the adolescent seems to get the idea. When he begins to offer illustrations of his own, concerning himself or others, these are accepted and the adolescent should be given credit for his wisdom. The simple comment, "I think you're right," from the therapist may encourage the adolescent to continue his objective scrutiny of interpersonal judgments.

A 16-year-old girl was panicky about her relationship with a special girlfriend. She lived in constant fear of offending the friend. This came to a climax when the friend called and dramatically demanded that the patient bring her drugs for a suicide attempt. When the patient refused, her friend became very angry and accused her of never wanting to help!

The patient was finally able to recognize that her friend was determined to feel rejected by others and had to engineer situations in which this would be unavoidable. Since the patient had similar tendencies both within therapy and with others, it was possible to use this insight productively later in her treatment. Whenever she was angry because the therapist had opposed self-destructive behavior, he would say, "Now you *know* I dislike you, since I won't even help you kill yourself."

THE ADOLESCENT WHO LIVES FOR POWER STRUGGLES

In some patients, there is little opportunity to build a background for acceptance of transference clarifications. These youngsters enter therapy with a flurry of hostile allegations about the therapist. They view the therapist as a computer, already programmed with preconceived ideas and attitudes about them and very definite plans for their future. Many of these youngsters come from families in which they have been the victims of just this kind of "externalization" (Brodey, 1965), or else have grown up in families in which virtually no limitations were set by parents. Instead, the parents have relied on cunning and underhanded techniques for influencing behavior. It is useless to deny the accusations of these youngsters, since experience has taught them that their parents deny their intrusive control while continuing to practice it. "We don't want to tell you what to do; we only want you to be happy. Now here's what you must do in order to be happy." It also does little good to ask what they themselves want to do. Their interest is only in opposing what they imagine to be the therapist's wishes, not in asserting their own. If you insist that you are interested in their wishes, they often reply that their wish is to quit therapy, run away from home, or take some other action which any responsible adult would have to oppose out of concern for their welfare.

It is difficult to relate to youngsters of this kind, since their whole existence is bound up in soliciting control struggles. Strictly speaking, their attitude toward the therapist is not an expression of transference so much as a symptom and a way of life. One can only empathically accept their anger and frustration while sharing in a friendly way the awareness that no therapist could please them, since they are determined to pick a fight. Therapy is designated then as a friendly battle (at least friendly on the therapist's side), and the therapist accepts his adversative role with as much grace and humor as he can manage. It is important to credit the adolescent with his victories in these sallies. As Holmes (1964) has pointed out, these victories will be numerous. Often in these cases, no true therapeutic alliance forms, and the therapist is actually conducting supportive psychotherapy, functioning more as an unaccepted and unsung guardian than a true psychotherapist. However, this role may be literally lifesaving for some of these youngsters. Some of them return, when they are older, with greater capacity to cooperate in therapy.

GARDEN VARIETY TRANSFERENCES

The more typical youngster shows transference attitudes which are subtle and related to the material which is emerging in therapy. Although the younger adolescents still tend to have difficulty in recognizing the internal origin of their transference attitudes, they can be prepared educationally to explore this possibility.

It is important to recognize and clarify transference as it appears. Often, the adolescent is reluctant to voice feelings about the therapist, especially if these are negative. It is usually up to the therapist to detect the tendencies implied in behavior and to verbalize them for the youngster at the proper time. For example, the adolescent may reveal a competitive oedipal transference by describing his accomplishments, only to diminish them quickly. The alert therapist notes this and assures the adolescent that he has a right to be proud of real accomplishments, noting that he behaves as though he expected the therapist to criticize either his accomplishment or his pride in it.

As in this example, it is usually necessary with the adolescent to point out his unspoken assumptions while simultaneously clearly disclaiming the projected distortions. Words alone are often not enough. After the transference attitudes are clearly demonstrated, one must actively show by attitude, words, and behavior that they do not accurately reflect the therapist's true characteristics. In short, the therapist tries to neutralize irrational transference distortions as quickly and totally as possible.

A 14-year-old boy was convinced that his therapist felt he was stupid. He was surprised when the therapist asked his advice about which make of automobile to purchase. The therapist asked for specific information which the youngster could easily supply from his extensive reading in this area. The youngster was especially impressed that the therapist actually wrote down the information he gave. Later, the boy expressed his amazement. The therapist said, "What's so strange about it? I know a lot about how people feel and behave. You know a lot about cars. You came to me for help; why shouldn't I ask for your help?"

In a similar way, the transference feeling that the therapist is disinterested may be offset by remembering the details of the patient's comments in a previous session or by actually offering practical help and advice.

Since the goal in adolescent psychotherapy is not to elicit regression and a transference neurosis but to increase ego control, these active interventions are indicated even though they would interfere with classical psychoanalysis. Transference is interpreted to the adolescent only to prevent interference with the therapeutic alliance. The therapist always acts to clarify the irrationality of the transference and to diminish its impact in the therapeutic situation.

This is not to say that transference attitudes are ignored or denied. The adolescent is not encouraged to pretend that his irrational feelings do not exist. These feelings are noted and brought to his attention. He is then helped to recognize that they originate in his own mind and is supported in his attempt to deal with them as creatively as possible. Every effort is made to interfere with the adolescent's tendency to deal with the therapist as a real object for his libidinal or aggressive drives. It should be recognized that this is a difficult technical problem, since only the older adolescent is capable of maintaining objectivity toward intense transference attitudes. The younger patient needs a healthy dose of reality and early intervention to prevent the development of an explosive and destructive transference.

There are certain types of transference patterns which regularly appear in the treatment of adolescents. All of them interfere with the therapeutic alliance and with ego growth in the adolescent and therefore require early recognition and active management.

The Erotic Transference

Sexual transferences are common in adolescent psychotherapy. They are extremely frightening to the younger adolescent who has developed neither a comfortable acceptance of his sexuality nor the subtle ego techniques for expressing these feelings with any finesse. As a result, open manifestations of sexual transference during the psychotherapy of younger adolescents are often panicky eruptions of a rather crude kind. At other times, the feelings are held in fearful secrecy. They are apparent only in the blushing, agitated confusion of the adolescent's behavior. Often, these youngsters simply cannot tolerate a young therapist of the opposite sex because of the overwhelming intensity of their sexual fantasies.

Even though older adolescents are better prepared to modulate their feelings, they still must face the incestuous implications of their responses much more directly than the adult patient who can partially rationalize his feelings since the therapist is an approximate age peer. The awakening of similar feelings in adolescents places them in the same fearful oedipal situation which they have been attempting to escape in their own family. If these stirrings are not actively managed, the result is often a precipitous flight from the danger represented by the therapy relationship.

A 14-year-old girl squirmed and twisted in her chair while telling her therapist of a fantasied relationship with an older boyfriend. During the recital, she was in an intense state of excitement. Her twisting and turning resulted in extensive exposure of her genital area. Her comments were crudely suggestive and her seductiveness was grossly evident. She seemed in a virtual frenzy of sexual excitement mingled with intense anxiety.

The therapist commented that her mind seemed to be more on fun than on the work of therapy. She agreed, giggling. The therapist stated firmly and gravely that the therapy hour was not a place for fun. She would have opportunities for fun with her friends, but the therapist was interested in understanding her feelings, not in having fun with her. This firm disavowal of interest in her seductive overtures allowed the girl to gain control and returned the emphasis of the session to therapeutic goals.

With great relief, she joked, "Boy, you're really square."

The therapist agreed firmly, "Yes. I am."

With older adolescents, the expression of erotic transference feelings is more subtle and approaches that seen in adults. Still, even the older adolescent can rarely handle sexual transference feelings openly. It would be unwise to focus attention on their origins or to encourage their elaboration. Instead, the therapist emphasizes their value in emotional growth and their defensive function, clearly and tactfully maintaining his unavailability as a real sexual object.

A 17-year-old girl left "gifts" for the therapist session after session. She forgot cigarettes, matches, change, and other small objects. During this time, she became more and more distant and quiet. When the therapist linked these two patterns of behavior, the girl blushed. She admitted to a fear that she might "get a crush" on the therapist. She did not want this to happen, since it would be humiliating and childish to have such a "puppy love."

The therapist assured her that she could feel friendly and emotionally close without necessarily developing a crush. He added that crushes were often expressions of liking and admiration which did not imply that the young person loved the elder in the same sense that she would someday love a person of her own age.

The therapist was attempting to offer himself as a friendly, supportive father figure who would not respond seductively to her.

The Omnipotent Transference

The omnipotent transference is even more seductive than the erotic transference with the adolescent. The expectation that the therapist will have answers to all questions and solutions for all problems bears enough similarity to some ordinary or at least fantasied relationships between the generations to be quite attractive. The therapist expects to offer some realistic advice and help to his adolescent patient in the normal course of conducting psychotherapy. It is easy to drift gradually into a relationship in which the adolescent presents as a helpless, idiotic emotional cripple, repeatedly rescued from disaster only because of the brilliance of the therapist.

As gratifying as such a situation may be to the therapist's narcissism and his own unresolved infantile omnipotence, it is catastrophic to the goals of psychotherapy. When these transference attitudes are challenged, the adolescent usually reacts with irritation or open anger. This occurs because the transference actually covers the adolescent's secret fantasy of personal omnipotence. After all, the adolescent grants the therapist his power! It is also the adolescent who enjoys its benefits. The therapist only serves as a dupe, fronting for the adolescent's defense against his fear of confronting reality without magical powers.

The Negative Transference

Adolescents, like younger children, can rarely tolerate continuing psychotherapy in the face of a strong negative transference. As indicated above, intense and pervasive negative feelings toward the therapist usually do not represent transference. They express, rather, an intensely negative attitude toward all adults in authority. Negative transference should also be differentiated from the defensive hostility which many adolescents flaunt. This "porcupine" attitude often covers painful feelings of shame, inadequacy, and anxiety. This type of negative attitude often disappears when the adolescent recognizes that the therapist will respect his feelings.

Some younger adolescents are so fearful of therapy that they cannot risk any positive attitudes toward the therapist. In this instance, the negativism represents an attempt to avoid therapy by forcing the therapist to reject them.

True negative transferences may appear early in therapy. This occurs when the therapist happens to resemble a disliked figure from the past. Such occurrences are rare. More frequently, early negativism results when intense ambivalence is split and the therapist is cast into the role of the bad parent. Often, the relationship with the parents improves superficially as a result of the split. If the parents cannot understand what is actually happening, they may consider the adolescent to be cured and withdraw him from therapy prematurely.

SOURCES OF NEGATIVE TRANSFERENCE FEELINGS. Later in therapy, true negative transference attitudes are usually more subtle and disguised than the global rejection described in the patterns above. The therapist may realize he is being slyly depreciated, pointedly ignored, or craftily maneuvered into ridiculous positions. These situations are marked by the collapse of the therapeutic alliance and disinterest in the therapeutic work.

These vague, unstated negative attitudes must be brought into the open for discussion. From the therapist's point of view, they should be explored objectively to determine their origin. We have already described the normal and ubiquitous angry reaction to those interventions which cause narcissistic injury to the adolescent. Any comment which interferes with a functioning defense, thereby increasing anxiety, naturally arouses some hostile feelings toward the disturbing influence. These angry feelings are not truly transference phenomena. They are affective reactions to the reality of the therapy situation. They are tolerated by the adolescent only because both his positive feelings for the therapist and his growth experience within therapy give him hope that the overall process will be beneficial to him. Because of this positive orientation toward the future, he can accept some pain in the present. Since he has a sense of trust in the therapist's positive attitude, he can forgive some injuries to his pride.

When faced with a hostile patient, the therapist must also consider the possibility that he has actually attacked the patient. Whether the assault has been direct, as in an angry or deprecatory response to provocation by the adolescent, or indirect, as in a subtle betrayal of confidence to the parents, the adolescent may be expected to retaliate angrily. To treat this reaction mistakenly as transference will only compound the therapeutic error.

THE THERAPIST AS FRUSTRATOR. True negative transference reactions occur when situations in therapy reactivate earlier experiences in which negative attitudes toward important loved objects predominated. They appear whenever the therapist, as a representative of reality, is seen as opposing gratification of libidinal (id) drives or appropriate "ego drives." They appear whenever the therapist himself seems to refuse to gratify emotional needs which appear legitimate and important to the patient. They also appear whenever the therapist is viewed as opposing appropriate drives for achievement, independence, and autonomy. Obviously, the feelings cannot be considered as transference if the therapist is *in fact* antagonistically opposed to his patient's wishes for pleasure and accomplishment. It is the inappropriate and incorrect projection of these attitudes originating from previous introjects which constitutes transference.

The therapist will, of course, unavoidably frustrate the adolescent. Therapy is designed to explore and investigate impulses, not to gratify them. However, the long-range goal of therapy is clearly to aid the patient to maximize gratification and minimize frustration.

The therapist may be seen as a frustrating parent when he questions the relative value of immediate pleasure as opposed to long-range goals. In the terminology of psychoanalysis, the therapist favors the reality principle over the pleasure principle. This stance is often mistaken for a generalized ascetic opposition to gratification. The adolescent has not as yet synthesized his drives with a wider appreciation of his own future survival and well-being. Often, he is willing to sacrifice prudent self-protection for the impulsive gratification of an immediate urge. Opposing this tendency frequently gains the therapist a reputation as a wet blanket with his adolescent patients.

Just as frequently the therapist can "spoil the fun" by interpreting the true motive behind certain "pseudolibidinal" activities. Pointing out that a planned seduction seems more hostile than sexual may produce intense resentment in the adolescent patient. Clarifying the destructive motives involved in helping a "friend" get drugs or run away from home can lead to rage at the therapist. In these instances, the therapist is calling attention to the hidden hostile pregenital components which the adolescent is attempting to "bootleg" under the guise of a loving act. It is this hidden hostility which is actually freed for expression toward the therapist. The therapist is accused of puritanical suppression to avoid recognizing that the rage actually belonged to the adolescent all along and was merely disguised, disowned, and projected.

On the other hand, the adolescent's anger because the therapist will not personally gratify his libidinal transferences is, from the adolescent's point of view, a justified response. The therapist is certain to let the adolescent down in this regard. The adolescent will direct many vague wishes and hopes toward his therapist. He may expect the therapist to fill various neurotic expectations magically. He may hope to become omnipotent, free of depressive feelings, or imbued with phallic power. He may hope for symbiotic nurture or libidinal gratification. Since the therapist cannot meet these needs, the adolescent will inevitably feel disappointed and even cheated. This, of course, produces feelings of anger toward the therapist, who may be viewed as spitefully withholding gratification.

"YOU DO NOT WANT ME TO SUCCEED." The adolescent patient who suspects the therapist of thwarting his ambitions is often struggling with strong destructive competitive urges. These may be oedipal or more primitive wishes to dominate or destroy the therapist completely. These urges cause guilt which may lead to fears of retaliation or to projection of the unacceptable impulses onto the therapist. These defensive maneuvers help to justify the hostile competitive feelings toward the therapist and partially relieve guilt and anxiety.

Management of the Negative Transference

In all instances of negative transference, there are basic rules which may help to restore the therapeutic alliance. First, the negative feelings must be accepted objectively as additional experiential data for therapeutic exploration. Objective acceptance implies not only the avoidance of counterattack, but also a quiet yet firm refusal to accept unrealistic blame. Occasionally, therapists, in a well-intentioned eagerness to appear fair and openminded, will accept excessive criticism and hostility from the adolescent without pointing out that the anger is irrational. This attempt to help the adolescent express his "true feelings" can interfere with the therapeutic process by implying that the feelings are justified by the therapist's personality or behavior. This obscures their intrapsychic and unconscious origin and confuses the patient. In addition, as Fromm-Reichmann (1950) has pointed out, inviting the patient to express his hostility actually serves to prevent the genuine expression of hostility and to protect the therapist from hearing honest anger from his patients.

As the adolescent is encouraged to explore the causes of his anger (or annoyance or irritation, if the adolescent prefers to soften his terms) in the same way that he has learned to study his other feelings in therapy, some clues usually emerge which help to clarify the general origin of the anger. The therapist can begin to guess whether he is being seen as a "spoilsport," a selfish withholding parent, or a competitive bully. These transference attitudes can then be countered by the therapist's words and actions as described above in the general section on management of transference. The question of how far the transference feelings should be allowed to develop before they are actively neutralized can only be decided by clinical judgment. Older, healthier adolescents can tolerate longer and more thorough exploration of negative transferences, whereas younger and more disturbed youngsters need quick and active aid in reality testing in order to sustain the therapeutic relationship.

A successful intervention which dissolves the negative transference reaction is often followed by a period of regression and depressive affect in the adolescent. In some instances, this depression may be obscured for a period of time by a defensive elation. The depression results from some degree of awareness of the personal origin of the frustrated wishes and a dawning recognition that the wishes are incompatible with reality and must be abandoned. It is always sad to realize, even dimly, that a gratification must be relinquished. During this period, the therapist must steer a close course between excessive sympathy and cold, unfeeling objectivity. When the adolescent is mourning a lost illusion, he needs both empathic understanding of his sense of loss and help in remembering that what was lost was, after all, always only an illusion. The pleasures of reality, although sometimes dimmed by complexity and responsibility, at least have the advantage of actually existing. The therapist gently encourages the adolescent to recognize that, with all its faults, reality is the only dependable source of pleasure.

The Therapist as Superego

Patients of all ages frequently see their therapists as superego figures. This tendency is especially marked in the adolescent patient. Indeed, the success of adolescent psychotherapy frequently hinges primarily on the skill with which superego conflicts are managed. These conflicts are strongly reflected in the therapeutic relationship and produce countless complex dilemmas. It is quite difficult to guide an adolescent toward a self-respecting sense of firm impulse control while also assisting him to relax the rigid, relatively passive, and asexual superego of latency.

Within the therapeutic relationship, the adolescent frequently sidesteps this developmental task by projecting his superego onto the therapist, as we have previously noted. All of the therapist's interventions tend to be experienced as superego sanctions. Because of his moral preoccupation, it is difficult for the adolescent to understand other rationales for foregoing the gratification of any impulse.

WHAT DOES YOUR CONSCIENCE SAY? The initial phase of the work with the adolescent's superego conflicts consists of recognizing and clarifying the pattern of his internalized moral prohibitions. It is crucial to demonstrate that these are the adolescent's own taboos, which he is attempting to ignore, externalize, or otherwise escape. The therapist insists, on the other hand, that the route to real freedom demands open and honest confrontation with these internal policemen. They can be altered only through conflict, not avoidance.

The techniques of confronting the adolescent with his own superego vary with the particular personality structures which are encountered. The most common pattern is the adolescent who rebels against his own conscience and then reveals his guilt through self-destructive behaviors. If the connection is repeatedly brought to the youngster's attention, he can gradually become aware of his sense of guilt and of the unconscious interdiction that he is violating.

Other superego restrictions produce only inhibitions and personality constrictions. These may reveal themselves in therapy as overcontrol of certain impulses or conversely as a defiant overemphasis on some aspect of life. For example, both the shy, inhibited adolescent and the brassy, insolently bawdy youngster may be revealing strong unconscious guilt feelings around sexuality.

Some youngsters present their superego problems more openly, clearly cognizant that their feelings of excessive guilt are irrational. Other adolescents expect to be relieved of guilt feelings while continuing to do things which are self-centered, exploitative, and destructive to others. There are also adolescents with defects in superego structure who require active confrontation. This is also necessary at times with youngsters who are attempting to escape superego pressures with various bribes and rationalizations.

A 17-year-old boy professed extremely high moral standards and was extremely critical of middle-class hypocrisy. At the same time, he did not hesitate virtually to blackmail his wealthy mother for money, utilizing the most flagrant and often dishonest manipulations to extort the cash that he wanted. This dishonesty was motivated by spiteful oral rage and rationalized on the basis that he had no respect for his mother and should get from her what he could. This behavior allowed the youngster to maintain a fantasy of symbiotic sustenance secretly while disavowing any sense of dependency. It gradually became clear that this secret delinquency was one source of the boy's nagging sense of inferiority.

He came to therapy one day nonchalantly planning purchase of a new automobile. The therapist asked where he got the money, since the youngster had been complaining of being broke. The boy explained that he had told his mother that he had learned he had a terrific "inferiority complex" which might be ameliorated by driving a flashy car.

"You implied that you learned that from therapy?" the therapist asked.

"No, but if she wants to think that, it's sure okay with me. It's not my fault she's stupid."

"It isn't okay with me. I don't want to be part of your con game. Besides, you are throwing away your chances in therapy for a bunch of chrome and steel. I can't go along with that."

"What do you mean?"

"Do you have any idea of how much that lousy car is really costing you? If you want to live the life of a con artist, that's your business, but let's at least be honest about what you're doing when you come here."

THE THERAPIST'S VALUES. It should be obvious that the therapist cannot remain completely neutral in moral questions. By the very nature of his work and his technical operations, the psychotherapist conveys a value system. Emotional honesty, self-awareness, fairness in interpersonal relationships, reasonable control of impulse, coupled with a tolerance of unacceptable fantasy and a preference for reality gratifications over neurotic gratifications, are values which are revealed by the therapist's general approach to the adolescent. Whether these values are derived from a scientific knowledge of the nature of man or merely represent a personal credo which characterizes most people who become psychotherapists is a debatable point. The therapist should be aware of the moral assumptions that he holds, regardless of their origins. London's (1964) book, *The Modes and Morals of Psychotherapy*, provides a thorough and enlightening discussion of many pertinent issues in this regard.

Since the adolescent therapist is even more of a pedagogue than his adult therapist counterpart, he should not hesitate to admit his moral biases frankly and to defend them energetically. Since the younger adolescent tends toward a "black or white," right or wrong view of morality based primarily on institutional sanctions, it is useful to him to discuss some of the more rational and informed foundations for moral conduct. Some degree of sexual restraint has more to recommend it than a puritanical fear of sin or a terror of the social stigma of illegitimate pregnancy. The dangers of exploiting others or of being exploited and the difficulties involved in accepting emotional responsibility for the sexual partner are only two of the issues which would recommend some degree of caution in sexual expression. It should be kept in mind, however, that the honest expression of one's own moral stance does not mean attempting to impose that morality on the adolescent patient. The youngster must reach his own definition of righteousness and live by that.

The adolescent is not only involved in a dramatic unconscious moral upheaval; he is also learning to think out his value system. The therapist must provide not only professional help in understanding the internal struggle, but a model as a rational adult with considered opinions regarding the proper conduct and meaning of life. He does not force these views on his young patient, but neither does he attempt to avoid his responsibility as an adult to offer his ethical conclusions based on a long period of considered experience and observation of human interaction. Such openness in discussion also encourages the adolescent to think about his own assumptions and to use his own powers of logic to the best possible advantage. Obviously, this kind of teaching should never deteriorate into self-righteous moralizing. The adolescent quickly loses interest when he feels that he is listening to a sermon. As Long (1968) has said, "In my own mind I think of therapy with adolescents as follows: The adolescent is alone and driving a car down the highway at 50 miles per hour, but has never driven before, has only watched others. I am in another car trying to shout advice to him. If he can make use of the advice he will, but he has to bring the car under control by himself. And I must first get across to him that I am not the 'fuzz.' "

SPECIAL TECHNICAL PROBLEMS

There are a few special technical problems which are regularly encountered in the psychotherapy of adolescents which deserve brief comment.

Embarrassment over Being in Therapy

Adolescents frequently feel intensely ashamed of their need for psychotherapy. This reaction is most common in the early stages of treatment, but may recur throughout the therapeutic encounter. The patient may complain either of a personal feeling of shame or of concern about what friends or others will think.

As we noted above, the adolescent is extremely ashamed of his dependency wishes. This developmental fact explains a large part of his discomfort in the therapy relationship. An exclusive emphasis on the normative aspect of this attitude, however, can obscure the specific meaning of the shame in particular patients.

Obviously, those adolescents who have the most intense dependency needs will tend to have the strongest feelings of shame. It is important to help them to see the wish for care which is hidden behind their fear of accepting help. This can be approached in the same way that other hidden wishes are gradually revealed, if the therapist is alert to its presence. What is important is the recognition that those adolescents who do not have marked dependency needs accept this part of therapy without undue fuss.

Some adolescents who express embarrassment are speaking for their parents. Although the social stigma associated with therapy has lessened in recent years, it has not disappeared. In addition to this cultural factor, many parents view the need for therapy as a negative reflection on their parenthood. The attitude is conveyed to the adolescent, who feels that his need for psychotherapy shames his family. Unless the parents can be helped to view the situation more objectively, therapy may be seriously compromised.

Finally, the adolescent who has marked feelings of social anxiety and inferiority may focus these on the therapy process. The youngster then blames psychotherapy for his lack of social success. One can only encourage these adolescents to persevere while gently refusing to accept total blame for their discomfort. The question of whether they should tell their friends that they are in treatment should be explored dynamically in the therapy rather than defensively answered.

Bringing Friends

Some adolescents, far from hiding their involvement in therapy, announce it widely in their peer group. This may represent, in addition to an expression of exhibitionism, an attempt to avoid serious involvement in therapy. Instead of a private and important relationship, therapy and the therapist become subjects of social chatter. However, there is some value in this sharing of the therapy experience. Often, the peer group can be helpful in lowering anxiety and the discussion may be a learning experience. In any case, as Easson (1969) has pointed out, it is pointless to forbid the behavior, since the therapist cannot enforce such a rule.

Other youngsters occasionally appear at sessions with friends whom they wish to bring into the treatment room. The motivations for such behavior vary widely, but, in my opinion, the action should be viewed as a transference behavior. If this is true, it should be treated as a communication to be examined and understood.

A 16-year-old boy appeared for his therapy session with a friend in tow. He asked if the friend could accompany him to the therapy hour. The therapist replied that the time was his and he could use it as he wished.

The two boys joked uncomfortably while the therapist watched quietly, occasionally commenting on the vaguely hostile tone of their conversation.

The patient finally asked his friend to wait for him in the reception area. When he was alone with the therapist, he asked, "Well, what do you think of my friend? My parents don't want me to run around with him."

"I don't really know him. What do you think of him?"

"I think he's fine."

"If you're sure of that, I wonder why you brought him here to get my opinion?"

The patient began cautiously to explore his feelings about his friend. He admitted reluctantly that the boy was immature, self-centered, and hostile to adults. He also began to look at similar traits in his own personality which caused him to be defensive when his friend was criticized.

In this instance, a friend was brought to therapy as a proxy. If the therapist criticized the friend, it would mean that it would not be safe to reveal certain unacceptable personal traits and attitudes in therapy.

The wish to refer a friend to the therapist, although often reflecting a positive attitude toward the treatment experience, may also express a wish for a smoke screen to divert attention from the original patient. Generally, it is wise to insist on exploring the motives behind the referral rather than to accept the new patient. If the friend clearly needs help and desires it, the patient may be directed to a competent colleague. Late in therapy, the referral of a friend may be an indication that the patient is ready to consider termination.

Requests for Special Attentions

Some adolescent patients develop intense dependency ties to the therapist. They may request extra appointments, telephone the therapist, or request extratherapeutic contacts of various kinds. When this type of behavior develops late in therapy, it often resembles the behaviors described by Balint (1968) in *The Basic Fault*. As Balint points out, there is little advantage to be gained by attempting to meet these primitive needs for nurture. What the patient does need is a quiet, undemanding therapist who can patiently allow the regressed patient to come to peace with his inner feeling of emptiness and deprivation. (For the genetic origins of this sense of inner emptiness and futility, see Winnicott, 1958.)

In adolescents, this sense of deprivation, of having lost something central to life, often leads to delinquent behavior. The adolescent feels that he has been gypped by life and demands to be recompensed. If the therapist can avoid being caught up in the flamboyant protest toward current conditions and can focus his attention on the inner state of incompleteness, the delinquencies often stop. The therapist must avoid, however, holding out a false promise of total gratification. As we have noted earlier, adolescence is not the time for extensive remediation of early fixation points. The therapist merely accepts the deprived adolescent's complaints and anger as emotionally legitimate while quietly encouraging the adolescent to confront the problems of maturity despite his feelings of emptiness and incompleteness.

Silence

Brief silences may represent productive and creative periods in psychotherapy with adolescents. In fact, the capacity to sustain a period of silence without excessive anxiety often marks a significant growth in self-confidence and acceptance of inner feelings for the adolescent. The therapist should not be quick to fill these silences.

More often, however, silences in adolescent psychotherapy are defensive. They serve to avoid the discovery and expression of angry fantasies which might appear if the adolescent spoke freely. The management of these defensive gaps in communication is extremely difficult with adolescents. It is almost impossible for an adolescent to tolerate the tension involved in remaining silent while confined in an office under observation. This tension is blamed on the therapist, thus increasing the hostile affect and further blocking communication.

In the older adolescent, silence can often be managed within the therapeutic alliance by interpreting the patient's fear of his angry impulses. In younger or more disturbed adolescents, it may be wiser to "let them off the hook" by talking to them or suggesting some activity after mentioning that they feel too upset to talk. This obviously means sacrificing some potential depth of therapy in order to salvage a tolerable therapy relationship.

In some adolescents, silence does not represent a transference phenomenon, but rather a character defense of inhibition and withdrawal. Some of these youngsters have never learned to view emotional communication in a positive way. These youngsters require skillful and tactful education in the value and techniques of conversation. During this period, the therapist must be prepared to carry the major burden of responsibility for the therapeutic dialogue.

Utilizing Dreams and Artistic Creations

Although the focus of adolescent psychotherapy is on ego functioning, this does not rule out the appropriate utilization of symbolic productions such as dreams, stories, poems, and paintings. The adolescent often is quite creative and we can learn a great deal from the study of his productions. This need not interfere with the emphasis on reality functioning if the therapist confines his comments about the symbolic materials to their relevance in the adolescent's attempt to achieve ego synthesis.

It is true that adolescents often offer their creative products to the therapist as a substitute for themselves. The unwary therapist may be drawn into a dispassionate intellectual discussion of the "ideas" contained in the art work as though these ideas were totally unrelated to the adolescent's life. Needless to say, adolescents should not be encouraged to retreat into autistic daydreams. However, dreams and creative fiction often reveal valuable information about the adolescent's real concerns even when he is attempting to avoid them.

Jimmy was a 16-year-old youngster with marked problems in adjustment. He abused drugs, totally rejected parental guidance, had dropped out of school, and showed little interest in the future or in any sublimated interests in the present. His conscious attitude was one of nonchalant disinterest in his plight. He said that the goals of adult life meant very little to him and that he intended to live merely for his immediate pleasure.

In the 10th therapy session, he reported the following dream:

"Our whole family was flying somewhere. My parents each had their own small private plane, but I was flying a B-17. I landed it on the first fueling stop, but then I became frightened. I knew that only one man had ever landed the B-17 alone, without a copilot or crew. I was afraid to take off again."

Discussion of the dream content yielded the information that Jimmy had taken a few flying lessons in the past, but had been frightened by some near accidents on landing. His instructor had to take over the controls to complete the landings. Jimmy felt scared and ashamed. He admitted that he had been questioning the importance of learning to fly. He easily accepted the suggestion that his loss of interest in flying was related to his anxiety about his ability to handle the plane. The therapist commented that people often convince themselves that they do not really want to do the things they are afraid they cannot do. Jimmy admitted that he really wanted very much to learn to fly.

"By the way," the therapist asked casually, "what was the name of your plane?"

"B-17," Jimmy replied.

"When is it that you'll *be 17?*" the therapist asked pointedly.

"Why, next month," Jimmy replied.

Then, the light dawned. "You mean you think the dream was about being scared to grow up, to be 17?"

"The prospect has been known to scare guys, especially if they feel they have to manage it completely alone," the therapist replied.

Then, he added with a grin, "Sometimes, they get so worried about it, they have to pretend they don't care at all."

Although Jimmy was somewhat skeptical, his own dream and associations were difficult to dismiss completely. Gradually, his derogatory attitude toward the goals of maturity diminished. He began to discuss plans to return to school with appropriate concern about his ability to handle age-appropriate tasks.

The therapist did not comment on the family fragmentation or the possible sexual implications in the dream, since these were not relevant to the current phase of therapy.

Similar therapeutic work may be accomplished by using the artistic creations of adolescents.

David was a brilliant and creative boy of 17. His considerable talents were severely dulled by obsessive rumination, intellectualization, and isolation of affect. He entered therapy because of chronic depression and gnawing fears of masculine inadequacy.

Although he forced the issue of psychotherapy by threatening suicide, he was initially extremely resistant to all attempts to link his behavior and feelings to his actual life situation. He was particularly opposed to any discussion of his feelings for his mother and father. He assured the therapist haughtily that he was in no real sense their offspring and that they no longer mattered to him in the least.

A few sessions later, David timidly brought a poem to his therapy session. It was an excellent literary effort.* The therapist told David frankly that the poem was good. David did not like the poem, however. He dismissed it as "egocentric adolescent raving."

The therapist asked David what the poem was intended to convey. After a supercilious lecture on the bourgeois mentality that sought a moral message in every work of art, David condescended to comment on a few of the "thematic images" suggested in the poem. He said that the poem "obviously" had to do with the complete solitude of the individual and his "terrifying isolation in the infinity of existential vacuity."

The therapist said that he saw a different theme. He read the poem slowly aloud, verbally underlining the numerous words and phrases in the poem that seemed to refer to birth symbols and to man's origin from his fellows rather than his isolation. The therapist stated calmly that the *poet* may have intended to emphasize man's separation from his fellows, but the *poem* seemed to say that no man sprang full formed, alone, and self-sufficient from emptiness.

David listened quietly, and then asked softly, "So I am my father's son?"

"What do you think?"

"I think that I am asserting through negation."

"Can you put that simply for me?"

"You know what I mean. He must really have a hold on me if I have to pretend I don't even know him."

The therapist's goal was not so much to call attention to the father-son relationship, but to help David move beyond

---

* The poem was so excellent that it was later published under the author's real name. Therefore, it cannot be reproduced here without compromising confidentiality.

his sterile autistic isolation and into affectively meaningful material. Once again, the adolescent's own words, written in a sense in spite of himself, were the agents of change.

ONGOING THERAPY AND THE ADOLESCENT'S PARENTS

Psychotherapy with the adolescent has an additional complexity which so far we have mentioned only briefly. Even when the therapist has a clear grasp of the therapeutic alliance, considerable skill at conversing with adolescents, and the ability to recognize transference and handle it therapeutically, he may still run into difficulties related to the adolescent's family. We turn now to a consideration of the technical problems raised by the complex interrelationship of the adolescent and his parents.

CITED AND RECOMMENDED READINGS

Adatto, C. P. 1966. On the metamorphosis from adolescence into adulthood. J. Amer. Psychoanal. Ass. 14: 485–509.

Balint, M. 1968. The basic fault: therapeutic aspects of regression. London: Tavistock Publications, Ltd.

Bibring, E. 1954. Psychoanalysis and the dynamic psychotherapies. J. Amer. Psychoanalyt. Ass. 2: 745–770.

Brody, W. M. 1965. On the dynamics of narcissism: I. Externalization and early ego development. Psychoanal. Stud. Child 20: 165–193.

Buxbaum, E. 1954. Technique of child therapy: a critical evaluation. Psychoanal. Stud. Child 9: 297–333.

Corday, R. J. 1967. Limitations of therapy in adolescence. J. Amer. Acad. Child Psychiat. 6: 526–538.

Easson, W. M. 1969. The severely disturbed adolescent. Chap. 3. New York: International Universities Press, Inc.

Fromm-Reichmann, F. 1950. Principles of intensive psychotherapy. Chicago: University of Chicago Press.

Gitelson, M. 1942. Direct psychotherapy of the adolescent (1941 symposium). Amer. J. Orthopsychiat. 12: 1–14.

Gitelson, M. 1948. Character synthesis: the psychotherapeutic problem of adolescence. Amer. J. Orthopsychiat. 18: 422–431.

Holmes, D. J. 1964. The adolescent in psychotherapy. Boston: Little, Brown & Co.

Josselyn, I. M. 1957. Psychotherapy of adolescents at the level of private practice. In: Psychotherapy of the adolescent. Edited by B. H. Balser. New York: International Universities Press, Inc.

London, P. 1964. The modes and morals of psychotherapy. New York: Holt, Rinehart & Winston, Inc.

Long, R. 1968. The observing ego and adolescent development. Rev. Inst. Nac. Neurol. (Mexico) 2: 8–21.

Winnicott, D. D. 1958. Primary maternal preoccupation. *In:* Collected papers. London: Tavistock Publications, Ltd. (New York: Basic Books, Inc.).

CHAPTER SEVEN

the parents of the adolescent patient

THE PARENT-CHILD RELATIONSHIP DURING ADOLESCENCE

Many parents would agree that adolescence is the most trying period in the experience of rearing a child. For the parents of the disturbed adolescent, this phase of growth may be virtually unbearable. Problems which have been latent become menacingly overt. Dependency problems blossom into pitched battles as the adolescent invites parental involvement and help by his maladaptive behavior, and then vilifies the parents for babying him and trying to live his life for him. Competition becomes vicious as the adolescent's overdependence on intellectualization and grand sweeping generalities lead him to view the parents as narrow, dull, and ineffective. Superego externalization causes the parents to be viewed as harsh and joyless on some occasions, as immoral and self-indulgent on another day. Any parental defensiveness, self-justification, or counterattack provokes a vengeful rage and a sullen sense of martyrdom.

There are basic elements of duplicity in both generations during this developmental phase. The adolescent is actually struggling against intensified dependent and sexual ties to his parents. At the same time, he wishes to gain autonomy and independence. This combination of increased emotional investment coupled with the urgency to escape the family is hardly conducive to openness and honesty in the adolescent's interactions with his parents.

On the other hand, many parents of disturbed adolescents are dishonest in their relationships with their children. Although consciously claiming to desire independence and maturity for their youngsters, they unconsciously undermine growth because of their neurotic needs. They act to prevent separation, heterosexual ma-

166

turity, or self-sufficiency in their child when these would threaten their own tenuous adjustment or result in an unbearable sense of loss to them. The degree of tenacity with which the parent clings to the adolescent varies with many factors including the extent of parental psychopathology and the realistic sources of substitute gratification available to the parent. The widowed mother, living alone on meager funds, obviously faces greater problems in relinquishing her last son than a happily married woman in comfortable financial and social circumstances, although both must deal with some sense of loss. Both the adolescent and his parents have reasons for obfuscating the terms of the unwritten contracts which regulate their interchanges.

ENTER THE THERAPIST

The therapist who ventures into this devious and supercharged intrigue as a catalyst to emotional growth can expect to become embroiled with both parties. In order to work successfully with adolescent patients, one has to accept this involvement with the parents. Even when the parents are referred to a colleague for therapy, they will usually still insert themselves directly or indirectly into the adolescent's therapy. This involvement should be expected and utilized. Attempts to avoid it or deny its occurrence are futile at best, at worst tragic. The probabilities of a successful treatment are increased by planning a constructive reaction to the welter of emotions between parent and child. Ignoring the certainty that these forces will be expressed in the therapy can only leave the therapist blindly reacting to the manipulations of both his patient and the patient's parents. Although the technical approach may be individual psychotherapy of the adolescent, the therapist must remember that the entire family is the real patient.

This does not mean that the therapist adopts a touchy and pugnacious determination never to be "sucked in" by neurotic family patterns. It does mean that the therapist is alert to the multiple determinants and implications of the communications which he receives from the parents or from the child about the parents. It means that this awareness is utilized to promote growth and independence and to protect the vulnerable and crucial therapeutic alliance with the adolescent. If this bond is sacrificed in order to pacify immediate strains in the parent-child relationship, the therapist has lost the effective foothold necessary to help the family. All attempts to influence and manipulate the therapist, whether they originate from the adolescent or his parents, must be received with the same respectful, objective, exploring attitude which is accorded all other relevant material. This analysis of underlying meaning determines whether the therapist reacts to the manipulation with interpretation, firm limit setting, or temporary acquiescence. The therapist tries to choose the response which offers greatest promise of promoting the long-range goals of the therapy.

THE PARENTS AND THE THERAPEUTIC CONTRACT

The effort to develop a workable therapy contract with the parents of the adolescent begins in the postdiagnostic family conference. The most common roadblock at this early stage is the therapist's failure to insist on the necessary conditions for an effective psychotherapy. This reluctance to "drive a hard bargain" may often be a response to parental ambivalence about the proposed psychotherapy. Their conscious or unconscious fears that the family homeostasis may be jeopardized lead parents to threaten, offer deals, or otherwise attempt to influence the conditions of therapy. These efforts will not be difficult to manage if the therapist keeps the minimum requirements of outpatient psychotherapy clearly in mind.

Basic Conditions of Outpatient Psychotherapy

1) The patient must have a real choice about beginning and continuing therapy after clearly understanding its nature and purpose. Of course, several interviews may go by before the adolescent has finished testing the therapist, sending up trial balloons, and generally "casing the joint." Only then does he have any real understanding of the nature and purpose of therapy. Simply telling him what therapy is all about accomplishes very little. It is sometimes useful to offer a negative adolescent a definite number of interviews in which to decide whether he wants to involve himself in therapy. Even if his decision is positive, his willingness to accept and to continue therapy may be evidenced only by his appearance

at his sessions. If he comes without being threatened, bribed, or physically coerced, this may be accepted as prima facie evidence of an interest in the treatment process even if he grumbles constantly and regularly questions the need for therapy. On the other hand, if he must actually be forced to attend the sessions, it is unlikely that progress is possible. Some modicum of responsibility for his own treatment must be assumed by even the very young patient. If a youngster is unwilling to accept this degree of responsibility for his behavior and his difficulties, it is likely either that the family is strongly invested in his problems, that his problems do not give him enough serious difficulty to justify therapy, or that he is so immature, irresponsible, and unable to accept guidance that his problems could best be managed in an inpatient setting.

2) The adolescent must be allowed to come to therapy for *his* problems. A psychotherapy program explicitly or even implicitly undertaken to shape the adolescent to some parental expectation or to persuade or dissuade him in regard to a particular action is doomed before it begins. The adolescent must be in therapy for himself. *His* reasons for coming must be accepted and therapy must begin with his concerns. Of course, in the long run, successful therapy may produce some or all of the results which would please the parents, but this happy circumstance must only be a fortunate byproduct of autonomous choices made by the emotionally maturing adolescent himself.

The adolescent must separate and individuate himself. His goals must be his own, neither arising from passive compliance to parental wishes or based on blind rebellion against those wishes.

3) The patient's communication with the therapist must be confidential unless or until the *therapist* feels that a clear danger to his patient or others exists. The parents can expect to be told whether therapy is progressing satisfactorily, but not the feelings, fantasies, and concerns which the adolescent voices in treatment. They have a right to know "how things are in treatment," but not "what is going on in treatment."

4) The therapist and his patient must have an honest relationship. The therapist cannot agree to lie to his patient. Although he will not "tell all" to the parents, he must feel free to inform

the patient of the occurrence of each contact with the parents and the content of these interactions at any time that this information seems therapeutically relevant or at any time that the adolescent wants to know. The therapist will "keep secrets" from the parents, but will, if it seems indicated, feel free to "tell all" to his patient.

5) In matters which pertain directly to the treatment process, there can only be *one* therapist. If the adolescent verbalizes feelings about the therapist at home, these should not be evaluated by the parent, but should be referred back to the next therapy session. If the adolescent expresses uncertainty about continuing therapy, he should be told to discuss this concern with the therapist as he would discuss any other idea or feeling. If the adolescent asks his parents' opinions of a comment or a procedure employed by the therapist, the parents should ask the adolescent what *he* thinks and whether he has discussed his reaction with the therapist directly. If the parent feels the therapist has behaved inappropriately, he should discuss this feeling directly with the therapist.

These requirements may sound autocratic, stringent, and unrealistic. Many parents react to them as if they were just that way. They feel that the therapist is intruding into the sanctity of their home to dictate their management of their own child. As a matter of fact, this is precisely what he is doing! However, it must be recalled that the therapist is assuming this authority at the request of the family. He has been hired to lead the family members in their effort to improve family functioning. He cannot perform this job as therapeutic leader unless the parents grant him authority in matters pertaining directly to the psychotherapy.

If the therapist is so passive, nondirective, or timid that he fails to explain the role that he must play, he is in no position to confront the parents when they trespass into his area. If he does not assume firm therapeutic leadership, he may soon find himself being utilized as family scapegoat. The family members may handle their hostilities, anxieties, and depressions by turning them on the therapist. That poor fellow may soon feel like the bystander who tried to break up a marital argument and ended up being attacked by the husband and wife, now comfortably united in their rage at the outsider.

Even more frequently, the adolescent will attempt to avoid limits and feelings of guilt by playing the parents against the therapist. The parents can avoid being drawn into such manipulations if they have a clear conception and acceptance of the therapist's temporary leadership role.

The parents are likely to become angry when the therapist sets limits on them, just as the adolescent reacts with anger when his acting out is questioned and opposed. This should not deter the therapist from doing his job. If the family is treatable, the parents will come to respect the therapist for his courage and his determination to assume his responsibilities. If they intended all along to employ the therapist only so long as he did not really interfere with the status quo, it is better to get that fact out into the open.

Of course, it is not necessary for the therapist to be belligerent or combative. He must remember that he serves purely at the family's pleasure. He is never in the position of telling the family what they must do, only what must be done if therapy is to succeed. Even in this, he must humbly remember that he may be wrong. However, it has been said that wisdom consists of acting on the basis of incomplete information. The therapist must be a decisive leader even though he cannot claim absolute certainty. If he has good reason to believe that a request for a vacation, a schedule change, or a family discussion about the therapist interferes with therapy or represents resistance, it is his duty to convey this opinion frankly and with conviction. If parental behavior continually interferes with therapy, it is his duty to explain that treatment will be impossible unless the parents are able to understand and change their disruptive actions.

Function of the Treatment Contract

The contractual terms discussed are intended as a guide for the therapist in making arrangements with the parents for treatment. A rigid demand for absolute compliance with these conditions would stifle the parents' interaction in the treatment process. The list of conditions is not presented as a binding package deal during the postdiagnostic family conference. Generally, only those points which are raised directly or indirectly by the family need to be emphasized. The others are merely mentioned in a brief, matter-of-fact manner. Even though parents agree to this compact, they are likely to break one or more clauses under the pressure of emotions stirred in the course of treatment. The previous explicit or tacit agreement, however, allows the therapist to highlight the motives involved in the breach, since the parent cannot claim simple ignorance of the proper helpful role in regard to the treatment process. The parent who cannot accept the contract, as well as the parent who accepts and then complains that the agreement is unfair, also reveals his family-bound pathology directly to the searchlight of therapeutic curiosity. It must be emphasized, however, that parents do deserve education regarding the goals and methods of psychotherapy. If they do not understand these goals and methods and their own proper role in facilitating their achievement, they may interfere with the therapeutic undertaking out of simple ignorance, which may be misunderstood as neurotic meddling.

The real importance of guidelines is to help the therapist to avoid falling unknowingly into unsatisfactory agreements. By holding firm ideas of the working conditions that he needs, the therapist is alerted to recognize those parental anxieties which lead to unwillingness to allow their youngster every possible advantage in the treatment situation. When parents begin to negotiate for unworkable contracts, the therapist has an alarm system that warns him not to defeat himself in his therapeutic effort before he even gets underway.

Enforcing the Terms of the Contract

Actually, the therapist has no power to enforce any of the clauses of the therapeutic contract with the parents. Their cooperation depends on their understanding of the reasons that the therapist makes certain requests and the extent of their trust in his professional competence and his benevolence toward the entire family.

In a very real sense, the therapist not only must maintain a shaky therapeutic alliance with the adolescent, but also must maintain one which may be even more tricky with the parents. The alliance with the parents is partially cemented by their mature wishes for their youngster to improve and attain self-sufficiency. Therapy cannot be conducted if the parents are totally devoid of this healthy desire. Fortunately, this bleak condition rarely exists in parents who seek treatment for their adolescent. Usually, this hope for successful maturation is present, but is opposed by a variety of anxieties, neurotic ties, and cultural expectancies. The therapist must appeal to the best in the parents in an attempt to strengthen the healthy portion of the parental tie with the adolescent.

Mr. and Mrs. Jones brought Janet, their 13-year-old daughter, for psychiatric evaluation because of poor school performance, a dawdling, passive refusal to perform household chores, and general "emotional immaturity." Mrs. Jones particularly complained of Janet's clinging, demanding attitude toward her.

A most cursory evaluation of the family relationships revealed serious strains and blatantly neurotic accommodations to many hidden conflicts between family members. Mr. Jones was an extremely successful television executive. Because of the pressures of his job and a poorly defined "heart condition," he expected and received remarkably solicitous treatment from all family members. Nothing was expected from him in the home. Janet and her sister understood that they must remain absolutely quiet when he was in the house. Mr. Jones's heart condition was especially sensitive to any angry sounds. The mother threatened the children with the responsibility for their father's death whenever they argued or fought while he was within earshot. Even if the mother became annoyed with them and shouted, she blamed them for this threat to the father's health.

In fact, the mother nagged the children and especially Janet, the older, constantly. She hovered over their every move and was preoccupied with the fear that they might be kidnapped due to her husband's prominence.

Janet was a timorous, anxious child. Her manner was obsequious and pollyannish to a degree which suggested conscious caricature of her mother's expectations. She spent her diagnostic interview explaining her many academic and social problems, besieging the therapist with demands for advice and instant help.

After diagnostic study, the therapist told the parents that Janet needed psychotherapy. The parents' role in the problem was approached warily and counseling was recommended for them. Mrs. Jones spoke for them and stated that she did not wish to have treatment. She explained that a friend of hers had become overly dependent on a therapist and that she felt therapy might "ruin" her. She also felt that therapy might be upsetting and "too much for Mr. Jones's delicate health." The therapist wondered if the couple had similar fears about Janet's therapy. Mrs. Jones admitted that she did, but expressed confidence in the therapist, whom she felt "seemed to understand what Janet needed."

Somewhat reluctantly, the therapist decided to try to work with Janet. His diagnostic hunch that Janet had considerable hidden strength proved correct. She moved rapidly into an active therapeutic alliance and made remarkable strides toward an increased maturity.

The parents were very pleased with Janet's initial changes, since they discerned a new openness and sense of responsibility at home coupled with considerable improvement in her schoolwork.

However, when Janet suddenly made friends with Dolores, a mildly rebellious and sexually aware girl, the mother's attitude toward therapy underwent a rapid and drastic change! She telephoned the therapist to tell him coldly and firmly that she thought Janet no longer needed treatment and, in fact, was afraid treatment was making Janet worse. With some difficulty, the therapist convinced her to come to his office to discuss the reasons for her change in attitude.

Mrs. Jones had calmed down by the time she arrived for her appointment. She said she recognized that it had been silly for her to say Janet should quit treatment. If she had stopped to think, she would have realized that Janet was mistaken in her notions that the therapist approved of the friendship with Dolores! Mrs. Jones was sure the therapist would clarify the matter and show Janet how harmful the friendship was to her.

The therapist agreed that this was one possible course of action. He wondered, however, what Janet's reaction might be if the parents and the therapist took over the responsibility of choosing appropriate friends for her. Would she perhaps be tempted to return to her old pattern of irresponsibility and total dependence on adults? Might it be better to permit her some freedom in this area, maintaining safeguards by structuring the time which Janet and Dolores spent together in a wholesome manner? The therapist admitted that this approach represented a calculated risk. Dolores might have a negative influence on Janet; however, if the parents and the therapist maintained a friendly relationship and showed respect for Janet's good judgment, she might discuss her interactions with Dolores openly and allow them to help her utilize the relationship constructively. The therapist empathized with Mrs. Jones's wish to help Janet avoid danger. He pointed out that he and Mrs. Jones were in total agreement on this point and need only discuss the best techniques for achieving this goal without causing excessive dependency. He also told Mrs. Jones quite frankly that he understood that it frightened her when she did not know exactly what Janet was thinking and doing.

Mrs. Jones began to cry. She confessed that she knew the therapist was correct. In fact, she knew all along that he would suggest this approach and that it was the proper one. She recognized that she had wanted to remove Janet from therapy to avoid discussing the emotions and family problems which caused her to want to "treat Janet like a two-year-old." Then, she said, "I realize I'm going to need to study that whole mess. Oh, well, I knew if I came here today, I'd leave with a psychiatrist's name in my hands."

Mrs. Jones meant that she had finally decided to accept referral for psychotherapy.

Preserving the therapeutic alliance with the parents frequently requires both encouraging the healthier aspects of the parent-child relationship and sympathetic acceptance of parental anxieties and needs. This combination of factors must also be utilized in helping the parents to involve themselves in collaborative therapy or counseling.

REFERRING PARENTS FOR TREATMENT AND COUNSELING

A purist might argue that all troubled adolescents come from troubled families and that therefore all parents should have personal therapy in conjunction with their child's treatment. In practice, however, many parents do not consciously recognize any relationship between family problems and the symptoms of their disturbed adolescent. A fierce resistance is the only result if these parents are arbitrarily forced into a treatment relationship.

The most important factor to be considered in deciding whether to refer parents for psychotherapy or casework is whether such a step is really necessary.

Do the Parents Need Treatment?

The presence of a clear relationship between parental attitudes or marital patterns and the psychopathology of the adolescent does not necessarily mean that it is crucial for the parents to have treatment. Some parental problems are the result, not the cause, of adolescent difficulties. It is hard to grow up, and there are enormous variations in the adaptive equipment which each child receives through the accidents of heredity, prenatal and neonatal illnesses, and uncontrollable environmental experiences.

Over and above these considerations is the fact that parents often grow over the years, whereas their children may carry some precipitates of earlier difficulties in the form of character defenses or symptoms. The father who was anxious and unsure of his competence at age 24 may be a much more relaxed and accepting father at age 36. His 16-year-old son may still need therapy because of defensive patterns which he developed at age four in order to deal with his father's excessive oedipal rivalry. Treating the father in the present would not necessarily assist the adolescent to resolve his (now internalized) problems with male authority.

Some adolescents may even be encouraged to evade responsibility for their own problems if the parents' need for treatment is overemphasized. It is obvious that many young people manage a satisfactory adjustment despite fairly marked psychopathology in their parents. Since effective psychotherapy with parents may well require two to three years and extend beyond the adolescence of the young patient, the therapist certainly cannot demand complete parental mental health as a prerequisite to the successful treatment of his young patient. Generally, it is wise to encourage the adolescent patient to accept his parents as "givens" and then to assume the responsibility for managing his own life productively. If the parents become healthier, with or without therapy, so much the better.

When Parents Must Have Help

Still, there are family situations which are incompatible with psychotherapy of the adolescent. The youngster who lives in a family which maintains itself by encouraging the adolescent to assume a role inappropriate to his age (such as an infantile or, conversely, an adult role), an inappropriate sex role, or a role which is clearly destructive (such as a criminal or "stupid" role) can rarely utilize a therapeutic approach which permanently excludes the parents. Curiously, these youngsters are often surprised by the recommendation that their parents receive therapy; in fact, they often oppose treatment for the parents. This observation may be useful in diagnosis and planning. The adolescent who shrieks, "Why don't you treat my parents? They're the ones who need it," may not be the youngster whose parents have drawn him into a comfortable neurotic impasse.

Those parents who do need treatment must often be brought gradually to a recognition of their need by their child's therapist. Careful preparation is often necessary if the parents are to utilize a therapeutic experience constructively. Therapy which is undertaken without a felt need is rarely successful. Some parents arrive for the diagnostic evaluation with a vague recognition of the family's involvement in the adolescent's problems. Others readily come to such an awareness during the diagnostic process in the postdiagnostic family conference. Still others, like Mrs. Jones in our earlier example, can recognize their enmeshment only after improvement in their child disturbs the family homeostasis. Because of this third group, it is often necessary to plan treatments which begin with only the child in treatment, but with clear knowledge that *eventually* the parents will need direct help. This help is offered when the parents are ready to use it. They are led to recognize their need through their contact with the child's therapist. These early contacts are discussed more fully below.

It should be noted that a valid recognition of involvement in a youngster's problems must be differentiated from the defensive offer to "do anything that will help our child." This passive offer to be "worked on" does not imply any usable awareness of the family pathology. The current sophisticated, "I know we must be doing something to cause all this," may also mask an unspoken blithe attitude of, "But I don't have the slightest idea of what it could be, nor do I really care to know!"

Needless to say, the task is far from completed when a successful referral for therapy is accomplished. The skillful cooperation of two therapists in a collaborative treatment arrangement is a complex topic in itself. The therapists must depend on mutual respect, open communication, and emotional honesty to avoid being manipulated into overidentification with their respective patients to the extreme detriment of the overall goals of therapy. When a collaborative therapist treats the parents, the interactions with the parents described below are kept between the parents and their own therapist whenever possible. In the following section, these interactions are presented primarily as they occur when the adolescent's therapist is working alone.

THE PARENTS AND THE ONGOING THERAPY
OF THE ADOLESCENT

The Telephone Contact

During the therapeutic work with the adolescent, some continuing contact with the parents is necessary to ensure their cooperation and support. The telephone is a useful instrument for much of this contact. The parents may be instructed to call if they have information or questions. They are told that they should let their adolescent know when they call and the general topic of discussion. Experience shows that most parents do not abuse this opportunity to contact the therapist ad libitum. Early in the therapeutic contact, the calls may be frequent; however, these calls usually decline fairly rapidly. If the therapist reserves a specific period in his day for returning phone calls, the arrangement need not be burdensome. The parents who do call with extreme frequency make up one group of parents who require direct treatment. In the course of these telephone contacts, along with occasional interviews, the therapist has the opportunity to create a trusting and understanding relationship with the parents. This will allow him to make referral for personal treatment a positive and meaningful recommendation. The parents often come to recognize their need for help through their relationship with the therapist and are more accepting and motivated for treatment. Although some difficulties may arise around transferring their therapeutic relationship, this gap can usually be bridged through the cooperative efforts of the two therapists. The parents' therapist must accept the early allegiance to the adolescent's therapist and avoid competitive responses and professional jealousy. The adolescent's therapist must respect the parents' therapist and assist the smooth transfer, tactfully resisting the parents' efforts to cling to him. Joint sessions involving the parents and both therapists may help to convey the mutual respect of the team and aid the parents to accept a team concept and approach.

Parents Who Never "Bother" You

It was mentioned that anxious, uncertain, or controlling parents, who tend to telephone frequently, make up a portion of those who need referral for treatment. Without this assistance, they find it difficult to provide the living area of maximum freedom and personal responsibility safely surrounded by firm boundary lines of acceptable behavior which the adolescent needs if he is to reap the benefits of psychotherapy.

Those parents who never call the therapist may need help even more. Most of them are so frightened of "doing the wrong thing" that they exclude themselves from their child's life. Some of them are merely displaying a lack of interest in the youngster or outright rejection of the child. Some of the parents have brought their adolescent for psychotherapy only as social insurance so that no one can ever accuse them of not "doing everything possible to help the child." Involving these parents is difficult, if not impossible. Even if the attempt is unsuccessful, it helps the adolescent to see and accept the reality of his family situation. It is difficult enough to grow up in a rejecting home without the additional burden of being deluded about the facts of the matter.

Telephone contact with the parents, then, has both therapeutic and diagnostic value. In utilizing this and other contacts with parents, it is worthwhile to keep Irene Josselyn's (1957) perceptive words in mind. "If anxious parents are not always equated with meddling parents and parents who remain remote from the situation until or unless the therapist appeals to them are not always seen as rejecting parents, if instead the parental attitude toward treatment is incorporated in the overall evaluation of the case, the relationship between the adolescent, his parents, and the therapist will have greater likelihood of success."

If the contacts between the therapist and the parents are handled openly with the adolescent, these contacts should not interfere with the therapeutic alliance between the therapist and the child. It is possible, of course, to create problems through the inappropriate management of the relationship with the parents. Parents usually call for advice on the management of adolescent behavior, for recommendations for dealing with family crises, or in order to seduce the therapist into an alignment with them in the neurotic family conflict. The motives for contact must be evaluated, not only with each family but in each individual instance, in order to respond appropriately.

The Value of Advice and Education

Often, the appropriate response is to provide the advice or information which is requested. Many parents have only the vaguest notion of what behavior to expect from an adolescent. They may be deeply concerned over one piece of behavior which is age-appropriate while blandly accepting other behavior which evidences severe distortion of normal development. The therapist should provide the parents with information regarding the developmental phase. This can be done directly and also by suggesting reading sources which may assist the parent. Our recognition of the central role of emotional factors in shaping parent-child relationships often leads to an excessive depreciation of the value of the intellect. In past generations, knowledge of normative child behavior was disseminated informally through the extended family and the cohesive wider community. Since this effective casual instruction is largely unavailable under current social conditions, it must be replaced by more formal educative efforts. Parents need models of family interaction and child behavior, not to adopt blindly, but to utilize as guidelines. Books such as those from Gesell and Ilg on normative behavior, as well as books like Ginott's (1969) *Between Parent and Teenager* and Missildine's (1963) *Your Inner Child of the Past,* which deal with emotional interactions within the family, are helpful to parents. These books cannot substitute for personal therapeutic contacts, but they may potentiate their value. The therapist should read carefully any book which he recommends to parents in order to be sure he agrees with its general philosophy. A complete knowledge of the book's contents will also allow the therapist to spot any parental distortions and discuss them with the parents.

The therapist also advises freely about matters which directly concern the psychotherapy. He is the expert on the subject and should not expect the parents to know whether the child can safely miss sessions, reduce their frequency, change therapists, or terminate. In these matters, he needs the observations and opinions of the parents to assist him, but the final decisions are his.

Advice to Avoid

There are traps to avoid in advising parents directly. These mistakes may be generally described as any intervention which accepts the "cookbook theory" of child rearing, that is, the overemphasis on parental behavior rather than parental feelings and attitudes. Specifically, this problem frequently arises around requests for advice on "discipline." The parents who need support in this area often are unable to use it wisely. If they are extremely unsure of their prerogatives, they may counter their youngster's angry reaction to limits by announcing that the limit was recommended by the therapist. This appeal to "expert opinion" has the effect not only of completely negating the adolescent's respect for his parents, but also of interfering with the nonauthoritarian therapeutic alliance. This devious exercise of authority merely causes both parent and therapist to appear frightened of direct communication with the adolescent. If the therapist must assume a limit-setting function with his patient, he should do so in a direct, person-to-person manner.

Other parents who ask advice regarding discipline merely want the therapist to join them in their effort to dominate the adolescent. Dispensing explicit advice on techniques of controlling the child is rarely in harmony with the therapist's goal of increasing the adolescent's autonomy and indepedence, regardless of the motive which drives the parents. It is wiser to explore the goals and aims of parental discipline, leaving the methods completely up to the parents.

Many parents do need help in understanding the purposes of limit setting. Fuller knowledge allows them to evaluate the complex reactions of their adolescent to family rules and to use these reactions as information which will help them to understand the teenager's real needs. They should be assisted to see the plea for control and structure which may be hidden in flagrant rebellion. Some of them can understand the ways in which their youngster may utilize "crime and punishment" to deal with his guilt. They are also helped to see that their anxiety about granting reasonable freedom to an adequately functioning youngster may represent envy of his vitality or fear of being deserted. As I have suggested elsewhere (Meeks, 1967), the management of limits is a delicate barometer of the emotional climate between adults and adolescents. It should be fully utilized in the therapeutic effort, not closed off by rigid directions from the therapist.

Helping Parents to Manage Crises

Any therapist who accepts the responsibility of treating adolescent patients must expect parental telephone calls announcing crises within the family. Parental anxiety is high, not only because of the adult's tendency to project and expect the worst from the adolescent, but because of the adolescent tendency, based on impulsivity, to deliver the worst. Many emergency calls from parents are disguised requests for support, muted complaints about the course of therapy, or subtle attempts to lure the therapist into a family intrigue. These can generally be recognized for what they are by the obvious disparity between the level of parental anxiety and the magnitude of the behavioral problem described. The therapist, of course, insists on a leisurely exploration of the questions raised; if necessary, he schedules a full interview for this purpose.

Mrs. Smith called her son's therapist in the evening. She apologized for bothering him, but rushed ahead breathlessly.

"I don't know what I can do with Jeff! He refuses to study for his midterms. I know I should let him handle this, but you can't just stand aside and watch them ruin their lives! What should I do? Should I force him to study?"

"How would you do that?" the therapist inquired.

"That's why I called you. What can I do?"

"I'm not sure you need to do anything. Jeff's been doing pretty well in his work lately, hasn't he?"

"Yes, but he's going to ruin it all. You must tell me some way to get him to work."

"What does your husband think?"

"Oh, he isn't here. He's out of town this week. I'm so mad at him! He's never here when I need him."

"Have you been feeling pretty alone?" the therapist asked.

"Yes," said the mother, crying. "I sure have. And now Jeff won't even let me help him with his work. He ordered me out of the room and said he'd study like he wanted to. I only wanted to help him!"

"I know that, Mrs. Smith. I guess some company would be nice for you, too. I think your loneliness and need for company when your husband is away are things you ought to discuss in your next therapy session."

"What about Jeff?"

"I believe it would be best to respect his wish to work alone. After all, you and your husband have just put a lot of work into helping him to take responsibility' for his own work—sink or swim."

"Well . . . I guess you're right. I may just call up a friend and visit a while to relax myself."

"That sounds like a pretty good idea to me. I do think this is something you ought to explore pretty carefully with Miss Jones [her therapist] next time you see her."

There are some situations, however, that do constitute bona fide crises. Most of these are discussed in Part Two of the book which deals with special problems in adolescent psychotherapy. Suggestions for dealing with the parents involved in such emergency situations are offered there.

When confronted with crises of any kind, the therapist often feels that he is walking a thin line between overinvolvement in the situation and a failure to assume appropriate helpful responsibility. It is obvious that a realistic emergency situation such as a suicide attempt or a runaway cannot be met with excessive therapeutic aloofness and cold objectivity. At such a time, parents need very direct emotional support and explicit advice on handling the problem. At the same time, the therapist must be careful not to be stampeded into an antitherapeutic action by parental anxiety and manipulation. It is wise to ask for full information before taking action. One does not wish to advise that the police be called in order to protect a runaway when the actual situation is merely one of the adolescent being out of the home for three or four hours without notifying the parents of his whereabouts.

The therapist also attempts to avoid usurping parental responsibility or permitting the parents to dump a trying situation entirely into his lap. An example might be the therapist's personal participation in a search for a runaway. Only in extremely rare and unusual situations would such a departure from the therapeutic role into direct care for the adolescent be appropriate.

This wavy and indistinct border between directing the therapy and directing the adolescent's daily life is the line of demarcation between parental responsibility and therapist responsibility in all matters pertaining to the adolescent. The adolescent patient himself should assume as much responsibility as he can on both sides of the line. When he is not able to take care of himself, the parents assume responsibility temporarily until he is able to handle the job again. When the lapse in responsibility directly affects his psychotherapy, the parents should defer to the therapist and be guided by him.

The therapist should never permit himself to be maneuvered into taking greater responsibility than he can realistically discharge. If the patient is suicidal, homicidal, or otherwise in real-life danger, the therapist must inform the parents and insist that they assume ultimate responsibility for their child. Of course, the therapist offers all possible assistance to them in this undertaking. Some explicit approaches to managing these situations are suggested in Part Two of the book.

TALKING WITH THE ADOLESCENT PATIENT ABOUT HIS PARENTS

Just as the parents of the adolescent need help in understanding and assisting their youngster through this turbulent phase, the adolescent needs direct assistance in dealing with his parents. The typical adolescent has many complaints about his parents which may be presented so convincingly that the beginning therapist is tempted to identify with the apparently victimized youngster, viewing all his difficulties as understandable reactions to parental unfairness. With greater sophistication, the therapist comes to realize that many of these complaints are unjustified in reality and represent primarily projected adolescent pathology. This focus, true as far as it goes, overlooks the interactional nature of family pathology. Although the adolescent may be entirely incorrect in his accusations, his basic sense that his parents are actively contributing to his psychopathology may be entirely accurate. Parents do have emotional needs and emotional conflicts and thse are often inappropriately expressed in the parent-adolescent interaction. Sooner or later, this portion of the adolescent's problem must be faced in his psychotherapy. It is unrealistic to ask the adolescent to face and accept painful realities about himself, his society, and his friends while protecting the parents from similar honest appraisal. In his role as guide, the therapist will be drawn into this exploration of parental personality and motivation. Often, he will have to accept or reject interpretive comments offered by the adolescent, and at times he will need to share his own impressions of unconscious family pathology.

It should be obvious that the therapist is on dangerous ground whenever he deals with any material which cannot be directly verified with his own patient. With the adolescent and his parents, the therapist runs the additional risk of being manipulated into taking sides in a neurotic power struggle. The adolescent may use therapeutic comments as ammunition to attack his parents. This misuse of information is more common early in therapy before the adolescent is able to face his personal responsibility for his problem, his conflicts, and the course of his life. The therapist should be sure of the therapeutic alliance and confident of his patient's growing maturity before verifying parental psychopathology to the adolescent. Even then, the adolescent must be helped to see that the existence of psychopathology in his parents does not excuse him from responsibility for managing his own life. To blame his parents for his failure and unhappiness may merely allow the adolescent to continue being miserable. To understand why his parents may have had some problems in parenthood may permit the adolescent to forgive them and concentrate on making the most of his own assets and liabilities.

The greatest hazard to the successful resolution of the adolescent's resentment toward his parents is the countertransference of the adolescent's therapist. There are some therapists who relate well to adolescents but who fail therapeutically with them because of their own unresolved (and often unrecognized) resentment of their own parents. These therapists are still locked in a chronic state of adolescent rebellion themselves. They often overtly or covertly encourage their adolescent patients to wallow in their refractory rage toward their family. The therapist and the adolescent may then avoid facing the inevitable need to accept the burdens of maturity. Unfortunately, they also forego maturity's gratifications and pleasures.

Perhaps, the core dynamic behind such prolonged spite is the stubborn refusal to accept the bitter fact that no one is omnipotent and that each human being must face the struggles of existence without a magic ally. As long as one can mesmerize oneself with complaints about "how it could have been if only my parents had been different," one can hold onto a dream of a nirvana that might have been.

Of course, there are other factors which may interfere with this therapeutic step. The therapist may overidentify with his patient, especially if the parents are hostile, rejecting, or irresponsible in their behavior toward the adolescent. It is helpful to remember, however, that these parental attitudes are shaped by the parents' endowments and experiences. If the therapist adopts a deterministic, causal view toward his adolescent patient's psychopathology, he should allow the parents a similar objective acceptance. All parents are doing their best with their children. There are no bad parents, only some who are unequal to the demands of parenthood. The therapist may need to offer firm restraint on some of the parents' destructive floundering, but he cannot permit himself the luxury of casting them in the villain role. His adolescent patient settles for this easy way out on pain of perpetual psychological invalidism. Some parents make it quite difficult for their adolescent to grow up, but this does not change the nature of reality. The adolescent must grow up anyway, or live with the misery of a lifetime of emotional infantilism. The therapist must help the adolescent to accept this difficult fact. He can be very gentle in this confrontation, but he must also be very firm.*

Rebellion versus Freedom

The adolescent also needs help in seeing that his perception of himself as a younger child and his wishes to enjoy a more dependent relationship with his parents frequently lead him to overreact to their expectations and wishes for him. Even when the parents are controlling and push the youngster toward preconceived goals, the adolescent must learn to be free to reject or (even more difficult) accept these goals according to his own needs and abilities.

---

* A widespread reluctance to force this issue is suggested by Masterson (1967, page 134) as one possible reason for poor long-range therapeutic results in his study of treated adolescents.

Often, the adolescent mistakes rebelliousness for freedom. He cannot choose any goals which happen to coincide with parental desires, even when the goals are identical with the adolescent's own ambitions. Obviously, under these circumstances he is not free to do what he wishes. The adolescent can sometimes grasp this through an allegory: "It seems to me that if you were ravenously hungry and your parents commanded you to eat a beautiful and delicious steak, you would refuse!"

The adolescent also needs help in recognizing that the parental tendency to "treat him like a child" does not actually make him childish. He is only in danger from his own childish wishes. The immature adolescent takes umbrage if his parents dare to remind him to drive carefully. The mature adolescent recognizes the concern and anxiety for his well-being implied in the warning and responds reassuringly to the parents. Even if he suspects that the overconcern has roots in suppressed hostility toward him, he still realizes that the hostility is not expressed because the parents also *love* him and are fearful that their anger will harm him. He is aware that he is a separate person with ambivalences and defenses of his own. This complex understanding is eloquently expressed in his simple explanation, "Aw, they're good parents. They're just worrywarts. Hell, I'm not perfect myself."

"If Only I Could Get Away From Them"

Frequently, adolescents express the desire to leave home. This wish is part of the fantasy that they could be mature if only they did not have to live with their parents. In some cases, there is a degree of truth in this idea. There are parents who undercut healthy adolescent independence. However, even in these families, geographical distance will not resolve the adolescent's ambivalence. Sooner or later, the adolescent must be willing to give up the regressive gratifications that the family offers in favor of maturity and independence. In other words, the adolescent's most dangerous opponent in his struggle for independence is his own wish for dependency. Some adolescents can understand the clarification, "Could it be that you want to run away from home quickly to avoid thinking about really growing up and leaving home?" This paradox can be expanded by pointing out that a poorly considered, precipitous departure from home may actually be designed to ensure failure, a parental rescue, and continued dependency. As Blos (1967) has commented, these youngsters are "doing the wrong things for the right reasons." In these adolescents, this conflict is often reactivated with the therapist as termination approaches. They are tempted to "quit" treatment prematurely to avoid openly facing the pain of separation which would appear during a planned termination.

SUMMARY

In many respects, the management of the complex relationships between the youngster and his parents and between the parents and the youngster's therapist is the most important and delicate task of psychotherapy during adolescence. The therapist must obtain and keep the trust and cooperation of the parents without compromising the adolescent's movement toward independence from the family. The parents must be mobilized to accept and support the eventual goal of the young person's emancipation. Often, they will need the support of their child's therapist, if not personal therapy, to bear the pain of releasing the adolescent and reestablishing family homeostasis without him.

After the qualified therapist has performed an adequate diagnostic study, chosen an appropriate candidate for outpatient psychotherapy, formed a therapeutic alliance with parents and child, and effectively responded to the ongoing problems of psychotherapy, he still faces one final crucial task. He must effect a termination at the correct time and in a constructive manner. Some of the issues and techniques involved in this phase of the therapy are considered in the next chapter.

CITED AND RECOMMENDED READINGS

Blos, P. 1967. The second individuation process of adolescence. Psychoanal. Stud. Child 22: 162–186.

Ginott, H. G. 1969. Between parent and teenager. New York: Macmillan Company.

Josselyn, I. M. 1957. Psychotherapy of adolescents at the level of private practice. In: Psychotherapy of the adolescent. Edited by B. H. Balser. New York: International Universities Press, Inc.

Masterson, J. F. 1967. The psychiatric dilemma of adolescence. Boston: Little, Brown & Co.

Meeks, J. E. 1967. Some observations on adolescent group leaders in two contrasting socioeconomic classes. Int. J. Soc. Psychiat. 13: 278–286.

Missildine, W. H. 1963. Your inner child of the past. New York: Simon and Schuster, Inc.

CHAPTER EIGHT

termination of psychotherapy with the adolescent

TERMINATION OF THERAPY AND THE ADOLESCENT PHASE OF DEVELOPMENT

In an earlier chapter, I suggested that the technically necessary process of forming a therapeutic alliance with the adolescent has the additional beneficial effect of strengthening the adolescent's observing ego. This therapeutic instrument, therefore, has a curative value of its own because it promotes a developmentally crucial task. The proper management of the termination of adolescent psychotherapy is perhaps even more important, since the basic function of all adolescent development is to complete a "second individuation" (Blos, 1967). The separation from the therapist, both physically and psychologically, is an integral part of the entire psychotherapeutic process. Many of the earlier gains of psychotherapy may be lost through unskilled management of the issues and technical problems raised in the termination phase. It is equally true that this part of therapy offers the opportunity for observing and partially resolving many adolescent dilemmas which may remain latent until the adolescent is confronted with termination. The series of decisions concerning the methods of ending an important personal relationship arouses important developmental conflicts. Often, the actual leavetaking in therapy comes to symbolize the process of loosening the bonds to internalized parental images and giving up the magical omnipotent and passive expectations which go with them. When the termination of psychotherapy becomes the microcosmic representation of this accommodation to young adulthood, it is indeed a momentous event in the adolescent's life. This is often the case in the treatment of youngsters in middle and late adolescence, especially the latter.

One may expect a wide gamut of defensive and regressive maneuvers as the adolescent attempts to deal with the anxieties which accompany the important psychic restructuring related to termination. Emotional upheavals, symptom recurrences, and episodes of self-destructive fantasies and even behavior (often calculated to provoke rescue and reinstatement of dependency) may alternate with wishes to flee prematurely or deny the importance of therapy and the therapist, to "run away from home to avoid leaving."

It follows from these developmental considerations that the termination of psychotherapy with the adolescent must be correctly timed, sensitively related to his particular needs, flexibly managed, and conducted with maximum alertness to complicating countertransference issues.

DECIDING TO TERMINATE THERAPY

In my opinion, successful psychotherapy contracts with adolescents tend to be unnecessarily prolonged. This may result in a blunting of the developmental thrust toward independence, which partially nullifies the positive impact of the therapy. Individuation, the goal of adolescent development, is best served by assisting the adolescent toward a workable character synthesis and then quickly moving aside so that the adolescent's new strengths propel him toward real and available objects outside of the sheltered therapy office. The problem of course is to have reasonable confidence that the synthesis is stable enough to permit continuing individuation in the real world rather than pseudoadult "shadow playing" of old and outmoded childhood relationships (Blos, 1967). It is my impression that the therapist frequently withholds this confidence too long from youngsters who have clearly found the right path to maturity out of an anxious desire to walk along and guard the adolescent all the way to the goal. Actually, much growth can occur once the previous "vicious circle" is converted into a "virtuous circle" (see Wender, 1968). There are other motives for unduly delaying termination which are discussed below. Even if the therapist accepts the premise of early termination, he still has to establish some guidelines for deciding when to consider its initiation.

General Patterns which Suggest that Termination Should Be Considered

Both Menninger (1958) and Fromm-Reichmann (1950) have offered excellent descriptions of the general changes in a patient which suggest that termination is near. Hiatt (1965) has elaborated these and offers explicit and useful guidelines for terminating psychotherapy. Even though these authors were dealing with adult patients, many of the basic ideas contained in their discussions of the problem of termination can be extrapolated to adolescent psychotherapy.

In the adolescent, as in the adult, one looks for symptomatic improvement, a heightened capacity for nondestructive pleasure (especially in interpersonal relationships), greater comfort with the acknowledgment and appropriate expression of a wide range of emotions in himself and others, a capacity to laugh at himself, and other quasi-objective phenomena which Hiatt (1965) has listed in detail. In addition, one expects a more objective attitude toward the therapist. Intensive transference reactions leading to expansive overevaluation of the therapist's skills, capacity to nurture, or wisdom, as well as hostile devaluation and belittling of his abilities, should be minimal and should be recognized as distortions by the adolescent patient when they do occur.

Normal Compared to What?—The Need for Developmental Norms

The problem of deciding when termination should be considered is complicated in the adolescent by the need to measure the characteristics mentioned in the above section against a scale of developmental norms. For example, some tendency to mild depressive episodes, interpersonal touchiness, and a slightly shy and coquettish treatment of the therapist are expected behavioral characteristics of the 13-year-old adolescent girl. They do not indicate a need for further therapy. Older adolescents gradually approximately the young adult model and consequently signal a readiness for termination with general behavioral patterns which resemble those described for adults. Reasonable levels of expectation for adolescents of various ages may be developed by observing the behavior of normal adolescents (every therapist should make the effort to become acquainted with some), reading descriptive studies of normal adolescent behavior, and to some extent by recalling one's own adolescent behavior and feelings.

There is another point which is obvious, but which may be forgotten in the heat of therapeutic ambition. It is impossible, even with the most skillful psychotherapy, to resolve emotional conflicts which are related to developmental tasks beyond the youngster's years. The 13-year-old girl described above cannot be expected to achieve final resolution of her oedipal attachments, since this maturational step normally occurs later in life, often not until young adulthood. She would be ready for termination when she could show a dawning appropriate interest in boys her own age (or slightly older), a budding capacity to identify with her mother's positive feminine traits without total fear of a homosexual bond, and a capacity to move in and out of regressive pregenital positions with relative comfort. The absence of paralyzing rigidities and inhibitions or defensive pseudoadult behaviors would indicate that she had "gotten back on the developmental track." Some writers on therapy of adolescents have not sufficiently emphasized this point (for example, see Corday, 1967). One does not try to accompany the adolescent on his entire developmental journey, only to guide him off sidetracks and back to his age-appropriate station on the main trunk of the developmental line.

At times, the therapist must point out the limitations of therapy to the adolescent patient himself. Despite the inner thrust toward independence, the youngster may find a comfortable therapeutic alliance hard to relinquish. The patient recognizes that the collaborative work with the therapist has helped him to free himself from many inner terrors. He naturally hopes that the same device can help him resolve other dilemmas, even when these are desirable "growing pains." The therapist must gently and firmly prevent the adolescent patient from using psychotherapy as a magic talisman to ward off or delay necessary developmental struggles.

Naturally, not all adolescent patients will be able to reach ideal goals even when these are corrected for developmental variation. Adolescents who have severe ego defects on the basis of constitutional or organic defects, severe emotional deprivation, or grossly disturbed family relationships will always show some distortions in personality functioning related to these basic defects.

Treatment in the above cases aims at establishing a workable synthesis which will probably include defensive patterns which are partially crippling. One attempts to work to a point where personality functioning provides some pleasure and sense of identity to the adolescent without seriously infringing on the rights of other people. If the underpinnings of the adolescent's personality have been crushed in early life, he will probably always move with a psychological limp. The therapist only hopes that he can help him learn to get around and take care of himself despite the disability.

Some Checkpoints for Termination

The only reliable basis for a decision to terminate therapy is a careful consideration of general behavior (in and out of the therapist's office) in comparison with developmental norms. When this global and partially intuitive assessment suggests that the adolescent is ready for termination, this impression can be checked against some specific behaviors which often appear in conjunction with an inner readiness for greater independence. The hunch that termination is near is reinforced when:

1) A growing appropriate involvement with peers results in a friendly and nonprovocative decrease in interest in therapy. The genuine gentleness and warmth toward the therapist which accompany this "drifting away" clearly differentiate it from the defensive avoidance of dependency relationships which one often sees early in therapy.

2) The adolescent wants to discuss the "hang-ups" of a friend without relating these to himself—that is, these problems are discussed without contrasting them with his own problems in an attempt to minimize his difficulties, divert attention from himself, or show his own plight as more serious or deserving of sympathy. In short, the adolescent appears to have the necessary emotional

energy and comfort with his own identity to concern himself about another person with reasonable objectivity and clarity of ego boundaries.

3) The adolescent suggests that the therapist could help this friend. When the expectation of what the therapist could offer the friend is reasonable, this often signals a willingness to share the therapist. Often, I suspect, it is also an unconscious attempt to deal with guilt feelings engendered by the wish to "abandon" the therapist by offering a replacement.

4) The adolescent shows a capacity for more objective evaluation of his parents, considering both their assets and their liabilities as human beings. He is able to accept their strong points as identification models while rejecting some of their weaknesses.

5) The adolescent uses fewer superlatives. Hiatt (1965) has noted this change in adults, and it seems to hold for adolescents. However, it should be remembered that the *normal* adolescent, may use more superlatives than the *sick* adult. In adolescents, one expects not a total avoidance of superlatives but a greater capacity for moderation than noted earlier in treatment.

6) The adolescent rarely acts out in regard to the therapy. He comes on time, does not battle over scheduling hours, does not haggle over stopping on time, and rarely needs to "play games" by teasingly withholding information, feelings, and ideas. There is a sense of simple forthrightness which is age-appropriate.

7) The adolescent inquires about the possibility of termination in a frank and comfortable manner. This is an especially good indicator of approaching readiness for termination if it is accompanied by appropriately mixed feelings delivered with typical adolescent sentimentality. "I really think I'm about ready to split this scene. Damn trouble is, I'm so used to you nagging me to look at why I draw every breath, I'm gonna miss you. Man, I never thought I'd say that!"

8) The adolescent's use of alloplastic defense mechanisms is less frantic and more realistic and shows greater consideration for the complexities of human needs and motivations. It would be neither reasonable nor desirable for the adolescent to give up his efforts to change himself or his environment (see Keniston, 1970).

It would be detrimental to our development as a society and a personal dereliction for the adolescent to accept the social status quo with all its defects calmly. Efforts to change malevolent social conditions, even if the efforts are disruptive and unpleasant, do not necessarily suggest that the adolescent is emotionally ill.

The healthy adolescent may even remain somewhat utopian and naive in his plans for social change. It is the single-minded demand that the environment accommodate completely to the idiosyncrasies of the adolescent that suggests a defensive utilization of social activism or cultural philosophy. A reasonably mature compromise in the choice between internal modification and alteration of outer reality is an acceptable point for termination. It is especially encouraging if the adolescent shows some recognition of both his capacity to change things and his limitations as an agent of social change, succumbing neither to grandiosity nor apathetic withdrawal.

THE THERAPIST'S PROBLEMS WITH TERMINATION

On "Letting Go"

Pearson (1958) has pointed out that adults have many motives for emphasizing the inadequacies of adolescents. Pumpian-Mindlin (1965) has described still other unconscious sources of envy which may lead to underevaluation of adolescent abilities. These generational factors, which may include protective and competitive elements in varying degrees, contribute to the therapist's reluctance to let his young patients handle things on their own. Of course, the adolescent patient can also lead the therapist to kick him out angrily and prematurely with an open or veiled prophecy that his attempted independence will fail and he will come crawling back. This, of course, is not really "letting go."

In addition to these generational distortions at the time of termination, the therapist faces the discomfort which every human being feels when he relinquishes a valued relationship. At the ending of a successful psychotherapy with an attractive adolescent, the honest therapist must often admit to a "forgotten parent" element in his complex of feelings. This aspect of his reaction might be stated as, *"Now* he wants to leave me, just when I get

him grown-up enough to be useful and enjoyable to have around."
The frequency of this countertransference attitude may be part
of the reason that many adolescents seem slightly guilty and apologetic about their appropriate wish to terminate and handle their
own affairs.

The therapist's problem in letting go probably explains the
frequency with which final sessions are taken up with Polonius-
like lectures and advice. Fortunately, the now-healthy adolescent
is usually indulgent and forgiving of the therapist's lapse into
pomposity. If the adolescent were not, the therapist might undo
much of his good work in ego building by this effort to reassure
himself of his importance to the adolescent.

Of course, there is one very practical reason that the therapist
has some reluctance to terminate successfully treated cases. Since
the therapeutic alliance with these youngsters is firmly established,
he anticipates their sessions with comfort and even pleasure.
When they are terminated, who will take their place?—probably
an angry, devious, defended, difficult youngster who will carry
little of the load of the therapeutic work for some time to come.
Small wonder that the therapist is tempted to hold onto his comfortable and cooperative youngster past the time when the adolescent really needs him.

On "Kicking Out"

I have emphasized the factors which tend to prolong therapy
unnecessarily. Countertransference problems may also lead to
errors in the other direction. Hostile feelings toward an adolescent,
especially if these feelings are unconscious, can lead the therapist
to exaggerate the patient's progress in order to rationalize an angry
rejection as an appropriate termination. A narcissistic or omnipotent need to achieve quick results may tempt the therapist to
skip over important and necessary therapeutic work. Parental
pressure based on realistic financial problems or emotional needs
may hurry the insecure therapist. Fear of erotic urges stirred by
closeness to the patient can cause a panicked wish to withdraw
and terminate in the interest of self-protection.

On both sides, the therapist must rely on his intellectual and emotional honesty, accepting the fact that he will invariably err in both directions on occasion.

TECHNIQUES OF TERMINATION

The key word in termination of the adolescent is flexibility. Rarely can the adolescent terminate smoothly and with finality in one try. The "open door" policy recommended by Buxbaum (1950) for analytic patients is almost mandatory for the adolescent patient. No matter how carefully one approaches the emotional reactions which termination stirs in the adolescent, it is usually necessary for the patient actually to experiment with physically leaving therapy, returning briefly, and going away again. One reason for this is the expected continuation of developmental storms which may trigger temporary regressive episodes that the adolescent knows the therapist can help to clarify and resolve. More often, however, it seems that the adolescent merely needs to visit home briefly. The purpose of these visits are considered below.

Introducing the Idea of Termination

Often, the adolescent will verbalize an appropriate interest in termination. When he does, Menninger's (1958) suggested reply, "I think you could finish up soon," is useful. It introduces the issues of termination in a definitive way without committing the patient or the therapist to any set time. The answer also implies that the adolescent and the therapist have further work to do within a finite time limit. It also maintains the focus on the adolescent's responsibility for finishing the job.

Many adolescents will not suggest termination in a direct manner. Many of them are too comfortable in a helpful dependency relationship, which is not inappropriate to their stage of life. Normally functioning adolescents still need understanding adult friends, adult listeners, and adult advisors. When all these characteristics are combined in a trusted adult who has stood by them through many very difficult periods, it is easy to see why they are not eager to give him up.

Although it is important to avoid the appearance of kicking the adolescent out of therapy or shaming him for his dependency wishes, it is also important to introduce the topic of termination as soon as the adolescent is emotionally ready. This need not be done abruptly or tactlessly. The patient will present numerous opportunities for the therapist to introduce the idea of termination in a positive light. The therapist's attitude should imply the calm assumption that he and the adolescent share a pleasant anticipation of a healthy, warm, and constructive parting of the ways, although both may have some mixed feelings about it.

The patient's pride in his independent functioning and his constructive use of object relationships which he has developed on his own are supported and approved as they begin to appear in the course of therapy. More and more, the adolescent says, in one way or another, "And here's another thing I handled well without your help." The therapist replies, in one way or another, "That doesn't surprise me or hurt my feelings. You're a rather competent person and I'm glad of it."

Very gradually, the adolescent is encouraged to rely on his own resources with less help from the therapist. It is often useful to introduce brief discussions of one's own limitations and dilemmas in therapy hours. This does not imply a discussion of deeply personal problems or conflicts the therapist may encounter, since the adolescent is unprepared to face and deal with the full impact of adult problems and living. The goal is merely to help the adolescent realize that the strengths of maturity derive from skill at problem solving and the acceptance of reasonable personal goals. The therapist must be careful not to overwhelm the adolescent or to suggest that the therapist himself finds life too difficult.

Terminations of this kind may be rather prolonged. The therapist should not succumb to pressures or temptations to rush things.

Sarah, the 15-year-old girl with problems of promiscuity, academic difficulty, drug use, and poor interpersonal relationships who has already been mentioned several times before, had a long and difficult termination phase.

Strong dependency yearnings which were violently denied early in therapy came to be centered on the therapist. It became necessary to point out repeatedly Sarah's tendency to play at helplessness in order to elicit a supportive helping response from the therapist. When Sarah was able to see this clearly, she joked, "You know if you told me I could solve a problem by holding my breath five minutes, I'd try it, turn blue, and swear it worked!"

Although she gradually came to utilize therapeutic help more realistically, she showed little indication that she regarded her arrangement with the therapist as anything less than lifelong.

Around the end of the second year of treatment, Sarah was symptom-free and enjoying moderately good social relationships in and out of her family. Her first indication of an awareness that therapy would have an end came when she reported angrily that her father had asked her when therapy would be over. She regarded this as evidence that he wished to undermine her treatment (actually this had been a problem early in therapy). The therapist wondered if her father's present comment might be seen rather as a compliment, an indication that she seemed well to him. Sarah asked if the therapist thought she was ready to stop treatment. The therapist replied that he had not thought too much about it before, but, since she had brought it up, she had been handling things very well and if she continued to work hard the idea certainly would not seem totally unreasonable within the near future.

Sarah didn't say anything more about it in that session, but came to the next interview loaded with problems to discuss. "Everything," she declared, "is falling apart. I'm all strung out!" She then recounted a series of concerns that sounded rather trumped up. The therapist commented that perhaps she was feeling a need to work out all of her problems in a hurry, since the idea of termination had come up in the last hour. He added that he really suspected that Sarah herself was quite capable of dealing with most of the problems she had mentioned.

Over the next few months, Sarah vacillated between feeling that she was ready to "quit" and a panicked feeling that she could not deal with life without the therapist's help. The therapist confronted her with her tendency to confuse herself and tied this to her invariable use of the word "quit" to describe termination. He suggested that perhaps it was difficult for her to imagine two people parting in a friendly way. She seemed to have a need to "go away mad" or to imagine that the other person was angry with her, which tended to interfere with her comfort in functioning independently.

This interchange led to a more direct expression of a variety of ambivalent fantasies about termination. At times, Sarah accused the therapist of being tired of her and disgusted with her inability to handle her own life. At other times, she was sure that the therapist would not let her "quit—I mean stop. Oh, dammit, why do I always say 'quit'?"

Even the issue of the fee was raised again, although Sarah was able to decide she was glad the therapist was paid to see her. "I guess it keeps it all straight and on the up and up."

Again and again, the therapist discussed the concept of voluntary separation based on a mutual agreement that it was time for new kinds of relationships. Often, it was possible to universalize about the adolescent's wish to leave home, not because he hated his parents or they hated him, but because he was ready for another phase of life. The distortions and conflicts around this issue in Sarah's real family were discussed rather fully during this time.

A full six months after termination was first mentioned, Sarah took LSD again for the first time in over a year. She came to her next session a bit sheepishly, but approached the exploration of the "slipup" (as she called it) with a determined air. She mentioned that she realized she had no real desire to "trip." The experience was unpleasant and she felt annoyed with herself under the drug and could not achieve the state of pleasant "boundlessness" which she had previously experienced with the drug.

"I kept thinking, 'I'm only doing this for X's [her therapist's last name] benefit.' It was pretty lousy. I'd really feel silly except I know I'm trying to figure out how to stop coming here without being mad about it."

She continued to explore her behavior objectively and with

skill for several minutes, and then said angrily, "Well, aren't you going to say *anything*!"

Genuinely surprised, the therapist spontaneously replied, "Gee, I'd be glad to, but you were doing so well yourself!"

Somehow, this seemed to reach Sarah more than the voluminous explanations the therapist had offered earlier. She shook her head in wonderment.

"That's all there is to it, isn't it? You really don't mind helping me. You just really believe I don't need it any more."

"Yeah. That's it exactly. Wish I could have told you sooner."

"Oh, that's okay. I think you did. I just listen slow."

She paused for a moment, and then said softly, with tears in her eyes, "I'm ready to stop seeing you now, but don't expect me not to miss you."

Needless to say, the therapist did not escape the session dry-eyed either.

Sarah terminated in four more sessions, utilizing them primarily to talk of her feelings of sadness which were accompanied by a quiet sense of excitement. She was especially looking forward to leaving home for college and talked a good deal of her plans.

In the ensuing three months of high school and the summer vacation, Sarah did not contact the therapist. She wrote from college after three months to report that things were going well and that she had many friends. She said that she also liked her dormitory "mother" and occasionally liked to talk with her.

"... but," she added, "I don't lean on people totally any more. I can always use help, but mostly I lean on me."

The therapist returned a brief note congratulating her on being happy and stating that he enjoyed hearing from her. She did not write again.

Sarah's case illustrates many of the issues which tend to appear around termination of therapy. These include anxiety over separation, fears of rejection, anger over relinquishing omnipotent expectations of the therapist, and a desperate struggle toward personality integration. In adolescents who have needed a less intense attachment, the conflicts are often briefer and more easily resolved. Some of these conflicts may be fleeting and hardly visible. They are all usually there in some form, however. In adolescents with a less sound therapeutic alliance, more may be acted out. Instead of talking about "quitting" as Sarah did, these youngsters may actually quit, with a need to return later and deal with the issues more directly when they learn that the therapist will neither condemn them for bolting nor pursue and rescue them from their impulsive folly. Some adolescents also show a greater need to "return home" in order to relinquish lingering hopes that the therapist is omnipotent, the perfectly desirable sexual partner, or the source of unlimited gratification.

Mike was a 16-year-old who handled termination by denying his dependency and feelings of loss. He insisted on leaving therapy only two sessions after the therapist had agreed with his assertion that he had "pretty well worked out his problems."

Two months later, he called, insisting on an interview on that very day. The therapist said that he would be glad to see him, but did not have an opening for two days. Mike angrily accepted the appointment. He used the session to express his sad feelings over breaking up with a girlfriend he had been dating for six months. The therapist agreed that partings were sad, but indicated that he felt Mike was handling his feelings quite well. He added that he saw Mike's capacity to cry and feel sad about the breakup as evidence of emotional health and a necessary and appropriate preparation for dating again.

Mike seemed relieved. He expressed thanks for the help which the therapist had given him during treatment. When he left, he shooks hands with the therapist, smiled with some wistfulness, and said, "Thanks again. You're really okay." He seemed somewhat sad and left the office rather slowly.

Therapy—Interminable

Some adolescents cannot be totally terminated. Despite the best therapeutic efforts, they are unable to manage their dependency needs without indefinite support from the therapist. This may be due to an inability to see the therapist's insistence on separation as anything other than a rejection. These patients are so convinced that they are unlovable that any attempt to terminate them is seen as a wish to be rid of them. They cannot believe any explanation of termination as a vote of confidence for them and as a bittersweet separation experience for the therapist. Dewald (1965) described the catastrophic reaction of a patient to his announcement that he was terminating her because of a move to a different city. The amazing thing was that his only contact with her in quite some time had consisted of intermittent brief telephone calls designed to monitor her medication! It is also interesting to note that the patient was able to accept the termination and to reconstitute psychologically after an interview in which she expressed her intense feelings about being left.

Schizophrenic patients, including those described as "borderline," suicidal adolescents, and other adolescents who actually have no dependable family, seem especially likely to prolong therapy indefinitely.

The therapist may elect to reduce the frequency of therapy sessions gradually with these potentially interminable patients without pressing the issue of finalizing termination. If holding the therapist in reserve, as it were, allows the patient to make a more successful adaptation, there is no compelling need to withhold this support. It is a relatively inexpensive and harmless addiction. However, it would seem wise to reevaluate the overall situation periodically. If the patient's life situation or ego strengths improve sufficiently, it may be possible to bring him back into more frequent therapy sessions for a brief period in order to effect a true termination. Wiener's (1959) description of the results of forced termination on several chronic patients suggests we may occasionally classify patients as interminable when termination is actually possible. Pumpian-Mindlin (1958) has stated a similar opinion. Especially in the adolescent, we should make every possible effort to complete emancipation.

Unfortunate Endings

There are two situations in which termination cannot be handled as constructively as one might wish. These are the termination of unsuccessful attempts at treatment and those terminations which are caused by external events.

TERMINATION OF UNSUCCESSFUL ATTEMPTS AT THERAPY. In the termination of unsuccessful treatment contracts, those in which it has been impossible to establish a therapeutic alliance, one attempts to salvage as much as possible. Hopefully, these terminations will not be abrupt or come as a surprise to the adolescent patient. The honest therapist will have commented on the absence of a true alliance periodically during his contacts with the youngster. As we have seen earlier, the formation of the alliance is a necessary condition for dealing with other material. The therapist should avoid "going through the motions" of the therapeutic work before completing this essential task.

The patient's inability to form a therapeutic alliance should be approached sympathetically and in a spirit of benevolent inquiry, but the therapist should still make it clear that no useful work can occur without this alliance. If the patient's mistrust of others, defensive structure, or living situation make an alliance impossible, it is preferable to admit that and suggest termination. Often, the adolescent is as frustrated as the therapist and has mentioned interruption of treatment several times himself. One can only try to make the dissolution of the therapy effort as constructive as possible. If a different treatment arrangement such as inpatient care appears indicated, this recommendation may be made to the adolescent and his parents. If the youngster's problems are less serious, it may be more advisable to part as amicably as possible, hoping that the youngster will be able to return later in a more accepting frame of mind.

Martha was referred for psychotherapy against her will when she was 13 because of poor school performance, lack of friends, and passive-aggressive behavior toward all authority figures expressed by forgetting, procrastinating, and other techniques which tormented her energetic, domineering, and compulsive parents.

Martha was the family scapegoat. Her mother persisted in efforts to organize Martha's life completely despite her inability to counter Martha's passive opposition effectively. Martha's father was openly contemptuous of her and either avoided her or slashed at her verbally. Martha perferred this treatment to her mother's worried nagging.

Martha was impossible to involve in any meaningful therapeutic alliance. She seemed terrified that she would be controlled by the therapist and defended herself by denying that she had any inner motivations and feelings. She was, she said, "a very simple person." She made fun of the therapist's comments by caricaturing them into ridiculous pseudo-Freudian nonsense. If the therapist asked about an episode of forgetting, Martha would say, "Oh, yeah. I forgot my glasses because I detest glasses. You see, I was frightened by a pair of glasses when I was a little child."

In spite of this attitude toward the work of treatment, Martha seemed to like the therapist personally and rather enjoyed her hostile bantering with him. During the few months that she was in treatment, she made some improvements in her social relationships and in getting along with her parents. Martha herself tended to deny that things had changed, and, when she could not deny the changes, she made it very clear that she did not feel they were related to her contact with the therapist. Martha continually protested that she did not need treatment. The therapist finally decided that it would be wiser to accept the symptomatic improvement and stop therapy. This was done with the statement that the therapist felt Martha still had unsolved problems.

Almost three years later, the therapist was called to see Martha because of an impulsive suicide attempt. Martha had ingested poison and was in real medical danger for several days. During this time, the therapist visited her regularly in the hospital. He noted that Martha seemed less frightened of him, more relaxed, and able to be genuinely appreciative of his attention during this trying period.

Psychotherapy was reinstituted at Martha's request. Although she remained rigidly defended, she showed some interest in understanding her emotions and was less condescending toward the therapist. Some useful therapeutic work was possible under these circumstances.

Other adolescents return to therapy much less dramatically than Martha. Often, it appears that the therapist's willingness to release them allows these youngsters to return of their own volition.

Of course, some do not return. Sometimes, one hears that they have found another therapist with whom they can work more comfortably. Sometimes, one hears that they have been through several therapists without success. This may happen when the parents remain too involved in dictating the goals of therapy. It also happens when the youngster has insufficient trust and interest in other people to allow the development of any enduring human relationship.

FORCED TERMINATION. At times, therapy must be terminated because of the therapist's illness, death, or change of location. Adult patients' reactions to these losses have been well described in the literature (Ross, 1968; Dewald, 1965). The reactions of adolescents appear similar, from my observations. The response is one of grief. Anger is expressed toward any new therapist until the feelings toward the lost therapist are accepted and resolved. The patient works through his ambivalence toward the old therapist gradually and only then is able to form an attachment and a therapeutic alliance in his new treatment relationship.

SOME FINAL COMMENTS ABOUT TERMINATION

Do Not Expect a Rose

Adatto (1966) has described the narcissistic investment of the adolescent which prevents total analysis of transference during the adolescent period. From his patients who returned for analysis as adults, he also learned that he had been introjected to a surprising degree and had served as an important internal figure in the intervening years.*

I feel there is a valuable lesson for adolescent therapists in Adatto's observations. The therapist often helps his adolescent pa-

---

* "Analytic associations in the adult phase indicate that I not only became an object of transference but was also introjected as a new object who acted as a transition between the old and the future, growing 'organically' from the past, and actively used in restructuring and synthesizing the psychic apparatus." (Adatto, 1966, page 504.)

tients toward health without knowing it and certainly without their explicit acknowledgment. *He is often much more important to them than they can let him know!*

The adolescent does not wish to admit dependency. Still, he often takes the therapist's comments, reflective stance, and non-critical, exploratory attitude home with him. He may ignore, kid, and even deride the therapist in the office, but at home he secretly mulls everything over. He would rather, in the words of a popular television commercial "do it himself." The therapist should be prepared to allow him that face-saving maneuver, so long as "it" gets done.

When the therapist is able to see the growth and development that may continue even after psychotherapy has officially ended, he is amply repaid for his efforts.

At Last!—The Payoff for the Therapist

As valuable byproducts of his therapeutic efforts with adolescents, the therapist may collect a broadening sense of involvement in social conflict and social change as well as a more wholesome grasp of the mutual interdependence of the generations. The need to recognize and retain the enduring human bonds which transcend cultural change and social upheaval challenges the therapist's wisdom as the searching adolescent forces him into the problems of the immediate present. Ossification and ivory tower isolation are at least delayed, if not prevented. Treating adolescents may not keep one young, but it tends to discourage the worst features of aging—the impoverishment of thought and constriction of viewpoint.

As the therapist reflects on what the adolescent has given him, perhaps he will even be able to find the strength, enthusiasm, and faith to prepare himself for the next adolescent patient. And who will replace his departing young friend? As noted earlier, the new patient will probably be an angry, devious, defended, difficult youngster who will carry little of the load of treatment for some time to come. In short, in many respects and for everyone concerned, termination is always a new beginning. The adolescent begins again, more completely self-reliant. The therapist begins

again, not only with a new patient but with a new impetus to the
development of his own "ego integrity" (Erikson, 1950). As he
moves toward this goal, he avoids despair and the fear of death.
To the extent that he succeeds, he may be able to help his adolescent patients to avoid the fear of life.

CITED AND RECOMMENDED READINGS

Adatto, C. P. 1966. On the metamorphosis from adolescence into adulthood. J. Amer. Psychoanal. Assoc. 14: 485–509.

Buxbaum, E. 1950. Technique of terminating analysis. In J. Psychoanal. 31: 184–190.

Corday, R. J. 1967. Limitations of therapy in adolescence. J. Amer.
Acad. Child Psychiat. 6: 526–538.

Dewald, P. A. 1965. Reactions to the forced termination of therapy.
Psychiat. Quart. 39: 102–126.

Edelson, M. 1963. The termination of intensive psychotherapy. Springfield, Illinois: Charles C Thomas, Publisher.

Erikson, E. H. 1950. Childhood and society. New York: W. W. Norton
& Company, Inc.

Fromm-Reichmann, F. 1950. Principles of intensive psychotherapy.
Chicago: University of Chicago Press.

Hiatt, H. 1965. The problem of termination of psychotherapy. Amer.
J. Psychother. 19: 607–615.

Keniston, K. 1970. We have much to learn from youth. Amer. J. Psychiat. 126: 1767–1768.

Menninger, K. 1958. Theory of psychoanalytic technique. New York:
Basic Books, Inc.

Pearson, G. H. J. 1958. Adolescence and the conflict of generations.
New York: W. W. Norton & Company, Inc.

Pumpian-Mindlin, E. 1958. Comments on techniques of termination
and transfer in a clinic setting. Amer. J. Psychother. 12: 455–464.

Pumpian-Mindlin, E. 1965. Omnipotentiality, youth and commitment.
J. Amer. Acad. Child Psychiat. 4: 1–18.

Ross, W. D. 1968. Persisting transference after interrupted psycho-
analyses and other therapeutic relationships. Compr. Psychiat. 9:
327–343.

Wender, P. H. 1968. Vicious and virtuous circles: the role of deviation
amplifying feedback (DAF) in the origin and perpetuation of behavior. Psychiatry 31: 309–324.

Wiener, D. N. 1959. The effect of arbitrary termination on return to
psychotherapy. J. Clin. Psychol. 15: 335–338.

CHAPTER NINE

group psychotherapy of the adolescent

There is something inherently seductive about the idea of treating disturbed adolescents in a group. It is a well known fact that the age group has a spontaneous interest in getting together and the conditions of current social reality require adolescents to spend most of their waking hours interacting within formal and informal peer groups. Developmental pressures cause these groups to hold great fascination and importance for the young person (Buxbaum, 1945). Theoretically, group psychotherapy should lead to effortless success.

It has been reasoned that group therapy would take full advantage of this natural grouping in the adolescent period, converting a distraction from individual therapy into a powerful therapeutic alternative. The troublesome dependency-independency-authority conflict with adults would be diluted by the presence of other young people in the treatment setting. Prompted by friendship and mutual concern, group members would recognize and confront maladaptive behavior in one another, including self-destructive pathological clashes with authority figures. These interventions would have great impact since they could not be dismissed as "uptight adult hasseling".

Sounds reasonable, doesn't it?

It is—in theory.

Unfortunately in practice group psychotherapy with adolescents often does not unfold in that way. Group members do not settle into a friendly acceptance of one another. Instead they approach each other with silence, suspicion and defensive affectations. They may not approach at all. Many groups disintegrate after a meeting or two.

If the group survives, perhaps because of external pressure to attend, the authority conflict is not diluted. In fact, instead of struggling with a single snarling youngster, the therapist is confronted with an angry and disruptive mob. Therapists have been known to disband groups out of fear for their own safety or at least their reputation in their clinic or private office building. Naturally, this extreme is unusual, but there are plenty of frightening war stories around to alarm the uninitiated.

Some therapists have succeeded in coralling their group, only to find that their reasonable, cooperative patients expect them to do all the work. The therapist is clearly accepted as a powerful leader and is beseiged with requests for advice, practical help and infantile support.

These unfortunate experiences (and others even worse) follow from a failure to consider all aspects of adolescent development, psychopathology and the dynamics of group formation during adolescence as they affect the formation and function of therapy groups.

There are many youngsters who need psychotherapy who will either fail to respond to the group approach or who may even be damaged by this technique. These youngsters may easily be screened through careful evaluation prior to group placement. If diagnostic study suggests that the presenting complaint results from ego depletion with panic and disorganization barely contained, the youngster is not a candidate for group therapy (Josselyn, 1972), at least not before a period of individual therapy. In individual work, youngsters of this kind can utilize an extremely dependent transference to gradually strengthen and widen their defensive skills and to partially resolve the primitive conflicts which are dangerously near eruption. At that point they have the potential to utilize interaction with peers constructively. Earlier they would have merely experienced a lively, challenging group as another stress to an already over burdened coping system. (Sugar (1972) has described the utilization of self-selected peer groups in cases of this kind).

A second category of youngster who cannot benefit from group therapy is fixated at a level of development which does not value the opinion or support of peers. Such adolescents often present with psychosomatic or self-destructive behavior which seems clear-

ly motivated by a need to coerce nurture from adults. They
require an infantile feeding relationship with a caring adult to
maintain marginal functioning.

Ann, a thin, tense fourteen year old girl had been in
psychotherapy with three different therapists since age eight
when her multiple neurotic symptoms of school phobia, ab-
dominal pains, vomiting episodes, and multiple phobias first
became evident. Her mother was a narcissistic, infantile, and
extremely unhappy woman who had been in psychoanalysis
for eight years. She made no secret of the fact she experienced
Ann as an unlovable burden. Her father was distant and rigid,
confining his family interactions to occasional outbursts at
his daughter when she interfered with any of his plans and
criticism of his wife for not coping better with the children's
management and control. Ann's problems had been variously
diagnosed as an anxiety neurosis, borderline psychosis and
childhood schizophrenia. Psychotic diagnoses had been considered because of Ann's general disorganization and because
some of her phobic concerns were quite bizarre. For example,
she feared she might wet herself at school but responded to
this common worry by wearing four to six layers of under-
garments. She also was periodically fearful that her hair was
falling out, that she had cancer or that she had performed
acts that she had only thought about. Reality testing clearly
was shaky.

After a year and a half of therapy with her latest therapist
she had stabilized markedly and was symptom free. She
began to move toward adolescent concerns and behaviors,
but complained chronically that she had no friends at school.
The therapist tried to explore her role in this state of affairs
with very little success. Motivated more than a little by
countertransference annoyance, he pushed her to join an
adolescent group where her ways of relating to agemates
could be directly observed. She agreed reluctantly, insisting
on continuing individual sessions concurrently (though she
complained constantly that they were valueless).

In the group she was paralyzed with anxiety, developed a
blind hatred for the female co-therapist, and alienated the

other group members with her childish and demanding behavior. In one active session while being confronted by
another group member, her eyes rolled back in her head and
her neck muscles went into spasm so that she literally could
not "see what was being said". She had to leave the meeting.
The support of extra individual sessions allowed her to recover quickly and, after some ambivalence, she decided to
return to the group where by subduing herself, she was able
to attain a degree of acceptance. However, it was the therapist's opinion that she had only survived the group experience, not that it had benefited her. She remained in individual
therapy after the group was terminated, and maintained her
symptomless but constricted adjustment even as the frequency of appointments was gradually reduced to one a
month.

Similar failures, more dangerous to the group than to the patient,
may occur with unsocialized acting-out youngsters. Of course,
many adolescents who present with antisocial behavior are basically well socialized and are handling neurotic or developmental
problems in an alloplastic manner. They work out quite well in
group therapy. However, those youngsters who have never shown
evidence of adequate object relations and the capacity for affectionate attachment will not respond to group pressure and cannot
adapt to group expectations.

Fortunately, most youngsters who should not be in group have
some awareness of this fact. They, like Ann, resist the plan for
psychotherapy. Although some youngsters who do well in group
resist the idea initially, strong reservations should lead the therapist to review his diagnostic thinking carefully before pressuring
the youngster to enter group psychotherapy. As a rule, the appropriate group candidate is anxious about the prospect of group
work but is also fascinated and intrigued by his fantasies of what
may happen.

WHY ADOLESCENTS WANT TO BELONG

Some consideration must also be given to the nature of spontaneous adolescent groups. The developmental pressures which
drive the adolescent toward his peers and the emotional needs

which he hopes to satisfy in peer groups strongly affect the readiness with which adolescents will relate to one another in a therapy setting and the style of communication which will tend to occur. These developmental factors also influence the reception the therapist can expect as the therapy group's leader.

In early adolescence the youngster turns toward peers under the pressure of his need to emancipate himself from his family. It is more of a panicked flight than a positive quest. As the parents are rejected and devalued, their utility as sources of narcissistic support is weakened or lost. The youngster does not yet have a suitable substitute internal mechanism for maintaining his sense of worth. The peer group provides a temporary emergency support system. However, this means that the adolescent's friends must be people he can view as equals or superiors and that they must offer him a primarily positive reflection of himself. Naturally, he is willing to conform slavishly to group norms in order to obtain this acceptance. The adolescent is very particular in choosing his associates. His ties are somewhat fickle, since he will drop any friend who falls from favor with the remainder of his gang. It is the rare fourteen year old who will maintain an open friendship with a youngster who "everyone else" regards as "weird" or "queer".

As the youngster grows older, the peer group increasingly becomes important as a support system in the task of modifying the superego. The group shares guilty secrets with bravado and even encourages previously unacceptable behavior, particularly actions which defy adult authority. However, group members are not merely "partners in crime", they also offer one another limits based on the human rights of other members of the group. They may also persuade individuals not to "go to far" because certain behaviors may be dangerous to the individual or may threaten the continued existence of the group. Therefore the group serves both to loosen the constraints of the latency conscience and to provide an alternative, reality based, system of controls.

As these developmental tasks are mastered, the adolescent becomes increasingly interested in his peers as real people. Relationships become less narcissistic and attachments are based on positive attraction rather than flight from the family of origin. Bonds are still somewhat tentative and there is considerable role playing, but relationships are warm and enduring over relatively extended periods of time. Even friction and controversy are accepted as necessary and valuable aspects of a rounded experience in the group.

This progression is often interrupted or uneven in the troubled adolescent. Many patients, even in late adolescence, are still more invested in the search for "psychic bandaids" than in learning from an honest give-and-take relationship. This fact creates two kinds of problems in the early stages of adolescent group psychotherapy.

First of all, the troubled adolescent is reluctant to accept his fellow group members. It is difficult for the patient to idealize people who are gathered with him because they too "have problems". He is frightened by the prospect of losing self esteem through accepting membership in a group of "misfits". If some group members have strikingly different defenses, social styles, or socio-economic backgrounds, the patient's certainty that he is in the wrong place grows exponencially. Some patients are often lost to the group at this point. As those who remain begin to find some group members who seem acceptable as "friends", there is a strong tendency for the group to fragment and develop cliques and scapegoats. It is a trying time for the therapist whose goal is to promote total group cohesion.

A second problem is created by the narcissistic vulnerability of the adolescent. Because of the need to use peer relationships for narcissistic confirmation, the adolescent tends to hide his problems and to cooperate fully with the same strategy as it is utilized by the other group members. The patients desire to avoid criticism and are understandably reluctant to throw the first stone. Each patient pretends to offer what he hopes to receive—total acceptance and admiration. Any confrontations that occur tend to be directed toward scapegoats and are hostile and distancing. It is easy for the therapist to become the only one in the group who "hassles the kids who are okay". He must be careful also to avoid being the only one who "takes up for the dopey ones".

The adolescent's use of peers to assist in the modification of his conscience also carries a threat to the successful formation of a therapeutic group. Most groups will test the therapist in this area. In more subdued groups, the discussions of forbidden thoughts and actions will be carried on initially before and after the therapist enters the group. Sooner or later, however, some group member will be either brave or nervous enough to broach the topics in the therapist's presence. Other groups are much more bold. In either case the group must know the therapist's stance. Will he encourage acting out or will he come across as a parental-superego figure? Will he be corruptible, seducible and manipulatable or will he be repressive and rigid? Of course, the opportunity of therapeutic exploration is lost if the therapist is drawn into an unholy alliance with either the id or the superego. This problem has been considered earlier in regard to the development of the therapeutic alliance in individual psychotherapy and the principles of management are the same in groups. However, the counter transference pressures of facing a group involved in externalizing superego issues are greater than those encountered with individual patients, particularly when the group seems in danger of transforming itself into a vicious, salacious street gang before one's eyes. Skilled group therapists have managed to navigate this risky period spontaneously, but many problems may be avoided by utilizing some of the technical structuring patterns suggested later in this chapter.

This brief discussion of developmental issues which influence the achievement of group cohesion underlines the fact that the natural tendency of adolescents is indeed to form groups, but not groups that are inclined to explore the meaning of behavior (Meeks, 1973). Of course, groups can be helpful, even therapeutic in the broad sense, without investigating the meaning of behavior. One successful strategy of group therapy with adolescents is to simply accept the basically narcissistic, supportive patterns of spontaneous groups and to harness these forces for constructive goals. This technique does not encourage introspection and will be described briefly. A second approach which utilizes structural techniques intended to encourage introspection, investigation of motives and scrutiny of the emotions which underlie interpersonal transactions will be discussed in greater detail. Many groups actually develop some characteristics of both types of group structure.

THE OPEN-ENDED SUPPORTIVE GROUP

Therapeutic groups which focus on changing self-destructive behavior by embracing and manipulating natural patterns of adolescent behavior in groups have been rather successful in a variety of settings (Sadock and Gould, 1964; Franklin and Nottage, 1969; Kraft, 1968). These groups have certain characteristics in common although there is considerable variation in their membership, specific procedures and goals. Initial membership is often compulsary and enforced by outside agencies such as probation agencies or the officials of a residential treatment institution. The groups are open-ended, and, in fact, often define the addition and successful assimilation of new members as their primary function. Members are selected primarily on the basis of their symptom or because of their presence in a particular institution. The group, then, is rather homogeneous, either for symptom (drug usage, delinquency, etc.) or through their common experience in daily living circumstances. The work of the group is oriented toward fairly circumscribed goals, usually either altering the common symptom behavior or improving the adaptation to the common living situation.

The basic force for change in these groups is a core of committed "old members" who have been converted from a prior involvement in the symptomatic behavior to an alternative life style. They credit the group and its leader for their success in changing. They are familiar with the gratifications and temptations of the negative behavior and recognize immediately the common defensive patterns and attitudes that insulate the new group member from awareness of the destructiveness of his maladaptive symptoms. Since they have decided that the symptomatic behavior is unwise and self-destructive, they are quite willing to confront the new member. Their self-esteem now depends on maintaining the wisdom of their decision so the new member's defense of the rejected behaviors represents a personal threat and is vigorously attacked. However, since they have also "been there", the old members tend to temper their assault with empathy, support and open confession of their own shortcomings.

The technical devices utilized by leaders in these groups are primarily inspirational, supportive and directive although group members may actively pursue hidden motivations. Exploration is primarily directed toward subtle manipulations of the group and its leader by the unrepentant new member. Interpretations and confrontations are mainly aimed at unmasking the new member, helping him to "shape up" and stop "playing games". On the other hand, extended discussion of personal genetic and dynamic material tends to be viewed with suspicion since such material may be used as a justification for the unacceptable behavior, an excuse to avoid essential change, a "cop out".

In many ways the leader of these groups serves primarily as a consultant and support to the old members who carry the main thrust of the rehabilitative work. He is there to help if the old members become discouraged or if they are manipulated into an unnecessarily punitive or overly permissive position in relation to a particularly difficult new member. The leader assists the group in maintaining focus on its tasks and values. Usually he does this without commenting on the motives or problems of the old members. The leader points out that the old members may temporarily lose sight of the purpose and correct procedures of the group because their task is difficult. He avoids criticism or discussion of the old member's psychopathology since this might weaken their loyalty to the group and lessen their influence on the new members.

The narcissistic value of being "right" and "cool" are usually sufficient reward for the old members' work in the group, especially as these values are continually reinforced by the successful conversion of new members to the group ethic. The group provides an opportunity to obtain admiration from a peer group which is acceptable (i.e., the members are street wise, tough, know the drug scene, etc.) without engaging in behaviors which are dangerous and self-destructive. The group also provides a reasonable new superego model divorced from childhood and the parents. The almost evangelical drive to help other youngsters provides an important sense of worth and mission which can substitute for the need to prove one's self in daring and illegal actions.

Although these groups are powerful agents for change, there are many limits to their application. It may be that some environments are so brutally unfair and destructive that adolescents subjected to their viciousness are unreachable. However, skilled workers with honest committment can ameliorate some of the damage in the worst environments (Stebbins, 1972). The difficulty of finding therapists with sufficient empathy, skill, toughness and concern to activate the group and form the original pro-therapy core of "old members" is an important limitation. Many are called, but few succeed and persevere.

Some youngsters cannot respond to any form of group therapy. Those so socially immature as to be immune to group pressure and group rewards cannot respond to a therapy based on these factors. Open-ended support groups are also relatively ineffective in correcting symptomatic behavior which is grounded in severe neurotic conflict, particularly when the behavior is part of a generally masochistic pattern.

Even with an appropriate leader and members who fit, there are potential problems. Failure to influence one or more new members is demoralizing and can erode collective self-esteem. Trusted old members can relapse in response to increased stresses in their lives with an even greater disruptive impact on the group. Charismatic new members may tempt the entire group to return to old value systems. In short, the group ties are basically narcissistic and therefore somewhat unreliable when pressures mount. The group leader's own charisma, flexibility and clinical wisdom will be severely tried as he attempts to maintain a positively functioning group entity over time.

THE CLOSED, EXPLORATORY THERAPY GROUP

The developmental impediments to adolescent group work may also be circumvented by altering the structural characteristics to encourage the development of a group ethic of emotional openness and exploration. The model described here does permit the addition of occasional new patients at infrequent intervals, but is basically designed for a group with constant membership and a reasonably prolonged existence. It is basically designed for out-patients. Under these circumstances, further modifications are necessary to insure continuing parental cooperation in the group work.

The open ended group described above can afford to neglect parental involvement since the group basically substitutes for the family and discourages extensive discussion of family relationships. In contrast, the dynamically oriented group is virtually certain to consider in detail the impact of family problems on the attitudes, feelings and interpersonal quirks of its members. These discussions will tend to activate latent family conflicts and may lead the parents to sabotage treatment or even terminate the adolescent's group membership. The needs of the parents must be considered if the group structure is to be successful. This parental involve-ment in the group will rarely substitute for specific therapy direct-ed toward their marital or personal problems. Although some parents benefit personally, the primary goal is to enlist their en-lightened support for the work of the adolescent group.

We can now turn to a description of the model. As in the remainder of the book, the procedures will be described explicitly with the clear recognition that other therapists have utilized other techniques successfully. Models must be altered to fit treatment conditions and personal preferences.

GROUP SELECTION

Members must be chosen carefully for outpatient dynamic group psychotherapy with an eye to both the needs of the individual youngster and the overall composition of the group.

The criteria of group selection are hardly scientific, but some principals seem clinically sound. We have already mentioned some youngsters who should be excluded from groups. Additional cri-teria should be mentioned. It seems important for the prospective member to have parental permission and, preferably, parental encouragement to join the group. Good group work produces anxiety and resistance. If the parent is poised to support flight from the experience, it is unlikely that most adolescents will be able to resist this invitation to escape immediate pain in the interest of long term benefits.

The youngster himself should have at least a modicum of positive motivation for the group experience, perhaps limited initially to a mixture of interest and anxiety with an agreement to try the group for a month or two. The youngster's motivation will be evaluated in more depth during the evolution of individual treatment contracts, a process which will be described later.

Some attention should be given to choosing a group population which will be socially compatible within broad limits. Early impressions of other group members are important and adolescents are often harsh in their judgement of superficial characteristics. For example, a psychotic youngster with the same style, vocabulary, dress, and social experience would probably be less threatening to an adolescent group than a healthier youngster with a disfiguring physical defect or a background and life style which seemed "weird" to the other members.

An adolescent group jelled with surprising rapidity except for Bill, a seventeen year old who remained withdrawn and uncomfortable through the first four meetings. He requested an individual interview where he told the therapist the group wasn't helping him. The other kids seemed strange and unfriendly and he intended to quit. When pressed about his discontent his complaints were vague. The therapist commented on Bill's uncharacteristic silence in the group meetings and wondered if he could really assess the other members' friendliness without being more open. Bill responded with angry tears. "I can't".

"Why not?"

"You're stupid. Why did you put me in a rich kids' group?"

Though the therapist hadn't realized it, every member of the group except Bill came from very affluent families. They spoke casually of their cars, going out to dinner and attending concerts. Bill's father was a university professor who couldn't afford such luxuries.

In this case, Bill's educational and social background were actually quite similar to those of the other group members.

They were quite prepared to accept him although he felt very "different" from them.

Bill was able to resolve his discomfort and work success-fully in the group. His reaction is described merely to illus-trate the adolescent's exquisite sensitivity to superficial social differences.

Some attention must also be given to the "balance" of the group. Passive and silent members must be offset with some "talkers". Youngsters inclined toward "acting out" solutions to conflict should be placed in groups which include some youngsters who reflect or even ruminate on their feelings before acting. Mostly one must depend on an intuitive sense of how the group will fit together. This sense is never infallible, but the chances for success are increased by knowing the individual youngsters reason-ably well. This kind of knowledge can only be obtained through fairly prolonged pre-group individual evaluation.

PRE-GROUP EVALUATION

The diagnostic advantages of pre-group evaluation have been mentioned but these sessions are central to group success in other ways as well. The early stages of group therapy are extremely anxiety producing for many adolescents so it is important for each group member to have a stable, trusting relationship with the therapist prior to the first group meeting. Many youngsters should be started in group only after a period of individual psychotherapy with the therapist. Others may be referred by therapists who do not do group work themselves but believe the patient would be helped by a group experience. If the colleague's assessment is correct, these youngsters may require only a few individual ses-sions to get acquainted with the therapist and learn something of the pattern of group work he follows. Of course, the group therapist also uses these meetings to assure himself that the young-ster is ready to function constructively in the group. If he does not think so, the patient can be referred back to the original therapist for further individual work.

If the group will have co-therapists, they can divide the evalua-tive work between them. This has practical advantages since most therapists do not have group evaluation time in their normal schedule and are somewhat overburdened by the extra work involved in preparing to begin a group. The procedure does produce some technical problems since group members may resist group involvement and cling to their individual relationship to the co-therapist who evaluated them. However, this problem is preferable to the risk of early group dissolution. In any event, this excessive attachment to the therapist quickly diminishes as the group members become acquainted and form attachments to one another.

Pre-group meetings also allow patients to elaborate their anxieties and fantasies about group therapy. The therapist can correct frightening misconceptions and explain the goals and procedures of the group. The ground rules of the group such as prohibitions against physical contact, the desirability and limitations of confidentiality, the need for regular attendance, the procedure for quitting the group, and the expectation that each group member will formulate a treatment contract for the group can be discussed fully. The youngster has the opportunity to consider his treatment goals and to solicit the therapist's help in shaping a treatment contract which he would be comfortable in sharing with the group. This is important since many youngsters wish to discuss very sensitive topics in the group, but would be understandably reluctant to disclose these fully in an initial meeting of the group. For example, the fifteen year old boy who has never had a date and is terrified of girls may need permission to limit his first treatment contract to "I would like to improve the way I get along with girls". At the other extreme from youngsters who might say too much are those who require pressure and assistance to come up with any personal treatment goals. The pre-group individual sessions provide an opportunity to explain that comments like "I'm only here because my parents sent me" or "I was just curious about what happens in groups" will not suffice.

Pre-group meetings also permit the therapist to clarify his expectations about how the group will proceed. Comments such as "when a group really gets going, you get pretty involved with the other people" both explains the importance of regular attendance and sets the expectation that group members *should* comment on each others' absences, consistent lateness, or precipitous desire to quit the group. The therapist has defined these behaviors as evidences of concern rather than meddling in someone else's business. Similar double duty is accomplished by predicting some of the problems the youngster may expect in the course of the group experience. "If this group really works like others I've had, there will be pretty open talking about how people feel about one another. Sometimes you may not like what people say about how you're coming across". "You know, there may be things about people in the group that annoy you. Now at school you might just avoid that person, but in a group it's important to talk about how you really feel even if you're afraid the other person may get mad or have their feelings hurt. Do you think you can do that?" Of course, these comments are tailored to the dynamics and relating style of the individual youngster. The diagnostic evaluation often allows a fairly accurate prediction of the types of group interaction which a given youngster will find most uncomfortable. Naturally these structuring comments do not guarantee that the group will actually move toward confrontation, emotional openness, and exploration of interpersonal processes, but it begins that process by presenting the possibility for such interactions and implying that the therapist expects these possibilities to occur.

The therapist predicts the patient will be emotionally accepted in the group and also states a rule when he explains, "the reason we make a fuss about someone stopping is because a lot of times the group wonders why someone quits, maybe even blames themselves. If you decided to leave the group—let's say you got your problem worked out—it would be important to explain that. The rest of the members would probably hate to see you go and they might wonder if it happened because of something they said or maybe they weren't interesting or good enough. So we ask anyone who thinks about quitting to bring that up at the start of a meeting and to tell why they're thinking of leaving the group. The other good thing about this is for you, the person who's thinking of quitting, it gives you a chance to hear what the other people think about your reasons for quitting and gives you a chance to think it over. And that's good, because stopping the group is a pretty important decision and you'd want to think about it pretty seriously".

OBJECTION! Your honor, Dr. Meeks is leading the patient.

You bet your sweet id.

And that's only the beginning.

THERAPIST ACTIVITY

The leader of an adolescent group must work actively at promoting spontaneity and intimacy (Anderson, 1972). The therapist's activities include structuring group tasks and procedures and the usual group leader's activity of conceptualizing and verbalizing the group experience (group process) as it unfolds, but these professional activities are not enough. The therapist must also be active as a person, alive and involved in the group. He needs to share his own feeling responses to the meaningful emotional interactions which develop between group members.

Obviously this activity poses potential dangers of encouraging excessive dependency in group members. The therapist may be seen as a guru, a teacher, a good parent. These developments need not be unhealthy if they are recognized and discussed openly. If the therapist is alert and free of excessive needs for power or status, there will be plenty of chances to support emerging leadership in the group. The therapist's overt and explicit interventions can often decrease as the group's momentum grows, but he must remain an actively interested and emotionally invested observer.

In the seventh session of an adolescent group the therapist confessed his discomfort.

"I don't know. It seems like I'm talking too much in here. I don't think I'm giving other people enough chance to talk and that's really bad, because I'm not even getting to know you guys well enough to know whether I'm saying the right things".

Mike, a previously silent sixteen year old, said, "You're not. I'm sorry, but we need to get the kids talking. Me too, I guess. I haven't said much myself. I think we ought to interview each other, like take turns being the patient. Everyone could ask three questions—Course if you don't think—"

"Sounds great to me, but maybe you'd better ask the other kids".

"Okay, but Mike has to go first". Everyone chimes their agreement that Mike had to be the first "patient".

Everyone has their own style of activity. The important point is that passive, detached, dispassionate scrutiny may have great value in some scientific settings. The adolescent psychotherapy group is not one of them.

THE GROUP CONTRACT

The group contract or the group rules of the group are nothing more than a set of conditions which group members agree to follow in order to achieve treatment results they desire. This quality of informed consent and mutual committment needs to be emphasized to offset any fantasy that group contracts are made in heaven or in the therapist's head. The anticipation of possible control problems in adolescent groups may lead the therapist to focus on a long list of prohibitions as the primary content of the group contract. The adolescents correctly perceive this as a frightened insistence on a superego alliance and respond according to their particular pathology. Overly inhibited youngsters slavishly obey the rules and youngsters in rebellion fight them. Neither group becomes involved in treatment.

The fundamentals of the group contract have already been discussed with each youngster during his pre-group individual sessions. Each therapist must decide for himself the basic working conditions under which he can conduct meaningful group therapy. Many would consider most of the following rules important for the reasons given.

1) No hitting in the group. The therapist explains the obvious fact that people cannot speak honestly with one another unless they are assured that the therapist and the group will neither permit them to hit or be hit. Some therapists extend this rule to "no physical contact" to rule out physical expression of positive feelings (kissing, sitting on laps, etc.) along with the expression of aggression. This may be questioned on the grounds that it introduces some confusion by including "hittin' and huggin' " in the

same category as though they were somehow interchangeable or related to the same emotional origin. Secondly, the vagueness of the general rule suggests that the therapist is reluctant to confront adolescent sexuality directly. Finally, from a practical viewpoint, some physical contact (i.e., embracing a crying fellow member) may be decidedly constructive.

2) Regular attendance is expected. If it is totally impossible to attend a session, it is the patient's responsibility to contact the therapist and explain why the absence is unavoidable. The therapist explains that the members need to get to know one another very well in order for the group to be helpful. This requires very regular attendance. In addition, the unexplained absence of a member wastes valuable group time as the present members speculate on the reasons for the absence. Some members may even inhibit their group participation out of concern that some interaction with the absent member drove him away.

3) Any member who considers leaving the group should announce his intention at the beginning of a group session and permit full discussion of the decision. The reasons for this rule have already been discussed. Some therapists require a group notification of two sessions or more. Theoretically this makes sense, however it may invite passive aggression if some group members perceive the rule as a disguised attempt to force members to remain in the group when they have definitely decided to quit.

4) Each group member will be expected to make an individual treatment contract. This expectation will be discussed further below.

5) The group is told that the group will function best if there is no discussion of the group proceedings with others. Some therapists feel that this rule is impossible to enforce and add, "If you must discuss something that occurs in here with your parents or anyone else, at least don't use names".

The therapist (or co-therapists) may also wish to explain their position regarding confidentiality, namely that they will not discuss things that occur in the group or information revealed there unless, in their judgement, a group member is in danger of harming himself or others. Some therapists also reserve the right to answer parental questions regarding treatment progress. Most adolescents seem to accept their parent's right to know if the youngster is utilizing treatment appropriately, but some therapists feel uncomfortable with "sending home report cards".

6) The group is told that any contact between members outside the group sessions should be reported in the next group meeting. It is explained that important group issues may be missed if group members have discussions which exclude the remainder of the group.

Some therapists forbid outside contact, but there are serious difficulties in taking this position. It is a rule that cannot be enforced, seems artificial, and invites rebellion. Also, many therapists have observed that much extra-group contact is supportive, pro-therapy, and conducive to the development of group cohesion.

These conditions are not presented as a list of dogmatic regulations. They are discussed with the group as important issues which require resolution. This does not mean they are totally or even primarily negotiable. For example, few therapists would consider working with a group that could not agree to refrain from striking one another. The therapist must press for the conditions he needs, attempting to convince the group of the therapeutic necessity of each rule. There is no reason to avoid "sales talk". The resulting contract is designed to benefit everyone, especially the group members.

THE INDIVIDUAL TREATMENT CONTRACT

The practice of requiring each group member to formulate a personal treatment goal and verbalize that goal to the group has several advantages. It is not an unreasonable expectation when the adolescent receives assistance with the difficult job of thinking through his contract in the pre-group individual sessions. It is probably true that any youngster who is suitable for outpatient group work is able to make this degree of commitment. However, the therapist must be willing to permit some face-saving reservations. For example, it is probably acceptable for the adolescent to say, "Well, the *real* reason I'm coming to the group is because my father says I have to, but since I'm here, I might be interested in learning more about how boys should treat girls".

The group presentation of individual treatment contracts is taken up as soon as the group completes consideration and acceptance of the group contract, often in the first session. The therapist introduces the topic by saying, "Okay, since we've agreed on those things, let's get on to people's individual contracts. Remember we said everyone would tell the group why they're coming here and what they hope to accomplish in the group. Who wants to go first and get it over with?"

Usually someone will volunteer, but if not, the therapist can ask a member to begin. Each contract is open to discussion by the group and the therapist and may be accepted or rejected as inappropriate. Generally speaking, any serious goal which seems neither destructive or foolishly grandiose is accepted. One does not expect or need psychologically sophisticated contracts at this stage in adolescent group work.

The two primary purposes of requiring contracts in the initial sessions are to open problem areas for group discussion and to provide the therapist with legitimate, neutral instrumental authority. Since each member has asked for help with a specific problem, the "mutual protection pact" of denial which often characterizes adolescent groups during their formative period is less likely to develop. The open admission of difficulty and the request for help give both a focus and permission to the other group members as they consider commenting on a fellow-member's verbal or non-verbal behavior in the group. For example, if a youngster has stated that he is coming to the group because he wishes to learn how to make friends, the group feels more free to confront him with his silence, sarcasm or egocentricity without feeling they are intruding or merely being hostile. "Maybe the reason you have trouble making friends is that you're always cutting people down. At least you do here".

The therapist is also in a better position to avoid the unholy alliances with either id or superego. The process of making individual treatment contracts defines him as a consultant to the group; an expert given the responsibility for guiding the group toward behaviors which will permit the individual members to accomplish their chosen goals. If it becomes necessary to set limits on group behavior the therapist does this as a leader exercising his duty to help the group accomplish its aims, not as an offended uptight parent figure. His function is executive and oriented toward promoting better ego functioning with the group.

Any contract which is sincere will accomplish these two purposes. As the group work continues, contracts may be altered and refined. The therapist may suggest changes or new definitions of the problem may be offered by the patient or other group members. For example, the therapist may comment to a patient, "I would like to suggest a change in your contract now that I know you better. I don't think you exactly have a problem in making friends. I think you should consider working on your tendency to expect too much of friends and the way that causes you to be disappointed in people and overly critical". Later yet the contract may evolve to, "Trying to stop setting people up to prove they don't like me and that I'm better than they are".

The treatment contract is only a tool so its value will depend on the skill with which it is used to further the group work. Some therapists are worried that adolescent patients will not accept this condition of group work. They might consider the possibility that a group so resistant to the treatment process is unlikely to be successful in any case. Perhaps it is better to dissolve an unworkable group early in its course so that more suitable treatment approaches can be attempted. In actual practice, most adolescent groups will accept this condition of treatment. Naturally some of the more resistant members will hold back, but as more and more group members commit themselves to a treatment contract, the pressure to "get aboard" grows. The contracted members point out that it is only fair that all members reveal their problems and aspirations to the group.

THE PARENTS

Many patterns of parental involvement have been utilized in group work with adolescents. Some therapists conduct concurrent treatment groups for the parents or arrange for such groups to be conducted by a colleague. Attendance at these groups may be required as a condition for accepting the adolescent in the group.

These groups are sometimes quite difficult and unsatisfactory because the parents are unmotivated and do not recognize a need for treatment. However, a skillful therapist can often make these groups effective by permitting the parents to focus on their youngsters initially, gradually using common themes and problems to build group cohesion and a capacity for personal therapy work.

Another successful approach involves periodic family meetings, basically an adolescent group meeting with the parents invited. The adolescents may also be seen individually with their families. These approaches are effective and are well received by the parents. The only potential disadvantage is that family work closely linked to the group may dilute the intensity of the attachments formed within the group. If the aim is to maximize group intimacy so that the group can serve as a microcosm of emotional life, this may be a disadvantage too serious to accept.

Another alternative is to approach the parents as collaborators in the group process, leaving any direct therapy they may require outside of the group involvement. A parents' meeting is called just prior to beginning the adolescent group. The therapist or co-therapists present the aims and methods of the group didactically, explaining all aspects of the group procedure in detail. The parents are told that their youngster's individual problems will be approached indirectly through the creation of a human relationships laboratory experience in the group setting. The parents are offered examples to demonstrate how this experience serves to develop the capacity for self-awareness and skill in relating to other people in a fair and honest way.

The parents are told of the problems and disadvantages of this approach. The therapist admits that this kind of work creates considerable anxiety which may cause their youngster to express desires to leave the group. They are warned that youngsters often attempt to manipulate their parents to support their flight from the group by suddenly claiming all problems have been solved, being amazingly cooperative in the home, expressing concern about the morality and mental health of other group members, or trying to imply that the therapist is hostile toward the parents. The parents are assured that they are not expected to force their youngster to remain in group. The desire to quit may be appropriate. The therapist merely wants their support in asking the youngster to discuss his decision and the reasons for it in the group setting. The parents are asked to refer any complaints their adolescent may have about the group or the therapist to a group meeting, encouraging the open expression of negative feelings in the group setting so that the youngster's emotional experience within the group can be as complete as possible. The parents are told that if *they* have any questions about the group or the therapist's behavior, these should be discussed directly with the therapist.

The importance of confidentiality is discussed so that the parents can understand why the therapist cannot fully disclose the happenings in the group to them. The therapist also explains why he needs their permission to talk openly with their youngster about any contacts the parents and therapist may have. Parents are encouraged to call the therapist with any questions or information but to inform their youngster that they are calling. They should also tell their adolescent the general content of what they intend to say.

Group fees and policies around absences are discussed along with an explanation of the importance of regular attendance.

The parents are encouraged to ask questions and to be sure they understand and agree with the plans for the group. The therapist tries to discourage entensive discussion of individual problems except when these lend themselves to illustration of general group concerns and techniques. Some questions may be referred to the other parents and some worries, such as fears that a particular youngster may not speak in group, may be generalized. The therapist can then talk in a general way about the way the problem will be handled in the group.

Similar meetings may be held periodically during the life of the group. They are always announced in advance to the adolescents. The parents develop considerable camaraderie and an atmosphere of mutual support for the adolescents' group work as these meetings continue. Some group interaction often develops among the parents. Frequently this is of both diagnostic and therapeutic value. In all meetings the therapist maintains the confidentiality of the group, but permits the parents to share information they may have regarding the progress and behavior of group members including their own youngster.

THE WORK OF THE GROUP

Once the tasks of developing cohesion and open communication are achieved in an adolescent group, the observed interactions are very similar to those seen in adult groups. The words and issues differ, of course, but the work of recognizing, confronting and resolving interpersonal blocks to group progress is technically similar to adult work. The therapist gradually becomes less of an active structuring agent and moves toward a more reflective, interpretive stance in the group.

There are two rather common patterns in adolescent group work which do differ somewhat from the typical adult group. The first concerns the frequency and intensity of direct competition with the therapist. Of course, similar interactions occur in adult groups, but the adult patient is usually less frightened by his effrontery than is the adolescent. Often the adolescent can express his new strength only in the context of totally discounting the therapist's importance to him. Frequently he announces his desire to leave the group. The persistence of occurrences of this kind in adolescent groups is related to the adolescent's need to utilize adults as identification figures. With the support of the group, the adolescent goes through a cycle of testing the therapist, accepting (or even idealizing) him, challenging the therapist and testing him again at a less dependent level, and then accepting a new relationship on this more equalitarian basis. No special group techniques are necessary in the management of this pattern of behavior. The cycle merely needs to be recognized as a natural growth experience which is basically constructive for the adolescent involved. If the group therapist can comfortably accept the challenge and support new strength in the member, the remainder of the group can usually remind the challenger of remaining problems and prevent his precipitous departure from the group.

The second problem results from the adolescent's relative lack of conceptual skill with which to describe the subtle and intricate nuances of interpersonal transactions. This deficiency can usually be countered verbally if the therapist can develop the capacity to describe complex social phenomena in words and images familiar to the adolescent. This kind of translation is sometimes insufficient or unconvincing. In these situations, judicious use of psychodrama and gestalt techniques to concretize the impasse may be indicated. These experiments often permit the group to comprehend the emotional factors beneath surface behavior and to feel the power of hidden forces operating in the group.

Pat, age 15, was silly and disruptive in a group that had decided to work seriously. He fended off efforts of group members to engage him in serious talk with clowning and flippant remarks. The group was angry and wanted Pat ejected since he was "just goofing off".

Pat had made an individual treatment contract but had described considerable anxiety about joining the group during pre-group individual sessions. The therapist was sure that the clowning reflected this anxiety rather than lack of motivation, but comments to that effect did not decrease the group's anger at Pat or change his defensive style.

The therapist proposed a "psychological exercise" which he said "might help the group members to understand one another better". One member (a popular boy) was blindfolded. He was asked to choose someone to lead him around the room. Without hesitation he chose one of the attractive girls in the group. After they had traversed the room without incident, they were asked to describe their feelings. The boy laughed and said it was fun—"A good excuse to hold hands with Cathy". The girl said she'd worried a little that he was walking too fast. Once or twice she thought he might bump into things and blame her.

"Okay, we'll talk some more about how you reacted later. Right now let's try someone else. How about you, Pat?"

"No siree, you're not gonna put that snot-rag on my face. Germs. Germs!"

"Yes, come on Pat".

Pat ambled up slowly, rolling his eyes in mock terror.

"Stop clowning, Pat," a member said.

Pat ran his hand over his face as though to wipe off a smile and pulled a solemn expression. The handkerchief was tied in place and he was asked who he wanted to lead him. He named the female co-therapist. She declined and told him he had to ask a group member. Pat began to look tense and worried beneath the blindfold as the silence lengthened.

"Come on, Pat, who do you pick. Hurry up".

Pat abruptly tore off the blindfold and rushed to his seat, clearly troubled and upset.

"You look scared," the therapist commented.

"They'd run me over something. They hate me anyway". Pat was obviously serious.

"God, he's really scared," a member said.

"Yeah, he doesn't trust anyone but the doctor".

Pat continued to have problems in the group, but the members were more sympathetic and were able to sense and explore his very real fear of people his own age.

ADOLESCENT GROUP THERAPY IN PERSPECTIVE

It seems that therapists are increasingly eclectic in their choice of treatment techniques. This would appear to be a reasonable development in a field where no single treatment approach has been demonstrated to have clear superiority. One benefit of this eclecticism is that it permits various combinations of treatment approaches tailored to the individual needs of a specific adolescent and his family. The combination and integration of individual and group therapy with the same therapist as described by Kaplan and Sodock (1971) for adults is gaining deserved popularity among adolescent therapists. The two forms of treatment appear to catalyze movement in each.

Group work may also be combined with family therapy or utilized to assist in dealing with a specific problem in on-going therapy. For example, a group experience may provide a transition between successful but extremely dependent individual therapy relationship and termination. Placement in a group may help an adolescent who is excessively enmeshed in his family to emancipate during the course of family therapy.

In short, group psychotherapy is a technique which can be

helpful or disastrous to the troubled adolescent. Careful initial and continuing diagnostic evaluation should dictate when it is used and decide which other techniques need to be combined with it for maximum benefit.

The method of beginning and conducting group therapy described here is only a skeleton. It is useless even dangerous, without training and experience both in group therapy and work with individual adolescents. There is no substitute for supervised experience in a live encounter with real adolescents.

TERMINATION

The issues involved in termination of group psychotherapy differ from individual work because group members are at various points in their development, yet the group must stop at one moment in time. In practice, termination of group therapy can occur because of clinical progress for the individual, but entire groups are usually terminated because of external events. Many therapists designate the life of the group at its very outset. A common pattern is to start groups in September and terminate them in June since many adolescents are unavailable in the summers. Individual decisions are made at termination as to whether a youngster should return for another group in the fall, continue in individual work, or leave treatment entirely.

Regardless of how this practical issue is handled, it does seem important for the group to have a clear and definite point of cessation. If the group is permitted to merely drift apart, the therapist deprives the members of the opportunity to face and learn from their idiosyncratic responses to separation. There is also considerable value in the process of reviewing the group's progress and assessing its benefits to each member. This can be organized around the individual treatment contracts of each member. The opportunity to address both the triumphs and failures of the members and the therapist offers both a chance for consolidating gains and for identifying areas that require further attention, in or out of formal therapy.

CITED AND RECOMMENDED READINGS

Anderson, R. L. 1972. The Importance of An Actively Involved Therapist. *In*: Adolescents Grow in Groups. Edited by I. H. Berkovitz. New York. Brunner/Mazel.

Buxbaum, E. 1945. Transference and Group Formation in Children and Adolescents. Psychoanalytic Study of the Child. 1: 351-365.

Franklin, G. and W. Nottage. 1969. Psychoanalytic Treatment of Severely Disturbed Juvenile Delinquents in a Therapy Group. Int. J. Group Psychother. 19 (2): 165-175.

Josselyn, I. M. 1972. Preclude: Adolescent Group Therapy: Why, When and a Caution. *In*: Adolescents Grow in Groups. Edited by I. H. Berkovitz. New York. Brunner/Mazel.

Kaplan, H. I. and B. J. Sadock. 1971. Structured Interactional Group Psychotherapy. *In*: Comprehensive Group Psychotherapy, Edited by H. I. Kaplan and B. J. Sadock, Baltimore. Williams and Wilkins Co.

Kraft, I. A. 1968. An Overview of Group Therapy with Adolescents. Int. J. Group Psychother. 18: 461-480.

Meeks, J. E. 1973. Structuring the Early Phase of Group Psychotherapy With Adolescents. Int. J. Child Psychother. 2: 391-405.

Meeks, J. E. 1974. Adolescent Development and Group Cohesion. Adolescent Psychiatry. 3: 289-298.

Sadock, B. and R. E. Gould. 1964. A Preliminary Report on Short-term Group Psychotherapy on An Acute Adolescent Male Service. Int. J. Group Psychother. 14: 465-473.

Stebbins, D. B. 1972. "Playing It By Ear," in Answering the Needs of a Group of Black Teen-agers. *In*: Adolescents Grow in Groups. Edited by I. H. Beckovitz, New York. Brunner/Mazel.

Sugar, M. 1972. Psychotherapy with the Adolescent in Self-selected Peer Groups. *In*: Adolescents Grow in Groups. Edited by I. H. Berkovitz. New York. Brunner/Mazel.

CHAPTER TEN

family therapy

INTRODUCTION

Family therapy has come of age as an important treatment modality in the management of troubled adolescents during the past two decades. An early neglect of the developmental and intrapsychic aspects of family therapy has been rectified by the involvement of many child psychiatrists and analysts in family work. The intricate play of developmental pressures, family structure and family communication patterns have added both theoretical and clinical richness to our understanding of personality development (Minuchin, Montlavo, Guerney, Rosman and Schumer, 1967). An early emphasis on the form of family therapy (for example, narrow insistence on having every family member present in every session) has matured to a recognition that the essence of the family therapy approach is a clear conceptualization of emotional disorders within their family context. The most effective family intervention at a given point in therapy may consist of an individual interview with an adolescent child or that youngster's placement in group psychotherapy. Frequently it may be separate interviews with the parents to strengthen the husband-wife relationship.

The family therapist appreciates the fact that these direct therapy contacts with individuals or subgroups of the family have great effects on the entire family structure. For example, the therapist makes a strong statement supporting the importance and legitimacy of the husband-wife relationship apart from the couple's parenting function merely by scheduling an interview which will focus exclusively on this subgroup and role relationship within the family. This message will reverberate throughout the family

239

influencing or perhaps threatening previous configurations of family priorities, alliances and status distributions. The family oriented therapist attempts to anticipate these repercussions, arranging those interventions which will accomplish the family alterations which further family growth, flexibility and effective communication.

This brief introductory comment is intended to convey a sense of the increasing clarity of therapeutic conceptualization in family therapy. The therapist proceeds methodically through several steps in his approach to the family. First he works to obtain acceptance as a temporary and yet important member of the family group. Minuchin (1974) has referred to this crucial step as "joining". Its successful accomplishment is necessary to the next step of re-defining the "emotional illness" in an individual family member as instead a family problem, a problem in family functioning which is partly manifested through the symptomatic behavior of the designated patient. This step is quite difficult in some families. Certainly it is rarely accomplished by mere theoretical insistence. The family must be *shown*, not told, that the family system, not the symptomatic member, is in need of help and change. As Rabiner et al (1962) have noted, even the scheduling of family therapy tends to increase the guilt and defensiveness in the family members.

Once these two steps are accomplished, the therapist is able to use his special role in relation to the family to block maladaptive patterns of relating within the family and to encourage exploration and experimentation with styles of interaction which may be more satisfactory. In this effort he may utilize the entire range of psychiatric interventions, perhaps emphasizing interviews with the entire family, but certainly not restricting himself to this format. The choice of interventions is guided by a tentative diagnosis of the family patterns and pathology, a conceptual framework which is constantly revised and refined to include the data which is revealed by the family's response to those interventions which the therapist attempts.

This process is quite complex. In many ways it is a more difficult skill to master than is individual therapy, since it requires greater activity on the part of the therapist and is therefore more prone to induce errors, both because of countertransference and the ease with which subtle verbal and nonverbal cues can be missed in the turmoil of an active family session. The family therapist is truly a participant observer and very busy at both jobs. These statements should not be construed as a warning against the dangers of doing great damage through family therapy. As Wynn (1965) has noted, family systems are very resilient and, in fact, hard to change. Still, effective work in the area requires careful study and supervised experience. One of the best introductory texts is Minuchin's (1974) *Families and Family Therapy* which is clear and concise and highly sophisticated.

The purpose of this brief chapter is merely to whet the appetite of those adolescent therapists who have not considered the positive applications which family therapy offers in adolescent psychotherapy. Family therapy as a formal approach has some particular indications which will be considered now, followed by a more complete explication of the steps in family therapy mentioned earlier.

INDICATIONS FOR FAMILY THERAPY

Conjoint family therapy with the entire family seems to be the treatment of choice in certain situations and for certain kinds of emotional disorders.

Crisis situations in adolescence, including many runaways, suicide attempts and illegitimate pregnancies often are best approached through family interviews. These sessions are of value in encouraging the family to find more adaptive ways of responding to the immediate problem, and, in addition, may reveal the chronic family problems which resulted in the eruption of symptomatic behavior in the adolescent. In many of these families the underlying excessive closeness of the adolescent to one or more family members may be the cause of a runaway or delinquent action which represents an ill advised attempt at emancipation. Unfortunately, many families do not seem motivated to continue in therapy once the immediate crisis is resolved (Morrison and Collier, 1969).

Even in the absence of crisis, the adolescent whose difficulties seem primarily related to problems in separating from his parents is probably best treated in conjoint family therapy. These youngsters may present with clear developmental immaturities including social anxiety, academic difficulties, and overt clinging, childish behavior. They may disguise their excessive dependence, with the family's collusion, as psychosomatic illness and complaints of illness. Of course, this family pattern may be precipitated and potentiated by the presence of actual physical disease, particularly chronic illness, in the child. As mentioned earlier, these families may come to therapy only at the time the adolescent tries to extricate himself from the excessively close family bonds. Occasionally the family is pressured into therapy by external agencies such as the school who detect the adolescent's social immaturity.

The basic problem in many of these families is an unsatisfactory marital relationship leading to inappropriate utilization of the adolescent to satisfy parental affectional needs or to provide a buffer between the parents. Therapy efforts are directed to strengthening the husband-wife subgroup if possible. If this seems impractical, the dissatisfactions can be rendered more explicit and the parents can be assisted to meet their needs outside the family while the adolescent's desire to separate is strengthened and supported. The therapist needs honest empathy for the "holding-on" parent in these families in order to keep the families in treatment and permit the eventual release of the adolescent. It is very easy for therapists with a special interest in adolescents to over-identify with the youngster. Merely blaming the parent and lecturing about the adolescent's right to a life of his own will only increase anxiety and perpetuate the frightened clinging pattern in the family. Many of these parents know at some level what they are "doing wrong". They need help in discovering alternatives.

Another group of adolescents who may be assisted through family therapy are those who live in families who externalize problems. In these families each member is preoccupied with the shortcomings of various other family members, and tends to feel that whatever unhappiness and adjustment problems he is having actually results from shortcomings of another family member. If individual sessions are held they are dominated by complaints directed against other members of the family. If the therapist sees two family members separately and discusses a recent upset with each, he is often left wondering if the two people were actually involved in the same event. There is virtually no introspection and the capacity for self-observation seems as limited as the skill in finding faults in other family members is hypertrophied.

Diagnostically, adolescents from these families often present as behavior disorders or personality disorders. Usually the pathology is relatively ego-syntonic and the adolescent rejects designation as a patient. However, since he clearly sees the pathology in other family members, he may accept family therapy as necessary.

Family therapy in these cases is difficult and trying for the therapist who is constantly being sought as an ally against other family members. However, with patience and dogged perseverance, it is possible to gradually require these families to communicate in ways that diminish the need for cycles of recrimination and blame. For example, the therapist, after assuring himself that he has effectively "joined" the family, may prohibit critical statements between family members. All communications must be translated into personal requests and statements of personal need. For example, if the father wishes to complain that his wife is not affectionate, he must say, "I feel lonely and I need affection. Is there any way I can help you show me more warmth?" In previous family discussions he probably would have said, "Our trouble is that you're a frigid bitch." The therapist may also require the parents to sit together and even request that they hold hands. The purpose of these maneuvers is not to forcibly graft these new behaviors on the family. The goal is merely to block previous stereotyped interactions which serve to avoid awareness of internal feelings by displacing them on other family members. Of course, many other techniques will be utilized in the tedious and prolonged effort to change destructive relationship patterns. The examples offered are merely illustrative of the way in which the therapist actively moves to alter family tradition.

A final kind of adolescent who may be best treated through family interviews is the youngster whose pathology is required to maintain a neurotic family homeostasis. This includes youngsters with "superego lacunae" but also a variety of other situations in which the adolescent is scapegoated by his family. In some of these cases it is necessary to provide a period of individual therapy to the scapegoat, in order to raise his status in the family group and to discover and activate personal goals which lie outside the scapegoat role. Without this special assistance, the scapegoat is often unmotivated to give his central role in the family. Like the man who has been ridden out of town on a rail, he feels the procedure is uncomfortable but more of an honor than merely walking like everyone else.

FAMILY DIAGNOSIS

The family therapist is interested in assessing family functioning in a number of interlocking dimensions. The first of these considers the family boundaries. The therapist tries to determine if there are clear generational boundaries, boundaries between individuals in the family, clear boundaries between the family and the surrounding society, and clear sex role boundaries. Pathology may result from excessively rigid boundary definitions or from boundaries which are vague or capriciously changeable.

The second structural feature of the family which is observed is the nature of the subgroups within the larger family. For example, a common dysfunctional subgrouping consists of mother and children allied against the father. The result is that the father is rendered ineffective in the parenting role and is lost to the wife as a gratifying husband. In normal families subgrouping occurs in a variety of patterns determined by the emotional or practical issues which occupy the family at the moment. There is flexibility and alliance patterns shift without strong family efforts to resist the changes.

The therapist also studies the family patterns of communication, noting both the conceptual clarity and the affective range. Normal families have relatively open communication which tends to be clear and determined by present needs rather than defensive maintenance of family myths or the need to deny particular affective states. Some disturbed families cannot permit the expression of angry feelings. When these threaten to emerge, communication may be blocked by irrelevant expressions of mutual concern or warmth. Other families block expressions of tender feelings.

During the diagnostic period of family therapy the parenting skills and styles of the family are also delineated. Do the parents provide appropriate nurture? Are they able to set limits? Can they provide information in a form which is useable and accurate? Can they deal openly with husband-wife conflict or do they utilize the parenting function to fight one another? Have they relegated parenting partially or wholly to one of the children? These and many other questions must be answered if one is to plan an effective treatment approach for the specific family.

Finally the therapist observes the family's style of problem solving. He is interested in seeing whether the family permits wide involvement in reaching decisions and planning actions or depends on one autocratic leader. If there is a single leader, is he supported or is there implied rebellion and contempt behind the apparent passivity of other family members? The therapist will encounter other families who seem incapable of reaching a decision. In these families there is no leadership or the process of problem solving is so contaminated by raging affective conflicts that it becomes chaotic and inconclusive.

FAMILY TREATMENT

After diagnostic evaluation it is possible to arrive at treatment goals for a specific family. These goals may have levels of priority although the therapist considers the entire picture in all his interactions with the family. For example, the therapist may decide that a family's confusing style of communication is a basic problem which must be actively confronted early in treatment. At the same time, however, he may be aware that one purpose of the disjointed communication is to disguise the fact that the overtly respected father is actually powerless in the family. He may chose then to focus on the communication problem by utilizing the father as his ally, thus simultaneously attempting to improve the father's status and reveal the family's use of confusion to block the father's competence.

As the therapist intervenes to change the family, his approach must constantly respond to the countermeasures the family mobilizes to prevent change. The process is not static but interactive.

Throughout the treatment contact, the therapist focuses primarily on family strengths and skills. Even behavior which must change is usually relabeled positively even while it is questioned and blocked. An intrusive, domineering mother may be told that she is taking too much responsibility and pressure in the family. Her husband may be asked to take over some of the work, "to give your overburdened wife a little rest from all her worries." A general expectation that family members will help one another is regularly voiced by the therapist. The value position that mutual support is the function of the family is clearly ennunciated, even when the needed support is a limit. "Johnny has a problem in that rules sometimes make him angry. Now you need to help him with that by making rules clear and not arguing about them or trying to explain them when he's angry. It might really be a help to him to know that he can talk with you about the rules later, when he's calmed down."

Needless to say, the focus in family therapy is on the present. When the family begins to recount past history they do so in order to refocus on the individual designated patient as the "real" problem in the family. Talk of the past is usually, therefore, defensive; a countermeasure aimed at neutralizing therapeutic activity. There are two exceptions to this general rule. Occasionally, the family will bring up the past in order to reveal a family secret to the therapist. Of course, this is not defensive, but a step in opening the family interactions to the work of therapy. The clear differences from defensive use of the past is that these past occurrences continue to have a strong impact on the entire family in the present and knowledge of them helps to clarify current issues and conflicts.

The second exception tends to occur late in family therapy when an individual family member has dropped his defensiveness and has accepted personal responsibility for his role in the family problems. At that time, a member may focus on experiences from his past which serve to distort appropriate responses to present family reality. It may be useful at this point to refer the family member for individual therapy.

Since it is impossible to even mention the endless variety of problems and techniques which may mark the course of family therapy in this brief consideration of the approach, the reader will merely be offered a brief summary and a list of some of the important writings on the subject.

SUMMARY

Family therapy offers much as the primary therapy in certain kinds of adolescent problems and may be useful as a temporary adjunct to other treatment methods in many other cases.

It differs somewhat from other intensive therapy approaches in that it depends less on introspection and insight to achieve lasting change than does either individual or group psychotherapy. The family therapist, in his direct interactions with the family, is more of an actor and participant than an interpreter of events. He does not aim to help the family understand itself. He acts to change the family so that it no longer blocks the understanding and growth of its members.

Therapeutic activity, however, is not random or dictated by countertransference. It is carefully planned following a careful diagnostic study of family pathology. Family therapy is not anti-intellectual and intuitive in its conception. Although the therapist may reveal more of himself than is customary in more reflective therapies, this revelation is directed only partly by his subjective experience of involvement in the family. This spontaneity must be tempered by a precise understanding of the purposes for which he is utilizing himself as a living instrument. Arriving at this under-standing will require the best intellectual and professional skills he can command. Achieving the goals will require a combination of activity and restraint which equals the most challenging demands of any form of psychotherapy.

BIBLIOGRAPHY AND SELECTED READINGS

Ackerman, N. W. 1958. *Toward an Integrative Therapy of the Family*, American J. Psychiat. 114: 727-733.

Bell, J. E. 1963. *Recent Advances in Family Group Therapy, In:* Group Psychotherapy and Group Function. Ed. by M. Rosenbaum and M. Berger. New York. Basic Books.

Haley, J. (Editor) 1971. *Changing Families: A Family Therapy Reader*, New York. Grune and Stratton.

Minuchin, S., B. Montalvo, B. G. Guerney, B. L. Rosmon, F. Schumer, 1967. *Families of the Slums*, New York. Basic Books.

Minuchin, S. 1974. *Families and Family Therapy*. Cambridge, Mass. Harvard University Press.

Morrison, G. C. and J. G. Collier, 1969. Family Treatment Approaches to Suicidal Children and Adolescents. J. of the Amer. Academy Child Psychiat. 8: 140-153.

Rabiner, E. L., H. Molinsky, A. Grabnick, 1962. *Conjoint Family Therapy in the Inpatient Setting.* American J. of Psychother. 16: 618-631.

Satir, V. 1964. *Conjoint Family Therapy.* Palo Alto. Science and Behavior.

Spiegel, J. P. 1957. *The Resolution of the Role Conflict Within the Family.* Psychiatry 20: 1-16.

Watzlawick, P., J. H. Beavin and D. D. Jackson, 1967. *Pragmatics of Human Communication.* New York. W. W. Norton.

Wynne, L. C. 1965. *Some Indications and Contraindications for Exploratory Family Therapy. In: Intensive Family Therapy.* Edited by I. Boszormenyi-Nagi and J. L. Framo. New York. Hoeber Medical Division, Harper and Row.

Part

Two

introduction

This section of the book deals with special problems which may be encountered in the psychotherapy of adolescents. These topics are discussed separately to allow elaboration of the technical complications introduced by extreme behavior patterns. The suicidal adolescent, for example, requires particular precautions and introduces unique countertransference issues. These were largely omitted in Part One in order to avoid tangential excursions which might have detracted from the continuity of the presentation. Despite the separation of syndromes in Part Two, the basic techniques described earlier apply in these special cases as well as in the more "average" case.

Many of the topics discussed in Part Two are more controversial than the general treatment approaches described in Part One. Where disagreement does exist, I have tried to mention the points of controversy and to include bibliography references which may be consulted for more thorough explication. I have generally tried to offer a more complete bibliography on the specialized topics, since the experience of any one therapist with these cases is usually limited. One must rely heavily on the reported experiences of colleagues.

Part Two is intended primarily as a beginning reference source for the therapist when he is confronted with a case involving one of the symptom complexes which are covered here. The chapters are self-contained and may be read in isolation from one another.

As in Part One, I have generally recommended one specific approach as the best method of dealing with each clinical situation. In treating these difficult and complicated problems, suggesting that one technical method is best is even more risky than in the discussion of general techniques. As in Part One, the suggested "right" approach should be viewed as an orienting statement. Each

251

therapist must think out his own philosophy and technique, utilizing only that portion of the approach described here which
seems comfortable and useful in his own work. If my "orientation"
serves to catalyze this thinking process in the individual therapist,
it will have served its intended purpose.

CHAPTER ELEVEN

depression, suicidal threats, and suicidal behavior

Suicide is an important cause of death during adolescent years even without counting those "deaths due to accidental cause" which may be consciously or unconsciously suicidal. A case in point which is growing in importance is the mortality rate compiled by motorcyclists. Nicholi (1970) has explored the dynamics involved in this particular self-destructive behavior. The actual estimated adolescent suicide rate (3.6 per 100,000) is still much lower than the peak rate (up to 27 per 100,000 in the aged) (Weiss, 1966). The rate is higher in college students than in the general adolescent population. Ross (1969) estimates a rate of around 10.5 per 100,000 American male students and 19.3 per 100,00 British male students. Suicidal attempts in the total American population below 20 years of age are much more common and have been estimated by Jacobziner (1965) at 60,000 per year.

FACTORS WHICH AMELIORATE SUICIDE POTENTIAL IN DEPRESSED ADOLESCENTS

It is perhaps surprising that the rate of suicide attempts and successful suicides is as low as is estimated. The threat of object loss and punitive superego pressures, two important dynamic factors in suicidal behavior, are virtually endemic to adolescence. Suicidal ideation and fantasies of glorious death are probably extremely common among young people. Possibly, many adolescents are protected from their self-destructive impulses by a combination of felt parental concern and the relative ease with which new relationships can be formed during the period.

Another factor, to which we alluded in an earlier chapter, is the adolescent's alloplastic avoidance of depressive affect. The tendency toward depression is probably basic to many of the emotional disorders observed during adolescence. Certainly, it plays a major role in many delinquent behavior disorders, drug abuse, the run-away, and learning problems. This depression is related primarily to the state of object deficiency which accompanies the necessary decathexis of parental introjects. Often, the delinquent behaviors which serve as defenses against depression are clearly self-destructive "little suicides." Very frequently, they are accompanied by a conscious sense of self-loathing. The adolescent says, "I don't care what happens to me," but his behavior suggests that the un-spoken conclusion of the statement is, "but I hope it's something terrible."

Morrison and Collier (1969) have pointed out the multiplicity of symptoms in adolescents who were referred to their emergency service because of suicide attempts. The authors regarded "school refusal and truancy; sexual promiscuity, occasionally associated with pregnancy; boredom and withdrawal; a variety of physical symptoms; compulsive hyperactivity; threats of physical assault; runaway; and the use of drugs or alcohol" as "associated symptoms of depression" in their cases. Interestingly, suicide attempts were the most frequent reason for referral to their emergency service, a finding which was duplicated in a similar program in Cleveland (Mattsson et al., 1969). Both studies emphasized the role of family disruption in precipitating the suicidal behavior.

MOTIVATIONS FOR SUICIDAL BEHAVIOR

Toolan (1962) has stressed the "call for help"—an attempt to manipulate parents which motivates both the runaway and the youngster who attempts suicide. In many cases, however, the sec-ondary gains sought through suicidal behavior seem less important than its relationship to primitive internal conflicts.

Some combination of factors, usually including a chronic his-tory of dependency deprivation, reversal of child-parent roles, and threatened abandonment, gives rise to a sense of hopelessness, helplessness, and worthlessness.* The suicidal attempt then serves

---

* Some authors have suggested that suicidal behavior in adolescents is re-lated to genital conflicts. These do appear in the history as unsuccessful ro-mances, conflict over incestuous feeling toward parents, and the like. In my

as a "trial by ordeal" or "gamble with fate" whose positive verdict is (at least temporarily) accepted. Since fate (the primitive super-ego) allows life to continue, the youngster is reprieved (Weiss, 1957, 1966). Both aspects of the suicide attempt are essentially "magical acts" (Wahl, 1957) aimed at attaining irrational goals.

The above pattern has a tendency to repeat itself so that recurrences of suicidal behavior are not unusual, especially if the response of important loved ones is not supportive. King (1969) has underlined the importance of the therapist's concern in response to a suicide attempt. Sabbath (1969), speaking of family relationships in the suicidal adolescent, speculates that suicidal behavior appears when the child perceives himself as "expendable" because the family unconsciously wishes that he would disappear or "drop dead."

MANAGEMENT OF THE SUICIDAL ADOLESCENT

The management of suicidal behavior depends on the evaluation of a complex set of factors. One must first consider the seriousness of the suicidal behavior. If the youngster utilized an extremely lethal method (shooting, hanging), it may be that the attempt aborted by purest chance. If the attempt was planned without provision for discovery, it is clearly more malignant than an attempt carried out with built-in arrangements for being rescued. The clinical diagnosis is also important, since some studies suggest that successful suicide may be related to the nature of the psychiatric disorder (Weiss, 1966). Balser and Masterson (1959) described a higher incidence of successful suicide in schizophrenic adolescents and in those who have lost a loved parent through death. The latter youngsters often seem driven to "join the loved one."

Most adolescents who survive suicidal behavior fall clearly into the "suicide attempt" category, as opposed to the "aborted successful suicide" category. Still, there are marked variations in the ex-

---

experience, closer investigation usually shows that the romance failed because of overpossessive, demanding behavior and that the incestuous ties interfered with a previously satisfactory dependency relationship. The block to moving comfortably into heterosexual roles in the depressive adolescent is the unresolved primitive tie to the mother.

tent to which the adolescent must stack the cards against himself in his gamble with fate. He may need to make his odds so poor that a completed suicide is virtually a certainty.

In addition to assessing the adolescent's inner drive to self-destruction, the therapist must consider the extent of environmental stress, especially family disintegration. The possibility of family compliance or even encouragement of suicidal behavior should be investigated. Finally, the adolescent's wider social environment should be evaluated. Social isolation, poor school performance, parental loss (Greer, 1964), and disruption of important friendships and romantic alliances increase the likelihood of repeated suicidal attempts (Barter et al., 1968; Stanley and Barter, 1970).

After weighing the multiple factors involved, the therapist must make a decision regarding the advisability of hospitalization. Often, this decision must be taken on very incomplete data distorted by the chaotic and charged emotional atmosphere which surrounds suicidal behavior.

Hospitalization of the Suicidal Adolescent

Certainly, the therapist cannot afford to take undue risks with the life of his young patient. Although some authors suggest an almost laissez-faire attitude toward the possibility of patient suicide (see as an example Bosescu, 1965), most therapists feel much more responsible for the protection of their patients. Litman's (1965) study of therapists who had lost a patient through suicide demonstrated that the event had a stunning impact on the practitioner. We return to this issue during the discussion of countertransference problems with the suicidal adolescent.

In any event, most therapists agree that, if the patient appears to be actively suicidal, he must be protected through immediate hospitalization. However, one must remember that hospitalization itself is not free of risk. The therapist must consider not only the routine risk involved in hospitalizing any adolescent, but the particular problems associated with the suicidal patient. It has been observed that there is an extremely high risk of suicide during the period immediately following discharge from the hospital setting (Moss and Hamilton, 1955). It almost appears in some cases that hospitalization merely delays and perhaps intensifies the dangers which may exist in the outpatient management of suicidal adolescents.

Outpatient Treatment of the Suicidal Adolescent

Many therapists feel that unless the diagnostic picture suggests an overwhelming likelihood of imminent suicide, most cases of attempted adolescent suicide should be managed within the family. This home management includes three areas which require attention. These are: 1) "sterilizing" the physical home environment, 2) parental therapy, and 3) direct therapy with the adolescent.

STERILIZING THE HOME. Although people may point out that a determinedly suicidal patient can always find a way to kill himself, there are many advantages in clearing the home of all easily available lethal materials. The parents and the adolescent are told, separately or in joint session, that suicidal feelings come and go. Confidence is expressed that eventually the adolescent will be glad that he is alive. Because of this, he will be offered all possible protection to allow him the opportunity to reach this attitude toward himself. The therapist explains the necessity of making the home as safe as possible to decrease the possibility of impulsive suicidal behavior. All potentially lethal medications, poisons, firearms, and razor blades (electric razors are quite satisfactory) should be removed from the home. The suicidal adolescent patient should be restricted from driving automobiles or motorbikes alone. Although the adolescent may protest these measures, they represent tangible proof that his parents and his therapist want him to live. This reassurance may play a larger role in the preventive value of the "sterilization" than the relative absence of the means for suicide (Mintz, 1966). If the parents do not cooperate in this effort, the therapist may be sure of their unconscious or conscious participation in the suicidal behavior. Hospitalization is essential under these circumstances.

It is wise to advise against prolonged parental absences during the early phases of therapy with the suicidal adolescent. Youngsters who are struggling with suicidal thoughts should not be burdened with excessive solitude. In addition, separations from the parents are potent precipitants of suicidal ideation and behavior in these vulnerable adolescents (Levi et al., 1966; Margolin and Teicher, 1968). Anecdotally, one is surprised at the frequency with which suicide attempts occur shortly before parents leave on a planned trip. Perhaps more surprising, the parents often ask the therapist if they should go ahead with their plans!

PARENTAL THERAPY. Many parents of suicidal adolescents are themselves extremely depressed, even suicidal (Margolin and Teicher, 1968). Many are overtly or covertly rejecting of their child (Sabbath, 1969; Schrut, 1964). These problems are often associated with and intensified by severe marital conflict (Stanley and Barter, 1970). Even when the parents do not appear seriously disturbed, they need extensive support and help because of the intense anxiety engendered by the suicidal attempt and the difficulties of parenting a potentially suicidal child.

The treatment approach for parents of suicidal adolescents is basically supportive, since unmet dependency needs are common determinants of the rejecting attitudes toward their own child. In those who are clinically depressed, antidepressant medication may be a valuable adjunct. This medication should never be dispensed to the parent in a suicidal dose.

Often, it is wise to provide these parents with a therapist of their own. Despite themselves, they may tend to feel envious and rivalrous of their youngster if all share the same therapist. If collaborative therapy is arranged, the adolescent's therapist must remain alert to any evidences that the family is withdrawing from his patient. This suspicion must be quickly conveyed to the parents' therapist, whose active steps to reestablish family reintegration and at least minimal support of the adolescent may be literally lifesaving.

Both Morrison and Collier (1969) and Mattsson et al. (1969) have pointed out that many families with suicidal children can accept help only during the immediate crisis and lose interest quickly. Of Morrison and Collier's 30 cases, only eight came for further interviews and only two were in treatment one year after the suicidal attempt. In the Cleveland study, 15 of 75 families failed to effect any further study or treatment after the crisis contact, although it was recommended. It does appear that a crisis-intervention approach involving the entire family may often be effective therapy for these disorganized families (Schrut, 1968).

DIRECT THERAPY OF THE SUICIDAL ADOLESCENT. Somatic therapies seem to offer little in the treatment of the suicidal adolescent. Even medication appears to be of limited value. If antidepressant medications or sedatives are used, it is imperative that they be prescribed in nonlethal amounts. Automatic refills should not be permitted. Even with this precaution, some adolescents will stockpile pills, gradually collecting a suicidal dose. Before deciding to utilize medications, the therapist should consider not only these practical problems, but also the psychological overtones involved in prescribing psychoactive medication for adolescent patients. The uncertain self and body images, fears of dependency and external control, and suspiciousness of adults which are often part of adolescent disturbances may lead to bizarre and antitherapeutic reactions to psychopharmacologic intervention (Easson, 1969).

Whether or not drugs are utilized, the real key to successful therapy of the suicidal adolescent is the provision of understanding, acceptable dependency gratification, and a gradual opportunity for emotional growth within the therapeutic relationship. The initial task in the psychotherapy of the suicidal adolescent is to establish a dependency relationship which the adolescent can accept without "losing face." Many of these youngsters are extremely threatened by their intense dependency wishes. The therapist must often utilize humor, extreme tact, and vigorous support of independent behavior to help the adolescent tolerate being helped. The techniques of treating a special patient of this general group, the "wrist slasher," have been described by Grunebaum and Klerman (1967).

When the dependency relationship is established with the adolescent, the problem becomes one of gradually assisting the youngster to become more self-sufficient without stirring fears of abandonment. The pace of therapy is characteristically slow, and the intense needs of these patients exert a drain on the therapist. A study of suicidal behavior during psychotherapy has suggested that attempts often follow a perceived rejection or negative prognostic comment from the therapist (Wheat, 1960). The therapist must be alert to countertransference hostility toward the demanding suicidal patient. It is imperative that the youngster not become "expendable" again.

There are a number of reasons why therapists may tire of the suicidal adolescent. This youngster has little capacity to assume responsibility for himself and often indulges in a great deal of whining and complaining. He continually sees other people, including the therapist, as withholding and unfair. No matter how giving the therapist may be, it is never enough. The therapist often begins to feel that he is trying to fill a bottomless pit. At other times, he begins to blame himself for his inability to meet the patient's insatiable demands. Some suicidal adolescents add to the countertransference problems by continuing periodically to threaten or attempt suicide. Often, they use the veiled or direct threat of suicide to extract special considerations from the therapist such as dramatic late-night phone calls or extra appointments. The therapist senses that if necessary many of these youngsters would play their trump card—a real suicide.

The combination of sympathy for the patient's real despair and emptiness, competing with frustration and anger over the youngster's emotional blackmail, makes for a turbulent and uncomfortable countertransference. The therapist is in fact walking a tightrope in many cases. If he capitulates totally in the "suicide game" and guarantees to meet the adolescent's unrealistic, nonnegotiable conditions for continuing to live, he can actually drive the adolescent to suicide. On the other hand, if he refuses to negotiate at all, insisting that the adolescent must decide whether to live or die himself, his patient may commit suicide in pique and dejection over losing the game.

The therapist must remember that these youngsters manipulate and demand because they are unable to meet their needs in any other way. They are convinced that no one will give them anything freely. They also believe that without "gifts" they are nothing. They feel that all good things come from others and that they are hollow and bad. They must blackmail, threaten, and coerce others. For them, this manipulation is literally a matter of life-or-death. Only gradually can they come to see themselves as possessing any inherent strength and worth.

In the management of crisis periods with suicidal youngsters, consultation with a colleague is of inestimable value. The objectivity of an uninvolved fellow therapist helps to prevent any mismanagement of the case which might result from the primary therapist's emotional discomfort. Decisions of whether to hospitalize the patient, how to respond to one of the "life-and-death" deals which these patients often propose, and whether to allow the patient to take a trip or go away to college are better shared than made alone. The practical advantage of consultation in medicolegal terms is also readily apparent. There is an obvious additional dividend for the patient if consultation allows the therapist to be comfortable about his legal liability and his ethical responsibility.

In the later stages of psychotherapy, after the development of a reasonably stable therapeutic alliance, it may be possible to deal more directly with the patient's dependency needs and masochistic defenses. Premature interpretation of the adolescent's active role in creating his own misery tends to be felt by these patients as criticism, "Rather than giving me the understanding and sympathy that I need, you too say that it is all my fault." Feeling abandoned, the patient may again become suicidal. Some of these depressed and empty youngsters require almost indefinite support with the frequency of supportive sessions only slowly and cautiously diminished (Easson, 1969). As mentioned in the chapter on termination (see the section "Therapy—Interminable"), this arrangement should be periodically reviewed with an eye to the possibility of actually completing the work.

—And If You Lose

Sadly, even the most skillful therapy cannot always prevent the suicidal adolescent from killing himself. The therapist is then faced with the task of dealing with his feelings of grief, guilt, and inadequacy. Litman (1965) has noted that therapist responses in this situation range from defensive denial and rationalization to virtual refusal to accept a suicidal patient ever again. From Litman's observations, it appeared that the therapists who succeeded in mastering their feelings generally did so by presenting the case to professional colleagues with an attitude of trying to learn something about preventing a similar occurrence in the future.

SUMMARY

It is a frightful responsibility to become involved with a youngster who is struggling with the question "to be or not to be." The drama and finality of suicide conspire with the personality traits of suicidal youngsters to make treating the suicidal adolescent one of the psychotherapist's most exacting experiences. The wise therapist will recognize his limitations and refuse to treat more of these youngsters than he can manage. Most therapists find that two or three potentially suicidal adolescents are the upper limit that they can effectively treat. Therapists with depressive tendencies of their own may find it best to avoid working with any youngsters of this kind.

CITED AND RECOMMENDED READINGS

Balser, B., and J. F. Masterson. 1959. Suicide in adolescents. Amer. J. Psychiat. 116: 400–404.

Barter, J. T., D. O. Swaback, and D. Todd. 1968. Adolescent suicide attempts. Arch. Gen. Psychiat. 19: 523–527.

Bosescu, S. 1965. The threat of suicide in psychotherapy. Amer. J. Psychother. 19: 99–105.

Easson, W. M. 1969. The severely disturbed adolescent. New York: International Universities Press, Inc.

Greer, S. 1964. The relationship between parental loss and attempted suicide: a control study. Brit. J. Psychiat. 110: 698–705.

Grunebaum, H. U., and G. L. Klerman. 1967. Wrist slashing. Amer. J. Psychiat. 124: 527–534.

Jacobziner, H. 1965. Attempted suicides in adolescence. JAMA 191: 7–11.

King, J. W. 1969. Depression and suicide in children and adolescents. Gen. Pract. 36: 95–104.

Levi, L. D., C. H. Fales, M. Stein, and V. H. Sharp. 1966. Separation and attempted suicide. Arch. Gen. Psychiat. 15: 158–164.

Litman, R. E. 1965. When patients commit suicide. Amer. J. Psychother. 19: 570–576.

Margolin, N. L., and J. D. Teicher. 1968. Thirteen adolescent male suicide attempts: dynamic considerations. J. Amer. Acad. Child Psychiat. 7: 296–315.

Mattsson, A., L. R. Seese, and J. W. Hawkins. 1969. Suicidal behavior as a child psychiatry emergency. Arch. Gen. Psychiat. 20: 100–109.

Mintz, R. S. 1966. Some practical procedures in the management of suicidal persons. Amer. J. Orthopsychiat. 36: 896–903.

Morrison, G. C., and J. G. Collier. 1969. Family treatment approaches to suicidal children and adolescents. J. Amer. Acad. Child Psychiat. 8: 140–153.

Moss, L. M., and D. M. Hamilton. 1955. Psychotherapy of the suicidal patient. Amer. J. Psychiat. 112: 814–820.

Nicholi, A. M. 1970. The motorcycle syndrome. Amer. J. Psychiat. 126: 1588–1595.

Ross, M. 1969. Suicide among college students. Amer. J. Psychiat. 126: 220–225.

Sabbath, J. C. 1969. The suicidal adolescent—the expendable child. J. Amer. Acad. Child Psychiat. 8: 272–289.

Schrut, A. 1964. Suicidal adolescents and children. JAMA 188: 1103–1107.

Schrut, A. 1968. Some typical patterns in the behavior and background of adolescent girls who attempt suicide. Amer. J. Psychiat. 125: 69–74.

Stanley, E. J., and J. T. Barter. 1970. Adolescent suicidal behavior. Amer. J. Orthopsychiat. 40: 87–96.

Teicher, J. D., and J. Jacobs. 1966. Adolescents who attempt suicide. Amer. J. Psychiat. 122: 1248–1257.

Toolan, J. M. 1962. Suicide and suicidal attempts in children and adolescents. Amer. J. Psychiat. 118: 719–724.

Wahl, C. W. 1957. Suicide as a magical act. In: Clues to suicide. Edited by E. S. Schneidman and N. C. Farberow. New York: McGraw-Hill Book Company.

Weiss, J. M. A. 1957. Gamble with death in attempted suicide. Psychiatry 20: 17.

Weiss, J. M. A. 1966. The suicidal patient. In: American handbook of psychiatry, Vol. III. Edited by Silvano Arieti. New York: Basic Books, Inc.

Wheat, W. D. 1960. Motivational aspects of suicide in patients during and after psychiatric treatment. South. Med. J. 53: 273–278.

CHAPTER TWELVE

the runaway

Running away from home is a time-honored American tradition. Few people reach adulthood without having angrily marched out from their home (often at age five or six) with the intention of making their way in the world. Many teenagers of past generations chose this abrupt emancipation from home and made it stick. Americans, with their emphasis on early independence and self-sufficiency, have an amused respect for the plucky youngster who grimly sets out to make his fortune. We have all loved Huck Finn and a long list of other picaresque heroes.

In recent years, runaways have become much more common, and much less amusing. Almost every large city has its equivalent to Haight-Ashbury, some district where large numbers of preteens and teens flock to escape their home life.

Some of these older youngsters are merely liberating themselves from objectively cruel and unbearable living situations. For other adolescents, running away is almost purely a symbolic expression of unconscious conflict, a true neurotic symptom. Most often, the runaway child is signaling a family disturbance which involves both himself and his parents. The running away in this case serves both to discharge family tensions temporarily and to symbolize the conscious or unconscious wish of one or both parents to desert their family responsibility—to "walk off and leave it all." According to Jenkins (1969), "The home background of the chronic runaway child is typically one of parental rejection from birth or before birth and one of parental severity and inconsistency."

Most runaways are managed by various social agencies in the community. Occasionally, however, a runaway is the initiating

264

event in a psychiatric referral or occurs in the course of evaluation or therapy with an adolescent referred for other reasons.

The personal dynamics of the youngster who feels compelled
to run away from home usually centers around a dependency-
independency conflict. Typically, the youngster is confronted
with strong feelings of helplessness and wishes for dependency
in a context which makes these feelings appear shameful, dangerous, or incapable of fulfillment. The resulting sense of panic
leads to a desire to escape the painful situation, to prove self-
sufficiency, and yet secretly to seek out a benevolent helper. The
runaway is both running from something (a disappointing object) and towards something (a fantasied gratifying object). The
similarity between the dynamics of runaways and depression has
been noted in referring to the act of running away as a "depressive
equivalent" (Chwast, 1967; Morrison and Collier, 1969; Glaser,
1967; Toolan, 1962).

Jane, a rather well-behaved girl of 15, impulsively ran
away from home, leaving with a boy she knew only as a "guy
with a pretty bad reputation." She convinced herself that she
loved him and accepted "speed" and sexual advances, stating
that these experiences were "beautiful." She maintained this
view, even after the boy deposited her on a street corner and
failed to return for her. She was then picked up by a "nice
guy" who convinced her to return home.

Jane felt that she had run away from home because she
could no longer "talk to her father." She said that he treated
her "like a baby." She felt that he was very unfriendly to
boys who visited the home to call on her. She also complained
that he was contemptuous of her opinions.

The parents admitted that the home was very unhappy
for all family members. Both parents had frequent, strong
conscious wishes to escape from a situation in which they felt
trapped.

In a family session, Jane wept and asked her father, "Why
can't it be like it used to be?"

When asked how long things had been going badly, she

indicated a time which corresponded to her pubertal development.

Jane's mother was preoccupied with Jane's brother. The
father had been a major source of dependency support until
the biological changes of puberty forced awareness of the
sexual components within the relationship.

Parents react to runaways with varying mixtures of anger, guilt,
and shame. They cannot entirely ignore the runway's dramatic
denunciation of them as parents even when they have little honest affection for the child. The intense emotional reactions to the
accusations contained in the act make it difficult for parents to
respond rationally to the practical problems raised by a runaway.
Some parents may also unconsciously prefer to rid themselves of
the responsibility for the youngster's care. They are guilty over
the runaway, but not entirely displeased.

The following classification of runaway behavior is offered as
an aide to diagnostic treatment planning. Naturally the various
types of runaway behavior overlap. One should not substitute
labels for careful evaluation of the individual runaway
youngster.

TYPES OF RUNAWAY BEHAVIOR

1. *The Adventurer*:

A great many youngsters who run away from home for a short
period of time during mid-adolescence are basically emotionally
healthy. They seem to be seeking an opportunity to prove that
they are self sufficient and that they can survive without the
support of their parents.

Although it is obvious that many of the dynamics of separation
and individuation are exaggerated in these young people, the
actual runaway behavior seems to result primarily from cultural
factors. Most of these adventurous youngsters come from
suburban affluent families in which they have been sheltered,
perhaps excessively. Often they are taught directly or indirectly
that the larger urban world is extremely dangerous. The desire of
such youngsters to venture forth into this "urban jungle" may
represent little more that a self-prescribed rite of passage designed

to overcome fears of independence. Although many of these youngsters describe minor difficulties with their parents or with school authorities, these difficulties do not sound serious. Often the complaints contain a predominant theme of being underestimated and overly directed. On direct psychiatric examination these youngsters do not show evidence of severe psychopathology. Their families seem equally free of severe disturbance and the social history does not reveal evidence of earlier trauma or serious impairment of the developmental process.

Most of these youngsters do not show a repetitive runaway pattern. They return home feeling older and wiser and resume their previous pattern of adjustment, often maintaining that the runaway experience was a valuable and important part of their development. In many cases, the runaway experience leads to subtle or obvious changes in family dynamics. The adolescent may be treated with greater respect, given more psychological distance, and more clearly recognized as an individual agent.

2. The Hedonist:

These youngsters may superficially resemble the Adventurer described above since they too run without any evidence of severe conflict with family members or with other important adults. The frictions which have been present in their lives tend to center around issues of freedom and controversy over rules. Superficially the fights sound similar to those "normal" runaways. However, closer investigation reveals that these complaints have much less substance and that the Hedonist feels irritated and constricted by even the most reasonable restraints on their absolute freedom to do as they wish. These youngsters may not appear calloused or angry, their affability depends on the adult's willingness to give them their way on all matters that affect their immediate pleasure.

Although the families in this category appear to have genuine affection for their youngsters, a careful history often shows that limit setting has always been cursory and ineffective. The parents tend to fear the youngster's anger and displeasure and have a long history of indulging and entertaining the child. This approach worked satisfactorily in the earlier years of development, but when the youngster's appetites become more adult, conflict appears as the parents attempt to curb the youngster's pleasure seeking for the first time. Frequently this effort to set limits is instigated by external social pressure eminating from the adolescent's school or some other agency of the larger society. Family dynamics often reveal a reason for psychological over evaluation of the child by one or both parents. This excessive narcissistic investment is the source of the hedonistic colusion which interferes with appropriate discipline.

These pleasure oriented youngsters tend to run away to situations where they can find other youngsters who share their philosophy of life. As a rule they do not go to adult-organized refugees for the runaway, since their motive for running is not to find assistance in dealing with family problems, but to engage in activities which have come to be forbidden in the family and in the community where they reside.

In a psychiatric interview these young people do not present as severely disturbed. They often admit freely that they enjoy the freedoms that they have found away from their home setting. At times their basically infantile viewpoint leads them to illnesses caused by over indulgence in drugs, the uninterrupted and sleepless pursuit of pleasure, and sexual promiscuity. Although the negative effects of their pleasure-seeking may lead to superficial promises to reform, they are difficult to treat successfully in an outpatient setting even when the parents are cooperative and involved. Having tasted the joys of unfettered license, they tend to run periodically when temptations are particularly attractive. These youngsters may gradually mature as they are faced over the years by the demands of reality. This maturation is particularly likely to occur if the parents can be helped to deal more realistically with the youngster's self indulgence. In some cases, hospital or residential treatment may be necessary in order to assist the youngster in accepting the requirements of living within the constraints of the reality principle.

3. *The Loner:*

The next three categories of runaway behavior are basically drawn from Steirlin's (1973) classification of runaway youngsters based on family psychopathological patterns. His general classification is based on the conceptualization that there are three types of families which produce in the adolescent a desire to run away. The first of these he describes as the excessively binding family. These families tend to hold their youngsters too close either through excessive gratification of dependency wishes or through a process of "mystification" which prevents the youngster from becoming aware of his own wishes and desires. As the youngster reaches adolescence, he finds his emerging sexual and aggressive drives cannot be contained within the family and experiences the desire to emancipate himself.

However, since his knowledge of the external world and his capacity to relate to peers are extremely deficient, his skill in adapting to the world outside the home is markedly impaired. If he does attempt to run away, the absence is brief since he is unable to find, attract, or utilize alternative sources of gratification. His loneliness and extraordinary dependency forces a quick return to the family, but the adjustment there is also unsatisfactory so that the wish to run again occurs sooner or later.

Family therapy in these cases is essential but is difficult to arrange. Inpatient therapy is almost always needed but is difficult to maintain. The parents of these youngsters are extremely threatened when their child is removed from the family. They are driven by their desperate need to maintain their unwholesome bond with the child to disrupt and undermine treatment. Often they become hostile toward the residential staff and are prone to sign the youngster out of the hospital against medical advice.

The therapist who hopes to succeed with these families must be patient and persistant. Often therapy must be interrupted and started many times before successful treatment can proceed. This degree of effort is indicated, however, since the situation is malignant. The family situation is extremely unstable and dangerous since the youngster's inability to find satisfaction within or outside the family may lead to severe depression and impulsive suicidal behavior.

4. *The Hood*:

This runaway youngster is produced by a family configuration diametrically opposed to the family which produces the lonely runaway. Steirlin describes this family as one with an expelling mode. The child is experienced by his parents as an unwanted incumberance to their own desires and pleasures. He is rejected and neglected and forced to fend for himself and meet his own needs at the earliest possible age and in any way that does not require the parents' time and attention.

Such a youngster runs away from home basically because there is nothing at home for him. The long background of depravation and emotional coldness have their anticipated result and the child tends to be emotionally cold, predatory, and unscrupulous. He does not trust emotional ties of any kind and is well prepared to maintain himself and to succeed among the criminal element on the street. In short, he tends to be a successful runaway but a hazard to conventional society. Naturally, it is extremely difficult to interrupt the adjustment mode by means of any currently known psychotherapeutic approach.

5. *The Emissary*:

Steirlin's third family type does not bind or expel the child, but sends the youngster on a "mission". The youngsters from these families are subtlely encouraged to leave the home for a period of time to engage in activities which indirectly benefit one or both of the parents. Often these children act out id impulses which the parents' super-egos forbid them to express directly.

The dynamics are those originally described by Johnson and Szurak in their classic paper on "Super Ego Lucanae". Other family missions may be more related to the vicarious testing of ego possibilities as in one of Steirlin's cases in which a father who was frightened of changing jobs and moving to a new community seemed to utilize his youngster's runaway as proof to himself that the change was not as dangerous as he feared.

Diagnostically one may be alerted to this type of runaway when a youngster's behaviour during an absence from home is clearly marked by expensive involvement in a specific activity which the family mission requires. For example, the daughter who is being utilized to act out mother's inhibited sexuality may concentrate on active sexual behavior during her runaway. Another clue may be the parents' preoccupation with a specific behaviour. Most of these Emissary youngsters maintain some contact with the home and often report on their behaviour by telephone or on their return home. Often one is amazed to learn that the parents have rather complete knowledge of the youngster's location and activities throughout the runaway period. This information is especially surprising in view of parental inactivity in retrieving the youngster.

Actually, this particular pattern of runaway behaviour is unlikely to change without extensive alteration of the family dynamics achieved by direct treatment of the parents or through family therapy. Inpatient treatment accompanied by intensive family work may be necessary in order to help the dynamics become conscious.

FIRST YOU MUST FIND THE CHILD—

The therapist's task falls into two phases. The first is to assist the parents to focus on the concrete situation. The parents' attention should be turned to seeking the child actively, since the likelihood that the youngster will engage in dangerous behaviors is quite high. The adolescent's denial of panic and dependency often results in a defensive sense of omnipotence. Under the spell of this sense of magical power, the adolescent may attempt extremely daring and hazardous activies such as stealing, sexual excesses, or drug experiments. It is wise therefore to attempt to locate the runaway as quickly as possible. This is especially important in the case of the preadolescent and younger adolescent in whom immaturity and poor judgment increase the the probability of hazardous behavior.

In recent years, some youth communities have organized themselves to provide care for the runaway. In many cities, these groups actually encourage the disgruntled youngster to leave home with the promise of satisfactory alternative living arrangements. In spite of the destructive effects of such pied pipers, the current social arrangements have some advantages. An experienced policewoman comments, "There was a time when almost every girl who ran away would end up pregnant by the time we found her. This isn't true any more. The kids tell us they don't have to take up with men now to earn their way, that they can go to the hippie communes and there they all live like brothers and sisters" (Birdwell, 1970).

Many hazards remain however and parents should be encouraged to contact the police as soon as they are sure that a runaway has occurred, with instructions to bring the youngster home when he is located. In addition, the adolescent's friends should be contacted, since adolescents rarely run away alone. Often, these friends have no intention of revealing the whereabouts of the missing adolescent. Their statements should be taken with a grain of salt, since they usually are actually trying to mislead the parent to cover the runaway's tracks. Still, instances do occur where the friend is not sure his friend's decision to run away was wise. He may be willing to help if he feels that it is in his friend's best interest. Needless to say, if the parent's call is angry and threatening, the friend is likely to conclude that any sensible person would run away from such a mean person and keep going. The parents should also contact those agencies located in the areas of the city where runaways are known to congregate.

None of these approaches would have any chance for success except that most runaways want to be found. They expect to be searched out and need to save face by making some effort to avoid detection and return to the home. They want to come home only if the parents really want them back and will show it. Once this assurance has been convincingly demonstrated, they often return quite easily after putting up enough resistance to maintain the respect of their friends.

The parents also need explicit advice on how to treat the adolescent when he is found. The may also require help for their own feelings in order to carry out the advice. Since the goal is to deal with the runaway event in a therapeutic way, the parents are asked to adopt an attitude of trying to understand why a runaway was necessary. The parents should avoid angry, accusative, and punitive attitudes as well as apologetic, self-accusatory, guilty comments. The therapist should offer an early appointment, preferably within 24 hours, for the family to consider together the reasons for this particular attempted solution of the family's conflicts. The therapist should convey to the parents an openminded desire to understand, neither assigning blame nor permitting the parents to finalize unchallenged any premature and oversimplified explanations which merely cast blame on the child or on themselves.

—THEN YOU MUST TREAT THE FAMILY

When the family arrives for the emergency family conference, the second phase of the therapist's job begins. This phase includes both diagnostic and treatment-planning tasks. The therapist attempts to evaluate the factors involved in the runaway. To what extent is the child responding realistically to impossible family circumstances, struggling with a neurotic conflict, or scapegoating himself to accommodate a family conflict? The answers to these questions suggest the type of help which should be recommended. The chronologic and psychologic immaturity of the adolescent also plays a role in deciding on the best approach in a given case.

In many instances, it is wise to arrange placement for the child whose home is realistically unsuited to adolescent needs. Confinement accompanied with active psychotherapy may be necessary for youngsters whose ego resources are limited. These youngsters will need external controls to avoid running away again when they feel stressed. Usually, the parents require concomitant therapy during the child's placement to avoid having the youngster return to the same setting which produced the problems originally.

A few runaways can be managed as outpatients. This group includes those who see their running away as an ego-alien symptom—an inner compulsion they would prefer to overcome. Some of the cases which closely approximate the "family neurosis" model may also be included, with a collaborative or a family psychotherapy approach. However, it should be recognized that symptoms rarely disappear magically at the initiation of a therapy program. One can predict to the parents that in outpatient therapy (or even inpatient care, for that matter) some repetition of the act of running away is a very real possibility. When it does occur, most therapists as well as parents have intense affective responses to this callous abandonment and indictment by the adolescent. Predicting the possibility of such an occurrence in advance may be helpful in attempting to maintain a therapeutic attitude.

CITED AND RECOMMENDED READINGS

Birdwell, R. 1970. Quoted in feature article by Maryln Schwartz, Runaway problem growing. The Dallas Morning News, Sunday, June 7.

Chwast, J. 1967. Depressive reactions as manifested among adolescent delinquents. Amer. J. Psychother. 21: 575–584.

Glaser, K. 1967. Masked depression in children and adolescents. Amer. J. Psychother. 21: 565–574.

Howell, M.D., E.G. Emmons, and D.A. Frank. 1973. Reminiscences of runaway adolescents. Am. J. of Orthopsychiatry. 43: 840.

Jenkins, R. L. 1969. Classifications of behavior problems of children. Amer. J. Psychiat. 125: 1032–1039.

Johnson, A.M. and S.A. Szurek. 1952. The genesis of antisocial acting out in children and adults. Psychoanalytic Quart., 21: 323.

Morrison, G. C., and J. G. Collier. 1969. Family treatment approaches to suicidal children and adolescents. J. Amer. Acad. Child Psychiat. 8: 140–153.

Stierlin, H. 1973. A family perspective on adolescent runaways. Arch. of Gen. Psych. 29: 56.

Toolan, J. M. 1962. Depression in children and adolescents. Amer. J. Orthopsychiat. 32: 404–415.

CHAPTER THIRTEEN
the violent adolescent

Vehement theoretical arguments flourish around the question of whether or not there is such a thing as an aggressive drive. The basic question is whether aggression is a learned reaction arising from frustration or whether it originates in an inborn instinctual drive. Waelder (1960) offers a detailed marshaling of the evidence which bears on the debate, but no definite answer seems possible. Currently, because of the recent flood of highly publicized violent acts, the proponents of the inherent drive theory seem to have the upper hand. There have been several popular books which have propounded this concept with varying degrees of scientific support (Ardrey, 1961; Lorenz, 1966; Morris, 1967). Golding's (1955) *Lord of the Flies,* a fictional account of the natural viciousness of a group of young boys isolated on a remote island, has had tremendous popularity among college students of the last decade, suggesting that there is ready acceptance of this view of human nature.

Actually, most research data suggest that aggressive behavior arises primarily in response to specific stimuli in the environment (Bandura and Walters, 1959; Dollard et al., 1963). Case studies of severely aggressive individuals usually contain much evidence both of severe frustration and of clear models of violence during the formative years (see Capote, 1966). Obviously, this does not settle the question, since it is clearly much easier to manipulate and research variables in the environment than to establish or disprove the presence of an innate biological drive. Some observations of the relationship between destructive behavior and the achievement of object relationships suggests that aggression is an inherent human tendency which must be socialized within the matrix of a loving and nurturing human relationship if it is to

275

be channeled into benevolent uses (Hartmann et al., 1949; A. Freud, 1949; A. Freud and Dann, 1951).

It may be that the most fruitful view of the basic nature of human aggression would regard aggression as a universal potential in human beings, yet almost infinitely variable in its expression. If appropriate growth conditions are provided for the young child, the potential for aggression is detectable primarily as an anlage of constructive capacities for active pleasure-seeking and problem-solving within the personality. Under less perfect developmental conditions, the potential may unfold in twisted and malevolent forms destructive toward the self and others.

No matter what position one takes in this controversy, it seems clear that adolescence is marked by an increase in aggressiveness. Some experts refer to this as a strengthening of the aggressive drive, whereas others emphasize the defensive and adaptive aspects of adolescent aggression. The flight from regressive passivity, the fearless sense of personal omnipotence, the weakening of superego controls, and the overburdening of the ego's adaptive capacities all favor excessively aggressive behavior in the adolescent. Much of the observable anxiety during this developmental period seems to be "instinctual anxiety," related to the adolescent's concern that he may be unable to restrain his destructiveness.

ADOLESCENTS WHO "THINK MEAN"

In the therapy of most adolescents, even those whose realistic potential for violence is minimal, violent fantasies, dreams, and threats are not unusual. The teacher who has crossed the adolescent is often tortured and mangled before being mercifully dispatched—all in the adolescent's ferocious daydreams, of course. A few days later, the same teacher is adjudged "not so bad after all." Usually, the therapist is laboring to help the adolescent realize that his murderous thoughts are harmless. As a matter of fact, the demonstrable harmlessness of these secret lethal fantasies is sometimes a valuable aid in proving to the adolescent that his thoughts are not so powerful as he thinks, and that he should be glad that this is so. A sparing and tactful use of humor may be a valuable tool in making this point.

ADOLESCENTS WHO FEAR THAT THEY MAY BECOME VIOLENT

Some adolescents may be much more threatened by their angry thoughts than those adolescents just discussed. Youngsters with borderline psychoses or severe personality disorders are frightened not by the imaginary power of their thoughts, but by concern that they may be unable to stop themselves from carrying their thoughts into action. These youngsters require a sensitive and supportive recognition of their fear of losing control. They are terrified of the damage that they might do and of the retribution which would follow. Some of them can be reassured by the symbolic promise of external assistance, whereas others need concrete evidence that they will not be permitted to run amuck. In both cases, the youngster's capacity and responsibility for self-control are underlined as necessities. The working defenses against hostile discharge should be respected and supported.

The therapeutic emphasis should be placed on recognizing and discussing the fear of loss of control rather than on the anger itself. The efforts which the patient makes to contain himself are accepted even if they are pathologic, illogical, or even emotionally crippling. These defenses should not be interfered with until it is clear that the adolescent is completely safe from the dangers of overt expression of destructive physical aggressiveness. The therapist never focuses therapeutic attention directly on the rage until he feels reasonably confident that the violent impulses can be vented and considered at a verbal and symbolic level.

Those youngsters who cannot feel safe without concrete evidence of external control may need inpatient treatment. Often, it is difficult to decide if this is necessary without a period of trial therapy.

Mark was a 16-year-old boy of sturdy build. He outweighed his therapist by 20 pounds and was in outstanding physical condition, since his fears of inner feminine and dependent strivings drove him to a herculean program of physical culture. He was referred for psychotherapy because of multiple minor delinquencies and a belligerent attitude toward parental discipline. On several occasions, the parents felt that Mark was forcibly restraining himself from striking them. His mother admitted to extreme fear that Mark might hurt her. However, Mark had never lost control.

Mark accepted treatment because of his concern over his inability to go to sleep without nightly calisthenics carried on until he dropped from exhaustion long after midnight. He worried about this symptom, since he recognized that it "wasn't good for health."

In an early session, Mark became very angry when the therapist commented that he seemed afraid to look at some of his frightening feelings. Mark took this as an insinuation of cowardice and immediately challenged the therapist.

"Can *you* admit that *you're* afraid of me?"

"Should I be afraid of you?"

"Don't give me that crap. What would you do if I came over there and knocked the shit out of you?" Mark said. He dramatized the comment by clenching his fist and half rising from his chair.

"Frankly, I think you are strong enough to keep from hitting me even when you're angry with me. I guess if I were wrong and it looked like you couldn't keep from coming after me, I'd holler for all the help I could get. I don't see that hitting me would help you. I'd try to get enough people here to keep you from hurting me or getting hurt yourself."

Mark relaxed visibly as the therapist spoke, but still seemed tense. The therapist continued, "Do you think I should get someone to sit in with us until you are sure that you can talk about being mad without throwing your fists?"

Mark looked at the therapist to be sure he was serious. When he was convinced, he relaxed.

"Naw, I'm not gonna hit you. You sure make me mad, though."

"Mark, I know it seems to you that I'm picking on you. That's not my aim. It's just that we've got to take an honest look at your hang-ups if we're going to get anywhere here."

"Go ahead, Doc. I'll try to behave myself."

THE HOMICIDAL ADOLESCENT

For most adolescents, violence is a feared thought or a frightening potential. Unfortunately, for others it is a very real possibility and a substantial risk. If these youngsters can be recognized prior to the eruption of homicidal behavior, tragedy may be averted.

There are some clues, gleaned from the study of youngsters who have committed extreme acts of violence, which may alert the therapist to the possibility that homicidal behavior could occur.

Most authors who have studied youngsters who commit acts of murderous aggression have described a family in which open violence is a commonplace (Easson and Steinhilber, 1961; Kaufman, 1962; Bender, 1959). Often, the child himself has been a target of physical abuse. If not, he has commonly witnessed brutal fights between the parents. Flagrantly seductive behavior, alternating with brutality, toward the child has been noted in many cases. Often, the child is encouraged to be violent. His aggressive assaults are not firmly limited. The parents may predict that he will eventually injure or kill someone. In several cases (Easson and Steinhilber, 1961), the parents permitted the youngster to keep and add to a collection of dangerous weapons even after he had shown assaultive behavior. Often, there is a history of dangerous aggressiveness toward family members or pets. According to Kaufman (1962), the violent acts are followed by calmness and a lack of remorse in the violent schizophrenic adolescent.

Many homicidal youngsters are willing to discuss their plans or fears of violent behavior if they are asked about them. The therapist should explore violent fantasies carefully. Does the adolescent have a particular person whom he wishes to hurt or fears that he may hurt? Has he thought of particular times when he might act or the weapons that he might use? Has he obtained these weapons? Has he practiced with them? Through a series of questions, it is possible to assess the current level of homicidal intent. The history helps to clarify the danger of an impulsive and unpremeditated homicidal act by illuminating the success that the youngster has had in controlling strong feelings and delaying action. Solomon (1967) feels that evidence of "poor rapport with the examiner" and "evasiveness" also indicates a more serious possibility of violence, possibly because this suggests paranoid tendencies. Scherl and Mack (1966) pointed out the active role of the victim in a study of adolescent matricide. The presence of a person who seems to be "asking for it" in the adolescent's environment increases the possibilities for homicide.

MANAGEMENT OF THE VIOLENT ADOLESCENT

The dangerously homicidal adolescent obviously needs immediate hospitalization. The family must be informed clearly of the seriousness of the adolescent's danger to others. Confidentiality does not hold when it appears likely that the adolescent will be unable to restrain himself from injuring others. The therapist should arrange for hospitalization under circumstances which assure his own safety as well as the safety of those who will be with the adolescent during the process of hospitalization. The quiet presence of several people reassures the adolescent struggling for control that he will be prevented from hurting anyone. The adolescent should be told that the therapist is hopeful that he can control himself without help. It is important to be honest and open with the potentially violent adolescent, especially if he has paranoid tendencies. He should be told directly and firmly that the therapist feels that any eruption of violence would be terribly damaging to the adolescent himself as well as unfair to others. The adolescent should be assured that the therapist will take all possible precautions to prevent this from occurring. Of course, it is only with the extremely precarious adolescent that such elaborate cautions are necessary. In most instances, the firm statement that hospitalization is necessary will be sufficient to calm the adolescent, since it promises the early availability of external support and control. Needless to say, it is important to avoid any provocation, physical competitiveness, or unkindness toward a youngster who is on the verge of an aggressive outburst. Any individuals who are brought in to help are there to strengthen restraint and control, not to offer counteraggression.

As a rule, the violent adolescent should not be treated as an outpatient until the threat of violence has abated. The failure of his defensive mechanisms and his fear of his own destructiveness make it difficult for him to explore his feelings without the structure and safety of an inpatient setting. For a description of the philosophical issues of patient control and practical procedures utilized in one college mental-health service, the reader is referred to Halleck's excellent paper (1967).

Stubblefield (1967) has written a concise, yet inclusive, summary of the relevant issues in the assessment of antisocial behavior. The entire group of antisocial patients deserves very careful attention. Robins (1966) has clearly documented the appalling adulthood which generally awaits the youngster with serious antisocial behavior problems.

CITED AND RECOMMENDED READINGS

Ardrey, R. 1961. African genesis. New York: Atheneum Publishers.

Bandura, A., and R. H. Walters. 1959. Adolescent aggression. New York: Ronald Press Company.

Bender, L. 1959. Children and adolescents who have killed. Amer. J. Psychiat. 116: 510–513.

Capote, T. 1966. In cold blood. New York: Random House.

Dollard, J., L. W. Doob, N. E. Miller, O. H. Mowrer, and R. R. Sears. 1963. Frustration and aggression. New Haven: Yale University Press.

Easson, W. M., and R. M. Steinhilber. 1961. Murderous aggression by children and adolescents. Arch. Gen. Psychiat. 4: 1–9.

Freud, A. 1949. Aggression in relation to emotional development; normal and pathological. Psychoanal. Stud. Child 3: 37–42.

Freud, A., and S. Dann. 1951. An experiment in group upbringing. Psychoanal. Stud. Child 6: 127–168.

Golding, W. 1955. Lord of the flies. London, Faber.

Halleck, S. L. 1967. Psychiatric management of dangerous behavior on a university campus. Amer. J. Psychiat. 124: 303–310.

Hartmann, H., E. Kris, and R. M. Loewenstein. 1949. Notes on the theory of aggression. Psychoanal. Stud. Child 3: 9–36.

Kaufman, I. 1962. Crimes of violence and delinquency in schizophrenic children. J. Amer. Acad. Child Psychiat. 1: 269–283.

Lorenz, K. 1966. On aggression. New York: Harcourt, Brace and World, Inc.

McDonald, M. W. 1938. Criminally aggressive behavior in passive, effeminate boys. Amer. J. Orthopsychiat. 8: 70–78.

Morris, D. 1967. The naked ape. New York: McGraw-Hill Book Company.

Robins, L. N. 1966. Deviant children grown up. Baltimore: Williams & Wilkins Company.

Scherl, D. J., and J. E. Mack. 1966. A study of adolescent matricide. J. Amer. Acad. Child Psychiat. 5: 569–593.

Solomon, P. 1967. The burden of responsibility in suicide and homicide. JAMA 199: 321–324.

Stubblefield, R. L. 1967. Antisocial and dyssocial reactions. In: Comprehensive textbook of psychiatry. Edited by A. M. Freedman and H. I. Kaplan. Baltimore: Williams & Wilkins Company.

Waelder, R. 1960. Basic theory of psychoanalysis. New York: International Universities Press, Inc.

CHAPTER FOURTEEN

the adolescent in legal difficulty

The problem of delinquency is much too complex for thorough discussion here (see Stubblefield, 1967). Some authors (Offer and Sabshin, 1963; Offer et al., 1965; Grinker, 1962) have found that a relatively high percentage of "normal" adolescents have committed one or more delinquent acts. Other authors (Masterson, 1967; Douvan and Adelson, 1966) have not found such a high incidence of "acting out" in their adolescent groups. However, in disturbed adolescents overt antisocial acts are common. These illegal activities appear in youngsters with a variety of diagnostic pictures. They may accompany psychoses and personality disorders of various types. Even basically neurotic youngsters may on rare occasions behave in a delinquent manner. Because of this propensity for alloplastic expression of conflict, the adolescent therapist is frequently faced with the family crisis produced when an adolescent is arrested and threatened with possible legal action.

The therapist is often expected to assume the role of the omnipotent protector who will rescue the adolescent from the throes of the legal process. Since the legal position in regard to the adolescent offender is somewhat ambiguous, the therapist is sometimes actually offered this power by well-meaning legal authorities. Judges, probation officers, and others involved in juvenile correction are well aware of the role which family and individual psychopathology plays in many cases of juvenile delinquency. If a qualified and respected psychotherapist makes a strong plea that a particular child be managed medically rather than legally, charges are frequently dropped and the youngster is simply released from any legal responsibility for his delinquent behavior.

In the case of some basically normal and neurotic youngsters

283

whose delinquency represents an isolated symbolic act, dropping of legal charges in favor of medical management may be an appropriate action. Unfortunately, the youngster who is struggling with a general problem of impulse control or the specific defects associated with superego lacunae is poorly served by such a failure in legal process. His pathologic sense of infantile omnipotence is strengthened. Society seems to be too frightened, just as his parents have been, to oppose his destructive impulses firmly. The adolescent feels this timidity as hostility and secretly believes that he is being given more rope with which to hang himself. The result is often a frightened repetition or intensification of testing behavior.

Youngsters with problems of impulse control need the external limits and structure which the legal apparatus may provide. An example of effective cooperation between probation officers and psychotherapists has been described by Kimsey (1969). Although the psychotherapist should never encourage or support vengeful, punitive approaches to the antisocial adolescent, he must recognize the value of the law and its official representatives in helping the adolescent master his impulses. Parents must be assisted to accept a similar attitude.

Parents will often be tempted to alleviate their feelings of guilt (which may be quite justified) by interfering with the process of law. Such ill-considered "help" may prevent the adolescent from recognizing his responsibility for his own behavior. It is hard for the adolescent to come to grips with himself if the parents tell him that their past mistakes "caused" his current legal problems. It is more productive for the parents to explore carefully their past and present contribution to their child's problems with rules, accepting and dealing with any guilt in an adult and mature manner. Confessing their "failure" to the child and begging his forgiveness can only compound previous errors and problems in the parent-child relationship.

Adolescents in trouble do need sympathy and help. However, the sympathy should be for the personal problems which tempt or force these youngsters into behavior that leads to loss of freedom and a lowering of self-respect. Help should be directed at encouraging personal growth and protecting both the adolescent and society realistically until a safe level of maturity and self-control is obtained.

Often, the therapist will not have the opportunity to deal with the adolescent or his parents until after an unrealistic "rescue" has been accomplished. In this case, the implications of corruption should be actively pursued in the therapy of both the adolescent and his parents. If such subtle encouragement of acting-out behavior is allowed to continue, the eventual results are always therapeutically disappointing and often literally tragic (Johnson, 1965; Millar, 1968; Leventhal and Sills, 1963).

THE DIFFICULTIES OF THE PROFESSIONAL

Parents and legal authorities are not the only people who have great trouble in dealing constructively with delinquent youngsters. The history of professional interest in delinquency suggests that we have had great difficulty in understanding and treating youngsters who act out. Eissler (1949) has suggested that the many confusing statements made regarding delinquency result from the fact that alloplastic expressions of psychopathology are very similar to normal behaviour in that in both cases action is utilized to alter reality. He also notes that while neurotic and psychotic patients show clear evidence of discomfort, the "delinquent" appears to be having a very good time with his disability. Although most modern psychiatrists would agree with a theoretical position which stated that delinquency was the result of psychopathology, there does not seem to be any comparable eagerness to treat this particular pathological condition. For example, Robins (1966) study of youngsters evaluated in the St. Louis Child Guidance Clinic revealed that those youngsters with severe behaviour problems were less likely to receive extensive treatment. The follow-up study also demonstrated that this group of youngsters was at a high risk for the development of psychiatric disorder in later life. Careful psychiatric evaluation of delinquent youngsters by Lewis and Balla (1976) has demonstrated that many youngsters in legal trouble are in fact seriously psychiatrically ill. It is also true, however, that many people are reluctant to recognize the presence of genuine psychopathology in youngsters who commit anti-social acts.

The relative neglect of this significant group of disturbed youngsters has many roots. It is more difficult to engage these children and their families in meaningful therapeutic work and they are often quite unpleasant to work with. In addition, the behaviors which characterize delinquent adolescents stir strong and uncomfortable feelings in the professional. The temptation to respond with punitive attitudes if not punitive actions is merely human. The view that the delinquent youngster is willfully bad (and enjoying it at that) is the historically traditional way of understanding delinquency. In fact it is only in very recent years that problem youngsters have been viewed in any other way. Prior to the twentieth century, anti-social youngsters were viewed as criminal and their misbehaviors were severely punished.

Of course mental health professionals rarely think about human behavior in this way, or certainly become uncomfortable if they realize that they do. It is possible that some notable tendencies to deny the reality and seriousness of anti-social personality problems may be partially the result of reaction formation against punitive attitudes such as those described above.

EVALUATION AND TREATMENT

In order to effectively treat the delinquent, we must recognize his serious ego defects. Superficially this defect in ego functioning seems primarily related to a "weakness" which interferes with impulse control. However, it may be more useful to see the erruption of impulses in the delinquent as a final desperate effort to compensate for other ego deficiencies.

The ego of the anti-social youngster is highly dependent on external agents for a variety of functions including management of stimulation levels, directing and maintaining attention, modulating affects, and a whole range of subtle operations related to the regulation of inter-personal relationships, particularly those that are emotionally important. Of course, these are the skills which enable one to master the environment and to maintain secondary narcissism and a sense of adequate selfhood.

It may be that the deficiency in these skills, whether it results from tempermental characteristics, constitutional or organic defects in the ego apparatus, or deficient parenting, is the core disorder in delinquent youngsters. Clinical experience often leads one to feel that the differences between the impulse-ridden youngster and the so called neurotic disorder is quantitative rather than qualitative. Even a youngster who expresses an internalized conflict through anti-social behavior is revealing a failure in internalization and socialization.

If we assume a basic defect in mastery skills in delinquent youngsters, we can expect that there would be efforts to compensate for such a basic deficiency. Some compensatory mechanism can be observed in the super ego pathology of these youngsters, in their persistant efforts to alter reality, and perhaps in some aspects of their relationships within their families. Lacking a capacity for mastery, they must attempt to maintain a sense of omnipotence.

The clinical evidence for super-ego defects in anti-social youngsters is obvious. There is often a lack of remorse and conscious guilt regarding actions which are clearly harmful or unfair to other people. There is also research evidence that delinquents show a lower capacity for self critical guilt than do controlled adolescents.

Other youngsters who act out appear to have indirect evidence of harsh and punitive super-egos. The basically self-destructive quality of much of their behavior, their frequent tendency to apparently arrange detection and punishment, and their vulnerability to periods of self hatred and depression suggest that some delinquents expend a great deal of energy in attempting to avoid strong feelings of guilt. One is also impressed by the extreme lengths to which these youngsters will go in order to maintain a sense of grievance against the world in order to justify their hostile and destructive behavior. Redl (1951) has been particularly articulate in describing the almost delusional quality of the delinquent youngster's sense of unjust treatment and the reluctance he demonstrates to relinquish this interpretation of the motives and actions of others. The youngsters will insist he is being mistreated even in the face of repeated demonstrations of trustworthiness, friendliness, and kindness. This kind of behavior suggests that the youngster is attempting to avoid an internal sense of guilt regarding his anti-social behavior.

This is not to suggest that delinquent youngsters have normal super-ego function. It is obvious that they do not. However, it may be that much of the super ego distortion observable in anti-social youngsters may be secondary to a basic defect in coping skills rather than the proximate cause of the anti-social behavior.

The limited adaptive skills of behaviorly disordered youngsters are also reflected in their attitude toward reality. Superficially, delinquent youngsters are clever, shrewd and manipulative. They are often quite effective in forcing other people to accomodate to them. Delinquents often appear willful and controlling; determined to have things their own way. For example, the normal youngster is willing, perhaps after a bit of grumbling, to adjust to his teacher's assignment of the difficult project, while the youngster with a behavior disorder may expend considerable energy avoiding the task or convincing the teacher that her expectations are too high. Many times the problem youngster may avoid the task and may be viewed as someone who gets away with things while other youngsters are forced to produce. What is often overlooked in this analysis of the situation is the fact that the healthier youngsters superior coping mechanisms allow him the luxury of accepting the teacher's demand while the behaviorly disordered youngster is forced by desperation to persist in his efforts to avoid a task that he feels he cannot master. The delinquent youngster fears change, novelty, and being overwhelmed. He develops one aspect of his coping skills, those that relate to adapting reality to his limited skills, to a fine art. Unfortunately, this emphasis on controlling others actually leads to a continuing and growing atrophy of other skills.

It is well known that most delinquent youngsters tend to view themselves as helpless and out of control. They feel that they are the victims of fate and bad luck. They have very little sense that they can control their own destiny. Frenzied efforts to control individuals, events, and situations may be recognized primarily as efforts to gain some illusory sense of impact and personal importance.

From the psychological point of view, the antisocial youngster's assessment of his place in the world is correct. In fact, he is not master of his fate because of the previously mentioned ego defects. Although he misunderstands the reason for his lack of self direction, his compensatory efforts to prove that he is running the show (of his own life) are as understandable as they are ineffective in improving his situation.

Finally, it should be recognized that many delinquent youngster's use their parents as ancillary ego agents while denying that their parents' interventions are desired or helpful in any way. Many delinquent youngsters are masters of techniques for eliciting an unusual degree of parental support, direction, and even intervention in the youngster's interaction with his environment. At times this help is requested or demanded openly but more commonly delinquents provide an indirect invitation for assistance through constant failure in adaptation and apparent lack of concern regarding their dangerous situation. Obviously, the parents feel that they must step in and save the youngster.

Often the delinquent youngster can gain a measure of success with the direct assistance of his parents, but there are other defensive advantages in involving them in his affairs in any case. If the youngster continues to fail in spite of parental aid, he can define that aid as interference, babying, or domination, all of which may then be utilized as explanations for the failure.

Specific treatment techniques may be individual, group, or family. The selection of a treatment approach or combination of approaches will depend on the specific case and the nature of the motivation for change. Regardless of the approach, however, one needs to keep in mind the basic deficiency of the delinquent described above and the primary defense that he utilizes in order to avoid facing his deficiency. This defensive structure will surely lead the delinquent patient to act out again, to attempt to involve the therapist in a direct power struggle of some kind and in efforts to corrupt the therapist. If one is able to patiently avoid becoming enmeshed in these defensive operations while continuing to provide affectionate acceptance coupled with reasonable limit setting, the delinquent youngster is provided with an atmosphere in which he can once again resume emotional and psychological growth.

CITED AND RECOMMENDED READINGS

Douvan, E., and J. Adelson. 1966. The adolescent experience. New York: John Wiley & Sons, Inc.

Eissler, K.R. 1949. Some problems of delinquency. *In:* Eissler, Searchlights on delinquency. Int. Univ. Press, Inc., New York, p. 9.

Grinker, R. R., Sr. 1962. "Mentally healthy" young males (homoclites). Arch. Gen. Psychiat. 6: 405–453.

Johnson, A. M. 1965. Sanctions for superego lacunae of adolescents. *In:* Searchlights on delinquency. Edited by K. R. Eissler. New York: International Universities Press, Inc.

Kimsey, L. R. 1969. Out-patient group psychotherapy with juvenile delinquents. Dis. Nerv. Syst. 30: 472–477.

Leventhal, T., and M. Sills. 1963. The issue of control in therapy with character problem adolescents. Psychiatry 26: 149–167.

Lewis, D.D., D.A. Balla. 1976. Delinquency and psychopathology. Grove and Stratton, N.Y.

Masterson, J. F. 1967. The psychiatric dilemma of adolescence. Boston: Little, Brown & Co.

Millar, T. P. 1968. Limit setting and psychological maturation. Arch. Gen. Psychiat. 18: 214–221.

Offer, D., and M. Sabshin. 1963. The psychiatrist and the normal adolescent. Arch. Gen. Psychiat. 9: 427–432.

Offer, D., M. Sabshin, and D. Marcus. 1965. Clinical evaluation of normal adolescents. Amer. J. Psychiat. 121: 864–872.

Robins, L.N. 1966. Deviant children grown up, The Williams and Wilkins Co., Baltimore.

Redl, F. and D. Wineman. 1951. Children who hate. Free Press, Glencoe, Ill.

Stubblefield, R. L. 1967. Antisocial and dyssocial reactions. *In:* Comprehensive textbook of psychiatry. Baltimore: Williams & Wilkins Company.

CHAPTER FIFTEEN

the sexually active adolescent

THE HETEROSEXUALLY ACTIVE ADOLESCENT:
A RELUCTANT LIBERTINE

Many young adolescents have sexual experiences. Even more youngsters would like their friends (often including their therapist) to imagine that they have an active sex life. The virile pursuit of girls is a socially sanctioned part of male adolescence. In recent years, in conjunction with the "sexual revolution" a similar readiness for experimentation of an overt kind has come to be expected of girls, at least in some cultural settings.

Without doubt, this social expectation is strongly reinforced by an increased biological thrust toward sexual maturity. Observation suggests however that personal anxiety about adequacy and peer-group pressure institute premature sexual behavior with greater frequency than any inner surge of lusty passion. Usually, early adolescent sexual drives are fairly well balanced by interpersonal anxiety and intrapsychic guilt, unless the anxiety is offset by a greater fear of being branded, by self or others, a sissy, chicken, wienie, square, or queer. Many of the adolescent boys who are seen in psychotherapy are either consciously plagued by doubts about their masculinity or driven to aggressive sexual exploitation to ward off the emergence of these doubts from the unconscious.

Some girls turn toward frantic sexuality during early adolescence to combat the regressive homosexual tie to the mother (Blos, 1963). They show more interest in scandalizing their mother and manifesting their complete scorn for her rules of behavior than in the boys that they pursue. They are not interested in any emotional relationship with the boys that they seduce. Often, they are more masculine than feminine in their aggressive conquest of males. They show virtually no tenderness toward the boys and often prefer to have many boyfriends on the string. Many of these girls engage in group sex with a number of boys, the "gang bang." In all of their sexual behavior, they exhibit a swaggering, triumphant, and spiteful attitude, both toward their mother and their sexual partners. When they become comfortable in therapy, they readily admit that intercourse itself gives them little or no pleasure. They do however, enjoy shocking people with their prodigal sexuality. They also take pride in recounting their "track record," the number of boys that they have seduced. Particular pride may be shown over success in seducing a boy who was generally considered shy, innocent, or morally upright. One gets the uncomfortable feeling that they are displaying their collection of scalps when they list their sexual conquests. Any kind words are reserved for boys who treat them with indifference and contempt. "He don't give a shit about *anything*" is a highly complimentary description of a male companion.

Other adolescents, male and female, utilize sexual behavior self-destructively in the service of a punitive superego. In these instances, the sexual behavior may serve more to prevent true pleasure in sexuality from emerging than to move toward its attainment.

The goal of these youngsters is to solicit external control and condemnation. This censure reinforces the faltering primitive superego and reinstates its domination over the instinctual life.

The overt sexual behavior of these adolescents is marked by exhibitionistic display and subtle contrivance to be caught. Often, they blame their sexual partners for "leading them astray." It is not unusual to see this pattern repeat itself in a cyclic fashion with periods of prudery alternating with episodes of complete license.

In short, there is considerable counterfeit sexuality in word and deed during early adolescence.

In therapy, heterosexually active youngsters may attempt to maneuver the therapist into a stand against their sexual behavior on moral grounds. If the therapist opposes their sexual involvement because they are "too young" or because they are unmarried, the youngsters are usually satisfied to argue, relieved that they do not have to face their real problems. There are few adolescents who would not prefer to see themselves as precocious, daring, and immoral rather than frightened, childlike, or hamstrung by a rigid conscience.

Even the late adolescent, the college student, may use sexual behavior more as a defense against anxiety than as an expression of mature, responsible affection. This topic is discussed more fully in the Group for the Advancement of Psychiatry report on *Sex and the College Student* (1965).

Psychotherapeutic Management of the Heterosexually Active Adolescent

It is very easy for the psychotherapist to be drawn into a subjective response to the adolescent patient's report of sexual activity. He may view the adolescent boy's flight into hostile "making out" as a healthy move toward masculinity, ignoring its defensive, sadistic, pregenital nature. Conversely, unconscious envy and competitiveness may lead to an excessively suppressive attitude toward a budding comfort with male assertiveness of an appropriate kind. With adolescent girls, the therapist may panic over the possibility of pregnancy or may slip into a subtle seductiveness. Powerful myths surround the subject of adolescent sexual behavior, and these influence the adolescent psychotherapist along with the remainder of society. When these social forces act in synergy with serious unresolved adolescent conflicts within the therapist, the result can be either an explosive unconscious sanctioning of destructive sexual acting out or, equally harmful, a stiff moralism which merely suppresses sexual strivings and stunts the adolescent's emotional growth.

ON BEING AN OLD FOGY. There seems to be general agreement that a "sexual revolution" is occurring, although there is considerable disagreement concerning its exact nature and its desirability (Shainess, 1968; Halleck, 1967; Lief, 1968). More than ever, the adolescent patient will be disposed to view his psychotherapist as morally old-fashioned. The therapist usually cannot avoid revealing his values regarding sexual behavior even if he tries to remain scrupulously objective. It is probably unwise to remain morally "faceless" with an adolescent. At the appropriate point in treatment, it can be very helpful for the therapist to discuss his moral views frankly with his young patient. This is especially valuable if the therapist will differentiate between those views which have some support in experience and those which "just feel right to me."

Most psychiatrists value honesty and genuineness in human relationships, responsibility for one's behavior, avoidance of exploitation of others, and the relative superiority of long-term intense emotional commitments over casual, hedonistic attachments. Halleck (1969) has pointed out that today's youth often value style, "coolness," and nonpossessive relationships with a limited emotional commitment. Obviously, there are some points of congruence and some diversions when the two lists of values are compared. As a rule, the points of congruence offer a "value agreement base" solid enough to support psychotherapy. Our young people do not advocate exploitation of others, interpersonal dishonesty, or self-deception. This common ground is usually sufficient for the exploration of symptomatic, pseudosexual behavior in psychotherapy. This is possibly as far as the psychotherapist should venture in evaluating and assessing the sexual behavior of our youth. If there is a detectable note of resignation in this position, it is due to my personal belief that Deutsch (1967) is correct in stating, "It has been my observation that an adolescent who invests his entire libido in genital gratification, for an over-long and energy-consuming period, suffers with regard to his capacity for sublimation, which may not fully recover during the process of maturation." Unfortunately, at this point in our history, American society offers little assurance of the value and desirability of extensive sublimations. In many communities, it seems almost quixotic to expect our young patients, already anxious and vulnerable, to delay gratifications which are virtually pressed on them by prevailing social mores in order to achieve a kind of personality richness and subtlety which seems of questionable adaptive value in their surroundings. At any rate, we may have to relax our pursuit of the ideal sufficiently to accomplish the possible—again, the exploration and treatment of *neurotic distortions* of sexual behavior.

If we accept this limitation and agree that it is not the function of the adolescent therapist to dictate or enforce moral codes, sexual behavior may be evaluated as any other interpersonal transaction. A few of the questions which must be asked in the attempt to evaluate the authenticity of any sexual activity are offered in the next section.

EVALUATING THE MEANING OF SEXUAL BEHAVIOR. Do the stated goals of the behavior match the adolescent's actual management of the situation, or does the adolescent appear to be deceiving himself? Does he desire sexual gratification or punishment for sexual behavior? Is he demanding an adult prerogative verbally while clinging to childish irresponsibility and dependency? To what extent does the sexual behavior serve the defense of "misdirection?" —that is, does the emphasis on sexuality hide a depression or a hostile, aggressive attitude toward other people? Does the sexual behavior appear relaxed and integrated in the personality or forced and counterphobic? Is the adolescent leaping into sexual behavior to avoid anxiety-producing sexual fantasies? To what extent are these frightening sexual fantasies related to oedipal involvements at home or with the therapist? How closely does the adolescent's relationship to his sexual partner approximate a mature, realistic human sharing? How much is the relationship still colored by identification with the partner, projection, idealization, narcissism, and other factors which diminish the humanness and autonomy of his lover?

These questions are complex and difficult to answer. They are offered only to concretize some of the issues implied by the truism that sexual behavior is an expression of the entire personality, not an isolated phenomenon which is to be viewed only from biological and moral perspectives. A broad view of the total developmental position of the adolescent permits the therapist to respond appropriately to the relevant growth problems of the adolescent without falling into futile efforts to dictate "proper" behavior.

Usually, however, it is necessary to set limits on sexual behavior in order to deal effectively with the real concerns which are being defended and disguised in the sexual acting out. For those adolescents who are deeply regressed or flagrantly self-destructive, it may be necessary to provide temporary or prolonged external control through hospitalization. In many cases, however, it is possible to establish a therapeutic alliance which is strong enough to manage the behavior. Interdictions are then based on technical considerations and are accepted because of the adolescent's wish to cooperate in a therapeutic process which already promises to provide greater benefits than those conferred by the conflicted sexual activity. The technique of limit setting is more fully discussed in Chapter Four.

The therapist must trouble himself with one further question. Does the sexual acting out, even though it contains elements of neuroticism and immaturity, represent a progressive movement in development? The adolescent must experiment in real life. Often, he must learn by making his own mistakes, even in a potentially dangerous area such as sexuality. If the adolescent seems to be honestly evaluating his experiences and profiting by his errors, it may be unwise to emphasize prohibition. When the adolescent can decide for himself that a style of behavior is unsuited to him, he has accomplished a greater strengthening of ego functioning than when he merely desists to "please" the therapist.

It is usually possible to distinguish between acting out for purposes of learning and acting out which is defensive and regressive, although the distinction may not be easy in many cases. Usually, the therapist can sense whether the prevailing tone of therapy is exploratory or evasive. The therapeutic alliance is a useful barometer to watch during episodes of sexual activity. Its fluctuations often gauge the extent to which the flurry of activity represents a turbulent storm of change and growth, or merely more hot air.

The reader is referred to Rexford's (1963) thoughtful paper, "A Developmental Concept of the Problems of Acting Out," for a thorough exploration of the importance of acting out in psychosexual maturation.

HOMOSEXUALITY IN ADOLESCENCE

There are few data regarding either the nature or treatment of adolescent homosexuality in the psychiatric literature. This is somewhat surprising, since homosexual behavior is fairly frequent in the adolescent population. It is well known that many adolescent boys fear passive wishes within themselves which they interpret as "homosexual tendencies." As we have noted, a similar fear often provokes inappropriate heterosexual behavior in the girl. Homosexuality appears to be more easily accepted among some subcultures of older adolescents than it has been in the past.* However, the vast majority of adolescents remain terrified by the prospect of sexual inversion.

The Pseudohomosexual Adolescent

In adolescence, most "homosexual" feelings actually resemble "pseudohomosexuality" as described by Ovesey (1955). The adolescent boy is uncertain of his masculinity and tends to react to any personal setback as a castration which diminishes his security as a male. These defeats also increase dependency feeling which are especially likely to be directed toward strong masculine figures. This combination of factors is often interpreted by the adolescent male as evidence of homosexuality. The resulting anxiety often precipitates a further cycle of failure → sense of castration → dependency yearnings → greater fears of homosexuality. Obviously, the boy who is caught up in this sequence finds it very difficult to approach girls with the necessary degree of self-assertion, masculine pride, and self-confidence to attract them. His lack of success in dating perpetuates the vicious cycle of masculine failure. Youngsters caught in such a pattern may develop straightforward symptoms of depression and anxiety or may attempt to disguise their concerns from themselves and others by hyperaggressive acting out. It is important to distinguish "delinquent" behavior of this kind from that which results from basic defects in socialization.

TREATMENT OF THE PSEUDOHOMOSEXUAL ADOLESCENT. If the ado-

---

* For example, complete acceptance of homosexuality (indeed polymorphous perversion) is implied in the popular musical *Hair*.

lescent presents with a facade of acting out, this must be managed first through the techniques described in Chapter Four (in the sections on developing the therapeutic alliance). When the fears of homosexuality are openly expressed, the therapist can begin to deal with them as outlined in the present section.

The origins of pseudohomosexuality in the adolescent male may include family constellation (such as the absence of an adequate male model), family dynamics (such as a mother or father who is frightened by normal masculine assertiveness), accidental traumas (physical disabilities or homosexual seduction by an older male), or tempermental inclinations toward passivity. It is important for the therapist to understand the beginnings of the heightened sensitivity to failures in masculine functioning. These may be useful later in therapy as the adolescent begins to define and synthesize his own style of male functioning. In this undertaking, he will need to assimilate his personal experiences with maleness in all its idiosyncratic richness.

Early in therapy, the above approach should be avoided. It will not help the adolescent if he interprets a genetic reconstruction as an explanation of how he came to be "queer!" The immediate goal is to reassure the adolescent that he is *not* homosexual.

It is important for the therapist to provide a model of active, assertive, and effective masculine functioning from the onset of therapy.* The pseudohomosexual boy often responds to this by forming an immediate (pseudohomosexual) dependent, positive, passive transference. This bond may then be utilized to redefine the adolescent's problem as masculine self-doubt rather than incipient homosexuality.

If the timing is correct, the adolescent's revulsion toward his homosexual thoughts and his frustrated yearnings for success with girls may be used to prove his heterosexual orientation to his satisfaction. In addition, the "powerful" therapist should not hesitate to use his status as an expert to state flatly and with conviction that the adolescent is a worried heterosexual and in *no way* homosexual.

---

* Although I have some scepticism regarding the overriding importance of the sex of the therapist in adolescent psychotherapy, pseudohomosexual youngsters probably do need a concrete model of sex-role functioning.

After the therapist convinces the adolescent that he is heterosexual, it is safe to explore the misconceptions which the youngster
harbors both about himself and the nature of masculinity. Many of
these young men have been rejected by fathers who have defined
masculinity in narrow and sometimes unattractively cruel, cold,
and combative terms.* A corrective redefinition within the treatment relationship can often literally free the adolescent to be "his
own man."

Usually, therapy must include active encouragement of appropriate heterosexual behaviors. Often, it is necessary to be quite
active in teaching basic dating and conversational skills as well as
supporting worth and attractiveness. The occasional misgivings
that the boy may be performing heterosexual behavior because of
his homosexual attachment to the therapist are usually dispelled
rapidly when the youngster begins to have some success with girls.

While supporting masculine assertiveness in the "outside"
world, the therapist gradually becomes less active in the therapy.
With as much subtlety as possible, the therapist allows and encourages the adolescent to become more assertive and aggressive
during therapy sessions. If the boy is able to disagree with a comment, the therapist may allow himself to be convinced, if the
comment is not essential to the goals of therapy. Occasionally, the
therapist casually defers to an area of expertise which the adolescent possesses. In many small ways, he demonstrates his respect for
the younger man's masculinity. The therapist is not pretending
that his masculine competence is inferior to the adolescent's. The
goal is merely to show the adolescent, as Maurice Levine is fond of
saying, that there can be *two* men in the same room.

Since many of these young men have secret wishes to be powerful and to dominate other men, it is important for the therapist
to insist on his own worth. The therapist has a further opportu-

---

* The play *Tea and Sympathy* provides a sensitive portrayal of such a
young man, although the treatment approach employed by the heroine cannot be generally recommended. She is the wife of the hypermasculine coach—
one of the men who disparages the hero's masculinity. She finally offers herself
as a sexual partner to the hero in a desperate and successful effort to prove
his adequacy once and for all. The story clearly states the unconscious fantasy
of the passive male who wins the oedipal contest through gentleness and
passive suffering.

nity in this phase of treatment to correct the distorted picture of masculinity which these young men harbor. They need to learn that men can be self-respecting, assertive, and competent without being cruel, overbearing, or domineering. In the therapeutic relationship, neither individual dominates or is dominated.

A note of caution should be added. The therapist will find it fruitless to tell the adolescent directly to "be more aggressive" (or "be less passive") toward him. Such a request is a double bind, since by definition autonomous activity cannot be required by another person. Pseudoassertion, which is actually a phony and involuted form of passive compliance, is the only possible result of such a request. The adolescent's self-assertion must germinate and grow spontaneously from his own inner strengths. The therapist can only provide climate control, protection, and applause for the first tender buds.

The Overtly Homosexual Adolescent

The psychiatric literature offers very few accounts of psychotherapy of the overt homosexual during the adolescent period. This may be due to a reluctance to define the adolescent as a homosexual. This caution is reasonable, since overt homosexual behavior during adolescence does not necessarily eventuate in a homosexual life pattern. Identity is fluid during adolescence and experimentation does occur (A. Freud, 1965). It does not follow however that overt homosexual relations during adolescence should be taken lightly. Such relationships, especially if repeated with any regularity, do interfere with the development of an adequate sexual-role identity. They are indicative of an unusual degree of anxiety about heterosexual behavior and suggest serious underlying developmental pathology.

Most investigators of homosexual behavior feel that the basic disorder is a phobic avoidance of the female genitalia (Ovesey and Gaylin, 1965; Socarides, 1960). As in the case of other phobias, most successful therapeutic approaches appear to contain major elements of behavioral modification, alone or in conjunction with an exploration of emotional factors (Bentler, 1968; Thorpe et al., 1963). Although we have a great deal still to learn, the most promising approaches appear to utilize an early phase of conventional exploratory therapy followed by an active effort to encourage appropriate heterosexual behavior and to extinguish the learned pattern of homosexual arousal (Ovesey and Gaylin, 1965; Fox and DiScipio, 1968).

As with the pseudohomosexual youngster, the therapist should make every reasonable effort to discourage the overtly homosexual adolescent from viewing himself as finally and irrevocably homosexual. This crystallization of sexual identity may be tempting to many adolescents who are deeply troubled by guilts and anxieties about heterosexuality. Even the the self-definition of homosexuality may be somewhat repugnant, it may at least offer the relief of a deliberately chosen defeat and retreat.

As always, the therapist can only offer as much help as the adolescent wants. Confusion arises because the adolescent's "wants" are often ambivalent and disguised. It is impossible to work with an adolescent who is predominantly satisfied with homosexuality, no matter how upset his family and others may be regarding his choice. It is often quite possible to work with an adolescent who *says* initially that he is satisfied with homosexuality. The therapist decides whether a trial of therapy is indicated after evaluating the adolescent's personality development and functioning, basing his decisions on both verbal and nonverbal communications from his young patient.

A 17-year-old boy managed to convince his parents to arrange psychotherapy for him by telling them that he was worried about possible academic failure.

He quickly told the therapist that his real concern was related to homosexual behavior, which he had engaged in for the past two years. He carefully explained that he enjoyed this behavior and had no intention of giving it up. When confronted gently with the apparent contradiction between his stated attitude and his request for psychotherapy, he explained that he wanted to know more about why he had homosexual feelings. He knew that he would face the possibility of military service soon. He wanted to be sure he understood himself sufficiently to suspend homosexual activities temporarily during this period in order to avoid "dishonorable discharge" and "scandal." The therapist accepted this "contract" with the provision that it would be regarded as a tentative starting point.

In actuality, therapy soon revealed that homosexuality was ego-alien to the youngster. The patient formed a therapeutic alliance quickly and actively explored his inner feelings. Later, he cooperated fully in efforts to direct him into a heterosexual adjustment.

His initial assertion of commitment to homosexuality appeared in retrospect to serve the function of protecting him from both the fear of change and doubts that he would be able to find other satisfactions. It was easily relinquished when the therapeutic relationship was solidly established.

There is still a great deal that we do not understand regarding the origins and development of sex-role identity and functioning. The interested reader is directed to the extensive publications of Money and Stoller for new developments in this fascinating research area (see especially Green and Money, 1966, and Stoller, 1967, in connection with this discussion). Current studies may well revolutionize our understanding and therapy of many distortions of sexual development in the future. It is already clear that we can no longer satisfy ourselves with simplified theories of "family configuration" to account for the development of homosexual behavior (see Kremer and Rifkin, 1969). Certainly, at this point we must approach the therapy of homosexuals with an attitude of openminded inquiry. Clinical research regarding both etiology and effective therapeutic approaches is urgently needed.

CITED AND RECOMMENDED READINGS

Bentler, P. M. 1968. A note on the treatment of adolescent sex problems. J. Child Psychol. Psychiat. 9: 125–129.

Blos, P. 1963. On adolescence: a psychoanalytic interpretation. New York: Free Press of Glencoe.

Deutsch, H. 1967. Selected problems of adolescence (with special emphasis on group formation). New York: International Universities Press, Inc.

Feldman, M. P. 1966. Aversion therapy for sexual deviations: a critical review. Psychol. Bull. 65: 65–79.

Fox, B. and W. J. DiScipio. 1968. An exploratory study in the treatment of homosexuality by combining principles from psychoanalytic theory and conditioning: theoretical and methodological considerations. Brit. J. Med. Psychol. 41: 273–282.

Freud, A. 1965. Normality and pathology in childhood. New York: International Universities Press, Inc.

Green, R., and J. Money. 1966. Stage-acting, role-taking, and effeminate impersonation during boyhood. Arch. Gen. Psychiat. 15: 535–538.

Group for the advancement of Psychiatry. 1965. Sex and the college student. Vol. VI, Report No. 60. Formulated by the Committee on the College Student.

Halleck, S. L. 1967. Sex and mental health on the campus. JAMA 200: 684–690.

Halleck, S. L. 1969. Address to Student Health Personnel, Southern Methodist University, Dallas, Texas.

Kremer, M. W., and A. H. Rifkin. 1969. The early development of homosexuality: a study of adolescent lesbians. Amer. J. Psychiat. 126: 129–134.

Lief, H. I. 1968. Discussion of Shainess article. (See below.) Amer. J. Psychiat. 124: 1081–1084.

Ovesey, L. 1955. The pseudohomosexual anxiety. Psychiatry 18: 17–26.

Ovesey, L., and W. Gaylin. 1965. Psychotherapy of male homosexuality. Amer. J. Psychother. 19: 382–396.

Rexford, E. 1963. A developmental concept of the problems of acting out. J. Amer. Acad. Child Psychiat. 2: 6–21. Reprinted in: Monograph No. 1 of J. Amer. Acad. Child Psychiat.

Shainess, N. 1968. The problem of sex today. Amer. J. Psychiat. 124: 1076–1081.

Socarides, C. W. 1960. Theoretical and clinical aspects of overt male homosexuality. J. Amer. Psychoanal. Assoc. 8: 552–566.

Stoller, R. J. 1967. Gender identity and a biological force. Psychoanal. Forum 2: 317–325.

Thorpe, J. G., E. Schmidt, and D. Castell. 1963. A comparison of positive and negative (aversive) conditioning in the treatment of homosexuality. Behav. Res. Ther. 1: 357–362.

CHAPTER SIXTEEN
illegitimate pregnancy

Teenage pregnancy out of wedlock is a growing social problem despite improved methods of birth control (Wright, 1966). The personal embarrassment and shame which illegitimate pregnancy causes in some families is still most commonly resolved by frequently ill-advised marriages (Gebhard, 1958). The divorce rate is extremely high in adolescent marriage (Osofsky et al., 1967; Semmens and Lamers, 1968); thus the original problem is often further complicated by the trauma of divorce.

Although the majority of reported illegitimate pregnancies occur in youngsters from economically and socially deprived backgrounds (Wright, 1966), teenage illegitimate pregnancies are quite frequent in other social classes. In the upper social classes, they are usually handled secretly, through precipitous marriage, abortion, or private arrangements for leaving the community during pregnancy and delivery.

The management of teenage illegitimate pregnancy is complex and involves the cooperative efforts of several professionals. A few programs have been instituted which attempt a comprehensive approach including quality obstetrical care, social work planning, and psychiatric counseling (Wright, 1966; Kaufman and Deutsch, 1967; Osofsky et al., 1967). In many communities, however, the psychotherapist will be called on to manage the crisis of illegitimate pregnancy. Certainly, when the pregnancy occurs in the course of psychotherapy, the therapist will need to be intensely involved in planning and managing for his patient.

The etiology of teenage pregnancy is complex, involving social, cognitive, and family forces as well as unconscious motivational forces within the adolescent girl (Young, 1954; Vincent, 1964). Semmens and Lamers (1968) have described and illustrated three categories of teenage pregnancy according to the degree of conscious participation by the girl: 1) the intentional, 2) the accidental, and 3) the unknowing. The unknowing class involves primarily youngsters who either have not been exposed to information regarding conception or have inadequate intellectual ability to understand the consequences of sexual behavior. The psychotherapist will have occasion to deal primarily with youngsters in the first two categories.

The conscious, intentional teenage pregnancy is usually manipulative. The usual goals are either to escape or drastically to change an unacceptable family living situation. Pregnancy may be used to force parental agreement to a marriage which is regarded as unsuitable. Other youngsters use pregnancy as a conscious and deliberate spiteful attack on the parents. Even in these adolescents, other motives may be active at an unconscious level, although obscured by the conscious design. Of course, these unconscious motives are of central importance in the cases which belong in the "accidental" category.

Blos (1963) has described the pseudoheterosexual adolescent girl who utilizes heterosexual behavior to combat a regressive, homosexual attachment to the mother. There is evidence that illegitimate pregnancy occurs in girls who have serious ambivalent dependency conflicts with their mothers and absent or weak fathers (Young, 1954; Barglow et al., 1968; Cattel, 1954). These dependency needs are often displaced onto the unborn child who is fantasied as "someone who will love me as I have never been loved." This dynamic constellation often interferes with plans for adoptive placement of the baby (Meyer et al., 1956, Barglow et al., 1968). As Barglow et al. (1968) have stated, "The depersonalized, unsatisfactory quality of the sexual experience and the immediate termination of sexual relations after pregnancy are consistent with a pregenital sexuality."

At times, one feels that the illegitimate pregnancy serves as a device to "get the parents off the hook." The adolescent girl seems to be living out her assigned family role as the scapegoated "bad" child. The fulfillment of the prophecy that she "would come to no good end" retroactively justifies the mother's long-standing neglect and hostility toward her. In these cases, the pregnancy may actually lead to apparent improvement in family relationships. The mother, fully exonerated, may relax her efforts to force the child into actions which define her as unlovable.

One final factor which must be considered in evaluating illegitimate pregnancy is the role of resurgent infantile omnipotence in the adolescent years. This force in mental life leads the adolescent to scorn reproductive reality by taking unwarranted chances, and its collapse is a major factor in the depressions which are seen in pregnant adolescents. The fact of pregnancy is often denied for a varying period (Semmens and Lamers, 1968; Barglow et al., 1968), but eventually it must be faced. The acceptance of the pregnancy completely shatters the adolescent's faith in her personal omnipotence and the omnipotence of her thought processes. This collapse adds to the adolescents despair and heightens her sense of total helplessness. This is an obvious setting for a suicidal "ordeal" aimed at reestablishing a magical sense of unity with powerful inner and outer forces.

ANOTHER POINT OF VIEW

Aug and Bright (1970) have challenged many of the traditional views of unwed motherhood. These authors conducted a study of 24 unmarried adolescent mothers and 22 married adolescent mothers to determine their degree of psychopathology and their attitude toward motherhood. Aug and Bright divided the patients into four groups described as follows:

"Group I: Group Description

"This group of married girls gave a history of a family of origin with stability and warmth of interpersonal relationships, clear-cut family role patterns, and a constant relationship to surrounding social and cultural norms. There was a typical high regard for infants, and in general a substantial amount of positive affective interchange among family members. "Mothering" experience prior to marriage usually consisted of assistance by the patient to her mother in care of younger sibs. Familial and religious sanctions against sexual activity were marked. History of premarital intercourse was rare.

"The interviews of these individuals brought out much more discussion of the mate than occurred with any other group. They described the husband with a fair amount of detail, not only in terms of his being a provider, but also a person who evidenced love for wife and offspring, set limits for children in a reasonable manner, etc. These men held down steady jobs (tenant farming, coal mining, carpentry, etc.) but often spent many hours away from home at the job because of their general poverty. None of these men had prison records or other evidence of antisocial behavior. Families of origin were discussed in much less detail than they were in any other group. Much more pertinent was their autonomous family unit. . . ."

"Groups II: Group Description

"This group of unwed girls are well adjusted with reference to their particular environments. The subculture in which these girls lived was tolerant of out-of-wedlock pregnancy (it was common for these girls to have sisters and friends with an illegitimate child.) A few of these girls were consciously 'trying' to become pregnant. Most of them expressed the attitude that they 'didn't care' whether or not they became pregnant, although they were having regular coition, and were conscious of the fact that they could become pregnant. None of them were using contraceptives, although all of them had at least heard of 'the pill' and most of them had heard about the 'loop,' the condom and contraceptive foam. These individuals also reported that they were 'happy' when they found out that they were going to have a baby. There was no report of concern regarding marriage to the putative father. Many girls reported that they might marry at some time in the future, but most felt that they were 'not ready' to take on the responsibility of living away from home. The putative father's offer of marriage was turned down because the girls wanted to finish school, or felt that they were too young. Although the putative father was pictured as 'kind' and generous with gifts and money for the expenses incurred by the mother, he was not a serious candidate for marriage, at least at that point in time.

"These girls were members of 'extended family groups.' They reported a substantial amount of positive affective interchange among family members, with a special emphasis on infants. They had a closer personal relationship with their mothers. The mother role was well defined, and was shared by all the postpubescent females in the family (in helping with the care of sibs and sibs' offspring.) It was common for the girls to have sisters with an illegitimate child. The usual picture was for a sister to have *only one* illegitimate child, and the girls in this group were primigravidas themselves with but one exception.

"Relationship with the putative father tended to be of long standing, though on a superficial level of personal involvement. Putative fathers tended to be about the same age as the girl, they were usually students, or held steady jobs in manual labor, food service, etc. The fathers had 'clean records' regarding antisocial behavior.

"All of the girls in this group kept their babies, and reported that they, as well as their family group, were pleased with "having a new baby in the family.' All these girls reported that they did not intend to have another baby in the next few years, and that they would use some contraceptive measure (usually 'pills') in the future.

"There were scattered minor instances of embarrassment, etc. reported by these girls, but all individuals in this group fitted well with the generally accepted norms of their subculture...."

"Group III: Group Description

"This group of both wed and unwed individuals showed pronounced disturbance of interpersonal relationships. They presented a picture of deprivation not only of financial resources, but also of practically any positive affective cues in their environment from the time of birth. Parents, when not separated, were often openly abusive verbally, physically, and occasionally sexually, toward each other and the children. These girls during early years were not uncommonly 'farmed out' to relatives for years at a time. Spontaneous 'trips' away from home (amounting to running away) were common during early adolescence.

"The putative fathers and husbands in this group were often heavy drinkers, either younger or considerably older than the girl. They were unemployed or passed rapidly from job to job, and they had histories of a variety of antisocial behavior, including prison records for car theft and armed robbery, military records of having gone AWOL for many months.

"The husbands in this group were often verbally and physically abusive of wife and offspring, and in certain instances had histories of difficulty with local authorities for lack of support of the family. The putative fathers were occasionally married men, and almost universally abandoned the girls upon discovery of their pregnancy.

"The attitude of these girls toward their offspring was ambivalent or openly negative. They often expressed intense 'need' to have children, and at the same time conveyed thinly veiled hostility toward them. It was flatly stated at times that 'they [the offspring] should have it hard like I do.' These women did occasionally place their children for adoption, but it was uncommon even in this group. The 'mother' and 'child' roles for these women were very poorly defined. Apart from any consideration of middle class norms, girls in this group were at odds with the generally accepted norms of their own subcultural group. . . ."

"Group IV: Descriptive Data

"This group was comprised of married Negro girls. These girls, who exhibited marked disturbance of interpersonal relationships, were between four and seven months pregnant with their first child at the time of their marriage. Two had been living with their husbands-to-be for a period of months prior to pregnancy. The dominant theme in these people was that of very keen social conflict. They were quite conscious of those 'middle class' values which conflicted with the mores of the environment in which they were reared. The families from which these girls came were unstable and were splintered rather than extended family groups. Notably was the presence of conflict and lack of communication between these individuals and other members of the parental family. A paternal figure was seldom present for extended periods of time during the girl's early years. The person to whom these turned with their problems was often the puntative father and husband-to-be, occasionally an aunt or grandmother, rarely their own mother. The husbands of these women were similar to the putative fathers of the Group III girls.

"All of these girls were illegitimate children, and were very sensitive about having illegitimate offspring themselves. They did, however, express much anxiety about 'having to get married.'

"A sentiment often expressed was one of displeasure with marriage because it was an imposition upon their freedom, and they were very uneasy about the degree of intimacy which marriage required.

"These girls were ambivalent toward themselves, their husbands, their children, and their marriage. . . ."

In reference to the general literature on unwed motherhood, Aug and Bright note,

"In light of the findings reported above, we should like to reexamine certain generalizations made elsewhere regarding out-of-wedlock pregnancy, in order to determine whether these generalizations hold true for our population. One generalization holds out-of-wedlock pregnancy to be the signal of a life gone awry. Without intervention such a girl is doomed to a 'downhill spiral' of failure. In its mildest form this attitude sees all out-of-wedlock pregnancy as pathologic, or at least symptomatic of serious disturbances (Herzog, 1969).

"Other generalizations which are at least implicit in current programs for unwed mothers are (1) that the unwed population under study is largely homogeneous and (2) that the majority of problems are found in the unwed mothers, and not in their wed counterparts. . . ."

Aug and Bright disagree with these generalizations. They propose instead a sociological and developmental evaluation of the meanings which illegitimate pregnancy may carry for various subcultures.

"In Group III, unwed motherhood does indeed seem an expression of psychopathology at both an individual and a family level. But in Group II, unwed motherhood seems to be a manifestation of an *intermediate stage* of psychosocial *development* which, although not yet mature, is quite normal for the subculture in which it occurs. In both of the subcultures which we have described (white Appalachian and urban Negro Bluegrass) the unwed mother may belong to a closely-knit 'extended family' which consists of *her* mother and a number of her sisters, plus their illegitimate offspring. The mother role is shared, and the children are 'communal' to some extent. Younger sisters get considerable experience at helping to 'mother' these children, prior to conceiving their 'own'. Such mothering by the younger girls is *not* at the expense of their own emotional supplies, and is *not* done in an atmosphere of deprivation.

"Furthermore, in these two subcultures there is a marked dichotomy between the role of *mother* and the role of *mate* (sexual partner and helpmate). The notion of mother is quite important, definite, and extensively elaborated, even in the minds of 14-year-olds; but the role of *mate* is not definite, not elaborated. The male is merely a 'pollinator' who may also contribute some financial support. Although these girls usually had a 'better' relationship with the putative father than the girls of Group III (less conflict, more continuity), nevertheless the girls of Group II did not relate in depth to the putative fathers *as* mate, and would typically decline an offer of marriage, as irrelevant, as interfering with plans for school or work.

"Thus we have the puzzling phenomenon of girls who have become mothers, and who accept their mothering role and responsibility and do a reasonably good job of it, . . . while not yet having mastered certain developmental tasks of adolescence and young adulthood which we ordinarily assume must be mastered *before* the individual is ready for the psychosocial role of *parent*. Examples of such developmental tasks which have *not* been mastered (by Group II girls) are:

1. The attainment of separation and independence from parents (followed by a partial return to the parents is a new relationship based on a relative equality).

2. A capacity for *intimacy* (in Erikson's sense) with a mate.

3. A commitment to work.

4. A commitment to an ideology; and the development of one's own personal moral values instead of merely incorporating the parent's values.

"On the other hand these girls *have* progressed on the important developmental task of being able to give considerable nurturance as well as simply receiving it. They are still nurtured by their own mothers, but are much more capable of giving sustained genuine nurturance to their infants than are the mothers of Group III. Incidentally, this capacity to continue accepting nurturance from their own mothers stands in sharp contrast to the situation from most middle- and upper-class urban unwed mothers, namely that the latter patients have intense conflict over their dependent ties (in fact *all* pregenital ties) to their own mothers, and usually are desperate to deny such ties and needs, e.g. by running away, defiance, etc.

"This idea of a normal developmental sequence in which motherhood occurs when other aspects of development are still incomplete is not a new concept. Therese Benedek (1959) discussed the further development which an individual undergoes as a result of the experience of being a parent: development which can proceed along either normal or pathological lines.

"Benedek's formulation of the *sources* of this further development was largely in terms of libido theory. We might add an additional source, namely that the bearing of a child (in a subculture that places great emphasis and value on the infant) by, say, an unwed 14-year-old girl *confers a meaningful positive status* within the family, for Group II girls. This is a situation in marked contrast to upper- and middle-class (and some lower-class) families. The multiple supports of such positive social feedback from this meaningful status would seem to aid immeasurably in sustaining a healthy psychological balance.

"Previously, out-of-wedlock pregnancy was often studied from a 'middle class' viewpoint. This may have been appropriate since many studies involved middle class populations. Since in the middle class illegitimacy seems to be a problem, however, studies with the above point of view tend to see out-of-wedlock pregnancy in general as a form of sexual delinquence. At the outset of such works there seems to be the assumption that out-of-wedlock pregnancy is a 'deviation' from the 'normal' pattern of development. The data which we have presented seems to indicate that for certain people, out-of-wedlock pregnancy is an accepted (by the subculture) and entirely 'normal' part of 'growing up'. The importance of illegitimacy, therefore, may vary greatly between individuals. One has to look at the individual existentially, as a person, as a family member, and as a member of a particular subculture group. . . ."

Aug and Bright also point out the dangers of overgeneralization of similarities and differences within patient populations.

"Similarities:

"It is not surprising that data on out-of-wedlock pregnancy varies between different class groups. It is tempting, however, to group the individuals in a *small* subculture under what appears to be a 'dominant theme'. It has been shown elsewhere that differences exist within low socioeconomic groups that are demographically homogeneous. The data which we have presented indicates that great variability can exist even in relatively small and stable subcultures. In our study, the designation of low socioeconomic status urban Negro applies to individuals who manifest a high degree of healthy psychological adaptation and continuing personality development. It also applies to individuals who manifest a high degree of social pathology and psychopathology. Knowledge of the subculture is useful in explaining certain factors in the behavior of people belonging to that group, but designation of an individual as unwed mother of a particular group gives no information regarding the degree of fit to the subculture, the presence of disturbed interpersonal relationships, or the prognosis for illegitimacy in the future.

"*Differences:*

"Most works on illegitimacy have been exactly that, i.e., they have ignored legitimate pregnancy in similar groups of people. This, of course, may be misleading. If the unwed mothers are selected from a population which has a high baseline of psychopathology, one could easily get a distorted view of the 'problems' of these people. Without a control population, one might get the idea that the problems seen in these unwed mothers are somehow part and parcel to being an out-of-wedlock mother. A control group, however, might well show that many of the problem seen are widely distributed through the subculture, so that they are coincidental to, rather than directly related to, illegitimacy. In the data which we have presented, it is seen that the 'problem' of disturbed interpersonal relationships is well represented in both wed and unwed groups. Conversely, there are a sizeable number of well adjusted people in both groups. It therefore seems that it would be wise to take a broad look at the entire subculture if one is to assess the import of illegitimacy as a 'problem' or as a symptom of 'problems' for a particular group. . . ."

It would seem clear that our understanding of the implications of illegitimate pregnancy would be greatly expanded by further objective studies of this kind. It would be particularly useful to the adolescent therapist to have comparable data on the varieties of illegitimacy encountered in girls from middle-class families.

MANAGEMENT OF ILLEGITIMATE PREGNANCY IN ADOLESCENT PATIENTS

Emotionally disturbed adolescent girls (such as those in Aug and Bright's Group III and the neurotic variety described earlier) are frequently reluctant to inform their parents of an illegitimate pregnancy. One strong motivation for seeking criminal abortion is to avoid the dreaded confrontation with enraged or wounded parents. The therapist should not only encourage the adolescent to tell the parents of the pregnancy as early as possible, but should offer his assistance in breaking the news if the adolescent needs and wants it. Some adolescents prefer to have the therapist tell their parents. Others want the therapist in attendance when they convey the information.

Once the fact of pregnancy is known to the family, the therapist needs to provide assistance in dealing with the parents' emotional reactions as well as making practical plans for the girl. The parents can be permitted and encouraged to ventilate their feelings of anger, shame, rejection, and guilt. The therapist must serve as a representative of reality and of the needs of the adolescent without condemning the parents. The parents must be gradually assisted to accept the reality of the pregnancy as well as the fact that their daughter has the ultimate responsibility in decisions concerning the pregnancy. Their role is to provide support, information, and counsel. Since many families in which a teenage pregnancy occurs have never functioned in this constructive and helpful way, extensive parental counseling is often necessary. In addition to this psychological help, both the parents and the adolescent will need factual information which may be best provided by referring them to professionals who devote themselves to the management of illegitimate pregnancy.

Abortion

The first decision which the adolescent girl and her family must face is whether to abort the pregnancy. State laws regarding therapeutic abortion vary widely. In some states, the conditions under which legal abortion is permitted do include those instances of teenage pregnancy in which there is serious danger of psychiatric complications in the mother. In other states, it is virtually impossible to establish psychiatric grounds for therapeutic abortion. Naturally, the adolescent therapist should be familiar with the laws and customs of medical practice in his locality. He must also consider his own attitudes toward abortion and convey these honestly to the adolescent and her family (Peck, 1968). Medical opinion is divided in regard to the psychiatric sequelae of abortion. Some authors (Muller, 1966; Kummer, 1963; Simon and Senturia, 1966) have suggested that serious disturbances may follow the procedure. Recently, several investigators have been unable to demonstrate serious psychiatric complications in aborted women (Anderson, 1966; Peck and Marcus, 1966; Ekblad, 1955; Marder, 1970). Most evidence appears to support the statement by Heller and Whittington (1968) regarding one of their cases: "Forcing the young lady to go off, bear the child, and give it up for adoption, we are strongly of the opinion, may be more traumatic by far than abortion is likely to be." A recent Group for the Advancement of Psychiatry report (1969) has strongly recommended the total removal of medical abortion from the domain of criminal law.

Criminal abortion of course should always be forcefully opposed by the therapist. The adolescent's involvement in a criminal act cannot conceivably be helpful to healthy emotional development. In addition, the medical risk is extremely high in these clandestine procedures, which are usually performed by inept and poorly equipped individuals. It should be borne in mind that abortion bears a modest risk of uterine rupture and infection even under the best of circumstances.

Marriage as the Answer

If abortion is impossible or unwanted, the possibility of marriage to the baby's father is often considered. It is obvious that a forced marriage, undertaken only to avoid the shame of unwed motherhood, is rarely indicated. Usually, such a decision merely expands the problem. Of course, in some older adolescents marriage is desired by the couple. Often, the pregnancy was deliberately sought to force parental consent or to overcome rational misgivings within the couple themselves, such as economic considerations. The therapist can serve only as a supportive counselor, helping the adolescent and her family to avoid a foolish decision based primarily on a panicky overconcern with public opinion.

Placement

If neither abortion nor marriage is planned, the adolescent must decide whether to place the baby for adoption or to keep the child and care for it herself. This question may be settled by circumstances outside the adolescent's control as in the disadvantaged minority groups where few prospective adoptive parents are available. When a true option exists, the facts usually favor placement. By placing the baby, the adolescent girl is free to continue her education and maturation until she is truly prepared to accept the responsibilities of parenthood. As a rule, the baby is benefited, since most adoptive parents desire the child with less ambivalence than may exist in the unwed adolescent mother and her family.

Despite the above practical considerations, many adolescent mothers are reluctant to part with their baby. The need to keep the child may be based on a projective identification with the unborn baby in which the adolescent fantasies that the infant will feel abondoned and rejected, as she has. Guilt feelings about the sexual behavior which led to pregnancy may cause the adolescent to feel she should "take her medicine" by accepting the responsibility of child care. She is often strongly reinforced in this opinion by the generally punitive attitude of society toward the unwed mother.

Other complex emotional patterns may make it difficult for the unwed mother to accept adoptive placement (Eisenberg, 1956; Schmideberg, 1951; Meyer et al., 1956). The therapist's job is to deal with these feelings with the same exploratory objectivity that he brings to all other issues in psychotherapy. The adolescent has the right to make the final decisions regarding her child, since she must bear the emotional and practical consequences of the choice. The therapist should make it clear that he will continue to offer his therapeutic aid no matter what the girl decides to do. Psychotherapy must continue following delivery, since there are difficult adjustments regardless of which plans are followed. The unwed mother and her parents need continued treatment, since there is a high probability of further pregnancies among girls who have one illegitimate birth.

CITED AND RECOMMENDED READINGS

Anderson, E. W. 1966. Psychiatric indications for the termination of pregnancy. World Med. J. 13: 81–83.

Robert G. Aug, Thomas P. Bright, and International Universities Press, Inc., Excerpts from "A Study of Wed and Unwed Motherhood in Adolescents and Young Adults", The Journal of the American Academy of Child Psychiatry, Volume 9, Pages 577 — 594, 1970.

Barglow, P., M. Bornstein, D. B. Exum, M. K. Wright, and H. M. Visotsky. 1968. Some psychiatric aspects of illegitimate pregnancy in early adolescence. Amer. J. Orthopsychiat. 38: 672–687.

Benedek, T. 1959. Parenthood as a developmental phase. J. Amer. Psychoanal. Assoc. 7: 389–417.

Blos, P. 1963. On adolescence: a psychoanalytic interpretation. New York: Free Press of Glencoe.

Cattel, J. 1954. Psychodynamic and clinical observations in a group of unmarried mothers. Amer. J. Orthopsychiat. 11: 337–341.

Eisenberg, M. S. 1956. Psychodynamic aspects of casework with the unmarried mother. In: Casework papers. New York: Family Service Association of America.

Ekblad, M. 1955. Induced abortion on psychiatric grounds. Acta Psychiat. Scand. (Suppl.) 99: 1–238.

Gebhard, P. 1958. Pregnancy, birth and abortion. New York: Harper and Bros.

Group for the Advancement of Psychiatry. 1969. The right to abortion: a psychiatric view. Vol. VII, Report No. 75. Formulated by the Committee on Psychiatry and Law.

Heller, A., and H. G. Whittington. 1968. The Colorado story: Denver General Hospital experience with the change in the law on therapeutic abortion. Am. J. Psychiat. 125: 809–816.

Herzog, E. 1969. Families out of wedlock. In: Family dynamics and female sexual delinquency. Edited by O. Pollak and S. Friedman. Palo Alto: Science & Behavior Books, Inc.

Kaufman, P. N., and A. L. Deutsch. 1967. Group therapy for pregnant unwed adolescents in the prenatal clinic of a general hospital. Int. J. Group Psychother. 17: 309–315.

Kummer, J. H. 1963. Post-abortion psychiatric illness—a myth? Amer. J. Psychiat. 119: 980–983.

Marder, L. 1970. Psychiatric experience with a liberalized therapeutic abortion law. Amer. J. Psychiat. 126: 1230–1236.

Meyer, H. J., W. Jones, and E. F. Borgatta. 1956. The decision by un-wed mothers to keep or surrender their baby. Social Work 1: 103–109.

Muller, C. 1966. The dangers of abortion. World Med. J. 13: 78–80.

Osofsky, H. J., J. H. Hagen, B. Braen, P. W. Wood, and R. DiFlorio. 1967. Problems of the pregnant schoolgirl: an attempted solution. New York J. Med. 67: 2332–2343.

Peck, A., and H. Marcus. 1966. Psychiatric sequelae of therapeutic interruption of pregnancy. J. Nerv. Ment. Dis. 143: 417–425.

Peck, A. 1968. Therapeutic abortion: patients, doctors and society. Amer. J. Psychiat. 125: 797–804.

Schmideberg, M. 1951. Psychiatric-social factors in young unmarried mothers. Social Casework 32: 3–7.

Semmens, J. P., and W. M. Lamers. 1968. Teenage pregnancy. Springfield, Illinois: Charles C Thomas, Publisher.

Simon, N. M., and A. G. Senturia. 1966. Psychiatric sequelae of abortion: review of the literature, 1935–1964. Arch. Gen. Psychiat. 15: 378–389.

Vincent, C. E. 1964. Unmarried mothers. New York: Free Press of Glencoe.

Wright, M. K. 1966. Comprehensive services for adolescent unwed mothers. Children 13: 171–176.

Young, L. R. 1954. Out of wedlock. New York: McGraw-Hill Book Company.

CHAPTER SEVENTEEN
acute psychotic episodes

Acute psychoses appear rarely during psychotherapy of adolescents. When they do appear, they are usually due to the emergence of an unrecognized chronic psychotic illness or directly precipitated by toxins. Only rarely do acute psychotic episodes represent a transient situational reaction of adolescence or "adolescent turmoil" (Masterson, 1967). The therapist must also be aware of the defensive use of psychotic-like behavior which may occur in some severely disturbed adolescents. Cain (1964) has delineated the various meanings which "playing crazy" may have for these children.

Schizophrenia is often difficult to diagnose during adolescence. The differentiation from depression, psychopathy, or other personality disorders may be very unclear (Masterson, 1967; Sands, 1956; Bender, 1959). If the basic schizophrenic illness is overlooked in the diagnostic process, further stress arising from life circumstances, or even the employment of inappropriately vigorous psychotherapeutic techniques, may precipitate an overt psychotic disintegration. The treatment is that of any acute schizophrenic episode, utilizing psychologic support (usually including hospitalization) and antipsychotic medication (major tranquilizers). Follow-up treatment should succeed management of the acute episode. This follow-up period tends to be prolonged and primarily directed toward suppression of symptoms, improvement of socialization and work skills, and assistance in successfully managing current interpersonal distortions and emotional crises. The basic schizophrenic illness is rarely altered. The adaptation to the illness can be greatly improved by appropriate supportive, suppressive, directive therapy. Easson (1969) feels that this holds true even in the prolonged inpatient treatment of the psychotic adolescent.

PARENTS OF THE PSYCHOTIC ADOLESCENT

The parents of the schizophrenic adolescent tend to be markedly disturbed and to express their pathology in their interaction with their child. These disturbed patterns are usually tenacious, stereotyped, and difficult to influence therapeutically. Parental management must often be firm, directive, and very specific to prevent overt parental sabotage of the adolescent's tentative gropings toward independence.

Toxic psychoses may appear postoperatively, and in deliria of various etiologies. In most of these, the management is the same as that of any delirious process. However, far and away the most common organic psychosis of our time follows the deliberate ingestion of psychoactive drugs. Since these psychotic episodes represent only one small part of the problem of drug abuse in adolescents, their management is discussed in the next chapter, "The Adolescent on the Drug Scene."

CITED AND RECOMMENDED READINGS

Bender, L. 1959. The concept of pseudopsychopathic schizophrenia in adolescents. Amer. J. Orthopsychiat. 29: 491–512.

Cain, A. 1964. On the meaning of "playing crazy" in borderline children. Psychiatry 27: 278–289.

Carter, A. B. 1942. The prognostic factors of adolescent psychoses. J. Ment. Sci. (London) 88: 31–81.

Easson, W. M. 1969. The severely disturbed adolescent. New York: International Universities Press, Inc.

Masterson, J. F. 1967. The psychiatric dilemma of adolescence. Boston: Little, Brown & Co.

Sands, D. E. 1956. The psychoses of adolescence. J. Ment. Sci. (London) 102: 308–318.

CHAPTER EIGHTEEN
the adolescent on the drug scene

It is with humility and considerable trepidation that one ventures any comments as a psychiatrist about adolescent drug usage. The whole area provokes heated debate. Opinionated radical controversy seems to rule the day.

It does seem clear that the current adolescent fascination with psychedelic drugs cannot be understood within a purely psychiatric frame of reference. Large numbers (approximately one-third in a recent carefully conducted study of *high school* students in Dallas, Texas) of youngsters in the age group between puberty and late adolescence are at least experimenting with these agents (Lewis, 1970). Most of them use the drugs colloquially referred to as "head" drugs (marijuana, LSD, amphetamines). A much smaller group use the "body" drugs (heroin, cocaine, barbiturates) (Hinckle, 1967). Any fad of this magnitude obviously reflects a complex social process involving a general discontent with achievement value systems, a disenchantment with established social organization, and a general turn toward individual goals of personal gratification rather than group dialectics which stress the partial surrender of the individual to a transcendental social ethic (see Riefe, *The Triumph of the Therapeutic,* 1968).

Many critics have decried our culture's colorless and crushing preoccupation with cognitive skills at the expense of human passion and spontaneity (Keniston, 1965; Roszak, 1969). Many adults (including some who seem "well adjusted" to life in our times) appear to our youth as soulless robots who have sacrificed their humanity for efficiency and technological competence, accepting the bauble of material affluence as a tinseled consolation prize. This negative judgment on our style of life has led not only to a questioning of the sufficiency of reasoning and rationality as bases for planning human life (Leary, 1968; Cox, 1970; for a more balanced view, see Hartmann, 1964), but to the questioning of whether reasoning and rationality have any value. "Reality," youth cries, "is a crutch!" It seems reasonable to assume that this attitude is not limited to young people. Perhaps, the young people are reacting to a general sense of cultural confusion and widespread discontent with our social system. Maybe, at this point in time, we are all muttering or moaning, "Reality is a hard mother."

There is an awakening interest in mysticism, magic revelation, and intuitive whim as more reliable guides to a fulfilling human existence (Cox, 1970; Leary, 1968). The similarity of these attitudes to those exhibited by the gnostics and romantics of past turbulent eras is quite striking (Adler, 1968, Sarbin, 1968). The quasi-religious nature of the "hippie" movement is apparent, and it is clear that the psychedelic drugs serve a central ritualistic and sacramental role for the movement (West and Allen, 1968; Brickman, 1968). The drug user often claims a "revealed" comprehension of the meaning of life. He is contemptuous of the "straight" people who cannot hope to understand his global grasp of beauty and truth. The narrowing effect of such doctrinaire provincialism (Mamlet, 1967) resembles other instances in which the faithful derogate the infidels. Eventually, it may be clear that the "dropped out, turned on, and tuned in" portion of our youth are another edition of the romantic tradition of dandyism. Of this type of revolutionary, Camus (1956) has said, "The dandy, therefore, is always compelled to astonish. Singularity is his vocation, excess his way to perfection. Perpetually incomplete, always on the fringe of things, he compels others to create him while denying their values. He plays at life because he is unable to live it."

We must also recognize that the widespread cultural expectation that relief from psychic tension can and should be available through pharmacologic agents undoubtedly serves as a backdrop to the ease with which youth accepts the illusion of "better living through chemistry."

It would be pretentious to suggest that this book offers any satisfactory account of the social factors involved in rising drug usage or the specific pharmacology of the various drugs. The issues involved are extremely complicated and are freely interwoven in the very fabric of our lives. Possibly, we are still too enmeshed in them to understand clearly what is actually happening. An excellent and intelligent attempt has been made by Hughes (1969). I will limit my remarks primarily to exploring some of the issues surrounding drug usage which will confront the psychotherapst who works with adolescents.

THE ADOLESCENT PATIENT WHO USES DRUGS

If, in any real sense, the current drug culture represents a quasi-religious movement, our patients appear to provide its martyrs. Some of them sacrifice their psychologic life, or at least the chance for full psychologic development, to the psychedelic drugs, whereas others have tragically sacrificed everything through suicide while under the acute influence of drugs. Others have destroyed their health by neglecting their body's basic needs because of chronic drug usage. Some others are more fortunate and merely sacrifice their freedom to be of the world, retreating instead into monastic communes peopled only by other "heads."

Of course, not all adolescent patients who use drugs have such perilous experiences. As Esman (1967) has demonstrated through case examples, the meaning of drug usage and its impact on psychotherapy show enormous variation from one patient to another. One might divide adolescent drug users into "experimenters" who are either healthy or suffering from pathology which the drugs appear not to influence, the sociological users, and the "sick" users (see also Keniston, 1968, on "heads" and "seekers").

Casual Use—The Experimenter

The experimenters use marijuana, the most common of the "head" drugs, sparingly primarily to solidify peer-group membership and to allay partially the developmental anxieties associated with emancipation from the family. In fact, except for the real legal risk involved in the possession of marijuana, this behavior would be analogous to the way in which earlier adolescent generations utilized alcohol. One moderate author has wondered if a total refusal to experiment with marijuana during the entire college experience might represent a rigid fear of the impulses carried to a pathologic degree (Liebert, 1967). Unfortunately, in addition to the negligible danger of actually being arrested and charged with a felony, the young marijuana user is damaged by the adult society's punitive hysteria* which, as Margaret Mead has pointed out, has produced a situation in which every young person is approached by law enforcement officials as a criminal, guilty until proven innocent. The grimness of the paranoid game which is forced on the adolescent, summed up in the cry, "Who's the narc in the park?", is relieved only by gallows humor which recognizes the ghastly penalty that will befall a losing player. This state of affairs tends to force the "developmental user" (our experimenter) to join an alienated subculture for self-protection, to obtain some sense of belonging, and in compliance with a socially prescribed "negative identity."

In this way, even the casual experimenter tends to be pushed toward polarization. The adolescent often feels he must be "straight," "square," and suspect to a large proportion of young friends, or a card-carrying "head." One is impressed with the extreme difficulty which our adolescent patients encounter when they resist being cast into permanent membership in either camp or when they try to change groups. Serious problems are encountered in making and keeping friends in some settings unless one is willing to sign the membership book in one warring clan or the other.

The Sociological Drug User—The Seeker

The so-called "counter-culture's" core membership derives from some of our most capable young people. Many of these youngsters are not only much more attuned to social realities than previous generations, they seem to complete their personal identity only through their active interaction with the social process. They appear partially fused with their environmental surroundings. In a very real sense, they feel society's shortcomings and inadequacies

---

* In a Gallup poll, 40 per cent of respondents felt that a convicted marijuana *user* should receive a minimum jail sentence of two years. Fourteen per cent of these favored 10 years or more, with one per cent favoring life imprisonment. For "pushers," 16 per cent favored life imprisonment and 2 per cent favored the *death penalty!* (*The Cincinnati Inquirer,* Sunday, April 26, 1970).

as their own. During this period of turbulent upheaval, they can feel complete only by forming a separate community of spirit, unified by a style of speech, an ethic of detached benevolence, and often the use of drugs to aid their separation from a social system which they view as evil, ugly, and destructive.

Liebert (1967) has suggested a specific defect in the ability to identify and express inner-need states which gives rise to a constant, tense boredom in those "seekers" who tend toward increasing use of marijuana. Their discomfort is relieved partially by the drugs and partially by membership in a loosely structured social group in which narcissistic loneliness is partly compensated by a grandiose sense of mystical revelation and the group-sanctioned myth of conflict-free fusion with others.

Fortunately, there are increasing opportunities for some of these youngsters to find acceptable and meaningful slots within or near the cultural mainstream. If they are successful in negotiating some of their developmental problems and avoiding a total retreat into narcissistic gratification, they often move in this direction, maintaining their social awareness and their activism. Indeed, there is growing evidence that the noblest of their discontents are having an impact on the ideals (if not yet the practices) of our larger society.

Sick Users—The Heads

The task of a psychotherapist is to distinguish the youngsters who use drugs primarily for sociocultural and moderately neurotic reasons from those youngsters who use drugs in a desperate effort to hide or correct a malignant deficiency in personal maturation. This distinction is difficult not only because we are dealing with a seamless continuum but because the "sick" drug users mingle freely with their healthier counterparts, wearing the same uniform and speaking the same tongue. Although they say the same things, the professions of cultural concern by the "sick" drug users may be as unrelated to the sincere involvements of counter-culture members as the religious ravings of a psychotic are to the convictions of a healthy believer.

Keniston (1965) has reminded us, "Knowing the psychodynamics of an ideology helps little in judging its consequences or merit, for unmotivated beliefs do not exist." Despite the truth of this statement, it is often possible to evaluate the degree to which personal motivations have been mastered by the ego and related to external realities.

The "sick" drug users may often be identified by observing several characteristics:

1) Serious deficiencies in interpersonal relationships (Carson and Lewis, 1970; Liebert, 1967; Walters, 1967) which are poorly compensated by avid group membership in a "head" subcultural group that is united only by a shared narcissism and a grandiose overevaluation of the drug experience. Common interests in such groups are largely limited to mutual concerns regarding the procurement, usage, and concealment of the drugs and the celebration of a vague and almost mystical narcissistic fusion with one another.

2) A high frequency of drug usage or a periodic tendency to turn heavily to drugs in times of stress. Often, the "sick" drug user will admit that episodes of drug usage are related to periods of emotional discomfort—often the vague "tense boredom" described by Liebert (1967).

3) A relative preference for the pleasures of drug intoxication over the pleasures derived from interpersonal relationships. Often, this includes a loss of interest not only in competitive endeavors, but also in sexual contact—at least sex as related to any affectionate bond to another person.

4) Even though the "sick" drug users may show more acumen as critics of society than in their ability to describe what is happening within them (Liebert, 1967), their criticisms often appear more stereotyped and related to their personal problems than those offered by activists whose personalities have a sounder base. After listening for a time, one begins to hear more externalization and self-justification than realistic social analysis in their comments.

WHAT DOES IT ALL MEAN?

The meaning of drug usage to the individual disturbed adolescent is often difficult to discern. A promising hypothesis suggests that specific pharmacologic properties of each drug may serve as a psychodynamic-pharmacogenic "prosthesis" (Wieder and Kaplan, 1969). Wieder and Kaplan state, "When an individual finds an agent that chemically facilitates his pre-existing preferential mode of conflict solution, it becomes his drug of choice. The drug induces a regressive state, but the drug taker supplies the regressive tendencies." The authors have reported several cases in depth which provide preliminary support for this hypothesis. According to this view, the opiates provide gratification of early oral fixations; hallucinogens such as LSD are related to the transitional period between autism and symbiosis, serving either to "crack the autistic barrier," permitting some object-relatedness or encouraging fantasies of symbiotic union; amphetamines are related to problems in the separation-individuation phase; and marijuana seems to lower inhibitions against sexual and hostile impulses.

Certainly, even if this rather refined and highly specific theory is not precisely verifiable,* one cannot avoid being impressed that many adolescent patients use the drugs both to obtain immediate and conflictless gratification of instinctual needs at a regressed level, and also in an effort to master a sense of inner incompleteness and vulnerability, that is, to bolster a sense of ego mastery. Many users of LSD and other hallucinogens who appear psychotic or borderline appear to be "turning passive into active" by deliberately distorting their perception of reality. Cottle (1969) has described this technique as deliberately throwing away what was already lost. Although this maneuver may appear rationally pointless, it does bestow a spurious sense of self-control and self-direction. This feels better to the frightened adolescent than being helplessly dominated by dark, inner forces. As one actively schizophrenic boy of 16 explained, "I trip because I need some *good* hallucinations, at least part of the time." We could add that perhaps he was also comforted by knowing *when* the hallucinations would appear and knowing that he had willed their appearance.

Of course, this stratagem can go awry. Some studies (Hensala et al., 1967; Frosch et al., 1965; Blumenfield and Glickman, 1967) have found a high incidence of psychotic or borderline premorbid

---

* It has been pointed out that the addicting agent seems generally less important than the personality of the addict. Addictions to inert substances such as water and nose drops have occurred (Pearson and Little, 1969).

adjustments in youngsters who required hospitalization because of adverse drug reactions.

It is doubtless true that classic adolescent rebelliousness (actually primarily directed against the internal parental images—the superego) is a motivating force in drug usage. Deliberately breaking the law may serve to externalize internal states of guilt, focusing the adolescent's concern on real life "narcs" and policemen, which he can at least hope to elude. Even if he is caught, the punishment at least has some limits, unlike the formless dread which is provoked by the primitive superego.

The adolescent's turn toward a peer culture, deliberately defined as deviant from adult norms, is also a factor in spreading drug usage. In a very literal sense, the adolescent must "sin" to test the penalties and mitigate his terror before his internal inquisitor. He much prefers to sin in a group. Perhaps, this is an important reason for the ubiquitous tendency of the adolescent drug user to recruit others evangelically to his habit. It is safer to have "partners-in-crime" to share and lessen the sense of guilt. The hostile aggressiveness of the superego may be displaced in angry attacks on the "straight people" and (often sadistic) efforts to seduce or trick the "straightest" into "turning on." When the adolescent user is determined to conquer a "straight" enemy, his efforts do not remotely suggest any friendly sense of sharing a good thing. Instead, he embarks on a calculated experiment in chemical warfare with the same fanaticism that has led some tightly pious missionaries to vow that they would bring salvation to the natives if they had to kill every last one of them to do it!

MANAGEMENT OF THE ADOLESCENT PATIENT WHO USES DRUGS

Many adolescents who present themselves to psychotherapy today will at some point administer psychoactive drugs to themselves and report this to their therapist. A recent contribution has noted that the psychotherapeutic work itself, if it activates pregenital strivings in the transference, may actually trigger drug usage (Hartmann, 1969). The adolescent therapist must be prepared to deal with this issue. Simple approaches such as forbidding drug usage seem destined to fail frequently if they are applied across the board.

Getting Your Head Straight

There are a few general attitudinal sets which may be useful to the therapist:

1) Each adult generation tends to look for a scapegoat to explain its failure (real or imagined) to socialize its youth adequately. It is easier to blame Socrates, marathon dancing, gangs, pornographic literature, or bathtub gin for corrupting and alienating youth than to deal with a personal and collective sense of anxiety and guilt. To a large extent, psychoactive drugs (especially marijuana) are the current scapegoat, serving to purge our nagging fears that we have not fulfilled our obligations and to justify continued intrusions and suppressions of the young.

The therapist must remember that rarely has any drug "ruined" an otherwise intact adolescent. At most, a drug may divert an emotionally crippled adolescent from his desire to overcome his disability or potentiate and prolong the periods of regression which are natural during adolescence.

2) The therapist must realize that *all people,* not just the adolescent drug user, tend to prefer immediate pleasure to the demands of reality. A brief glance at adult cigarette smokers, stock-market investors, the entertainment industry, and the approaches successfully utilized in advertising should be sufficient to convince any sceptics. If doubts remain, try a brief period of honest introspection with special attention to your fantasies and/or behavior at the last cocktail party you were really in the mood to attend.

3) Emotional maturity implies not a repudiation of pleasure seeking, but its integration with the more subtle fulfillments of intimacy and mutuality with other people and the objective requirements for self-preservation imposed by conditions of social and physical reality. In the mature person, pleasure-seeking impulses are tested, at a largely unconscious level, to assess their impact on valued object relationships and survival of the self. If the price of admission is not too high, the mature person still goes to the circus!

Keeping these facts in mind allows the therapist to evaluate the adolescent's use of drugs from the viewpoint of what is really best for the adolescent and to assess the adolescent's felt need for the

drug within a development framework. A self-righteous condemnation of the adolescent, often thinly disguising a sense of envy for
what the therapist fantasies to be unbridled and carefree hedonism,
may be avoided. Only by honestly holding such a neutral and benevolent attitude can the therapist hope to establish a therapeutic
alliance with the drug-using adolescent. As Liebert (1967) has
pointed out, we must not approach our young patient as a "pot-
head," but as a total growing personality.

Naturally, it also follows that the therapist cannot merely sanc-
tion blind submission to a drive for immediate and total gratification as a realistic mode of life and still call what he is doing psychotherapy. One does not support drug usage, but explores it motivational origins. Traditional dynamic psychotherapy respects and
values instinctual drives, intuitive hunches, regressions in the service of the ego, and the glorious, irreducible irrationality of human
life. Still, it recognizes that these vital forces must be harmonized,
conserved, and structured if they are to fuel successful and pleasur-
able living among other people. Just as human beings can be
drained of color, interest, zeal, and joy by excessive control of their
instinctual drives, they may be fragmented, cheapened, and eventually jaded and emptied by at total and one-sided surrender to a
chemically induced state of total narcissistic gratification.

Those Who Cannot Be Treated

Some adolescent drug users have totally committed themselves
to a value system which is incompatible with any realistic therapeutic contract. Usually, this hedonistic surrender is born of a
despair sired by a chronic sense of personal deficiency. It is closer
to a walking suicide than anything else. Unfortunately, even when
the adolescent can admit this, he may be too devoid of hope and
inner strength to tolerate the painful struggle toward wholeness,
which is all the psychotherapist may honestly offer him. Such a
prospect may appear pale and grim indeed compared to the instant
comforts of his drugs. Most youngsters of this type gravitate toward the "body" drugs and eventual oblivion.

It would appear obvious that it would be pointless to offer
outpatient treatment to a youngster who is totally immersed in

the drug scene, who is forced into therapy by others, and who has no wish to change. Still, it may be worthwhile to offer a trial period of therapy. Since most youngsters are ambivalent about heavy drug usage, it may be possible to awaken latent interest in a more complete approach to life if the youngster can form a meaningful human relationship with the therapist. If this does not appear, or cannot be sustained, the therapist must remember that no psychotherapy can occur unless the adolescent has something *he* wants treated and some hope that he can bear the cure. No matter how much pressure parents or others may place on the therapist to change the adolescent, it is useless to continue without a mutual contract. The value of forced abstinence and treatment in an inpatient setting is not clear as yet. Still, inpatient care probably must be prescribed for humanitarian reasons. It is the only possible course of action, and slow suicide is no better than fast suicide. However, in these instances the therapist must be sure that he has clear evidence that the adolescent is involved in a pathologic use of drugs, that he is really a "sick user." The psychiatric hospital should not be subverted to usage as a political prison serving to impose parental value systems on a basically healthy adolescent.

And Those Who Can Be Treated

The situation is somewhat more complex when the adolescent plans to continue drug usage, but does wish to be treated for other complaints. This is the most common pattern among self-referred adolescents. Often, a workable contract can be established even when the therapist recognizes that drug usage is actually blocking emotional development and therapeutic progress. Since the adolescent does have a goal, he may be motivated to give up drugs as the work of therapy demonstrates their interference with something that the adolescent wants for himself. It seems to me that no adolescent has ever been convinced by another person that he should give up drug usage. Many youngsters have convinced themselves for various reasons and have then used the help of adults to reach their goal. We must remember that they often ask for our help in very disguised ways.

In the cases treatable by outpatient therapy, drug usage is managed as any other kind of acting-out behavior. Its interference with therapy is noted matter-of-factly as the material indicates and the therapist, through the therapeutic alliance, acts to discourage its continuation in the interest of mutually accepted therapeutic goals.

Evans (1970) has offered a penetrating discussion of the influence of current youth subculture values on the developmental problems of adolescence. He describes factors which must be considered in setting therapeutic goals and evaluating the progress of the adolescent patient. These issues are especially important in the adolescent who champions the values of psychedelic drugs.

Esman (1967) has described a case in which he retrospectively felt that he should have forbidden his patient to use marijuana. The patient's personality structure may be sufficiently clear that the therapist can predict that drug experimentation will lead to dependence and a loss of interest in previously accepted goals of therapy. If the therapist is convinced that this is the case, he might consider making abstinence from drugs a condition of continuing therapy. Obviously, if the therapist is correct in his conviction, he may have nothing to lose by placing the therapeutic relationship in jeopardy.

In general, however, such arbitrary decisions cannot be recommended. Even if we may trust our predictive judgment, it may be more useful to modify the therapeutic approach toward meeting the adolescent's needs within the treatment relationship rather than to take the chance that the adolescent will interpret our stand as a dare and turn to a narcissistic solution to his pain.

Finally, we must recognize our relative ignorance of the natural history of drug usage in adolescents. Although we cannot avoid acting on incomplete knowledge as we deal with today's adolescents, we must continue to collect data and share our experiences with one another. In many ways, the abrupt arrival of the "drug scene" has made the psychotherapy of adolescents a "whole new ball game." We are understandably reluctant to play, since we are poorly grounded in the rules. We must enter the fray however whatever our anxieties, since for today's adolescent, whether he plays for the "straight" team or the "heads," it is literally "the only game in town."

DRUGS, CONFIDENTIALITY, AND THE ADOLESCENT'S PARENTS

In the section in Chapter Three on confidentiality in adolescent psychotherapy, we discuss the limitations of the confidential relationship with adolescent patients. These issues are often extremely relevant in dealing with adolescents who use drugs. Many of these youngsters' parents are unaware of the drug taking. Often, one feels that the parents are utilizing considerable avoidance, denial, and rationalization to prevent themselves from seeing the evidence before them. With equal frequency, especially in adolescents of high-school age and younger, one is impressed that the adolescents seem to be ambivalently hopeful that the parents will discover their drug activities and help them deal with their problems.

In my opinion, the adolescent should be told if the therapist feels his utilization of drugs is dangerous to his health or if his sale of drugs seems potentially dangerous to other youngsters or to the patient's legal status. The therapist must clearly explain that he will do whatever he can to interrupt these destructive activities. No reasonable therapeutic alliance could exist in a setting in which the therapist permitted clearly self-destructive behavior without opposing it. This does not mean that parents are automatically and quickly appraised of the details of their youngster's behavior. One must assess the ability of the parents to deal with the situation constructively and be willing to explore other alternatives for control of the behavior with the adolescent. If the therapist decides finally that the parents must be brought in as aids in the treatment situation, the adolescent should be informed in advance that this will be done and allowed an opportunity for full discussion of his feelings and reactions to the planned revelation.

The important point is that the therapist should not let commitment to complete confidentiality trap him into committing greater sins of compliance with superego corruptions, self-destruction, and exploitation of others. Correct decisions in this area are difficult to make and should be fully talked out with the adolescent patient. The final responsibility belongs to the therapist however and he must attempt to use his mature judgment and broad understanding of the adolescent's needs to choose the best course of action.

Naturally, when parents must be informed of drug usage, the therapist does everything possible to help them to a constructive management of the problem rather than a frightened and punitive overreaction. Sometimes, this is best done through a family conference on the subject.

THE BAD TRIP

Occasionally, the adolescent therapist will be confronted with the necessity of helping an adolescent who has become psychotic, terrified, or assaultive following ingestion of a drug. True "bad trips" occur almost exclusively with the hallucinogenic drugs, primarily LSD, but also with drugs from the belladonna family. They appear to be largely unpredictable and poorly correlated with dosage, previous experience with the drug, or personality structure (Ungerleider et al., 1968). Most youngsters experiencing "bad trips" are probably managed by their friends. They are usually brought to medical care when the reaction does not respond to the supportive care available in the drug user's immediate environment.

Treatment is primarily supportive, since the drug reaction is usually time-limited. The physician should offer calm assurances of a good outcome and comments which help to orient the adolescent to reality—especially the reality that his distorted perceptions are caused by the drug he has ingested. Chlorpromazine may be useful in counteracting the LSD effect (Report of the American Academy of Pediatrics, Committee on Youth, 1969; Ungerleider et al., 1968). Many drug users are aware of this and refer to the drug, along with others, as a "downer."

Chronic use of amphetamines may lead to a psychotic episode which is very similar to functional paranoid psychoses. Treatment is supportive, and caution must be exercised in prescribing any medication which has sedative properties, due to the generally overtaxed state of the nervous system.

The belladonna alkaloids in large doses may also produce an acute manic-like psychotic state which may include hallucinations. Several cases have been described which resulted from the ingestion of Asthmador, a proprietary preparation for the treatment of asthma. The clinical picture resembles a severe state of "twilight sleep," often with a fluctuating level of mental acuity. Atropine-like side effects of dry mouth, blurred vision, and tachycardia may be observable. The toxic state clears spontaneously with supportive care. In massive doses, there is the possibility of respiratory collapse. Chlorpromazine may worsen the psychotic state and potentiate the cardiovascular and respiratory side effects. It should be avoided (Louria, 1968).

Naturally, in all cases definitive treatment should follow detoxification. It is directed to the predisposing emotional problems of the involved adolescent if he is motivated to explore his basic personality problems.

CITED AND RECOMMENDED READINGS

Adler, N. 1968. The antinomian personality: the hippie character type. Psychiatry 31: 325–338.

American Medical Association Committee on Alcoholism and Addiction. 1965. Reports on dependency on amphetamines and barbiturates. 193: 673.

Blumfield, M., and L. Glickman. 1967. Ten months experience with LSD users admitted to county psychiatric receiving hospital. New York J. Med. 67: 1849–1853.

Brickman, H. R. 1968. The psychedelic "hip scene": return of the death instinct. Amer. J. Psychiat. 125: 766–772.

Cameron, D. C. 1968. Youth and drugs, a world view. JAMA 206: 1267–1271.

Camus, A. 1956. The rebel. New York: Random House.

Carson, D. I., and J. M. Lewis. 1970. Factors influencing drug abuse in young people. Texas Med. 66: 50–57.

Cohen, S. 1964. The beyond within: the LSD story. New York: Atheneum Publishers.

Cottle, T. J. 1969. Parent and child—the hazards of equality. Saturday Review, 52: No. 5, 16–48.

Cox, Harvey. 1970. The feast of fools: a theological essay on festivity and fantasy. Cambridge: Harvard University Press.

Dimijian, G. G. 1970. Clinical evaluation of the drug user: current concepts. Texas Med. 66: 42–49.

Esman, A. H. 1967. Drug use by adolescents: some valuative and technical implications. Psychoanal. Forum 2: 340–346.

Evans, J. L. 1970. The college student in the psychiatric clinic: syndromes and subcultural sanctions. Amer. J. Psychiat. 126: 1736–1742.

Frosch, W., E. Robbins, and M. Stern. 1965. Untoward reactions to

LSD resulting in hospitalization. New Eng. J. Med. 273: 1235–1239.

Hartmann, D. 1969. A study of drug taking adolescents. Psychoanal. Stud. Child 24: 384–397.

Hartmann, H. 1964. On rational and irrational action. In: Essays on ego psychology. New York: International Universities Press, Inc.

Hensala, J., L. Epstein, and K. Blacker. 1967. LSD and psychiatric inpatients. Arch. Gen. Psychiat. 16: 554–559.

Hinckle, W. 1967. The social history of the hippies. Ramparts 5: 5–26.

Hughes, H. S. 1969. Emotional disturbance and American social change, 1944–1969. Amer. J. Psychiat. 126: 21–28.

Keniston, Kenneth. 1965. The uncommitted: alienated youth in American society. New York: Harcourt, Brace & World, Inc.

Keniston, K. 1968. "Heads" and "seekers": student drug users. New York State District Branches APA Bull. 10: 8.

Leary, T. 1968. The politics of ecstasy. New York: G. P. Putnam's Sons.

Lewis, J. M. 1970. Report of the ad hoc committee on drug abuse, Dallas Independent School District Report, Dallas, Texas.

Liebert, R. S. 1967. Drug use: symptom, disease, or adolescent experimentation—the task of therapy. J. Amer. Coll. Health Assoc. 16: 25–29.

Louria, D. 1966. Nightmare drugs. New York: Pocket Books, Inc.

Louria, D. B. 1968. Some aspects of the current drug scene with emphasis on drugs in use by adolescents. Pediatrics 42: 904–911.

Mamlet, L. N. 1967. "Consciousness-limiting" side effects of "consciousness-expanding" drugs. Amer. J. Orthopsychiat. 37: 296–297.

Pearson, M. M., and R. B. Little. 1969. The addictive process in unusual addictions: a further elaboration of etiology. Amer. J. Psychiat. 125: 1166–1171.

Report by the Council on Mental Health and the Committee on Alcoholism and Drug Dependence of the American Medical Association and the Committee on Problems of Drug Dependence of the National Research Council. National Academy of Science, Reprints available from: AMA Council on Mental Health, 535 N. Dearborn Street, Chicago, Illinois 60610.

Report of the American Academy of Pediatrics, Committee on Youth. 1969. Drug abuse in adolescence. Pediatrics 44: 131–141.

Riefe, P. 1968. The triumph of the therapeutic. New York: Harper and Row Publishers, Inc.

Roszak, T. 1969. The making of a counter culture. New York: Doubleday & Company, Inc.

Sarbin, T. R. 1968. On the distinction between social roles and social types, with special reference to the hippies. Amer. J. Psychiat. 125: 1024–1031.

Tartakoff, H. H. 1966. The normal personality in our culture and the Nobel Prize complex. *In:* Psychoanalysis—a general psychology. Edited by R. M. Lowenstein, L. M. Newman, M. Schur, and A. J. Solnit. New York: International Universities Press, Inc.

Ungerleider, J. T., and D. D. Fisher. 1967. The problems of LSD[25] and emotional disorder. Calif. Med. 106: 49–55.

Ungerleider, J. T., D. D. Fisher, M. Fuller, and A. Caldwell. 1968. The "bad trip"—the etiology of the adverse LSD reaction. Amer. J. Psychiat. 124: 1483–1490.

Walters, P. A. 1967. Therapist bias and student use of illegal drugs. J. Amer. Coll. Health Assoc. 16: 30–34.

West, L. J., and J. R. Allen. 1968. Flight from violence: hippies and the green rebellion. Amer. J. Psychiat. 125: 364–370.

Wieder, H., and E. H. Kaplan. 1969. Drug use in adolescents: psychodynamic meaning and pharmacogenic effect. Psychoanal. Stud. Child 24: 399–431.

Part
Three

CHAPTER NINETEEN

the design of in-patient treatment centers

THE DESIGN OF IN-PATIENT TREATMENT CENTERS

The decision to remove an adolescent from his family or his surrogate family placement in order to provide residential treatment may be reached for a variety of reasons. It is impossible to design any single treatment center in such a way that it can meet the needs of all youngsters who require inpatient treatment. In addition, facility design is often dictated to some extent by practical considerations including sources of funding, available physical plants, availability of potential staff members, community preferences, local population needs, and other external factors which must be considered. It is obviously impractical and perhaps impossible to develop a small, long-term public facility for a community which has large numbers of troubled adolescents and no other treatment facility. The community and political pressures would almost force the development of a short term evaluation center. Later the community might be willing to consider the development of long term treatment facilities for some youngsters.

People who are planning inpatient programs for adolescents often have other practical questions. They want to know how you keep the kids from tearing the building down, maiming the staff or otherwise creating complete chaos. They are concerned, with good reason, about the techniques of behavioral control and safety. We will consider these questions later from a practical standpoint. The final answers to the overall success of an inpatient treatment program for adolescents are not simplistic or mechanical. Objective observations of existing programs suggest that many systems of clinical design can result in the successful treatment of emotionally disturbed adolescents. It is true that many of these effective programs share common features (Noshpitz, 1976) but it is also evident that there is considerable diversity between programs. In some cases the differences between successful programs suggest that the crucial aspect of program design is the process by which it is achieved rather than the form of the final product.

Basic Philosophy

When one reviews the successful programs mentioned above, one usually encounters strongly held theoretical opinions which the staff put forward to explain their effectiveness. When patients treated in these programs are interviewed they often echo these ideas and may even appear to speak in the jargon language which is commonly used in the day-to-day activities of the treatment unit. Resistant patients often appear to be rejecting these common beliefs and phrasings while those patients who appear to be improving embrace them and offer them as an explanation for their better performance. After a few days talking with the staff and patients at one of these centers, an outside observer often feels an enthusiastic sense of conversion and acceptance of the guiding principles of the treatment program.

The therapeutic approach used at this center seems to be the answer!

Unfortunately, there are many catches to this simple solution to design problems. Very often if one takes the successful design and attempts to copy it in another setting it is surprisingly unsuccessful. It is also rather confusing to study other successful programs and find that they embrace — with equal conviction — theories and ideas which differ markedly from those of the first treatment unit surveyed.

This puzzling and potentially discouraging observation is not so surprising if one remembers the need for diversity in inpatient treatment programs mentioned earlier. Different programs meet different needs, deal with different populations, and contain a complexity which defies the development of absolutes regarding the residential treatment of adolescents.

Like it or not, each adolescent residential treatment program must be custom designed to local conditions. Of course, the job of program planning is greatly assisted by familiarity with good programs. One can often draw valuable building blocks from the experiences of others. However, the final "whole" is somehow quite individual and always greater than the sum of its constituent parts.

The planning of any program begins with a careful survey of community needs, funding possibilities, and other practical issues which have been mentioned earlier. Once these have been determined the next important step in clinical programming is the construction of a philosophical or conceptual skeleton — a clear, sharply outlined description of the purposes and goals of the treatment center. This basic formulation of program goals and approaches must be strong enough to bear the weight of emotional dissension which will inevitably arise to test it. This is a crucial point to remember!

Without a clear philosophy which is backed by a strong commitment, any adolescent program will show a frightening and eventually destructive instability. No program design can prevent verbal criticisms, acting out behavior, treatment failures, and periods of chaos and relative unproductivity. These distressing events are simply part of the reality of treating adolescents. If there is no strong philosophical direction in the program, one often attempts to eliminate the distressing occurences by making programatic changes. Since the problems will continue to reappear there may be multiple confusing and disruptive false starts which can eventually lead to the collapse of the treatment effort.

This is not to say that blind faith in a theoretical position is the ideal basis for an adolescent treatment program. Long term evaluation of treatment results and gradual program modifications when they seem clearly indicated should be welcomed in any program. However, there should be a sufficient degree of conviction regarding the philosophic directions of the program, hopefully based on the relevant literature, to provide an air of confidence and an atitude of conservativeness regarding basic changes in the program. Due to the revolutionary tendencies of

disturbed adolescents as well as their propensity to externalize
problems and seek personal solutions in social change, there is a
great deal to be said for moving only grudgingly toward new
attitudes and techniques in adolescent treatment programs.

In speaking of philosophic guidelines I am not referring to a
highly theoretical or metapsychological construct of great
subtlety and complexity. On the contrary, I am suggesting that
one needs to think through in a very practical way, and in
language that all staff — regardless of professional background
— can understand, several basic questions regarding the nature of
the proposed treatment center.

First of all one needs to designate the place that the treatment
center plans to occupy in the world of the adolescent. This
usually involves some effort to limit the scope of what the
treatment program plans to achieve. Recognizing the program's
limitations requires some thinking about a number of facets of
the adolescent experience. This point can be illustrated by
beginning with one simple question.

What is the treatment center's relationship to the adolescent's
family?

Many philosophies of residential treatment imply that the
treatment center's function is to serve as a substitute family.
According to this view the emotionally disturbed youngster is
considered to be suffering from inept or distorted parenting. His
disability may then be corrected by providing substitute parent
figures so that the adolescent can internalize more appropriate
models. Subscribing to this viewpoint has obvious implications
for program design. A plan must be devised which will wean the
youngster from his pathological but intense tie to the original
parents. Often this means that the facility should treat youngsters
at some geographical distance from their family of origin. Often
it means that the program will severely restrict parental visits for
a fairly prolonged period at the onset of treatment. Further,
programming should provide every opportunity for one-to-one
interactions between staff and patients, preferably utilizing and
emphasizing natural alliances which may spring up between
patients and particular staff members. Allowances must also be
made for at least the possibility of extended periods of extreme

regression so that earlier pathological parenting experiences can be re-worked with the new parent figure. In programs of this kind the original parents are often viewed as almost "toxic" and the youngster is often protected from extended unsupervised contact with this source of his difficulty. Staff members are encouraged to appreciate fully their tremendous importance to the patient and may be expected to take extensive responsibility for providing care and nurture to the young patients in their program. If parents are treated, this work is usually carefully separated from the direct treatment of the disturbed youngster. Perhaps the program that most closely exemplifies this paradigm is the Orthogenic School as conceptualized and directed by Doctor Bruno Bettelheim.

Other treatment programs do not view themselves as substitutes for the family. They accept the family unit as their patient and feel that the adolescent is likely to show genuine improvement only if this entire social system of the family can be altered in a constructive way. These residential centers view themselves as a support system and a change agent for the family rather than as a substitute for it. In such a "family prosthesis" program, the design would be constructed to maximize direct parental involvement with the adolescent patients and with the treatment staff. In congruence with this view of the family as patient, treatment would include frequent visits home, relatively unrestricted parental visitation rights and active encouragement of staff-parent cooperation around everyday management issues in the treatment facility. Such a program would also place certain restrictions on the patient population which could be served. Only those parents who lived in relatively comfortable commuting distance could be expected to have the degree of availability required by the treatment approach.

These brief and somewhat oversimplified illustrations are offered primarily to illustrate the process by which program design is evolved. If policies and procedures are determined in this way by the goals and purposes of the basic treatment approach, form can evolve naturally from function. By proceeding in this way a multitude of important practical decisions are almost automatically shaped by a clear general and over-riding conceptual framework. The fact that there is then a clinically determined reason for program policies is extremely valuable in gaining consensual support from staff, administration, parents, and interested community members. This adds a basic consistency to program design and also provides a sensible answer to that constant question, "Why do the rules have to be as they are?"

Many other questions regarding a treatment center's place in the world of the adolescent patient must be answered in order to complete the philosophic design. The program must consider not only its relationship to the family, but also its relationship to the community. For example, some treatment centers regard themselves as havens from a basically destructive and pathological larger society. These centers function almost as psychological convents or monasteries where the adolescent may be purified and perfected in preparation for eventual return to an imperfect world that he will then be strong enough to withstand. Centers of this kind often plan their activities to emphasize the difference between the protected treatment society and the larger world outside. Strong emphasis is placed on internal communal activities and there are carefully constructed buffers between the program and the outside world. The treated adolescent may initially be permitted social experiences outside of the confines of the treatment center only in company with other graduates of the program. For example alcoholic adolescents may be transitioned outside of the residential alcoholism program by frequent and extensive contacts with Alcoholics Anonymous groups. Only when the youngster seems to have formed close and comfortable attachments within these groups are they actually discharged home. Many drug rehabilitation programs are designed according to this principle. Some of these require an entering youngster to cut his hair as a symbolic renunciation of his previous mode of existence. The youngster may not be permitted to listen to rock music since that art form is associated with the larger youth culture's easy acceptance of drug usage. The important point is that the program design in these centers derives from a feeling that the youngster's disability results from negative and corrupting social influences which can be corrected through immersion in a more sensitive, healthy and caring community in which all participants are embued with a deviant but nobler and superior value system.

Obviously another center which viewed its function to be a transmission of the best of community values and the re-integration of the youngster into the wider community as quickly as possible would be designed in a completely different way. For example a program with a strong community investment might use numerous community volunteers, the neighborhood public school and a work program which attempted to build strong ties between the treatment unit personnel and local employers.

Basic program planning is also affected by other philosophical issues. Convictions regarding the nature of psychic structure and the process of emotional healing are central to program decisions. Program directors who subscribe to a view that emotional growth occurs as a result of insight and intrapsychic reorganization will derive a program design which is quite different from that which will be designed by a director who views behavior primarily as a response to external pressures and conditions. The dynamically oriented program will place greater emphasis on individualized treatment plans which are designed to maximize emotional expression and psychic exploration. Deviant behavior will be acceptable as a behavioral expression of the internal conflict which can be utilized in the process of exploration and resolution of previously internalized conflicts. Staff will be encouraged to deal with patient behavior within a framework of acceptance and psychological curiosity and may be helped to develop intense individual relationships with the patients. Strong peer group interactions may be viewed to some extent as a resistance to the treatment process and secondarily as a source of information which can be utilized in individual formal psychotherapy.

On the other hand, a program that emphasizes the concept that maladaptive behavior results from poor learning in the past or improper management in the present will require a greater emphasis on the necessity for following group norms and expectations. Staff will view their job primarily in terms of the entire patient group. They will be expected to maintain the unit's traditions and values and to assist new patients in accepting these and in conducting themselves accordingly. Although individual difficulties may be viewed sympathetically, they are not pursued extensively due to the fear that the patient may use his internal problems as an excuse for failing to live up to group expectations. In addition to direct staff structuring, various sophisticated behavior modification techniques may be utilized to shape behavior in adaptive directions.

In practice, of course, most inpatient treatment centers are somewhat eclectic. That is, many centers utilize both insight psychotherapy and behavior modification. However, the ways in which these modalities are utilized and the relative centrality they occupy in the treatment program is dictated by an underlying sense of what is really important in the treatment process. For example, very few people would see value in allowing adolescents to act out in a totally uncontrolled manner within a treatment program. Control is necessary, but control may be viewed as an end in itself or merely as a way to prevent dissipation of anxiety which is needed for fruitful insight psychotherapy. In centers where acting out is viewed as learned maladaptive behavior, acting out is often actively and strenuously opposed even to the extent of using adversive stimuli. In centers where acting out is viewed as a defensive operation, programming tends to be designed to discourage the behavior through persuasion and appeals to the therapeutic alliance. In short, in the first kind of center the patient is told that his acting out *is* his illness, while in the second he is asked to desist from acting out so that he can be helped toward cure. The style and techniques of limit setting will be strongly influenced accordingly.

Even these philosophical issues may be influenced by practical considerations. One must look at staffing patterns, both in terms of numbers and in terms of the types of professional persons who will be available to implement a philosophical program. For example, it would be pointless to attempt to design an extremely sophisticated psychoanalytic program without staff members who were adequately trained in the intricacies of that theoretical model. The availability of sufficient funds to permit a high staff patient ratio might allow a greater degree of behavioral freedom than that which would be practical in a program which could be only marginally staffed. Of course, one has to make a decision at some point as to whether a program is possible under existing conditions. There is no real service to adolescents in providing a facility which is improperly staffed or inadequately funded to the point that acceptable care is impossible.

The Development of the Therapeutic Philosophy

So far we have spoken of this basic program design as though it could spring full-grown from the fertile brain of the program director. In fact, at inception the philosophic skeleton is often rather sketchy and still quite flexible in regard to its details. The design usually emerges in a clear and stabilized form only in response to questions and issues raised by patients and staff when the program actually begins. However, some basic design must be present even at the outset and the elaboration of the finer points cannot be delayed indefinitely. As mentioned earlier, an adolescent program will be seriously stressed and will not exist for long unless it is protected by a strongly held philosophy. As a rule this philosophy will be quickly embodied in one individual who is viewed consciously or unconsciously by the entire staff as the emotional leader of the program. It is important that this leader have a strong conviction that the basic plan is a good one and that it will help adolescents to grow. This conviction must be strong since the purpose of the unit will be tested and shaken to its very foundation by adolescent rebelliousness and by the adolescent's relentless search for integrity, consistency and meaning.

The author is aware that this assertion regarding the importance of a central leader in an adolescent program may offend some mental health practitioners who believe strongly in a process of decision making by staff consensus. However, practical reality requires this kind of centralized leadership. Democracy is a great ideal for political organizations, but consensus alone can never provide the conceptual foundation, the necessary inner stability, and the consistency over time needed in an effective adolescent treatment center. However, to emphasize the need for a strong leader with a clear sense of purpose and basic techniques is not to suggest a dogmatic rigidity which rejects other opinions and ideas. On the contrary, it is extremely important to be able to hear and understand the ideas and innovations presented by staff members. This process is extremely valuable to the success of the program, not only because open communication helps other staff members to feel important and included in the decision making process, but also because many specific suggestions will be valuable in their own right. The point is that all ideas should be tested against the basic understanding of what the treatment center is trying to accomplish so that policies do not change erratically in response to every clinical emergency, period of staff unrest, or other temporary expediency. As a matter of fact, comfort with one's overview of the program permits a relaxed consideration of any and all staff ideas, no matter how extreme they may sound at initial hearing. Since the stability of the program is based on "the big picture", it is possible to relax and consider many alternatives without excessive anxiety.

Over more extended periods treatment programs tend to absorb their tradition, particularly when the approach is blessed with positive treatment outcomes. As this gradually occurs, many staff members adopt and assimilate the basic philosophy of the program and its successful continuation becomes less dependent on the active presence of a single individual leader.

Assembling the Treatment Staff

If the conceptual framework described above provides the skeleton for the living organism of the treatment center, the staff provides the flesh and blood necessary for functioning. A great deal has been written and even more has been said regarding staff selection and qualifications for inpatient adolescent work. Many guidelines have been advanced, but anyone who works in the field sees daily exceptions to every rule. Unfortunately, it seems that the only real test of effectiveness as a staff member is to function for a period of time in that role. Even successful experience in other treatment centers is no guarantee that a staff member will work well in a new treatment program. For this reason most centers formalize a probationary period of three to four months during which the new staff member and the treatment center regard their relationship as tentative, temporary, and exploratory.

Although there is absolutely no proof, the author has the personal feeling that there are advantages to having a staff composed of individuals of varying age. The enthusiasm and empathy which young staff members bring to an adolescent program often need to be balanced by the wisdom and perspective of older staff members. However, a staff composed only of very mature people may lack the energy required to keep up with the almost frenetically active adolescent patient group. Needless to say, age requirements pale in importance compared to issues of professional qualifications and experience.

There are also advantages in having staff members of varying socio-economic backgrounds if their professional credentials and experiences are comparable. In fact, a staff of divergent origins along many axes of human experience provides the widest possible range of empathy and potential identification models for the adolescent patients. However, the staff members must be able to respect one another's competence or personal diversity can lead to destructive dissension and splitting.

In this regard, some balances are difficult to achieve. Ideally, a unit would have similar numbers of males and females for example, yet there are few available male nurses. In some parts of the country, racial and ethnic balance is difficult to achieve. The program director can only do what is possible, always using adequate professional qualifications as the primary selection criterion. In any case, staff training and supervision are always crucial.

Some mention should be made of a recurrent problem in the nursing staff structure of inpatient treatment centers. Those centers which are situated in hospitals usually have a patient-care staff composed partially of nurses and partially of non-medically-trained attendants or psychiatric assistants. These two groups of individuals with their strongly divergent educational backgrounds frequently have problems working together. The background of most nurses is medical and highly professional.

For some of them psychological mindedness comes with some difficulty, particularly when it seems to conflict with sensible behavioral standards. On the other hand, many young persons who are attracted to psychiatric work without professional training have had some training in psychology or other behavioral sciences and very little experience or even sympathy with the medical model. Often they feel that they know more about psychiatric care and psychological functioning than the nurses who are their superiors. This is equally true when nursing assistants are untrained and purely "intuitive". On the other hand, the nurses frequently feel saddled with unprofessional and maverick staff members who have no grasp of the real meaning of the therapeutic relationship or of proper conduct within the heirarchy of the treatment center. Since both groups have extremely valuable contributions to make to overall treatment, it is worth a great deal of effort to maintain mutual respect and cooperation between the two groups. This task usually falls to the program director, or if he is fortunate, to an experienced and skillful nurse to whom he can delegate the responsibility. The task is one of preventing either group from prematurely closing ranks with a polarized sense that they are correct and the other group is wrong. The value and contribution of both groups must be emphasized along with the crucial need to find a compromise position which everyone can accept. This is of obvious importance in an adolescent treatment program in view of the adolescent's tendency to split staff members as a defense. The program director must be alert to factions within the treatment staff and quick to utilize everyone's shared experience to demonstrate the need for unity and compromise. Paradoxically, this unity can often be achieved only after permitting a period of open disagreement and verbal dissension. As a rule, it is not the verbalized and recognized areas of staff disagreement that create the most serious problems in a treatment program. Covert and secret staff conflicts have the greatest potential for creating chaos and anti-therapeutic disruption.

We shall return to this extremely important question of creating and maintaining open communication within the staff later in a more general context. At this point it is important to take a temporary detour to discuss staff training. The initial orientation of staff and continuing active educational programs for the staff provide the cornerstone for effective treatment throughout the life of any adolescent inpatient program.

Staff Training

Staff who are hired to work in an adolescent inpatient treatment center need many things. Even those who have received some formal education in the area of adolescent psychiatry are usually poorly prepared to utilize these basic skills effectively in any specific treatment setting before they have been trained in a program designed specifically for that treatment institution.

First of all the staff members need a great deal of information. This can often be best transmitted in a fairly dyadic manner. However, since there is frequently a "combat patrol" mentality among workers in inpatient units, this dyadic information must be given by individuals who are respected by the staff. As a rule this respect is given only to people who have worked successfully with inpatients. Specific examples are important, best drawn from recent experiences with patients known to the staff. If the staff regards a lecture as too theoretical or the lecturer as primarily "academic" they often discount the useful information which is being transmitted. Lecturers need to be brief and to the point, partly because many adolescent staff members are extremely practical and action oriented, but also because of the realistic need to staff the unit which precludes long hours of sitting in lecture halls. It is also wise to repeat basic lectures on a regular basis. New staff often cannot absorb certain information because they're not yet aware of its importance or relevance to their everyday work. In addition, because of the shift schedules, not all staff will be available at any given time a lecture is presented.

Examples of material which can be covered in lecture form include teaching the general philosophy of the treatment unit, its specific policies, basic characteristics of adolescent development, common psychopathological syndromes, psychopharmacology and certain basic skills such as the fundamentals of interviewing techniques.

No effort will be made to suggest the specific content of these lectures. This will vary with the orientation of each program and with the teaching skills of those who are available to transmit the information. As implied earlier, the lectures should be kept as simple, practical and as well illustrated as possible. The goal is to convey base line information which can be used in everyday patient work. Many people even deprecate the value of didactic instruction of this kind in staff training. However, others, including the author, feel that such instruction provides a basic security to staff, helps to prevent glaring gaps in knowledge and saves a great deal of everyone's time by decreasing the need for individual repetition of basic information. The lecture series creates a shared body of knowledge which is available for reference in the future course of supervised experiential learning and general staff discussions regarding patient care.

In addition to information, staff members require assistance in gaining certain skills. For example, the didactic instruction regarding interviewing techniques needs to be augmented with some opportunity to experiment through role playing or actual interview situations with adolescent patients. These training interviews may be observed or video-taped so that the staff member can receive immediate feedback. In reacting to these interviews it is important to reinforce strongly the positive aspects of the interview. One cannot ignore blatant errors in technique, but these can be approached with tact, understanding and empathy for the anxiety of the neophyte staff member. It is important to avoid the impression that interviewing an adolescent is an arcane and intricate process best left only to the most highly trained professional. On balance, it is better for a staff member to conduct somewhat amateurish but sincere and comfortable interviews with the patients on the units than for the staff member to be afraid to talk to the patients for fear of "making things worse" through lack of skill. It is also important to remember that most actual staff interviews will occur in a very different situation than the one contrived for training purposes. Often in their day to day work on the unit the staff is much more comfortable in talking with the patients regarding routine unit activities and interactions than they will ever be in a formal interview setting. None-the-less, teaching the staff to utilize non-directive approaches, comfortable silences, and emphatic responses to affective statements will increase the effectiveness of their interactions with the patients under any circumstances.

Even more important than training in interview skills is staff training around behavioral control. One of the most disruptive and paralyzing aspects of a new staff member's feeling about working on an adolescent unit is the fear of violence. Many disturbed adolescents are extremely threatening and intimidating. The potential for actual violence of a dangerous degree is very real on any adolescent unit. Not only does the staff member face the prospect of a single youngster going out of control in a dangerous way, he must also contend with fantasies regarding group violence because of the propensity for contagion when an adolescent unit is angry and upset. The unit's policies in regard to dealing with situations of this kind must be concise and clear. The average staff member not only fears that he may be injured, but that his personal response to a violent situation may be non-therapeutic. Most staff members who choose to work in an adolescent setting accept the idea that a youngster's dangerous behavior is a product of his psychopathology and they desire to respond helpfully when this particular portion of the problem is evidenced. They can feel comfortable in this only if they are directed by a definite set of procedures which are utilized in situations of this kind. Because of the drama and intensity of the moment one cannot expect staff to be creative and flexible at a time when they must act quickly and decisively. It is important to be sure that all staff are totally familiar with the policies regarding control of dangerous behavior and that these policies are reviewed periodically.

Control of the violent patient is a subject which should not be taught only with words. The techniques of subduing and restraining a youngster who is out of control should be practiced in a role playing setting so that the proper approaches and procedures become second nature to the staff members. The staff person who is playing the role of the patient should be encouraged to be sufficiently resistant so that the new staff members get a realistic sense of the degree of physical effort which will be required to control a real patient.

This description of the importance of training in the control of physical violence is not meant to imply that restraining, subduing, and secluding adolescents is an extremely common or desirable part of their treatment. On the contrary, other techniques of behavioral control including the general atmosphere of the unit, skills in utilization of the relationship with the youngster, interviewing techniques for dealing with angry or frightened adolescents and the appropriate utilization of patient group support are all more important on a day-to-day basis than are techniques for the physical management of the out of control adolescent. However, all of these approaches are utilized more comfortably and effectively if every staff member is quietly confident that, if necessary, they can handle any situation which occurs. The specific techniques for controlling violent behavior without injuring the patient or risking an injury to staff have been well described in the literature and will not be repeated here. (Frost, 1972; Penningroth, 1975)

In addition to dyadic training and the use of contrived experiential learning opportunities, all staff members deserve and need on-going supervision of their daily work experience. As a rule, it is best if this can be provided by more experienced individuals of their own discipline who are now performing comparable tasks on the unit or who have done so in the past. When such individuals are not available, it is important to develop a supervisory atmosphere in which the staff member feels comfortable in discussing their management of situations and their feelings regarding the patients and the treatment program. Supervision is useless if the staff member feels that it is directed primarily toward a critical review of every action. Anyone who has worked in the direct management of inpatient adolescents realizes that it is virtually impossible to avoid errors — even a multitude of errors. Decisions have to be made rapidly and often in settings which are at least noisy and distracting if not downright chaotic. Many factors, including the patients basic illness, the current atmosphere of the entire unit, the particular group of staff who are on duty at the time and an infinite variety of other variables all effect each decision. In the comfort and quiet of a supervision session, blessed with the clarity of the retrospectoscope, it is almost always easy to see how a situation could have been handled somewhat better than it was. Given these facts, a staff member would have every reason to resent a condescending or superior, carping, nitpicking attitude on the part of the supervisor.

On the other hand, there are many opportunities for spontaneous praise and even awe at the on-the-spot skill demonstrated by staff members in their daily dealings with adolescent patients. Needless to say, there is no reason for the supervisor to withhold this kind of feedback. There are many occupational hazards in working with inpatient adolescents, but a grandiose over-evaluation of one's skills and abilities is not high on the list. As one staff member said, "One thing for sure, the kids will keep you humble".

It should be noted finally that the luxury of formal scheduled supervision is rarely available in an inpatient setting for adolescents. There is simply not time. Supervision tends to occur in conjunction with daily reports, casual conversations at the nursing station and in other settings where the routine daily work is done. The author has not been impressed with the value of having a staff member designated purely as a supervisor and teacher. The comradeship of a good treatment staff often works to exclude and isolate any individual who is not actively involved in patient care. In at least two treatment settings with which the author is familiar, a unit "teacher" quickly became a professor who was scorned and actively avoided by his would-be students.

All of the training efforts described above are doomed to failure unless the training program teaches staff members how to recognize their own feelings and the influence of these feelings on their daily functioning. Staff members are likely to achieve this capacity for insight only if there is a strong sense of teamwork and group cohesion on the unit which supports an open, supportive, and realistic atmosphere. In the author's opinion, it is impossible for any individual to be so mature, well adjusted, and dedicated as to work effectively in an inpatient adolescent treatment program over an extended period of time without an active sense of involvement and mutual support from fellow staff members. The counter-transference feelings stirred by disturbed adolescents are so intense that sooner or later one will make a serious error in dealing with a youngster. Tragic examples of competent staff members being actually seduced by patients or losing control of themselves and striking patients are all too common. Perhaps it is not surprising that these tragedies often happen to some of the most talented and skilled of the staff group. Perhaps outstanding individuals come to feel somewhat superior to their fellow workers and do not feel as much of a need for ventilation, discussion, and sharing of feelings as more average staff members might. Since they usually "know what to do", they feel little need to talk about it. In adolescent psychiatry, pride often comes before the fall.

Similar failures to communicate may occur with somewhat weak staff members who anticipate that they will be regularly criticized for their faltering efforts to help the patients. It is important for the program director to be especially alert to the vulnerability of individuals at both extremes of apparent competence.

One of the best safe-guards for all staff members is the provision of regular opportunities for group discussion of patient management. It is difficult to attain the proper atmosphere for these group meetings. There is some tendency for them to degenerate into opportunities for the program director or other experienced staff members to hold forth on proper techniques, thereby demonstrating their skill and brilliance. On the other hand, if the meetings are equally worthless if they become "group therapy without a leader" during which staff members simply wallow in the range of feelings stirred in the crucible of an adolescent inpatient unit. Some structure is necessary but there must also be opportunities for sharing of intense and even professionally unacceptable feelings. Constructive learning can occur if one can establish a general attitude that professionalism is the goal at all times but that it cannot be achieved without many mistakes and false starts. One is also wise to encourage staff to teach one another and to share common and analogous experiences. Peer teaching both adds a richness of information and provides reinforcement of the team approach to the task of treatment. Rossman (1978) has described an excellent model of group staff training which he has evolved for his program.

Some Further Comments About Leadership and Philosophic Evolution

Earlier we had touched briefly on the management of tensions between nurses and psychiatric technicians. Of course, in adolescent inpatient treatment there are many other opportunities for cross-discipline conflict and other staff dissension. The leader's role in approaching these issues is very important. The proper management of conflicts of this kind is fairly obvious in theory. The program direction should be fair, impartial, and directed by the philosophy of the program. However, in practice dealing with staff conflict can be highly problematic.

One of the main reasons for this is the peculiar emotional stress which falls upon the program director. We have just spent considerable time discussing the need for staff members to ventilate their feelings and discuss them openly. They also enjoy the opportunity for friendships outside of the work situation and for candid, even irresponsible cathartic outbursts regarding particular patients or other staff members. There are, in short, many opportunities for venting the intense emotions stirred by the work. On the other hand, the program director's position must be somewhat more lonely. He still must face the intense pressures and worries generated by conducting an adolescent inpatient treatment center. He is likely to be frequently harried and upset. In this situation there are many temptations to form confidential alliances with individual staff members who are seen by the director as unusually able, compatable and sympathetic to his position. It is very easy with these trusted staff members to engage in cozy games of what Eric Berne would have called, "Ain't it awful!" These take the form of, "Ain't it awful how rigid and insensitive the teachers, nurses, or others are?" Obviously the program director must resist this temptation. One protection he can provide himself is to insist on discussing all staff differences in a group setting where favoritism is extremely unlikely to occur without detection. In these groups it is possible to stick to a policy of testing all disagreements against the basic philosophy of the unit. Of course, in dealing with all staff issues it is necessary to steer a careful course between arbitrary authoritarian control, which would defeat the sense of mutual commitment which we have said is essential to the success of the program and the equally dangerous course of a rudderless permissiveness which would invite chaos. Let us consider a concrete example.

A new adolescent program is preparing to open and the staff members are considering the question of the appropriate involvement of parents. This will include many questions such as visiting hours, management of passes, staff response to parental phone calls, and staff reaction to patients' statements and queries regarding their relationship with their parents. Many other questions may be raised. Should the parents give their youngster an allowance or should the parents provide the treatment center with money which would be given to the youngster by staff? Should there be combined meetings of parents and staff in a "town meeting" format which would permit and encourage direct parental involvement in management decisions? Should the parents or the staff have the right to final decisions regarding the length of passes or even the question of whether a youngster should have a pass at all? Is it the parents' responsibility to approve visitors to the child or does the staff make the decision regarding who can come to the hospital?

These questions need to be debated openly in staff meetings. Discussions of this kind permit the staff to become aware of attitudes and prejudices which they may hold regarding parents in general or regarding parents of emotionally disturbed children. Talking out these decisions also allows the staff to think through their peculiar position as temporary substitute parents or as agents for youngster's real parents. The program director will have the opportunity to evaluate his particular staff on their skills and interest in approaching parental involvement in particular ways. For example, some mental health workers are quite comfortable directing a town hall meeting which includes parents while others would feel hopelessly intimidated and overwhelmed by the task of attempting to deal with such a large group. This realistic appraisal of staff skills and limitations must be taken into account in choosing one or several of the potential techniques for involving parents actively in unit work.

However, many of the decisions would be determined by a previous basic philosophical position which the treatment program had decided earlier. That is, is this program designed to provide a substitute parenting experience for the adolescent or is it designed as a support to the present family structure? The implications of that decision have been described earlier.

What this example attempts to convey in a brief manner is the dynamic interaction between a relatively unchanging treatment concept and the rather fluid impact of staff and patients on everyday decision making. It is the interaction of these two elements which gradually weaves a distinct fabric of clinical planning individualized to the particular needs of a given center and the capabilities of its staff.

Other Important Issues

To this point we have not talked in depth about the developmental needs of the adolescent and the influence that these have on clinical programming. It is obvious that these are over-riding considerations since the adolescent *must* be provided with developmentally appropriate educational and social experiences, including such a simple and mundane thing as sufficient physical exercise. Adolescent programs cannot be totally serious, analytic and intense twenty-four hours a day. Adolescents need fun, opportunities for social interaction, and the chance to perform activities which they can feel proud of. A well designed adjunctive therapy program which not only permits outlets for the appropriate interest and energies of the adolescent, but also broadens skills of sublimation which is crucial to the success of any inpatient treatment program. Educational programs which can provide a range of assistance from remedial education, challenging academics, and pre-vocational training for youngsters with very weak academic skills are also a crucial part of any treatment program.

The task of melding all of these components into a coherent, cooperative, and consistent design is an endless and challenging task. Accrediting agencies such as JCAH perform a necessary function by reminding us of the many necessary elements which go into quality patient care. They can also study programs to insure that all the essential pieces are present. However, they can never really check the "heart" of any program. That almost indefinable portion of the puzzle is the esprit, confidence in the program, and sense of mutual endeavor which characterizes the effective treatment unit.

CITED AND RECOMMENDED READINGS

Noshpitz, J.D. 1976. The therapeutic aspect of residential treatment. Journal of the Philadelphia Association of Psychoanalysis, 3: 71-84.

Frost, M. 1972. Violence in psychiatric patients. Nursing Times. 68: 748-749.

Penningroth, P.W. 1975. Control of violence in a mental health setting. American Journal of Nursing. 75: 696-709.

Rossman, P.G. 1979. Hospital treatment for disturbed adolescents: a model for staff training. Journal of the Academy of Child Psychiatry, In Press.

CHAPTER TWENTY

the process of inpatient treatment

THE PROCESS OF INPATIENT TREATMENT

A. *The Therapeutic Milieu*

It is difficult to define precisely the concept of milieu therapy. The term refers for our purposes to the cumulative impact of all aspects of the treatment program aside from formally scheduled treatment sessions and adjunctive therapy activities. The milieu is composed of all the informal interactions between patients and between patients and staff in addition to the formal organization of the processes of daily life together.

Although this aspect of inpatient treatment may be difficult to define, it is of central importance. In fact, it is the milieu which cannot be duplicated outside of the residential treatment program. All other aspects of treatment such as individual therapy, group therapy, family therapy, psychopharmacology, and adjunctive therapy activities could be provided to patients without hospital care. Protective confinement and the structured life of a milieu program differentiate inpatient treatment from all other forms of care.

Some inpatient treatment programs have been organized with the conscious idea that the unit was to provide only humane protective confinement while the therapy occurred in formal psychotherapeutic interview situations. This concept of nursing care as glorified babysitting is not only demeaning to nursing staff personnel but an unrealistic denial of the true nature of life in a residential treatment center. The depreciation of nursing staff is an important issue since it tends to lead to a lack of investment in the program with resulting rapid turnover and general discontent. However, there are even more serious drawbacks to this approach.

Even if the program director does not realize it, both patients

363

and staff are aware that scheduled psychotherapeutic time makes up a very small part of their life. Emotional involvements with fellow patients and with the staff who provide basic care are often much more intense than the involvement with the assigned psychotherapist. Attachments with this degree of importance will inevitably be structured in some way so that people can live together and relate with a reasonable degree of comfort. If a milieu is not planned, it will happen anyway and exert a powerful influence on the overall therapeutic thrust of the program. If the program director is unaware of this fact of inpatient living, he will be deprived of essential information and will lose the opportunity to direct this powerful therapeutic force.

It is realistic to view the inpatient treatment setting as a small society which has a somewhat unusual pattern of membership. Ostensibly this society is designed for the purpose of benefiting one subgroup of its population, namely the adolescent patient. By this very definition the adolescent patient is placed at some disadvantage in the social organization that he is joining. He is the citizen who is in need of help by reason of a presumed mental or behavioral deficiency. His wishes are suspect, his behavior is open to speculative interpretation and his political actions are more to be understood than responded to. In addition to these disadvantages, the patient is likely to be the most transient member of the society, often leaving when his effectiveness in the small world of the inpatient unit reaches its maximum.

Another non-permanent citizen group is composed of the parents of the adolescent inpatient. Their relationship to the social order is even more complex than that of the patient. They are not officially designated as ill and in some programs may not be viewed as needing the help of the treatment program. However, traditionally the parents of hospitalized adolescents are viewed with some suspiciousness by mental health professionals and may implicitly be regarded as the "real" source of the adolescent's psychopathology. This confusion is compounded by parental guilt regarding the adolescent's emotional difficulties. Often the parent carries the secret conviction that they are indeed responsible for the patient's difficulties. Although some parents are able to discuss this feeling openly and thus convert themselves into "patients", many of them defend themselves against these painful feelings. Defensive maneuvers may include rejection of the youngster, passive withdrawal, active hostility toward the treatment staff, and regressive identification with the adolescent patient so that the treatment staff is viewed as the bad, failing parent.

In addition to the confusion produced by these psychological currents, the parent must try to gain entry to the inpatient society while often having minimal contact with the staff members. There may also be considerable confusion regarding the proper exercise of parental authority once an adolescent is hospitalized. Most parents view hospitalization as "turning over" the youngster to professionals. They may welcome this state of affairs and cheerfully relinquish parental authority or they may compete actively with the treatment staff in a way that is confusing and destructive to the adolescent patient.

The treatment staff in an inpatient program often has equally confusing attitudes toward parents. This is particularly true if the program has not clarified its philosophy regarding its appropriate relationship to the patient's family. If the treatment staff views themselves as surrogate, corrective parents, the presence of the real parents may be viewed as an evil intrusion into their treatment efforts. This intrusion may or may not be regarded as a *necessary* evil. Unfortunately such a state of affairs sets the stage for defensive splitting in which all of the adolescent's difficulties are viewed as originating from the parents. This splitting permits the staff to avoid their feelings of anger and frustration with the adolescent patient so that these are never directly joined in the therapeutic process. Instead, the adolescent is viewed as all good; a helpless victim of parental destructiveness, who must always be understood and helped. Even if the parental destructiveness is charitably regarded as psychopathological in origin rather than malicious and willful, the adolescent still avoids all responsibility for his own problems.

The staff of an inpatient treatment unit also faces a somewhat ambiguous status in the small society we are discussing. In some ways they are clearly the most powerful citizens in this world.

They are relatively permanent residents who understand the traditions and laws of the country. By definition they are the ones who give the help to the needy patients. Ostensibly they are motivated by a healthy desire to be therapeutic. Their decisions are based on a righteous desire to assist and are not officially open to personal interpretations based on their life experiences. Their privacy is protected and their feelings and subjective responses are open to consideration only if they volunteer them.

On the other hand, this privileged position carries strong prohibitions against abuse, a noblesse oblige which in practice can lead to an almost masochistic and sacrificial role. Since staff must only do those things which will be helpful to adolescent patients, they may be reluctant to insist on conditions of life and unit policies which are openly and honestly based on staff convenience. If carried to extremes, this attitude can be extremely destructive in an adolescent treatment program. Unrealistic expectations of staff altruism can lead to resentment, burn-out, and rapid staff turnover. In addition, staff "perfection" can have an infantalizing effect on the adolescent patient which merely reinforces a narcissistic, omnipotent defensive stance rather than promoting a responsible autonomy.

The opposite extreme is equally destructive. Programs which are designed to provide entirely for the comfort and well-being of staff may ignore the human and treatment needs of the adolescent patients. Since the patient has very little genuine political power in this small society the result can be an unfeeling, calloused suppression of the rights of patients which is extremely destructive to any reasonable treatment goals.

Fortunately these potential inequities in the social structure of an inpatient treatment program are often outweighed by the humanity, common sense, and normal relatedness of the various individuals who comprise the populations described. Patients, for example, are often so obviously appealing and able that staff focuses on their strengths and potentials rather than their defined social position. Many staff are very comfortably aware that they receive as many emotional supplies from the adolescent patients as they give. Patients and parents usually have sufficient ego functioning to negotiate constructively within the framework of the treatment community. Still, it is important for a program director and his staff to be aware of these potentially disruptive differences in status and position so that they can be controlled and utilized constructively in the treatment design.

It is also useful to consider the various interfaces where individuals of different political importance encounter one another. Obviously the interface between the staff and patient group is immediately apparent and is of extreme importance. It is also somewhat more delicate than is sometimes recognized. The staff's professionalism and their desire to function thera-peutically are essential and laudable characteristics which must be supported and constantly reinforced as noted in the section on training. However, it is probably true that most pivotal staff-patient interchanges occur in a framework where the professional-patient boundry becomes slightly blurred and is then reconstructed on a new basis. For example, instances where staff become intensely and personally angry with a patient may, if appropriately resolved, lead to extensive emotional growth in both parties. It is also probably true that very personal positive attachments play an important role in fueling emotional re-organization. If staff members are able to remain cool, detached and professional at all times they may well be too defended or emotionally isolated to work well with adolescent patients. Adolescents demand and need a personal response. The delicate balance of permitting oneself this kind of involvement while retaining some degree of professional objectivity and focus on the therapeutic goals is the most difficult task faced by the treatment team. Staff frequently require support in recognizing and accepting as appropriate their individual and idiosyncratic responses to particular patients. As noted earlier, this can rarely be accomplished by "psychoanalyzing" the staff in either individual or group settings. The appropriate atmosphere of openness and sharing is most likely to be achieved when the program director sets an example of reflective awareness of his own responses and promotes a guilt-free atmosphere of emotional genuineness balanced by realistic limits of pro-fessional expectations regarding staff behavior. The staff needs help in recognizing that it is entirely appropriate to have fantasies regarding adolescent patients which may be violent or erotic but that these must be entirely aim inhibited and utilized in the service of understanding and treating the adolescent.

The interface of patient-patient interactions is frequently underestimated in considering the important therapeutic occurances within a treatment unit. In an informal follow-up of 50 former inpatients, this author found that over half of them mentioned a relationship with another patient on the unit as the most important and helpful aspect of their inpatient treatment experience. There is a great deal of apprehension regarding the potentially negative impact of patient-patient interactions in the hospital setting. Parents are often openly concerned that their youngster will be influenced by others who may be more ill or anti-social among the patient group. Staff members often recognize that intense one-to-one relationships between patients serve a defensive function. Patients may use one another in the service of resistance or in order to gratify unhealthy and pathological or regressive drives. Obviously, these kinds of unhealthy interactions should be viewed both as potential impediments to the treatment process but also as a source of information and as an arena for therapeutic work. In a sense, they represent the externalization of internal pathological states which are the reason for the youngster's emotional difficulties. Staff should be equally alert, however, to the constructive potential of both dyadic relationships and the emotional interchanges in the patient group as a whole. It is only human for staff to occasionally feel twinges of envy in the recognition that members of the patient group are helping a particular youngster in a way that the staff has been unable to. The reaction is similar to that of the parent when they realize that their youngster is more invested in a peer relationship than in the parent-child bond.

We have already mentioned briefly the problems and interactions between staff and parents. This area requires constant attention and clarification if a constructive treatment effort is to be maintained. Staff require a great deal of help in understanding the motives and behavior of parents, particularly in programs that do not include extensive parental contact as part of their program design. The whole question of parent-patient interaction will be treated more extensively in the discussion of family therapy within inpatient settings.

In discussing the various aspects of the inpatient milieu of an adolescent unit, it is important to keep in mind a basic goal. All efforts to understand what is happening within the milieu are based on the desire to create a pro-therapy atmosphere which hopefully permeates the entire treatment program. This crucial element spells the difference between creating an extremely powerful treatment experience and the potential for strongly anti-therapeutic "mob" or gang behavior. A pro-therapy attitude is the most powerful deterrent against acting out and the strongest catalyst for production of relevant material in formal treatment settings. This pro-therapy atmosphere is difficult to describe. It does not imply a polyannish and superficial compliance seen only in the verbalization of the youngsters. In fact, most truly pro-therapy units are characterized by a great deal of grousing, challenges to authority, and other negative verbalizations. It should also be recognized that a pro-therapy atmosphere is not a static condition which can be once achieved and then forgotten. It is an elusive and delicate general attitude of anticipating and expecting growth which at the same time recognizes varying abilities within the patient group. Even though it is difficult to define or describe, it can be recognized in action. One observes youngsters speaking honestly with one another (in their own language and in a very practical way) about treatment goals, day-to-day behavior, and subjective personal responses to one another. In a program where a pro-therapy attitude is in the ascendency patient A says to patient B, "Bill, I know you're pissed at your parents and the staff and maybe you've got reason, but breaking ashtrays is a stupid thing to do about it." It should also be noted that most inpatient adolescent programs develop a jargon which may be utilized in a "snowjob" primarily aimed at conning the staff just as easily as it can be used as a legitimate shorthand for honest work. As in other aspects of psychotherapy, it is not so much the words as the affective tone which indicates the importance of what is being said.

It is generally recognized that group sanctions and group responsibility are necessary in order to create a pro-therapy atmosphere in an adolescent program. The natural narcissism of adolescence and the cultural emphasis on individuality must be actively countered if one wishes to create mutual involvement and group cohesion. These techniques have been well described by Lewis et. al. (1970) Although they are a necessary condition for creating a pro-therapy atmosphere they are not a sufficient cause for that happy condition to result.

The single most important source of a pro-therapy atmosphere is the success of the treatment program.

Youngsters who have benefited from subscribing to the goals, techniques, and traditions of the treatment unit will become strong proponents of a positive pro-therapy attitude. The program has worked for them and they will make active efforts to convince new patients to accept the conditions of treatment as potentially effective for them. This advocacy is based not only on a genuine concern for the welfare of new patients but also on the human tendency to defend value systems which are of personal importance when they are challenged. Unfortunately for the equinimity of the treatment staff, those patients who are the most effective spokesmen in behalf of the treatment approach are forever being discharged because of the very improvement which makes them enthusiastic. The good news is that new leaders usually emerge to both benefit personally from the experience of leading and simultaneously to maintain the best aspects of the program.

You will notice that very little has been said regarding the specific organizational structure of the treatment community. This kind of consideration has been avoided.because many different formal arrangements can accomplish the goals described above. For example, some units are organized around a government with elected officers who have a clearly defined relationship to staff sponsors. Other programs utilize the therapeutic community model where staff are included as members of the social system. Still other units are composed of several treatment teams each of which sends representatives to some central governing body. The specific pattern is not as important as is the need for clarity regarding the functional mechanics of the specific organization. It is important that the unit have clearly established procedures by which decisions are made and conflicts are resolved. It is also important that these rules be followed scrupulously and that the small society of the treatment unit function as a government of laws rather than a government of people. That is, staff, as well as powerful or favored patients, must be law abiding within the organizational framework of the program. Even when this appears to work a hardship in the present, it can forestall more serious long-range difficulties which may result when special exceptions are granted.

B.   *The Direct Therapy of the Adolescent in an Inpatient Setting*

(1).   *Group Psychotherapy in the Inpatient Program*

Almost all successful adolescent treatment centers utilize frequent group psychotherapy as an important constituant of their direct treatment program for the adolescent patient. Group therapy builds on the natural process of living together in the inpatient treatment center. It also provides a vehicle for shaping the group interactions of the entire unit in therapeutic directions. Because of the fact that the youngsters live together 24 hours a day, inpatient group psychotherapy has the capacity for extreme intensity which may provide the opportunity for very profound emotional changes.

Because of the nature of most inpatient treatment programs, psychotherapy groups in an inpatient setting are almost invariably open-ended. This has many advantages, particularly for the newly admitted patient. Working in a group setting with individuals who have already progressed in the program and who have learned how to utilize the therapeutic facilities con-structively smooths the entry process for the new youngster. In addition, many opportunities for dealing with issues of separation and loss are provided by the recurrent situation of discharge. Patients who are ready for discharge from the hospital are often very valuable members of the group and are themselves deeply invested in their relationships with other patients and staff on the unit. Working through these issues can be extremely valuable both to the departing patient and those that he leaves behind. This is particularly important in inpatient settings since so many hospitalized youngsters have significant difficulties in the area of separation-individuation.

It is often valuable to include nursing staff members as co-therapists in inpatient psychotherapy groups. Many relevant issues are raised around the behavioral activities of the patients. Nursing staff is often most familiar with these issues and are therefore in a position to bring them to the attention of the group. At the same time being part of the group psychotherapy permits the nursing staff member to view behavior in a wider context. The temptation to utilize group psychotherapy primarily as a behavioral control mechanism is off-set in this way. For example, the nursing staff may have an opportunity to view directly the core depressive state in an individual which has expressed itself on the unit in the form of defensive acting out. The co-therapy relationship in the psychotherapy group forms a natural opportunity for liason and a mutual working relationship which may avoid the extremes of dealing exclusively with either intrapsychic conflicts or their behavior manifestations. Obviously, the patient is best served by fusing these two views and recognizing their interdigitation.

The techniques of group psychotherapy in an inpatient setting are not basically different from those utilized in outpatient groups as described earlier in this book. However, there are a few differences which should be noted. First of all, the group has a great deal more information regarding each member than is typical of outpatient groups. Daily opportunities abound for observation and intimate discussion outside of the group setting. This can be either an advantage or a disadvantage. On the positive side, there is the potential for great richness of understanding based on the extreme intimacy of the living conditions of the group members. On the other hand, the lack of relative anonymity and the requirement to live together constantly may at times inhibit open interaction. For example, a youngster may be afraid to express strong feelings of anger toward a fellow group member when he knows that he must live with that person twenty-four hours a day over the next few weeks or months. Sexual feelings may also be blunted because of fears of over-involvement. The potential for pairing and clique formation is also strengthened in an inpatient group.

Another way in which inpatient groups differ somewhat from their outpatient counterparts is the pattern of expression of anger. Because of the relative safety of the inpatient setting, open expressions of anger toward adults are usually much more free in inpatient settings. The intense anger is amplified by the dual role of the mental health professional in an inpatient setting. That is, the therapist and other staff are viewed both as helpers and as "jailers". The fact that to some extent the youngster's freedom is being clearly restricted by the staff opens many opportunities for the expression of negative feelings. Much group therapy in an inpatient setting has to center around dealing with the issue of the patient's confinement, his hopes for discharge (which may in fact be extremely ambivalent) and his anger at being "forced" to remain in the treatment setting. Parenthetically, these feelings exist even in the treatment units where new "patient's rights" legislation have required all adolescents to sign in voluntarily in a very formal way. Even though the adolescent knows very well that he has admitted himself to the hospital and that he may leave on his own request at any time, he still may find ways to insist that staff is requiring him to remain. This author feels that illusion of externally limited autonomy is so essential to the development phase of adolescence that these patently distorted assertions should be calmly accepted. Staff energy should be directed toward pointing out to the adolescent the appropriateness of the decision to retain him in the inpatient setting rather than wasting time in an effort to replace emotional reality with logic. The essential point is to insist that the restriction of freedom is a necessary and reasonable response to the youngster's behavior.

As mentioned briefly above, the issue of group termination with adolescents who are being discharged from the treatment program is extremely important in inpatient group psychotherapy. Although one occasionally feels that the process becomes somewhat ritualized (and certainly repetitive to the staff who continually expend their energy in assisting youngster after youngster to face directly their feelings about leaving) the process is so important that it must be pursued anyway. Naturally therapists should make every effort to avoid using cliches and falling into stereotyped comments regarding this important event. Simple concrete personal references to relationships between the departing patients and other individuals are much more useful than psychological generalizations in mobilizing genuine discussion of separation issues.

(2). *Individual Psychotherapy of the Hospitalized Adolescent*

Some form of basic cooperation in the treatment effort is essential to the success in the individual psychotherapy of any adolescent in any setting. This cooperativeness is based on an agreement between the therapist and the patient (which may not be verbalized directly) that there is a psychological problem and that the adolescent will permit the therapist to assist in its solution. Many features of inpatient treatment obscure and complicate the development of this basic understanding even beyond its obfuscation in the outpatient treatment of the adolescent.

We have already mentioned the issue of the patient's confinement. We have also already noted that often this confinement is more psychological than real. Still, we cannot deny the fact that we do have unusual power and control over the adolescent in an inpatient setting. In some instances the adolescent is at least verbally opposed to this control and is in treatment only because the parents, the juvenile court, or other community agencies have forced his compliance. As noted above, even when the adolescent is a "voluntary" admission he will usually protest his status as an inpatient at some point in treatment. At these times if the therapist feels that inpatient treatment continues to be a necessity, the therapist is forced into a position of being the patient's "jailer" at the same time that he attempts to function as the patient's therapist. Obviously this is fertile ground for the popular adolescent defense against autonomy; the projection of personal responsibility. It is easy for an adolescent who is being held in hospital treatment against his verbalized wishes to insist that any observed problems that he may show are only the natural reaction to this abridgement of his civil rights. If this point is conceded there is no therapeutic alliance since the treatment is clearly the Doctor's responsibility and the patient can choose only between passively complying with expectations so that he can go home or bravely and independently resisting the ominous and unfair control being exercised by an institution over a helpless individual.

This set of circumstances requires modifications in the psychotherapeutic approach utilized in individual psychotherapy of the inpatient adolescent. Confrontation becomes more important since the patient must be continually faced with the internal origin of his problems. Fortunately, accurate confrontation is much easier in the inpatient setting than it is in the treatment of outpatient adolescents. There is a wealth of information available from the 24 hour observation of the patient's behavior and verbalizations. With this data, it is often possible to demonstrate convincingly to the patient that he cannot handle the demands of life outside of the hospital setting until certain problems are resolved. This process of confrontation is much more likely to succeed when one can obtain the support of the patient's peers in the inpatient group setting. The importance of creating and maintaining a pro-therapy atmosphere in the inpatient adolescent unit is of extreme importance. The techniques of creating this kind of atmosphere have been discussed earlier.

Another related feature of inpatient psychotherapy which often startles and confounds therapists inexperienced in that type of work is the intensity of anger routinely expressed by the patients. Often this is viewed as evidence of the more severe psychopathology present in the child who requires hospitalization. To some extent this is true but does not account entirely for the phenomenon. In addition there are the interacting factors of the safety of the structured inpatient setting and the "legitimate complaint" of having one's life rather completely monitored and controlled. Regardless of its sources, it is important to recognize that this routinely observed intense, and vehement anger in the treatment relationship does not suggest that the alliance is unworkable. To some extent all inpatient individual psycho-therapy must be organized around a sometimes angry negotiation regarding the youngster's readiness for discharge. It should also be noted that the therapist too can afford a more open and firm expression of expectations regarding the level of behavior necessary for successful treatment to occur. Since the extended staff network of an inpatient setting provides considerable safety and support, it is rarely necessary to "pull punches". An intense interchange which might make it difficult for the youngster to continue in outpatient treatment is merely another rather routine "tough session" in inpatient psychotherapy.

An inpatient adolescent psychotherapy group was avoiding important and depressing treatment issues by clowning, interrupting one another, teasing the therapist and generally producing chaos. The therapist made several efforts to comment on the defensive nature of the behavior and to deal with the problems in a more traditional psychotherapeutic way. These interventions were totally ineffective and in exasperation the therapist shouted, "If I had wanted to teach nursery school I would have gotten training for that instead of learning to be a psychiatrist. You're all behaving like a bunch of little brats".

The group did not take offense. They laughed, said "Wow, I've never seen you get so mad", and proceeded to settle down and work on important issues.

Similar, although less flamboyant, candor is possible in individual sessions also. These liberties can be taken because of the greater intimacy of the inpatient experience which makes it unlikely that patients will misunderstand the therapist's overall intentions toward them. Of course, as noted above there is also much greater support both from the many other staff members and patients with whom the patient relates.

Although the therapist should consistently confront the patient with his need for treatment and refuse to accept efforts to assign responsibility for the patient's welfare to himself, it should also be recognized that most adolescents cannot be expected to avow their need for treatment openly no matter how desperate that need may be. In fact, when patients speak too fluently of their need for psychotherapy, seasoned inpatient practitioners become suspicious that such talk is a maneuver to gain earlier discharge through an appearance of "insight".

Some comments should also be made regarding the importance and meaning of severe episodes of acting out which occur frequently in youngsters in inpatient psychotherapy. Often it is difficult to isolate any single factor, including the individual psychotherapeutic relationship, which can explain the youngster's behavior. The variety of concurrent important relationships which are impinging on the youngster in inpatient treatment complicate one's efforts to gain a clear picture of the relative importance of each. The patient's relationship with his family, with significant nursing staff personnel, with other patients and with friends outside of the hospital must all be considered in trying to understand why a youngster has run away from the hospital, errupted into physical violence, has brought drugs into the inpatient setting or in some other way has departed strikingly from treatment expectations.

The relationship with the individual psychotherapist is often underestimated in understanding the cause of these dramatic and disruptive behaviors. Acting out is a common form of resistance in the adolescent in outpatient psychotherapy. It becomes a much more potent method of avoiding further therapeutic work in the inpatient setting where the therapist is often viewed as "super parent" who can be angered, humiliated, or distanced by rejecting or disrupting the small universe that the therapist directs and controls, namely the inpatient treatment unit. In other words, the entire hospital situation may come to represent the therapist and thereby provide a broad stage for "acting in" an extended transference image.

It is obvious that episodes of severe acting out signal a disruptiontherapeutic alliance. They are drastic actions which are designed to force the therapist to assume roles with the patient aside from that of neutral therapeutic guide. It is often very difficult to be sure what the precise conscious or unconscious goal of the patient may be. One adolescent may be courting rejection in order to avoid a frightening growing closeness. Another patient may be attempting to elicit greater concern and protectiveness from the therapist in an effort to evade the unwanted psychological equality offered in the alliance. At other times the youngster may be tempting the therapist, attempting to provoke a punitive response which can be eroticized in sado-masochistic fashion. Often it is possible in an individual instance to gain enough information so that one can be reasonably sure of the dynamic forces which are in operation. However, even when the therapist understands some of the motives, there is rarely a good opportunity to interpret the meaning of the action in the period of time immediately following its occurance. Since the alliance has been disrupted, the treatment situation is not ripe for genuine acceptance of interpretations. In addition, the chaos created in staff and family usually lead to a variety of theories regarding the youngster's motivation, most of which mainly reflect the anger which the patient has stirred.

For example, if the prevalent theory among the nursing staff is that a youngster went AWOL in order to "show off" and appear a hero to his fellow patients, the therapist's notion that the patient went AWOL because his growing affection for the therapist raised fears of homosexual attachment is likely to be viewed as psychiatric nonsense. In fact, the therapist may be accused of being hoodwinked by his young patient. Nursing staff may feel the therapist is trying to protect the patient from the just consequences of his behavior. It is particularly difficult to make the appropriate interpretation convincingly when the young-ster's overt behavior during and after the AWOL fits the staff's description much more precisely than it fits the therapist's theories. The issue becomes very clouded if the patient himself states candidly that he ran away to prove that he could get away with it or "just for the hell of it".

In inpatient treatment it is particularly important to work backward from observable behavior and to raise questions which may permit both staff and patient to expand their understand-ings of the multiple causations of any particular act. In the example described above, the therapist may agree that the youngster was "showing off" but may raise thoughtful questions about why he might have the particular need at the present time to demonstrate his bravery, contempt for authority, and resourcefulness. In both the youngster's therapy sessions and in staff meetings it may become gradually more clear to everyone that the youngster's behavior was a counter-phobic defensive action.

In the effort to decipher the meaning of acting out in the inpatient setting the patient's expectations of the therapist's response can provide valuable clues. Has the patient anticipated that the therapist would punish him, criticize him, withdraw affection from him? Or does the patient expect that the therapist will now realize that the adolescent's complaints about the hospial were really serious and take better care of him? Often the patient does not verbalize expectations but shows in his behavior an anticipation of altered responses from the therapist. Commenting on these expectations may lead to a fruitful discussion of those transference feelings which disrupted the therapeutic alliance. The expectations often carry the fears and wishes which the patient has not been able to put into words.

It should be emphasized the therapist must simultaneously support the behavioral controls to prevent continued acting out at the same time that he is trying to understand the meaning of the behavior. Both the staff and the patient have to be helped to understand that recognizing the motives for an episode of acting out does not justify the behavior or give license for its repetition. This is a particularly important point with adolescents because of their tendency to distort permissiveness and understanding of feelings into an unjustified and dangerous permission to live out all feelings regardless of reality consequences or the rights of others.

It must also be recognized that some youngsters act out in ways so dangerous to themselves, staff or other patients, or to the design and cohesion of the treatment program that continued psychotherapy becomes dangerous or impractical. However, this decision should always be considered very carefully. The acting out adolescent produces intense negative feelings in both his therapist and in the nursing staff. As a rule of thumb, unless one can honestly say that the decision that a youngster is untreatable in a particular setting is genuinely reluctant and sad, the decision should be carefully reconsidered. If there are elements of satisfaction or even triumph in discharging a troublesome youngster from a treatment program, it suggests that the therapist or staff may be acting out anger, disappointment, or sadistic wishes toward the patient.

One must also remember in doing inpatient individual psychotherapy that the patient is intensely involved with many other staff members. One must also recall that many of these other staff members have a very different role with the patient and that the fact that their jobs are different may easily lead to problems. The nursing care staff and educational staff in an adolescent inpatient treatment unit have a difficult job. On balance they frustrate the adolescent patient much more frequently than they gratify him. Since they are entrusted with the behavioral management of the unit and with the education of young people who have frequently developed extremely negative attitudes towards school, these staff members cannot afford even the limited degree of permissiveness which the therapist can allow in his inpatient psychotherapy sessions. Frequently these staff members end up being the "bad guys" who do not "understand" that the patient is behaving badly only because he is angry, anxious, or in desperate need of a rebellious stance. In a very real sense these staff members cannot afford to "understand" these issues since they must first insist on a minimum level of appropriate behavior. In spite of the surging torrent of emotions and impulses which are stirred in the patients by the treatment process, nursing and teaching staff must reinforce ego control. They are the keepers of reality's demands, and that is frequently a thankless task on an inpatient adolescent psychiatric unit.

Because of these circumstances in hospital treatment the opportunities for "splitting" abound. The patient may appear to have a warm and cooperative therapeutic relationship with his primary therapist while continuing to act out the negative side of his ambivalence with other staff members in an unexamined and guilt-free way. Needless to say, a pseudo-alliance of this kind does not actually benefit the patient since important areas of psychopathology are excluded from the treatment process and expressed uncritically toward other staff members in everyday life on the unit.

The patient's tendency to split his feelings in this way may easily be reinforced by unexpressed and unexamined splits between the various staff members. Therapists frequently view nursing staff as controlling and insensitive to dynamic treatment issues. Nursing staff may view therapists as overly permissive and naive regarding the patient's genuine motives. They may even view therapists as subtlely encouraging acting out against their efforts to maintain social control.

The educational staff is frequently the object of resentment. Nursing staff may be jealous of school holidays which regularly rekindle the chronic suspicion that teachers have a much easier life than they do. Therapists may view teachers as inflexible and overly concerned with the youngster's cognitive development and conventional educational expectations at the expense of emotional growth. Staff members may carry consciously or unconsciously the fear and resentment of teachers which many of us develop during the anxiety of our personal educational experiences into present day efforts to work together collaboratively. These negative memories make it easy to identify with the adolescent's hostility toward teaching staff.

It is the responsibility of the therapist to understand and appreciate the contributions made by all disciplines and to recognize the interdependence of the entire treatment team. Opportunities for discussion of tensions and conflicts between staff members must be provided so that the patients are not used to act out staff problems.

In the direct individual psychotherapy with the adolescent patient it is crucial to insist on generalizing the therapeutic alliance. For example, the question of confidentiality in inpatient psychotherapy frequently provides a clue to the real strength of the alliance. Many patients try to create splits between the therapist and the remainder of the staff by offering to share information if the therapist will promise to keep it secret from nursing or teaching staff.

As a rule much more is lost than is gained by making such promises blindly. Of course, the therapist frequently makes choices regarding the kind of psychotherapy material which can be fruitfully shared with the extended staff. Often it is disruptive rather than helpful to discuss the patient's fantasies, dreams, and transference interactions in great detail with the staff. This is basically intrapsychic information which has its primary value in the one-to-one treatment situation. On the other hand, overt action, interactions with other patients, family issues, and aspirations in the real world are important data for the entire staff to consider. Not only should the therapist insist on the freedom to use his own judgment in sharing material from individual psychotherapy with the remainder of the staff, he should strongly encourage the patient to share sensitive information with other staff members so that the alliance is generalized and its gains are moved closer to ordinary daily living. That is, if the patient can discuss distorted attitudes and conflicts with the staff members that he lives with 24 hours each day, he is one step closer to the capacity for self observation and self direction in ordinary family life and social interactions outside the home.

The therapist also needs to be alert to the relationships that the inpatient adolescent has with his fellow patients. A similar fragmentation of emotional experience may occur in relationships with fellow patients as well as with staff. Intense positive or negative interaction with other youngsters in the treatment program may represent the true focus of the patients emotional investment, leaving the therapeutic alliance empty and bland though superficially cooperative and apparently constructive.

The patient may also utilize fellow patients to act out conflicts by proxy, collude with them in the avoidance of significant emotional issues, or use them to bolster up defenses in other ways. This is not to say that the therapist attempts to thwart these intense interpatient interactions. This would be an impossible task and probably not desirable in any event. However, it is important to be aware of what is happening between the adolescents on the unit and to utilize this information in formulating the patient's emotional patterns and intervening therapeutically.

3. Pharmacotherapy of the Inpatient Adolescent

Child psychiatrists have long had an extremely cautious

attitude toward any psychoactive medication. This caution has extended to the adolescent patient. There is justifiable concern regarding the impact of a psychoactive drug on a developing organism. There is also concern that the drugs can be easily utilized to squelch annoying behavior even when this behavior is age appropriate and adaptive.

Although these concerns are realistic they have often led to an unfortunate situation in which talented and competent adolescent therapists are reluctant to use medication at all. This is unfair to the adolescent patients who could benefit from appropriate pharmacotherapy. The strong emotional attitudes have also led to some polarization between dynamic psychotherapists who do not use medication and other psychiatrists who utilize pharmacotherapy as the primary treatment approach. There has also been a tendency for well staffed and dynamically oriented treatment programs to use little or no medication while poorly financed and minimally staffed institutions are grossly overmedicating adolescents. In these programs there is a scandalous use of medicine to obtund the youngsters in order to reduce management problems. The overall effect is to preclude any effective therapy or educational progress. Some of these situations have been brought to public awareness with the unfortunate side effect of producing in some sectors of the public a hysterical reaction toward even well designed and appropriate pharmacotherapy.

It is obvious that some adolescents require psychoactive medication if their illness is to be adequately treated. Schizophrenic adolescents as well as those with manic depressive illnesses should not be deprived of the indicated pharmacologic therapy.

A text such as this one cannot deal with specific drugs and their precise dosages. Active research and clinical trials are going on constantly. It is necessary to read current journals in order to insure appropriate and up to date use of medication. For this reason this section will deal primarily with general principles of pharmacotherapy. Occasionally we will mention specific medications which have proven their clinical efficacy, recognizing that they may well be supplanted by superior products at any time.

To begin with, most youngsters deserve a drug free period of evaluation when first admitted to an inpatient setting. If the patient has previously been medicated, the instructions for withdrawal of the specific medication should be followed carefully. Most drugs require a gradual reduction to avoid potential danger from rapid withdrawal. Even though the process of withdrawing a drug may be complicated by patient or parental anxiety, a drug free period can be extremely valuable. It is not unusual, for example, to encounter youngsters whose condition has been created or worsened by indescriminate outpatient drug therapy. This iatrogenic portion of their illness cannot be identified unless medication is withdrawn for a period of time.

It is also important to see what impact the inpatient treatment program will have without the use of medication. This is important not only because all use of medication carries some risk, but because maintenance drug treatment in an outpatient setting is difficult. If a youngster can be treated successfully without medication this is preferable for many reasons. As a rule a period of ten days to two weeks without medication is a sufficient time period to provide an accurate baseline and clarify the need for medication.

Obviously, if a youngster's symptomatology poses an immediate serious threat to himself or to other persons living in the unit, medication cannot be with-held. In these instances adequate drug treatment should be instituted immediately.

Whenever medication is instituted it is important to be sure that it is perscribed in adequate dosage. Since, as described above, there is often a timidity in regard to drug usage among adolescent therapists there is the risk that small doses will be prescribed and that drug therapy will be prematurely interrupted when these amounts are insufficient to produce a therapeutic benefit. The therapeutic dosage level varies widely in individual adolescents and often is on the high side of acceptable dosage levels. On the other hand, some adolescents respond strongly to relatively small doses of medication. Proper management consists of beginning the adolescent on a very small dosage which should be raised fairly quickly to a level where either therapeutic benefit or side effects are observed. If a therapeutic response is achieved it may be possible to reduce the dosage and still continue the benefit. Obviously, the goal is to provide the patient with the lowest possible dosage that will maintain the desired therapeutic effect.

Most practitioners now agree that the phenothiazines can be administered in a single dose at bedtime. This not only provides a practical convenience to the nursing staff and the patient, but may prevent some side effects such as drowsiness from interfering with daily activities. Other people still prefer to prescribe two doses a day with two thirds of the total medication given at night and one third in the morning. Many inpatient centers prefer the liquid concentrated form of the drug since patients may develop considerable skill at pretending to take tablets while actually sequestering them for suicide attempts or abuse.

Oral medication should be used whenever possible except in situations where the patient's behavior is dangerous and his cooperation cannot be obtained. In very rare situations injection may be preferred route of treatment in order to achieve a more rapid result.

One such situation where parenteral use is indicated is to provide rapid control of severely and acutely disorganized psychotic youngsters whose behavior is clearly dangerous. Chlorpromazine 50 to 100mg IM is a time proven choice in this situation. Careful attention to the possibility of a hypotensive response is necessary, however. The same medication may be valuable for other youngsters who are dangerously out of control even though they are not psychotic. Other practitioners prefer to use a sedative drug such as a fast acting barbiturate to control non-psychotic patients.

The value of antidepressant medication in adolescents is less clear. Most depressive syndromes in adolescents are reactive and relatively unresponsive to antidepressant medication. These youngsters require psychotherapeutic approaches. However, some adolescents who show persistant severe depressive symptomatology, especially if it is accompanied with psycho-motor retardation and somatic symptomatology, deserve a trial on the antidepressants.

Some inpatient treatment centers utilize PRN medications rather extensively. These may be given by nursing staff when they are concerned about the youngsters' behavioral controls. The patient may also request the drug at times when he fears that he is losing control. Although this practice cannot be condemned totally, it is wise to review carefully the utilization of PRN medication. On an ad lib basis the medication may come to serve as a substitute for the psychological interventions which can often accomplish the same or better results. There is also the risk that the patient will come to depend on a pharmacological prop when, in fact, their own psychological resources could suffice.

Medication may be used at times with large numbers of youngsters when group contagion threatens to produce an outbreak of mass violence or extreme disruption within the treatment unit. Such a use of medication is certainly preferable to permitting a total destructive breakdown of the ward milieu. However, such a state of affairs calls for careful evaluation of the entire treatment program. Often the near riot conditions on the unit are the result of staff unrest, confused communications or a general failure of appropriate treatment planning.

The question of utilizing medication in an effort to help youngsters who appear primarily characterological, immature or impulsive is complex. There are reports in the literature of beneficial results from Lithium and other psychoactive medications in this group of patients. On the other hand, it is with these patients that one can easily substitute chemical intervention for the more difficult but perhaps more valuable human interactions which could produce genuine emotional growth and maturation. For example, medication should never be used to suppress appropriate verbal anger even when the intensity of its expression is somewhat uncomfortable to the staff. It is also important to avoid using medication as a punitive control since "chemical warfare" of this kind not only fails to help the youngster involved but breeds an atmosphere of suspicion which will adversely effect the attitude of youngsters who actually need medication.

Although we now have available many potent medications, they can achieve their maximum benefit to the patient only if we remain sensitive to the psychological issues involved in their administration. Prescribing medication to an adolescent is a very important emotional event not only to the patient but to his parents. If the implications of using medicine are properly understood and supported by the adolescent and his parents, therapeutic benefit is maximized. On the other hand, even the most indicated medication may fail to produce the desired result if it is not administered in the proper psychological context.

As a rule medication is best presented as a supportive agent to the patient's efforts to benefit himself. The family or the patient should not be led to expect magical results which would obviate the need for continuing psychological treatment and efforts to improve family and individual functioning. As a rule it is possible to specify those symptomatic behaviors which are likely to benefit from medication. For example, a psychotic youngster may be told that a phenothiazine may help him think more clearly. An impulse ridden youngster may accept medication which is designed merely to allow him to delay action until he has considered various alternatives.

As a rule, except in emergency situations, it is unwise to administer medication when the youngster or the parents are intensely opposed to its use. If this resistance does not yield to psychotherapeutic efforts over a period of time it may be necessary to proceed without total support. This should be done only in cases where medication is clearly indicated and where other treatment approaches have been demonstrated insufficient.

These general suggestions by no means provide sufficient guidelines for the practitioner in the area of pharmacotherapy. By and large, it is advisable for the average psychiatrist to use only a few agents and to develop an in-depth knowledge of their indications, limitations and side effects. Consultation with a practitioner who has made a special study of the use of medication is indicated in unusual or difficult cases whenever such expertise is available.

C.   *Psychotherapy of the Parents of the Hospitalized Adolescent*

The relationship between parents and inpatient treatment

centers is notoriously troubled. There seems a natural tendency for competitiveness. Both parties seem to contribute to this negative interaction. Many mental health professionals tend to regard parents as the cause of emotional disturbance in adolescents. By and large the angry troubled adolescent is more than eager to support this hypothesis. On the other hand, many parents behave in ways that reinforce this bias.

The admission of an adolescent to an inpatient setting is invariably a complex emotional event for the adolescent's parents. To some extent they are relieved and grateful since the family's problems have usually become unbearable. At the same time, there are always elements of guilt and shame coupled with anxiety involved in the decision to turn over a portion of parental responsibility to the inpatient treatment staff. This complex set of emotions often leads to a regressive pattern in one or both parents. As a result the parents may appear childishly demanding, hopelessly inept, blindly critical, or in other ways rather irrational and unlikeable.

In spite of these inherent difficulties between the parent and the treatment program, they are forced to relate to one another. Most inpatient adolescent treatment programs insist on some parental involvement, feeling correctly that the adolescent's illness effects the entire family and may partially result from family psychopathology. The degree of involvement may depend to some extent on the program's philosophic decision regarding its appropriate role with the adolescent. If the program provides longterm care and is designed to substitute for the parents over an extended portion of the youngster's life, parental involvement becomes less crucial. Even in institutions of this kind, it is important to maintain parental support and cooperation at least to a minimal degree. Obviously, those programs that are designed to provide temporary support with the goal of returning the youngster to his family must provide much more active parental therapy. In any case, every effort should be made to respect the feelings of parents and to deal with them sympathetically and supportively. Even in situations where parental psycho-pathology interferes drastically with appropriate parenting, it is important for treatment staff to maintain a therapeutic attitude toward the parents rather than indulging in attitudes of critical reproach. Most parents are doing the best they can and need our help.

Adolescents who are disturbed enough to require residential treatment usually have reached a situation with their families which is a desperate one. The parents often feel defeated, confused and totally ineffective in the parenting role. The adolescent patients often are extremely angry at their parents either for sins of commission of for less well-defined sins of omission. Both the parents and the adolescent are deeply disappointed in one another as a rule. These attitudes may be disguised by excessive solicitude and denial of conflict or they may be flagrantly apparent. Many different approaches have been utilized in approaching the family relationship of the hospitalized adolescent. Some programs insist on an initial period of separation with individual treatment for the adolescent and concurrent parent counselling. Other programs move immediately toward family therapy involving the adolescent with the parents. To some extent these decisions should be based on the clinical picture although elements of program design and practical necessity may also have to be considered. Regardless of the format one usually must eventually consider the family structure and determine the degree to which it allows for the adolescent's maturation.

It is impossible to consider the great varieties of family dysfunction which are encountered in inpatient treatment settings. There are some families who seem in temporary crisis and who move toward a successful resolution without extensive alternations in family dynamics. I think it is safe to say, however, that most families encountered in inpatient practice have to face the need for extensive change in the course of inpatient care.

For example, some families include clearly deviant parents whose behavior plays a rather direct role in creating and maintainiadolescent's abberant behavior. One example is the anti-social parent of the severely acting out adolescent. Some studies have shown that the adolescent is much more likely to improve if completely removed from the influence of such a parent. (Stewart, et al 1978) Another example would be the adolescent who by reason of brain damage or other biological defect is unable to function within an average normal family without creating intolerable strains for other family members.

As a rule family changes are more subtle. In the majority of cases this need for change must be directly addressed in a persistant manner. Inpatient staff often feel that a high percentage of their adolescent patients would benefit from placement outside of the family. To some extent this probably reflects an overidentification with the adolescent and a competitive attitude toward the parents. As a matter of fact, the question is often academic. Most adolescents return to their families within a few months of discharge even when other placements have been recommended by the hospital staff.

Treatment staff should still feel free to address the question of whether the family is a potentially functionable unit. For one thing, as noted above, some families are not viable and the difficult decision to reorganize the family with different members may be necessary. More important, this question is in some way at the back of everyone's mind in most cases. There are great advantages in addressing it directly since considering the possibility of dissolving the family both focuses the discussion on relevant issues and permits consideration of whole new ways of interacting. To some extent the question of leaving one's family is central in all adolescents. Considering concrete issues of emancipation often allows open discussion of more subtle emotional components of family functioning. It is important for treatment staff to remember that the inpatient adolescent is already temporarily separated from his parents. This reality factor undoubtedly partially explains the frequency with which the issue of actual family disruption is raised in the inpatient treatment of adolescents and their parents. In any case, the possibility of actual disruption of the family should be viewed as tentative and symbolic throughout early phases of all such discussions.

One must also remember that families are typically resistant to psychological change. Even in situations where the family homeostasis is achieved at high group or individual cost, the prospect of altering the balance is frightening. One can anticipate not only the typical resistances encountered in other family therapy but extensive utilization of other opportunities for resistance which are offered in an inpatient setting. In inpatient programs which include an active family therapy component, family resistance is a frequent source of staff splits and conflicts. Harbin (1978) has described this phenomenon in detail.

In closing this discussion of family involvement in the inpatient psychotherapy of the adolescent, it should be emphasized again that not all problems with parents result from their individual psychopathology or from resistance to changing maladaptive family group dynamics. It is difficult to maintain a consistant and humane therapeutic approach in the face of the stresses involved in providing inpatient treatment for adolescents. The entire staff often feels strained and even overwhelmed by their task. Because the therapeutic committment to the adolescent is more immediate, and perhaps to some extent because staff who have chosen work in such a unit have particular sympathies for people in the adolescent age group, the parents are perhaps the most likely scapegoat for our frustrations. We must confront parents in the process of helping them and their adolescent children. Before we confront too actively it is important for us to be sure that we have treated parents with the therapeutic understanding, tact, and simple humanity that we would desire for ourselves if we were in their shoes.

CITED AND RECOMMENDED READING

Lewis, J.W., J.T. Gossett, J.W. King and D.I. Carson. 1970. Development of a pro-treatment group process among hospitalized adolescents. Timberlawn Report No. 40.

Stewart, M.A., Adams, C.C., and Meardon, J.A., 1978. Unsocialized aggressive boys: a follow-up study, The Journal of Clinical Psychiatry, 39: 797-799.

Harbin, H.T., 1978. Families and hospitals: collusion or cooperation? American Journal of Psychiatry, 135: 1496-1499.

Gossett, J.T., Barnhart, D., Lewis, J.M., and Phillips, V.A. 1977. Follow up of adolescents treated in a psychiatric hospital. Arch. Gen. Psychiatry, 34: 1037-1042.

Berman, S. 1976. Hospitalization of children and adolescents: the role of the referring child psychiatrist. Journal of the Philadelphia Assoc. for Psa., 3: 5-15.

Stubblefield, R.L. 1978. Indications for hospitalization of adolescents. Interaction, 1: 20-27.

Rabiner, E.L., Molinski, H., Gralnick, A. 1962. Conjoint family therapy in the inpatient setting. American Journal of Psychotherapy, 16: 618-631.

Gunderson, J., Psychiatry 1978 November Issue. "Defining The Therapeutic Processes In Psychiatric Milieus". Vol. 41, No. 4: 327-335.

Fong, J.Y., Schneider, M., and P. Walls-Cooke. 1978. Multiple family group therapy with a tri-therapist team. Nursing Clinics of North America, 13: 685-698.

Index